MOTHER
RUSSIA

Also by Bernice Rubens

Birds of Passage
Brothers
The Elected Member
A Five Year Sentence
Go Tell the Lemming
I Sent a Letter to My Love
Kingdom Come
Madame Sousatzka
Mate in Three
Mr Wakefield's Crusade
Our Father
The Ponsonby Post
Set on Edge
A Solitary Grief
Spring Sonata
Sunday Best

MOTHER RUSSIA

Bernice Rubens

CHAPMANS

Chapmans Publishers Ltd
141–143 Drury Lane
London WC2B 5TB

Grateful acknowledgement is made for permission to reprint
from Nikolai Chernyshevsky: *What is to be Done?* Translated by
Michael R. Katz. Annotated by William G. Wagner. Copyright
© 1989 Cornell University. Used by permission of the publisher, Cornell University Press.

A CIP catalogue record for this book
is available from the British Library.

ISBN 1-85592-020-4

First published by Chapmans 1992

Photoset by Rowland Phototypesetting Ltd,
Bury St Edmunds, Suffolk

Printed and bound in Great Britain by
Clays Ltd, St Ives plc

For Joshua and Dashiel Lilley

PART ONE

I

There are many ways of celebrating the turn of a century. Suicide is one of them.

Count Fyodor Larionov, owner of the great Larionov estates, had had enough. He considered that he had led a good life. His past had been rich, glorious, eventful. And his present was happy enough. But it was the future that terrified him. And he decided that he would be better off without one.

'God and the Tsar forgive me,' he said, crossing himself.

Fyodor Larionov was wont to travel the countryside to oversee his estates. Over the years he had taken much pleasure in his workers' servility, in their chronic obedience, and their right and proper sense of place. A serf knew his master and the regular touch of his forelock might occasionally merit his master's smile. The poor peasant readily accepted his poverty, and acknowledged without question the privilege of the rich. But of late the Count had noticed a change. Once, while examining a potato crop amongst his field-workers, he had heard murmurs of dissent. And even without eavesdropping. For some of the peasants didn't bother to whisper, but made known to each other loud and clear the matter of their discontent. They talked about the unfairness of their lives, of their poverty and lack of opportunity. And they swore against the rich for their exploitation. Why, one of them even cursed the Tsar, blessed be his name, and in an oath rather above a whisper. Poor Fyodor Larionov winced at the affront, and would have whipped the knave on the spot had he been able to identify him. But his voice, whoever it was, was the voice of many, for they were lily-livered cowards, Fyodor thought. Each and every one of them. The incident depressed him in the extreme, and he was anxious to go home, and be amongst his own kind. But he had first to call on his trusted foreman to discuss the season's planting.

He entered the little hut to the accompaniment of much bowing and scraping from the foreman, his wife and three children. He refused their offer of lemon tea, for he was anxious to be on his way. Whilst talking with his foreman, his eye fell upon a shelf above the cooking stove. Among the pots and pans, he was astonished to see a book. No attempt had been made to disguise it. It leaned arrogantly against a skillet, and its hard covers proclaimed rebellion. Louder and more serious than any murmurs of dissent he had heard in the fields. For the presence of a book in the house of a peasant was the sign of the utmost danger. It hinted at literacy, a condition totally unacceptable in an underclass. And God knows, Fyodor thought, what the book was about. But whatever its subject it was words, and words could ignite the sparks of revolution. He took it from the shelf and stuffed it into the inside pocket of his coat. He noted with some pleasure how his foreman trembled.

As soon as he settled in his troika, he ordered his driver to take the road slowly. It was growing dark and he had to lean towards the carriage window to catch the lanterns' light. Then he took the book from his pocket and in the safe and tight-lipped gloom, he read its subversive title. And shivered. *What is to be Done?* he read. *By Nikolai Chernyshevsky*. He recalled the title and its dire association. Over a decade ago an attempt had been made on the life of the Tsar. The perpetrators of the crime had been hanged and it was rumoured that it was this very book that had prompted their vile attempt. Indeed they were heard to recite some of its words even on their way to the gallows and until the very moment when the rope choked their treason. Fyodor quickly put the book back into his pocket. Safer there, he reassured himself, than on a shelf in a peasant's hut. He would put it in his own library where books belonged, even if they were never read.

On returning home that evening, Fyodor Larionov fell into a state of deep depression from which he never fully recovered. He could not sleep, plagued as he was with his fears of the future. A time when tenant would usurp landlord, when serfs would over-throw their masters, when the poor would plunder the rich, and the entire natural order would be destroyed. Such a future did not tempt him. So on the night when the century would turn, when the eighteens would become the nineteens, he would ensure that the future would go about its ruinous business without him. His son, Count Dmitri, was that night giving a grand ball to celebrate the century's turning. Fyodor pleaded a headache and fatigue. He would go to his bed, he told his son, and did not wish to be dis-turbed. He did not want to spoil their celebrations. He would be found in the morning when the party was over. He said goodnight to his grandsons, Nicolai and little Andrei, and inwardly pitied them both for their future. He climbed to the attic at the top of the house and he prayed for forgiveness from God and the Tsar. Then, with little ceremony, he took a rope and hanged himself.

There are suicides and parties. But there is yet another way to celebrate the turning of the year. A positive way, a lasting way, a way of faith in that future on which Count Fyodor had resolutely turned his back. That way is to create a new life. Above the chan-deliers and the swirl of ball gowns and below the lethal necklace of rope in the attic, sandwiched between the temporal and the eternal, Countess Tatiana Larionova was writhing in the last stages of labour. She called for chloroform, a privilege of her class. Dr Lvov obligingly applied an ether-soaked gauze to her nose.

'It won't be long now,' he said. He hoped the baby would arrive soon, and without complications. Then he could go downstairs and join in the revelry.

Dr Lvov had attended the Larionov family since he had first qualified as a doctor some forty years ago, and during that time he had become a close family friend. He had delivered their sons, Nicolai and Andrei, and he hoped that this would be the last. The Countess was not a strong woman. He would have a word with Count Dmitri, he thought. He stroked the Countess's hand, then gently raised her knees and pressed his fingers on her stomach. He signalled to Marfa, the children's nurse, who stood waiting at the foot of the bed, a cashmere shawl draped over her arm.

'We will need her help now,' he said. 'Come, Marfa, I will need yours too.'

Marfa lay the shawl on the bed. Gently she removed the gauze from the Countess's nose. She was familiar with the procedure, for like Dr Lvov, she had been in attendance at the two previous births, and had served the family as long as he. The Countess squirmed with pain. She would have wished to scream aloud, but she was mindful of the celebrations below, and did not wish to embarrass them. So she gave out a long and polite moan.

'Push, my dear,' Dr Lvov said. 'It's almost here. I can see its crown. A little harder. Yes. Yes.'

At that very moment the New Year's bells pealed their birth pang, loud and shrill, and the Countess was at last able to scream her heart out. And though her mouth was open wide with her release, not a human sound was heard in the bedchamber, drowned as it was in the pealing of a thousand bells across the land, ringing in a future that, once and for all, would proclaim the past century as over. And not only in time, but in spirit too.

'It's a girl,' Dr Lvov said. 'A fine healthy little girl.'

Marfa wrapped the child in the shawl. She knew that the Countess would be disappointed, more on the Count's behalf than her own. For the Count saw himself as a sire only of sons, men who would proudly propagate the Larionov name until the end of time. He would look kindly upon a daughter, but he would not regard her as a serious issue.

'She's beautiful,' Marfa said and placed the new-born in the Countess's arms.

'What will you call her?' Dr Lvov asked.

'Anna,' the Countess said. 'For my mother. Would you tell them downstairs, Doctor?' she asked.

It was his permit to join the revelries below. He went straight to Count Dmitri's side and whispered his joyful news. An announcement was made and glasses were raised to toast the arrival of Countess Anna Larionova and the twentieth century, both in their innocent infancy.

The Larionov manor house straddled the brow of the hill. Below them, and in their proper place, were the scattered huts and cramped hovels of their peasant serfs. The century turned for them as well, but there were few celebrations. There was no money for revelry, and suicide amongst the poor respected no anniversary. It was a common enough event on any day of the week. But new life there was, and on that same night as the year turned, Maria Volynina, mother of two sons, lay labouring on her cot, and prayed for a daughter. Avdotya, the peasant midwife, sat by her side. There was no chloroform and conversation was the only means to etherise the pain.

'I saw Dr Lvov on my way here,' Avdotya said. 'He was going to the Countess. She's expecting too. She wants a daughter. Just like you.'

'I will be happy with what the good Lord sends me,' Maria said.

'The good Lord and the Tsar,' Avdotya added. In her mind they were equal.

'The Tsar's got nothing to do with it.' This from Ivan, Maria's second son, who sat in the corner of the hut reading in the light of a quivering candle. One of the late Fyodor's dangerous rebels.

'Don't talk like that,' Maria said. 'Go and fetch your father.'

'Why do we need Vassily here?' Avdotya asked. 'This is no time for fathers.'

'He was with me when both the boys were born,' Maria whispered into her pain. 'I want him with me now. And where is Pyotr?'

'He's working up at the manor, Mama. They have a party.'

'Perhaps he'll bring back some food,' Maria sighed. 'But quick, fetch your father.'

Ivan wrapped his coat around him and went outside to harness the horse. It was bitterly cold. His was a reluctant errand. He knew his father would not wish to be visited. For he was ashamed of his habitation and his way of life. But it was forced upon him. Every winter the men of the village were obliged to travel to Vosrov, a small town only a few versts from the Larionov estates, and there to find work and sustenance. Ivan had been obliged to call upon his father one winter before, and what he had seen still haunted him. As he neared the outskirts of the town, he heard the first pealing of bells. He slowed down his horse to savour a while their sound. He heard a future of hope in their chiming, hope for better times to come, when he could shuffle off the yoke of his fourteen lean years and lead his people against the powers of darkness. He had read of Ivan the Terrible, but he would be Ivan the Kind. There was no harm in ambition, he thought. Else he would end up like his father.

He steered his horse and cart through the narrow streets. The smells of open sewers and human despair almost stifled him and he pulled his muffler over his nose to sieve their stench. He reached the end of an alley where it was clear that the way forward was too narrow for his cart to pass. He climbed down onto the cobbles and tethered his horse to a post. He heard noises, shouts and screams and scraps of a vicious argument, strangely at odds with the chiming bells of peace. As he descended the alley, the noise grew louder until he traced its source to an open door. The place was suddenly familiar and he shivered in its fearful recall. He fought his way through the stench and the smoke, the bodies propped against the wall or huddled on the floor. Women amongst them, some with ready-made children at their breasts, others in humping heaps on the floor in the process of creation. He side-stepped them, ashamed. He looked into each man's face, searching for his father's. But hunger and despair fastens a like image on every man, and he might as well have been called upon to identify a skeleton. Then he heard someone call his name, and again, 'Ivan'. It was a common enough name, but he dared hope it applied to himself. And then the voice called again, but this time with further proof that he was sought. 'Ivan Volynin,' it cried. The voice was frightened, ashamed, caught red-handed in its humiliation.

'Papa,' Ivan cried. '*Papa*.' But still the names did not meet and he crisscrossed the floor, his steps orchestrated by the 'Ivan-Papa' duet. At last he traced the source of the sound, and found his father huddled alone in a corner, as if he would isolate himself from his shameful surroundings. But his eyes could not hide their joy at seeing his son. Ivan knelt by his side and embraced him.

'You shouldn't come to this place,' his father said.

'The baby is coming. Mama has sent for you.'

With a sudden and surprising strength, Vassily Volynin sprang to his feet. 'Is Avdotya with her?' he asked.

'Yes. Mama is fine. She just wants you there.'

'Come. Let's go. Quickly,' his father said.

Ivan settled his father in the wagon and covered him with a rug. He was uneasy in the man's company. His father smelt of failure and it embarrassed him. Vassily, for his part, was uneasy too, sensing his son's disapproval.

'When you grow up, you will do better than I,' he said, almost by way of apology. 'You can read. You know numbers. You are clever. You will find a post where men can respect you.'

Then Ivan was able to touch his father and to embrace him without fear of infection. For failure, if resistance is low, is catching, and his father had acknowledged with pride that his son was immune. He drew a small bottle of vodka from under the canvas. He always kept it in the wagon against the cold, though he himself had never taken it. He handed the bottle to his father, and savoured his pleasure as he drank from it. And pitied him too, that so little should so greatly satisfy him.

'A happy New Year,' his father said.

'A different one,' Ivan whispered. 'A different century.'

The baby was clearly waiting for its father's attendance, for as Ivan unharnessed the horse outside their dwelling, they heard the birth-pang cry. Vassily rushed inside, and held Maria's hand.

'Now don't you be getting in the way,' Avdotya said. This was her domain, and she rather resented intruders. Especially fathers. Birthing was women's work. And private. She pressed on Maria's stomach. 'Another push, my darling,' she said. 'It's coming. Oh look. Look, look, it's a beauty.'

But Vassily could not bear to look. Nor Ivan, who was crouched in the corner.

'When it's all over,' Vassily said. He wondered how women could endure it. Their strength frightened him.

'It's a boy. A beautiful boy!' Avdotya said. She wrapped the baby in a shawl, and handed him to Maria. Then she cut the cord. 'Go into life and be well,' she said, as she said to every child she brought into the world, and each time she knew, in every hut and hovel, that her wish was often only a dream.

'What will you call him?' she said.

'Sasha.' Vassily spoke for the first time. His eyes were brimming with tears. It could have been the cold, the vodka, or his simple happiness.

Ivan then dared to come to the bedside. 'It will be a better world for him,' he said. He spoke with such authority, as if he himself would make it so.

Avdotya smiled to herself. She had heard such words before.

They heard a rustling outside the door. Then Pyotr's breathless voice. 'Mama?' He rushed into the hut panting, and laden with crumbs from his master's table. 'What is it?' he gasped.

'It's a boy,' his father said hugging him. He felt easier with this one, his eldest, the one who, like him, couldn't read. He could drink with him, swear with him, weep with him even, and all without shame.

'What's his name?' Pyotr asked.

'Sasha.'

He kissed his mother, and stroked her hair with infinite tenderness. 'Well done,' he said. 'Another boy. We're a family of men.'

Avdotya would see no virtue in such a family, but she held her tongue.

'How did you know the baby was coming?' Maria asked.

'Dr Lvov. He told me. He'd seen Avdotya. He was up at the house. The Countess had a little girl. They've called her Anna. And there's more news. But first, look what Katya found for me.' He pronounced the name with the gentleness of a lover. Which indeed he was, and had been ever since he had started as coachman at the big house. Katya was the kitchen-maid and their courtship was innocent and of measured pace but with an inevitability that would lead to their marriage. Katya could read a little and she was teaching Pyotr, but he was a poor pupil and sometimes, peasants though they were, both feared their inequality. He unwrapped his parcels. A half-bottle of vodka, a roast chicken, whole but for one leg, and a tin bowl of cold kasha.

'Let's welcome Sasha and the new century,' he said.

'This is the best new year of my life,' Vassily said.

'There will be better ones,' Ivan muttered from his corner.

'Come, Pyotr,' Maria said, pulling him to her side. 'What more news have you got for us?'

'The Countess wants you to feed her new baby. Will you have enough, Mama?'

'I shall make enough. And I shall be honoured. But first tidy our hut a little.'

'Nonsense,' Ivan said. He came over to his mother's bed. 'You don't have to be honoured, Mama. And we don't have to tidy our hut. This is how we live and they must take us as they find us.'

Avdotya could hold her tongue no longer. 'Ivan Volynin,' she said, 'I brought you into this world and you grew up an obedient, trusting child. But now you want to make trouble and you will bring sadness to your family.'

Ivan laughed and hugged her. 'Don't worry, Avdotya. I'm only thinking, and there's no law against that.'

'But it's your thoughts that will get you into trouble,' she said.

He coaxed her to some vodka. Maria put Sasha to her breast and Vassily started to sing.

'We're having a party,' Avdotya said, her speech already slurred. 'Just like the Count Larionov.'

'Careful, Avdotya,' Ivan laughed. 'You're having dangerous thoughts.'

It was indeed a party, and all the more joyful because of its surprise. Together they ate, drank and sang, and only Maria, who was sober, heard the carriage draw up at the door.

'Ivan,' she whispered, 'there's someone outside.'

Ivan staggered across the hut, and peered into the darkness. Then bowed, in drunken mockery, as he ushered an astonished and offensively sober Marfa into the hut. In her arms she held the cashmere bundle of the new Countess. She looked around her and viewed the spectacle with horror. Vassily, booted and filthy, was sprawled across the bed, oblivious of company and humming to himself in a haze of alcohol. Avdotya was sprawled on the floor, a chicken wing dribbling its fat down her chin. Pyotr slouched in a corner blowing on a tin pipe, from which an occasional and random salivated note emerged, meek as an apology. Though a peasant herself, Marfa had lived and worked long enough in the

17

Larionov household to be infected by its disdain, and she had it in mind to take the baby back and make it do with a bottle. But she knew that mother's milk promoted a good start in life.

She sniffed with contempt. 'The Countess Tatiana has asked that you would suckle her child along with your own.' She wanted to distance herself from the request, so she added with disdain, 'It was not my idea.'

Avdotya stirred herself on the floor. She was not yet drunk enough to have misheard, neither the words themselves nor their tone of contempt.

'But you're one of us, Marfa,' she said. 'In spite of where you live and what you do.'

In his corner Ivan smiled. Good old Avdotya was well on her way to the barricades.

'Bring the child here,' Maria said, weakened by embarrassment and shame. 'It will be an honour for me.'

Vassily grunted by her side.

Marfa placed the baby on Maria's arm. 'Is yours a boy or a girl?' she asked. Her voice had lost its air of disapproval. She was one sober woman talking to another.

'It's a boy. His name's Sasha.'

'And this is Anna,' Marfa said. 'I shall send a cot, and I shall come every day.'

'I shall be honoured,' Maria said again, and Avdotya actually raised herself from the floor and laughed aloud.

Marfa's departure was swift. And troubled. She would report nothing of the scene to the Countess. She would simply say that Maria Volynina had enough milk for two.

Inside the hut, nobody noted her departure. Not even Maria who had at once put the child to her breast. Little Sasha, who sensed a sharing of a domain he thought was all his own, let out a cry at the sheer unfairness of it all.

And so the first night of the new century passed, and slowly sobered them all. In the morning Ivan drove his father back to Vosrov, and both counted the days till the springtime when he would come home for the sowing. Avdotya went on her delivering way, and Pyotr returned to the manor house to help clear the débris of the year that had passed.

Katya was on breakfast duty and she knocked on the door of Count Fyodor's bedchamber, the breakfast tray in her hand. There was no answer. She was afraid to open the door – her station in life did not permit such an intrusion – so she called the head housekeeper, who by rank was entitled to open his door. Which she did, and stifled her gasp at the bed, which had clearly not been slept in.

'We should tell the Count,' Katya suggested.

'He is still sleeping,' the housekeeper said. 'We must look for Count Fyodor. Perhaps he slept in Nicolai's room. Or Andrei's.'

'No,' Katya said. 'I've already taken them their breakfasts.'

'Then we must look for him,' the housekeeper shouted, as if it was Katya's fault that Count Fyodor had gone missing. 'We'll look in all the spare rooms. You do this floor and I'll do the one above.'

They went their separate ways, and after a while returned to their departure point with nothing to report.

'Perhaps he's walking in the gardens,' the housekeeper said, but with little confidence. The Count was never known to walk for pleasure. Besides, the untouched bed was an ill omen. 'You look in the attic, Katya. I'll look in the gardens.'

'Can't I look in the gardens?' Katya asked. She was afraid of the attic, though she had never been there. But attics housed ghosts and evil spirits.

'Do as you're told, girl,' the housekeeper said, and went quickly away to prevent further protest.

Katya's knees were melting as she climbed the stairs. There was only one door at the top of the landing, so she had no pause for choice. She put her hand on the door handle, and out of time-honoured habit she knocked. The sound echoed down the stairwell, and did little to lessen her fear. Nevertheless, she knocked again, playing for time. Then she crossed herself, took a deep breath, and opened the door.

And closed it. And screamed. She tried to run, but her feet were rooted in her terror. Screaming was all that she could do. Which brought most of the household running to the attic, Count Dmitri amongst them, followed by his sons.

'What's the matter, girl?' the Count said.

She opened her mouth but speech served her no better than her feet. So she pointed to the door.

'Go downstairs. All of you,' the Count said. 'And Katya, you go and lie down in your room.' He sensed that whatever was behind the door was a matter from which one had to recover. And he sensed, too, that it was a private one.

'Shall I stay with you, Father?' Nicolai asked.

'No. Go, and take Andrei with you.'

Count Dmitri waited until the landing was empty and then he opened the door. His silence was as piercing as Katya's screams, and as full of horror. He stared at his father's body for a long while. He could not understand it, and he did not dare to try, because he suspected he could not deal with the consequences. In a while he was able to weep, but that too was silent, muffled as much by shame as by sorrow. He cut his father down, and laid him gently on the floor. Then, bewildered and confused, he stumbled out of the room. But about one thing he was clear: no one must ever know that his father had chosen to take his own life.

He rushed to Katya's room. He found her lying on her pallet curled up like an infant, clasping her head with her hands.

'Katya,' he called gently. He knelt by her side, and touched her arm.

She lowered her hand, looked at him, then, in servile reflex, sprang to her feet, horrified to find him kneeling. He rose. 'I'm sorry you had to find him, Katya,' he said. 'But you must put it out of your mind. It was a terrible dream that you had. You saw nothing. Do you hear me, Katya?' His voice was raised. 'You saw nothing. Nothing at all. My father died in his sleep. A natural death. From old age. You found him in his bed when you took him his breakfast. Do you hear me, Katya?' he asked again. Her vacant look seemed to have registered nothing.

'How did my father die, Katya?' he asked her.

'A rope,' she said.

He knew he had to be patient. The girl was in shock. But it was imperative that the truth were not rumoured abroad. Not that it would set a bad example to his peasants. They needed no model for that manner of quietus. It was possibly the only right they had. But noblemen were not supposed to take their own lives. In their privileged positions there was absolutely no reason for it, and when the Count had done with his crying, he would deal with his anger.

'My father died in his sleep, Katya,' he tried again. 'How did my father die?'

'In his sleep,' she said, parrot-like.

He rehearsed her over and over again, and her replies reeked of obedience.

'You're a good girl, Katya,' he said. He pressed a coin into her hand. He hoped she would not construe it as bribery. Then he left her and went to break the news to his family. To them he would tell the truth. He had to, for it was a burden he could not bear alone.

But neither could Katya. The image of that swinging rope seared her retina and no false words or wishful thinking would ever heal the scar. The image of Count Fyodor's pendulum would shadow her to the grave. She had to share it with somebody. So that evening in the stable yard, in the steam of the sweating horses, she whispered it in Pyotr's ear, and swore him to secrecy. But Pyotr could no more bear the burden than Katya, and he whispered it to his mother, who in turn off-loaded herself to Avdotya. And that was the end of the whisper. For Avdotya, the bush telegraph, bore it aloud to each delivery, and every ear received it with sorrow and surprise. And a small measure too of satisfaction, for it proved that even the rich and the privileged could tire of life as well.

Count Fyodor Larionov was buried quietly in the family vault, and the peasants doffed their caps when the bell tolled. Death was a leveller, and so, in a way, was birth, for in the Volynin hut, Sasha and Anna, worlds apart, suckled at the same breast.

Thus the century turned in birth and in burial and both were indissolubly linked. For the fears that had prompted Count Fyodor's dispatch would be more than warranted by the milk-children's rebellious future.

2

After six months of wet-nursing, the little Countess Anna was weaned from the Volynin dwelling and returned to her proper place. Little Sasha suckled alone, and both children were bewildered by the sudden emptiness at their sides, an emptiness that nagged their infancy, as shadowless, in their worlds so far apart, they ran and stumbled through their first years.

After Count Fyodor's offensive leave-taking, his son, Count Dmitri, had taken command of the estates. Unlike his father, who had died in fear of the future, Count Dmitri did not envisage any change. God was eternal, and so was Tsar Nicholas the Second, and both were on the side of the masters to whom the slaves were by nature in thrall. That was the way of the universe, a pattern as inevitable as the night that followed day. In this opinion he was supported by his eldest son, Nicolai, though Nicolai did not share his father's benign nature. If God and the Tsar were truly eternal, Nicolai in his time would make a harsh taskmaster. Like his grandfather, Andrei, the younger son, envisaged change, but unlike Count Fyodor, he did not fear it. Indeed he relished it, and would live to ensure that the Tsar, if not God, was temporal. And as little Anna grew, she favoured Andrei, who loved and spoiled her to distraction.

In the Volynin household – though light years away from the manners and the mores of the Larionov dwelling on the hill – a similar pattern emerged. Pyotr Volynin was, like Nicolai, fully accepting of the status quo. 'This is how it's meant to be,' he would tell his rebellious brother, and his father would echo his opinion.

But Ivan was like Andrei. He knew that things had to change and by that very same law of nature that Nicolai and Pyotr held so inviolable. And little Sasha clung to Ivan, who in some way filled that mysterious gap at his side.

Though the master and servant families kept strictly apart, pursuing their own ways of life, there were occasions when the two mingled, when the one acted as spectator to the rites and customs of the other. One such occasion was the ceremony of the cutting of the Cross, which took place every December, when the ice was at its most solid. Originally it was a religious ceremony, attended by communal prayers and thanksgiving. But over the years the prayers had been privatised, whispered to one's heart and probably not even that, as the ceremony took on more of the appearance of a pagan rite. The whole village assembled at the lake-side, amongst them Count Dmitri and his family. A small balalaika ensemble spread an authoritative chord, a signal that the ceremony would begin. Then Nicolai Larionov, who for some reason always seemed to be dressed in the uniform of a Cossack, unsheathed his sword and handed it to his father.

A peasant guided Count Dmitri to the centre of the frozen lake, where the Count lowered the sword and made the first hesitant incision into the ice. He was like a groom deflowering a wedding cake. Another chord from the balalaika ensemble signalled that the show was on the road. As they played, the Count etched the outline of a large cross into the ice. Then he retired and left the serious business of Cross-cutting to his peasants. An army of them, equipped with chisels, then hacked at the ice according to the Count's amateur outline. They hacked away alternating between the vertical and horizontal, thus maintaining a delicate balance between the two. The work was arduous and took some time, but the band played all the while, and occasionally the villagers broke into song. The bandmaster kept a sharp eye on the cutting operation, waiting for the moment when he would order the music to cease. Then in the ensuing silence they would wait until the Cross was almost severed from its lake moorings, when it would require just one *coup de grâce* to set it free. And in that deliverance would be heard the thundering bellow of freedom as the Cross assumed

23

dominion. Then prayers were spontaneous, loud or whispered, and of such variety and dissonance that it would be difficult to imagine that one God could fulfil them all. For how would He gently turn His ear to Nicolai's plea for the status quo, and at the same time favour Ivan's prayer for revolution. But none of the supplicants envisaged such a divine dilemma, and each fervently believed that God's ear was his, and his alone.

Those who had chiselled the Cross now prayed to that same God for the strength to lift it and to carry it to the river. And as they did so, they bore in mind He who had once carried it alone. And they became as penitents, in which guise they gathered strength for their Calvary. The band and the villagers followed them. Now the music and songs were solemn and even the children fell silent as the procession threaded its way across the valley and down to the river bank. But the sight of the river signalled their penance was close to fulfilment, and slowly the music shuffled off its dirge-like harmonies and the songs were of joy. The children loosened their parents' pious hands and ran down to the river-side. For it was there that they would have the best view of the launch of the Cross. Amongst them little Andrei, who stealthily unlocked Marfa's hand and clambered down the slope towards the river, elated in his freedom. Freedom from Marfa and her narrow world of manners and elocution, but above all the freedom to play with other children whose lives he sensed were so very different from his own. Close to the river bank was a tree, its branches shadowing the water, and an irresistible invitation to a front-row seat. Andrei climbed the trunk and settled on an overhanging branch. There he sat, and waited for the launch of the Cross. Most of the children had rushed to the source of the river, where the Cross would first be lowered and from where they could run along the bank pacing its course. Andrei watched the Cross bearers as they came to rest at the bank. He saw how they knelt, and raised the Cross high above their shoulders, then eased it gently into the water. Huge and heavy as it was, it made not a sound as it touched the surface, and it floated with the current in a sacred silence. A lone bird landed on one of the arms of the Cross and perched there as if in hope of a free ride to heaven.

24

The children were approaching Andrei's tree, their line parallel to the floating Cross. Andrei watched from his perch, and as the Cross floated beneath him it appeared to him like Arthur's sword Excalibur, that soared miraculously from the bowels of the lake. The King Arthur legends were Marfa's favourites. She prided herself on knowing them, for they were different from the Russian tales told to children. When asked how she knew of them she would hint at an English sailor acquaintance, and giggle and blush and weep, all at the same time. For a moment, Andrei was convinced that the Excalibur sword was no legend, and he leaned forward to study it more closely. As he did so, the bough broke and tumbled him, with little regard to his station, into the swiftly moving current below. There were screams from the river bank. The Count and his family, who had not moved from the river source, sensing that with the launch their duty was done, and that they were free to return to the manor, gathered their clan and retinue for the departure. And it was now for the first time that Andrei was missed. Marfa screamed, forgetting her acquired manners, but mindful of her undeniable responsibility. But above Marfa's screams could be heard the screaming from the river, and the connection was clear to all of them. Nicolai ran along the bank, but his sword impeded his progress, and he was too conscious of his rank to relinquish it. Soon he caught sight of his little brother, his terrified head bobbing up and down. Andrei's hand was stretched in a desperate attempt to grasp the life-saving Cross but it turned out not to be Excalibur after all. Someone threw a log from the river bank, but it landed yards from Andrei's reach. The Volynin family were gathered further down the bank, at that point in the river where the current was strongest and where the ice-sword of God Himself could no longer conquer Nature; at that point in the river where it was known from former years to lose its equilibrium and to shatter with little dignity against the rock. There was a faintly sinful pleasure in watching it float to its inevitable ruin, which was probably why that section of the river was peopled with those who dared to question God and the Tsar's infallibility. At the first sound of the screaming, Ivan had rushed to the bank, and waited there for a while, sensing the strength of the current. He would bide his

25

heart-throbbing time until Andrei, if he survived, would float at a specific angle to where he stood. Then he would dive into the foaming river and gather him in his arms. He took off his coat and his shoes, and he waited. And prayed, despite the rebel that he was, for Andrei's survival. The screaming from the bank did not abate, but Ivan was deaf to it as he chose his moment and plunged into the flowing current. His timing was exact, for as he raised his head from the dive, Andrei, his life breath almost spent, sailed into Ivan's arms and, out of his awesome terror, somehow managed a mischievous smile. Ivan held him close. He knew he must get Andrei back to the bank as quickly as possible, but the embrace held him there, and Andrei too did not stir, for each of them knew, with varying degrees of reason, that that embrace, despite the vast gulf between them, was a moment of declared brotherhood.

Nicolai was calling from the bank. Marfa had caught up with him, and a flurry of the Count's retinue carried blankets and concern. Ivan held Andrei with one arm and swam back to the bank. Once there he handed Andrei into Marfa's arms and dragged himself to the grass verge. There he lay shivering for a while, oblivious of the cold and his fatigue but savouring still that moment of brotherhood when a frontier had fallen. And as he lay there trembling, he heard the crack of the Cross on the rock, and for some reason he knew that that clap of thunder echoed the crumbling of the old order and the first fearful and possibly bloody steps of the new.

Someone threw a coat over his body, and pressed a glass to his lips. He looked up and saw Katya's face, that frame of forbidden beauty promised to his brother. Ivan loved Pyotr with a brother's irritating and passionate concern, but he knew that Katya and Pyotr were ill-matched. Each had been promised to the other in childhood and that promise was irrevocable. After Epiphany they would marry and Ivan would stand by, a helpless witness. For over the last few years he and Katya had grown very close. Their bond was one of literacy, and like Ivan, Katya was hungry for words and ideas. What few books they managed to acquire, they shared, and always with those shy looks of conspiracy, knowing that their subversive exchange embraced more than mere literature. From all this Pyotr was excluded. Despite Katya's efforts to teach him to read, he was not an apt pupil. Besides, he did not share Katya's appetite for change, and the sole point in literacy was to promote that change. But because they were promised to each other they would marry after Epiphany and to renege on that betrothal would be a revolution in itself.

Now Katya leaned over him, rubbing his shivering body.

'Take this,' she said. 'It's aqua vitae. Count Nicolai gave it to me for you.' She sat him up on the grass verge and urged him to drink.

'How is Andrei?' he whispered.

'You saved his life,' she said. 'They're taking him back to the house. You're a hero,' she laughed.

He managed to smile at her before she was led away. It was Pyotr who took her, fearful of their intimacy. Then his mother and father were suddenly at his side, Maria scolding him for his hero-ism, leaving the pride to Vassily, who crowed the joy of his son's courage. He carried Sasha in his arms. 'You will grow up like your brother,' he said, 'a hero,' and poor Vassily, had he given it any thought, would have been terrified at his own prophecy.

By now quite a crowd had gathered around Ivan, including Dr Lvov, that link between the peasants and their master. For Dr Lvov held regular clinics in the Larionov servants' quarters, tending to the needs of the villagers. He crouched down by Ivan's side, and put his ear to his chest.

'As strong as a bull,' he said. 'And as brave. Go home and rest yourself. Hot drinks and keep him warm,' he said to Maria.

Between them they helped Ivan to his feet. Then Vassily and Pyotr took over, and half-carried him over the fields.

Maria put her hand on Dr Lvov's arm.

'What is it, Maria?'

'It's a favour,' she said. 'It's for Ivan.'

'How can anyone refuse a hero a favour?' he said. 'What can I do?'

'I'm worried about him,' Maria confided. 'He's clever. I want him to be somebody. I want a better life for him. You know many people. You hear about things. Perhaps somebody could give him work. A job that would make use of his brains.'

Maria felt uncomfortable. She was not given to bragging about her children, but she feared for Ivan; she feared that without work that would interest him he would grow violent. She had already seen signs of his temper, when he sensed that his future would be no better than his father's.

'I know a printer in Vosrov,' Dr Lvov said. 'He might take an apprentice.'

'We would all be very grateful,' Maria said.

That year, the ritual of the ice Cross was celebrated for the last time. After the near tragedy, the Larionovs feared its ill omens, and the villagers themselves came to regard it with equal apprehension. It had, in any case, lost much of its religious provenance, and God and the Tsar would surely forgive its forfeit. The villagers would find less perilous avenues of celebration.

Katya's wedding fell into this category, and it was rumoured that those at the big house where Katya had worked since childhood, would arrange the celebrations. Katya was an orphan. Her mother, who had also done her kitchen duties in the Larionov manor, had died when Katya was a child. Her father was unknown, but there were rumours about that too. Indeed it was more than possible that when Katya screamed at the dangling rope in the attic, she was bewailing the loss of her father, and the final endorsement of her orphanhood. But she knew nothing of that, nor ever guessed at it, which was just as well, for suicide is a criminal legacy to leave to one's children. But when it was known that the great house would host her wedding, the villagers nodded their heads, or shook them perhaps, but both gestures expressed the same confirmation of what they had suspected all along. Katya's wedding expenses would assuage the Larionov guilt.

Little Sasha Volynin was counting the days to the ceremony. Along with Ivan, he was to be Pyotr's attendant. A suit of blue velvet had been sent down from the manor, and every day he tried it on to practise his peasant limbs in the alien refinement of its cut and style. He could hardly contain his excitement, not so much for the suit and the ceremony, but for the prospect of being once more at little Anna's side. For she was to be an attendant to Katya. Together they would carry the rings on white silk cushions, and every day he practised his porterage, using an old tin tray.

Pyotr was nervous. He did not doubt his love for Katya, a love he considered eternal. But he was aware of the disparity between them, a difference that could only increase with the years. Sometimes he despaired of their union and he dreaded his wedding day as much as he yearned for it. Above all he wanted it over and done with.

In the last week before the wedding, he spent every day at the Larionov stables. And kept strictly away from the kitchen door. He wanted to be near Katya, but he did not wish to speak to her. He was suddenly afraid of her, fearful of her futile expectations. One day, when he was grooming the horses, he was surprised by a visit from Andrei. Andrei rarely came to the stables. Unlike Nicolai, who visited daily, he had little interest in horses. He disliked their smell, and feared their size. He still could not ride, and he was already almost in his teens. Nicolai had tried to teach him, and so had Pyotr, but he had more trust in his own legs for covering the fields and the fences.

He stood shyly at the stable door. He was hiding something under his coat.

'What is it, Andrei?' Pyotr asked.

Andrei ran to Pyotr's side. 'You won't tell anybody, will you?' he said.

'Tell anybody what?'

'It's a secret,' Andrei whispered. He pulled out a book from underneath his coat. 'Will you give this to Ivan?' he said. 'And make sure you say it's from me.'

'What is it?' Pyotr asked. 'What's it about?' Although he couldn't read the title, he knew it was trouble. The secrecy that Andrei insisted on was proof of that.

'It's called *What is to be Done?*' Andrei whispered. 'Katya told me Ivan wanted it. I stole it from the library. Don't tell anybody. Promise.'

Pyotr was loathe to take the gift. Besides, he resented Katya's part in the transaction. He knew that she and Ivan met sometimes and that they shared books and talked about them. Neither Katya nor Ivan had ever made a secret of it to him. But now even little Andrei was involved in their conspiracy and he felt an outsider.

'What's the book about?' he asked again.

'I don't know. But it's important. Ivan told Katya.'

Pyotr hid the book in his saddlebag. 'I'll give it to him,' he said.

'Don't forget to tell him it's from me,' Andrei said again, then he rushed out of the stables. He ran into the house and upstairs to the library. Then he climbed onto a chair to reach the shelf that he had so sinfully depleted. He shifted the books to close the tell-tale gap that he had left. He looked at the titles that had shielded his purloined copy. Benign, each one of them. Two volumes of the history of the Larionov estates. Count Fyodor had considered such a placing as safe and undisturbable. Books on parade, to be seen, and admired even, but never closely examined. Thus, with the filling of that shelf, poor old Count Fyodor had made a small contribution to the future that he had so feared.

On her wedding day, Katya was taken to the Countess's room to be dressed. Marfa was in attendance. She fulfilled her duties with little grace, for she rather resented Katya's promotion to her mistress's quarters. She consoled herself with the knowledge that it was only temporary, and that after the wedding, Katya would return to the kitchen where she belonged. Marfa was aware of her own poor and needy origins. But in the luxury of her present condition, she had grown ashamed of them. Often she even denied them to herself and to reinforce that denial, she was sometimes more dismissive of the peasants than her masters themselves.

'I hope you're grateful,' she said, as she cruelly pulled at the laces of the stays around Katya's waist.

'It's too tight,' Katya squealed. 'And yes, I am grateful.'

She thought that an expression of gratitude might bribe Marfa into loosening the tapes, but she seemed to tighten them as if gratitude could never appease envy, and it was envy that prompted her cruel fingers. Envy that evoked the bitter-sweet memories of her English sailor with his King Arthur legends in his fractured Russian. And his promise to return. And now, like an ageing Madame Butterfly, her wrinkled wings pinned to her sorry expectations, she waited still, and consoled herself with his stories, giggling, blushing, and weeping the while. She pulled the laces tighter. This should have been *her* dress, so many years ago, and this wedding ceremony hers. She gave one final tug to the lace. Katya squealed in protest, and Marfa was satisfied.

Down the hillside, the Volynin dwelling was abustle with preparation. There were only two rooms, each of them used for living, eating and sleeping. But now there was only one room – one, that is, that was usable. The other had been curtained aside, cleaned, whitewashed and scented, its only furniture a pallet on the stone floor. This was the bridal chamber, and would remain so until time and familiarity allowed for sharing, with perhaps a draped curtain for occasional privacy. Now the one room that remained to them was abuzz with activity. Little Sasha had been ready since dawn, and he was sent outside the hut to practise with his tray. Maria and Vassily were also wedding dressed, or rather best dressed in that attire that was simply the alternative to their daily working clothes. Now they too took themselves outside the hut and looked at each other as strangers. They sat together on a wooden bench and were silent. Then Vassily took Maria's hand, and his gesture was an expression of the thousands of words that, over their years together, he had never been able to give her.

Inside the hut, there was a silence too. But of a different kind. Pyotr and Ivan were already attired, but both were fiddling with their cravats, braces and belts. It was as if both men felt entirely unready for the ceremony and they were translating that unpreparedness to their dressing. They needed to speak to each other, but not by way of discussion. Such a conversation would have led to argument and possibly quarrel and neither brother would risk such a consequence. All they wanted was a word of reassurance from the one to the other, but both knew that there were no grounds for optimism, and that the future boded ill for both of them.

'You look splendid,' was all Ivan could give his brother. At least that was the truth and with no innuendo. Pyotr's wedding suit, together with Sasha's, had been sent down from the big house. It was of white silk, an alien material, and inside its genteelness, Pyotr felt an outsider, and from that outsidedness he gathered a small comfort, as if it were another who was attending the wedding, and thus another who would have to take the consequences. The trousers were narrowly cut and braided along the outside leg. The coat was of tunic style with a high collar and buttoned across with braided frogging, thus giving the ensemble a military air, and, for some reason, this aspect gave Pyotr a certain solace. For a moment, as he had buttoned the tunic, he had felt at home, and he wished there would come a time when he would be called upon to serve his country.

'Are you nervous, Ivan?' Pyotr asked, projecting his own fears.

'You're the one to be nervous,' Ivan laughed. And both brothers knew that their repartee was interchangeable.

At last they were undeniably ready. Suddenly the first toll of the wedding bells echoed across the fields. Pyotr cringed in his finery. The bell was tolling the truth of his future. He could no longer pretend it was just a game.

'We'd better go,' he said.

They joined their parents, who had already prepared themselves for departure at the sound of the bell. Maria took Sasha's hand and put the tin tray aside. Sasha was loath to relinquish it. He was suddenly nervous, realising, like Pyotr, that the marriage was no longer a game. Ivan joined them, taking Sasha's other hand, and the three of them crossed the field leading to the church. Other villagers were on their way and gradually they all converged as the church came into their sights. Vassily and Pyotr walked at a distance. Maria had engineered that her eldest son and his father should spend a little time together before the ceremony. She had attempted the same ploy in the days before, but Vassily, though conscious of his duties as a father, did not know how to fulfil them. Now some sort of paternal advice was unavoidable. But he had no advice to give, let alone the words for it. He remembered how his father had sat with him the night before his wedding to Maria. He recalled how they had sat together for a long while, staring at the floor between them, and saying nothing. At last, his father had touched him on the arm. 'Good luck, son,' he had said. And that was all. Vassily had inherited his father's reticence, a silence that stemmed from the same sense of failure. For his father too had wintered in Vosrov, and in a similar dosshouse to his own. Finding work where he could, bringing summer-money home when he could, and drinking much of it on the way. He had hoped for better for his son, as Vassily now hoped for Pyotr, but with little confidence, for despite Ivan's prophecies, Vassily believed that nothing would ever change. He walked beside his son, scratching his mind for something to say to him. He presumed that Pyotr knew the fundamental facts of marriage. He himself had never been taught them. They had come to him instinctively as he hoped they would come to his eldest son. But he had no advice, no words of wisdom to pass on to him, no worthwhile knowledge that he had learned from his own experience. He loved his son and that love was all he could give him. He hoped it would be enough. Enough to offset the inheritance of a long line of failure. They had almost reached the church. Vassily put his hand on Pyotr's arm. 'Good luck, son,' he said.

The church was crowded. The whole village had turned out for the wedding and all were invited to attend the festivities in the gardens of the manor house. That section of the church reserved for the Larionov family was empty. They would arrive en masse with the bride. The Volynin family entered the church. But Maria stayed outside with Sasha, and waited for the bridal party. The carriages could be heard on the road that skirted the field, and then, in a while, the first of them came in sight. It was the family coach, white, with its gold Larionov crest. When both coaches arrived at the church, those leading alighted first: Count Dmitri, the Countess Tatiana, Nicolai, again in his Cossack uniform but in its ceremonial style, Andrei, and Marfa holding little Anna's hand. The coach then moved on apace to give room to the bridal carriage. Katya rode alone, the spaces beside her draped with the silken folds of the voluminous gown. The Countess Tatiana had worn that same dress at her own wedding, and that night it would be returned to its tissued storage to await the nuptials of little Anna.

Count Dmitri helped Katya out of the carriage and, taking her arm, approached the church door. There they waited while Marfa smoothed down Katya's dress and murmured her admiration out of her heart of stone. Little Anna was then placed in position and given her silk cushion. Maria led Sasha to Anna's side. She felt his little hand tighten in hers, and she knew he would be loath to let it go. And indeed, when he reached Anna's side he refused to release his mother's hand. Even when the cushion was offered to him with the gold ring clipped to its centre.

He turned his head away and buried it in Maria's skirts. He began to cry softly. It was all too much for him. He'd had long enough practice in his attendant's suit, and he'd been totally at ease with his tin tray. But now the silk cushion with its golden ring was too serious for him. But most serious of all was the person of Anna by his side. The reality of her. That nestling, suckling milk-sister of his, who over the years had become a hollow shadow, and later on a sweet recurrent dream. Now the flesh and blood of that shadow and that dream stood by his side, and the sheer surprise of it and its strange power made him tremble.

'Come along,' Marfa said. 'Everybody's waiting.' Her voice was gruff and impatient and did little to inspire trust in Sasha, whose only desire at the moment was to go home. Then Anna put out her hand. Gently she prised Sasha's from his mother's skirt and took it in her own. Her touch shipped him right back to their loving milkhood, and the terror drained out of him. She kept hold of his hand, and squeezed it a little as if reseeking their infant bond. 'We're ready,' she said.

And so the ceremony began. Katya stood by Pyotr's side, but neither looked at each other. Pyotr because he was stunned by the reality of his hopeless commitment, and Katya because she feared that in looking at Pyotr she would catch Ivan's eye. But Ivan stared ahead of him forcing his mind into dreams of revolution. For he knew that those dreams, though a poor substitute for the real longings of his heart, would serve to calm him. The crowns were placed over the heads of the bride and groom. Anna and Sasha proffered their cushions, and rings and vows were exchanged. All that was intended since their childhood was now fulfilled.

The guests repaired to the manor house. Under a marquee they celebrated, shy of their hosts and with reticent appetite. They danced, sang and feasted and all with measured decorum. It was

34

not like an ordinary village wedding where peasants' manners did not have to be left at home and where they could rejoice in their own way, free of the straitjacket of an alien host. Thus the party was subdued and in Pyotr's heart it was fitting. In Katya's too, but most of all in Ivan's, for whom the ceremony was more of a wake than a wedding. But for Sasha and Anna there was true enjoyment for neither as yet understood the discrepancy between host and guest.

'When I get married,' Anna said, 'I'm going to wear that dress. My mother wore it. Now it's Katya, and then it will be me.'

'Then I shall wear Pyotr's suit,' Sasha said.

Thus they were betrothed, without their knowledge, and with no one's interference. In their small unconscious way they were effecting the revolution.

That night Ivan could not sleep. Katya and Pyotr lay behind the nuptial curtain. Ivan turned his ear from their loving. He lit a candle and reached under the pillow for the book that Andrei had given him. He opened it at random. 'The Golden Age will dawn. We know that, but it still lies ahead. The Iron Age is passing. It is almost passed, but the Golden Age has not yet arrived,' he read. He read it over and over again, in the hope that it would take his mind off his cuckolding. But he was writhing in jealousy. He hated himself for his ungenerous feelings. 'The Golden Age will dawn,' he read again. Those words were more important than anything on earth. They had to be, even if his heart denied them. The revolution superseded everything, and he would, if necessary, deny himself love to further its cause.

3

Ivan was happy to leave the Larionov estates. Apart from his anguish in Katya's presence he knew that he needed to leave the small confines of his village to broaden his horizons. Vosrov was hardly a metropolis but it was a positive step towards St Petersburg, that hub of change and agitation.

When Ivan first entered the print shop, the sheer noise and bustle of it excited him. It was so different from the tranquillity and slow tempo of the village he had left. He asked for the owner but had difficulty in making himself heard above the noise of the presses. At last he located him in a back office, and reported himself for duty. Ilya Chernov was a man of middle age, gruff in voice and manner. Yet a steady twinkle in his eye belied his irascibility. He noted Ivan's battered light-weight suitcase. He smelt the village on him and that particular village hunger that assailed all peasant boys who had taken the trouble to learn to read. Dr Lvov had spoken highly of this one. He was eager, he said. He could be trained, and he wasn't only referring to the art and craft of printing. Dr Lvov and Chernov were close friends and had been for many years, but it was a secret friendship for, considering the doctor's professional connections with the aristocracy, it would have been imprudent for such a friendship to be known and acknowledged. For Chernov was a noted dissenter and constantly under surveillance. Dr Lvov was officially his doctor and they shared their political sympathies behind closed doors.

'I'm Ivan Volynin,' Ivan shouted. 'Dr Lvov sent me.'

'I know, I know,' Chernov said. 'Are you hungry?'

'No,' Ivan lied. He didn't want to show any weakness.

'There's no law against eating. Not yet,' Chernov laughed. 'Here.' He handed him a hunk of bread and a piece of sausage. 'Sit down,' he said. 'I'll get you some lemon tea.'

For the first time in many weeks Ivan did not think about Katya. The prospect of work, a little money, and perhaps even conversation was exciting enough to relieve his Katya pain. He ate with relish, and with high hopes for his future. After a little while Chernov returned with two glasses of tea.

'I'll take some with you,' he said. He sat down on the chair beside Ivan. 'Dr Lvov says you bury yourself in books. Tell me what you are reading now.'

Ivan was afraid to tell the truth. He knew that the Chernyshevsky book was frowned upon, and he was not sure of his company. 'Pushkin,' he said quickly. Pushkin was allowed.

'Good,' Chernov said. 'Pavlenkov – you'll be working with him, sharing his room too – he's a great reader. He'll teach you a lot. Learn from him. He's a good man.'

'I will,' Ivan said. He had a feeling he might have fallen amongst friends.

When they had finished their tea, Chernov cleared the cups, and as he did so, he said, 'Your father lives in Vosrov, I believe.'

'Yes.' Ivan was hesitant, for Chernov's tone inferred that the proximity of his father might prove a handicap.

'Will you visit him?'

'I suppose so,' Ivan said. He thought it politic to show a certain indifference.

'If you should, or rather, if you must,' Chernov said, 'it would be as well to say nothing about your work here.'

'I shall not see him,' Ivan said. And meant it. He considered that to avoid his father would be an act of loyalty to his employer. Chernov said nothing, but led him into the workshop. About a dozen men were working there. None acknowledged Ivan when he passed, so intent were they on their machines. But one of them, on seeing Chernov with Ivan in tow, silenced his press and waited for them to approach.

'This is Pavlenkov,' Chernov said. And to Pavlenkov, 'Lvov's new recruit, Ivan Volynin.'

Ivan studied him. He was possibly his father's age. And looked it. Though every crease on his face was alive and expectant, unlike his father's time-grooved resignation. He shook his hand.

'I'll leave you,' Chernov said. 'Just tell him what to do.'

Pavlenkov handed Ivan a broom. 'You can start by sweeping the floor,' he said. He touched Ivan's arm. 'Every job is important here. Even the most menial. For they all contribute to the work we are trying to do.'

Ivan did not ask what the work was. But he had a feeling he would heartily have approved of it. He swept the floor with an energy and enthusiasm far beyond the call of duty.

For the rest of that day, Pavlenkov kept Ivan by his side. In simple terms he explained how the presses worked, and as he did so it was as if he were discovering their workings for the first time. He seemed to marvel at their miracles. 'This machine is a door to the future,' he said, but he did not elaborate. Instead, he turned to Ivan and winked at him, as if inviting him into a conspiracy. Later that day, he introduced him to the magic of typesetting. He concentrated on the technique and there was little opportunity to decipher the actual words that were assembled. But one word did compose itself under Ivan's startled eye. 'Strike.' Ivan knew it could have referred to anything, but he preferred to think of it as a password to conspiracy.

After work, Pavlenkov took Ivan to the room they would share. It was one of many above the shop, and Ivan rightly surmised that the other workers lived there too. Chernov's establishment was more than a print shop. It was a small community and perhaps, Ivan dared to hope, something even more than that. The room was sparsely furnished: two beds, with a table in between, two shelves, and one small cupboard. Ivan noticed that one shelf was crammed with books, and the table too was piled high with pamphlets and files.

Pavlenkov lit a candle. 'D'you read, Volynin?' he asked.

'Whatever I can find,' Ivan said.

'Then you must buy your own candle,' Pavlenkov said.

Ivan unpacked his few belongings. Pavlenkov puzzled him. He couldn't understand the contradictions in the man. Sometimes he was friendly, and at others, and almost in the same breath, he was dismissive to the point of unkindness. Ivan suspected he was testing him. He opened his suitcase, crouching beside it. He took out a nightshirt. He was wary of unpacking his few books, uncertain whether or not they would be frowned upon. But the Pushkin was safe. He put it on his shelf, but in its utterly unprotected isolation, it seemed to have lost its innocence. Alone, it shrieked a statement. Its very detachment proclaimed its guilt. He laid it on its side in an attempt to dilute its aggression. He was shy of undressing in front of a stranger. Pavlenkov lay in bed reading, and Ivan was relieved that his back was turned. So quickly he divested his clothing and slipped the nightshirt over his head. As he got into his bed, Pavlenkov turned around.

'That was quick,' he said. 'Don't you say your prayers before you sleep?'

'No,' Ivan said. There was no way he would disguise his lack of faith.

'Don't you even pray for the Tsar?' Pavlenkov insisted.

Ivan considered that silence was the safest way to respond, and after a while Pavlenkov smiled at him. 'I have a feeling we're going to be friends,' he said.

Ivan settled himself under the blanket. Tomorrow he would unpack his books without fear.

The first month of his apprenticeship passed quickly. And rarely did he give Katya a thought. Neither did he miss his village. That life had been swiftly overtaken by his obsession with his work and his new friendships with his fellow workers. After a few weeks he was put in charge of his own machine and he was able in his own time to read and to marvel at the subversion he was committing to paper. It gave him a feeling of tremendous power, a feeling he relished with as much pleasure as shame. It fed his expectations and he wondered at times whether he was entitled to ambition at all. But these were village thoughts and he tried to dismiss them. They reflected a state of mind bred on apathy and inertia. He was above all that, he hoped, and he tried not to feel too proud of himself.

His life was full. His days were overfilled with work at the presses, and Pavlenkov took care of his spare time. In the beginning they stayed in at nights, reading. Occasionally other workers would come to their room and reading would give way to discussion. For the most part, Ivan listened. He knew that he had much to learn. Words that he had stifled in his village, words that he barely had had the courage to whisper to himself, now thundered across the smoke-filled room with shameless audacity. 'Lenin', 'democracy', 'scientific revolution'. All the talk, even those words that he didn't understand, seemed to confirm and to nourish those hopes he had harboured in his heart since childhood. Hopes that had been fed by each visit to his father, by every signal proof of inequality, by every syllable that singed the pages of his sparse reading. One day he would talk like these men. One day he might even lead them. Once again he felt the uneasy nudge of ambition, and he prayed that soon he would find that nudge comfortable.

Some evenings the men took him to a tavern, where the drink would oil their talk into whispers. Ivan did not drink, and these were the times that he liked best, playing the role of the privileged and sober witness of conspiracy.

'It's time that Volynin joined the Printers' Union,' one of the men suggested – this from Smirnov, a young peasant, who'd been apprenticed some years before. Smirnov was a sullen man, with a slightly superior air. Hitherto Ivan had disliked him, but now he warmed towards the man for his suggestion.

'Tomorrow we'll take him to the meeting,' Pavlenkov said. It was a token of their total acceptance of Ivan as a member of their circle, and the following night, he was proposed and accepted into the printers' fraternity. But the question of his membership was dealt with very quickly and was a mere preamble to the purpose of the meeting. Ivan looked around the room. It was a cellar. He had no idea where in Vosrov the cellar was located, for Pavlenkov had blindfolded him at their approach. He didn't complain. He understood and relished the need for secrecy, and he had no doubt that one day they would trust him well enough to lead the way. He could not count the number of people in the cellar, and he could barely see their faces, for the room was dimly lantern-lit. He sat amongst his printing friends, Pavlenkov, Smirnov, Golenko, Bazarov, when, out of the shadows, the figure of a man took centre stage.

'That's Golikov,' Pavlenkov whispered. 'He is the leader of our cell.'

Ivan stared at him, and recognised an unnerving likeness to himself. He had the same gaunt features, the same tightness about the mouth. He clearly was a man who shunned pleasure, who neither drank nor smoked, who had little time for women, and whose life was obsessed with the Cause. Yes, it struck Ivan as an unnerving likeness, but at the same time he was not displeased by it. He noted that Golikov sported a beard, the only signal difference between them, and Ivan considered that he might go for a while without shaving. When the man began to talk of Lenin, Ivan knew on whom he modelled himself. He could do worse, he decided, than use that same model for himself.

'Without revolutionary theory,' Golikov began, 'there can be no revolutionary movement.' The men murmured their assent. Smirnov was silent, taking notes, as if he would consider that premise at his leisure and in private. 'I want you to consider just two words of Lenin's pamphlet,' Golikov continued. 'Scientific Socialism. A simple concept. A notion of the leadership of an élite. A vanguard of wise men to proclaim the Revolution.' There were more cheers from the audience and more notes on Smirnov's pad. Ivan joined in the cheers though he was far from fully understanding Golikov's words. Pavlenkov nudged him. 'I'll explain it all later,' he said with a smile.

Later the talk turned to the role of violence, and what part, if any, it should play in the Revolution. There was much heated discussion. Clearly the group was not unanimous in its opinions, while Smirnov scribbled like a demon. Eventually, the meeting broke up. Ivan was once more blindfolded and led to a tavern, where the blind was removed and he saw himself surrounded by his print shop friends.

'To our new comrade,' Bazarov was shouting, a glass of vodka

41

in his hand. So they drank to Ivan's initiation and to the success of the Revolution. For an arrogant moment Ivan felt a prophetic certainty that the two were indissolubly linked.

For subsequent meetings, Ivan was trusted without the blindfold. Slowly he began to understand Lenin's revolutionary theories, and every night, either in the tavern or in their room, he and Pavlenkov would split hairs in discussion. He was happy. For the first time in his life he felt useful. He wondered at times whether he would ever return to his village. And at such times, he would think of Katya and he realised that with all his work, his readings, and his meetings, she had never entirely slipped his mind.

There was suddenly an overwhelming amount of work in the print shop, for there were rumours of war. For many years Russia's foreign policy in Eastern Siberia, that terrain that abuts Japan, had been an expansionist one. Their colonising eye had settled on the Kamchatka Peninsula, a strategic jewel in anyone's crown. But it rightly belonged to Japan. Then Japan, troubled by the Tsar's belligerent covetousness, declared war. The Tsar, who referred to the enemy as 'little short-tailed monkeys', responded with the whole might of the Russian army and navy and with an overweening certainty that swift victory was his. But in the print shop and elsewhere amongst the dissidents, they prayed for the Tsar's overthrow.

'There is nothing more calculated to help the Revolution than the loss of a war,' Pavlenkov told Ivan. 'We must pray for the Tsar's defeat.' These words he whispered, for they were treason.

One morning, shortly after the declaration of war, Dr Lvov paid a visit to the print shop. It was the first time Ivan had seen him since he had left Larionovka. On meeting him, Ivan's heart flooded with a nostalgia that surprised him, and he made a decision to go back and visit his family. And Dr Lvov in his first words gave him cause.

'You must go home, Ivan,' he said. 'Pyotr is going to join the army. You must try and stop him. He should go into hiding. This will be a bloody and terrible war. I shall take you back with me today. I have arranged it all with Chernov. Just a few days, and then you can return.'

Ivan was stunned by his words. He had always considered the doctor as a Tsar-worshipper and here he was propagating desertion. But he would say nothing to anybody. After his months' work at the print shop he knew the vital importance of secrecy. The Security Police, the Okhrana, were zealous in their arrests and their network of spies spread from factory to farm, taverns to bars and even within families. The dissidents of the time were a nation of whisperers, but sometimes the very whisper betrayed them, for its muffled tone hinted at camouflage and discontent. Silence was a safer weapon, its only risk being a label of stupidity. So in his village he would play the idiot, Ivan decided, though he knew that with Pyotr it would be difficult to hold his tongue. He said his farewells to his workmates. Although they had never been close friends, Smirnov, for some reason, seemed most anxious for his return, and Ivan ascribed his affection to their common village background. Pavlenkov was the hardest to part with, although his village visit would last only a few days. As they took leave of one another, Ivan realised how close he had grown to that man, how much he owed him in friendship and teaching. And for his fathering. For that is how he loved him.

Pavlenkov, for his part, was as much moved as Ivan. Despite the fact that he knew little about Ivan, about his family, his background – such personal trivia were irrelevant to the Cause – despite that ignorance, and Ivan's like ignorance of himself, he looked upon Ivan as something more than a comrade. He was a friend, that old-fashioned and dangerous term, a term that hinted at personal intimacy. There was an abyss between the concept of 'comrade' and that of 'friend', an abyss one bridged at one's peril, but it seemed that both men longed for a meeting point. They embraced each other fondly.

'It will only be a few days,' Ivan said.

'Take care of yourself,' Pavlenkov said. 'And hold your tongue.'

In Dr Lvov's carriage, on the way home to Larionovka, Ivan tried not to think of Katya. The business of his visit was Pyotr, and to persuade him to go into hiding. He could not stifle the thought that, whether in hiding or in the army, Katya would be on her own. He tried to persuade himself that he would act only for Pyotr's

43

sake, and that he would respect his absence whatever its nature. He thought of his parents and little Sasha, those easy and comfortable welcomes in which whispers could be tokens only of affection, and when the carriage drew up outside the Volynin dwelling it was the three of them who stood outside to welcome him. Ivan scooped little Sasha in his arms.

'I can read, I can read, Ivan,' Sasha said. 'Katya taught me.'

Ivan shivered at her name and disguised his tremor in Sasha's embrace. 'But you're only four years old,' he said. 'I couldn't read until I was ten.'

'Then I'm cleverer than you,' Sasha laughed.

Ivan kissed his mother. Although he had not seen her for only four months, she looked a lot older. He ascribed it to her anxiety over Pyotr.

'He won't go, Mama,' he said. 'I shall stop him.'

She looked at him, astonished. 'He must fight for the Tsar,' she said. 'It's his duty.'

He remembered that he must hold his tongue, so he let it pass. His father, truanting from Vosrov, slouched at the door, eager to greet him, brimming with love, yet shy of him, shy of his learning, of his profession, and his audacious breaking of the failure chain. But proud too. Bewildered by all his irreconcilable feelings, he clung to the doorpost, longing for, and fearing, greeting.

'Papa,' Ivan shouted. 'Are you not pleased to see me?'

He rushed to his side, and embraced him. He noted his father's tears, but he was not moved by them, for in his eyes they were but a symbol of weakness, of docility and servile obedience, all desperate enemies of revolution. He put Sasha down and went into the hut.

He saw her back first. Perhaps on hearing his arrival she had turned her back to the door. She, too, feared their meeting. But he would deal with Katya later, for the sight of Pyotr in his soldier's uniform demanded his immediate and urgent attention.

'You mustn't go,' Ivan said. He couldn't be bothered to whisper. He would not be argued with. His decision was final.

It was then that she turned around. 'Ivan,' she said. There was no censure in her voice. No anger. Nor even pleasure. It was simply an acknowledgement that she was aware of his presence.

44

'Katya,' he said, with the same acknowledgement. Like her, he could afford no elaboration. He turned his attention once more to Pyotr. 'You cannot go,' he said again. 'You must go into hiding.'

Pyotr laughed. 'You're foolish,' he said. 'You and all your ideas.' There was a trace of contempt in his voice, and Ivan despaired of convincing him.

'Forget my ideas,' he said. 'You're my brother and I love you. I want you to live, and this is not a cause worth dying for.'

'We've been attacked,' Pyotr said. 'I'm fighting for the Tsar. That's a cause, isn't it?'

'But is it worth it?' Ivan tried to be patient. 'What do we need Kamchatka for? Isn't Russia big enough? Are you prepared to die in the name of greed, the greed of an oppressor? The Tsar's a monster.' He thought of Pavlenkov then, and his promise to hold his tongue. But it was too late. It was out, so he might as well repeat it. Besides, it gave him a certain pleasure. 'He's a monster,' he said again. 'A brutal despot. D'you think he gives a fig for people like us?'

'God help you.' This from Maria, who stood at the door.

And a sigh from Vassily, who was but her echo.

'Don't you dare say things like that in this house,' his mother said. 'Pyotr is right. He is going to do his duty. The Tsar is our protector.'

Ivan could stand it no longer. 'He's a beast!' he screamed. 'I wish him dead. Him and all his rotten family.'

The words were barely out of his mouth when Pyotr's clenched fist landed on his lips, bruising each syllable of his blasphemy. Ivan staggered, reeling against the wall. He did not think of fighting back. Pyotr was no enemy. He loved his brother and desperately wanted to keep him safe. And at home. For he was terrified of being saddled with Katya's availability. And now she was beside him, wiping his lips, her eyes misted with a disturbing tenderness.

'I'm going,' Pyotr said. He slung his kitbag over his shoulder.

Ivan sprang to his feet. 'Please,' he said. 'Pyotr. Please. You can come back to Vosrov with me. Katya too. I'll hide you both. I know people.' He was fearful of the promises he was making, but he had to keep Pyotr by Katya's side.

'I'm different from you,' Pyotr said calmly. 'I love my country, and I love my Tsar. I shall fight for them both.' He turned to Katya. 'Are you coming to the square?' he asked coldly, and Ivan wondered whether his brother was joining the colours less out of patriotism than as an avenue for escaping from an ungiving, unloving wife.

'We're all coming,' Maria said. 'You too, Ivan,' she ordered. 'The priest will bless the soldiers, though you are in greater need of blessing.' She took Sasha's hand and they left the hut. Vassily followed in their shadows.

'Well, are you coming or not, Katya?' Pyotr said.

She took his arm. 'Of course. And Ivan will come too.' She pulled him to Pyotr's side. 'Please,' she said, 'don't leave each other in quarrel. Pyotr,' she gripped his arm, 'take your brother's hand.'

Ivan stretched out his arms. Pyotr fell into his embrace.

'Take great care,' Ivan said. 'Don't be a hero.' Over Pyotr's shoulder he caught sight of Katya's face, that temptation trap of his brother's absence. 'And come home soon,' he pleaded.

The square was crowded. Young men from neighbouring villages had assembled in front of the church, their mothers weeping beside them, and their fathers wishing they themselves were young again. The village boys stood in a crowd apart, circling their priest with their proprietary rights. Their church had been chosen as the assembly and departure point for the whole region. They had a sense of playing host, and they chided their mothers for weeping. Pyotr joined them, standing in a position where he could keep his family in his sights. There was an air of expectation amongst the crowd and when the Larionov carriage came in sight over the brow of the hill, they offered up a doubtful cheer of relief and impatience, a cheer that orchestrated the last stage of the journey to the church portal. There the liveried coachman opened the carriage door.

The first to alight was little Anna, her excitement curbed by a mournful Marfa, who followed close behind. Nicolai was next, resplendent in a naval officer's uniform, his lower lip curled and his eyes lowered in contempt. He imagined that this was the look of a hero, which role, cock-a-hoop and full of confidence, he intended to play. Count Dmitri followed him with Andrei at his side.

The Countess Tatiana was last to alight from the coach. She was aware that she must set an example to the other mothers, and though her heart was as heavy as theirs, her eyes were dry. She even managed a manufactured smile. With their arrival the priest was at liberty to begin his round of blessings. He started with Nicolai, sprinkling holy water on his forehead, and murmuring a prayer. He lingered with him awhile, then moved on swiftly to other ranks. But these he did not bless separately, but in groups of three or four. In this manner he did the rounds of the whole company, then signalled to the several drivers of the horse-drawn carts that stood on the perimeter of the square. Now was the time of leave-taking.

Ivan watched the procedure, sickened by it all. Sickened by the hypocrisy and the utter futility of the ceremony. He knew it was an unjust war, and he feared that the battle was lost before it was ever waged. That thousands of men would not return to their homes. That villages like his own would be orphaned and widowed in the Tsar's overweeningly proud time. But not Pyotr, he prayed.

His brother was coming towards them, suitably blessed, and safe from the enemy's fire, as safe as his enemy who had no doubt been blessed in their own fashion. He went first to Katya, and held her close. She cried in his embrace, fearful for his safety. She wept for their past together, for their shared childhood. For their games and mischiefs and their growing limbs. She wept for the bright colours of that landscape, that countryside of innocence. But she could not weep for the cold and rooted stand-still that it had all become, the colours faded, the laughter a hollow echo. So she caressed him for the past and prayed for his future, whoever he might share it with. Pyotr held on to her with one arm, and with the other he embraced Ivan. It might have been because he was the nearest to hand, or perhaps, in holding them together, he was putting his sad signature to abdication. He held them close for a long while, without saying a word. Then he took Maria and Sasha in his arms, another wordless embrace, but most silent of all, and most loving, was his farewell to Vassily. His father he would miss most of all, for he was the echo of his own failures, his own frustrations and his own punctured innocence.

47

They moved towards the wagons. As they passed other enlisted men from the village they said their neighbourly farewells. Then they walked in patient line to where the Larionov family were gathered, to offer their peasant blessings to Nicolai, and their prayers for his safe return. A line of homage, and Ivan quietly detached himself from it, taking little Sasha by the hand, so he could join in the play of the other children who had, out of impatience, ignored the line.

Amongst them was Anna, who had deftly untied the sash about her waist, and had left Marfa a silk blue ribbon, unaware of its detachment. Wandering amongst the children, Anna made sure of accidentally bumping into Sasha. Ivan smiled. Though only four years old, she knew a woman's wiles. 'My brother's an officer,' she said. 'And yours is only a soldier.'

So young, Ivan thought. And already corrupted.

'But soldiers do all the fighting,' Sasha said, holding his little own.

'What do I care?' she said, skipping around him, bridging that sorely felt gap at her suckling side. Then Marfa was upon her, the loose blue sash dangling from her hand, and she was swept away with much tutting and disdain, back into her own class.

'Anna!' Sasha shouted in dismay. It was a cry of longing and pain, a pain illegal for one of his small years. Ivan scooped him in his arms, caressing him. He himself could have cried 'Katya' with the same longing, despite the years that separated him from his little brother.

The men were mounting the wagons and the village band began to play martial music, as was fitting for the occasion. Mothers and sweethearts took their last farewells, and waved the wagons out of the square. Last to leave was the Larionov carriage. As it passed, Sasha waved furiously, though the curtains on the windows were firmly drawn. In a short while all the wagons were out of sight, and the band wound down in an apologetic coda. Then the weeping began in earnest. Even the men, hitherto dry-eyed, now shamelessly acknowledged the reality of their loss. Maria clung to Ivan, and Vassily to Maria. Katya stood alone and wondered what she ought to be feeling.

Slowly the square emptied. They were loath to return to their homes and to the palpable absence at table, so they dawdled and comforted each other. The men, fathers too old to fight, who had long relinquished their seat at the head of the table in favour of the eldest son, now found themselves the men of the house, and were fearful of their lack of practice. Vassily, conscious of his status, and conscious, too, of his painful inadequacy to play the role, now timidly approached his middle son.

'Ivan,' he said timidly. 'Perhaps you should stay here. Your mother will need you.'

It was out of the question. Apart from Katya, whose presence would have been disturbing enough, he had a life elsewhere. And with others of his kind. He had outgrown his village. Larionovka belonged to his past, and now was but a target for nostalgia. He thought suddenly of Pavlenkov, and longed for his company. Then he looked at his father and rued his disloyalty. He didn't know what to say to him. A refusal would have been too cruel. And any explanation would have been beyond his understanding. So he simply put his arm around him and hoped he could not smell the pity in his touch. But his mother saved him from words.

'When you go back to Vosrov,' she said, 'you must take Pyotr's blanket with you. It will soon turn cold.' She took Vassily's arm. 'I have my old protector,' she laughed.

With this encouragement Vassily felt able to assume his old role. 'I'm a bit rusty,' he apologised.

'Come, Ivan,' Maria said. 'We shall go home and eat. And you shall tell us all about Vosrov.'

That evening, Ivan opened the bottle of vodka he had brought from Vosrov. Smirnov had given it to him on his departure. 'To drink to your brother's safe return,' he had said. And now they did just that. Katya was glad to drown whatever sorrow she should have felt, and Vassily drank greedily, for only in a vodka haze could he envisage himself as the head of the family. Ivan in his sobriety regaled them with stories of Vosrov. But he gave no details. He told them about his community of friends, about the tavern and their talks. But he did not elaborate on the matter of their discussions. He told them about the marvels of printing machinery, but he did not mention the matter of their output. He told them about Smirnov and the others in the print shop, but for some reason he noticed that on Pavlenkov he held his tongue. During his whole recital, Katya said nothing. She stared at him, but Ivan had the feeling that she was not seeing him. Maria plied him with questions. She was concerned about how he was eating and whether his mattress was comfortable. Sasha wanted to know about the letters and how they were put together. So Ivan drew him the likeness of a typesetting machine. In its composition, he assembled the first words that he had deciphered at Pavlenkov's side. The letters of 'strike'. Sasha studied it carefully and curled his lips over the letters. Then after a while, his brow puckered. 'Strike,' he said.

'Sasha!' Ivan exclaimed with delight.

Then Katya spoke for the first time. 'He's a good pupil,' she said. She smiled at him, and for a moment he thought he might stay in his village.

Vassily rose, staggering a little, and started to clear the table. So out of practice was he, that he thought that such a gesture would establish him as the man in the house. Maria gaped in astonishment. Then roared with laughter, then rose herself to help him. Ivan watched them together, and envied their easy loving. He was glad he would have such a memory to take back to Vosrov. It would soft-pedal the pain of leaving Katya.

In the morning Ivan rose early. Dr Lvov had calls to make in Vosrov and he would take him there. He said goodbye to his village, pressing a little money into Maria's hands. She was loath to take it, but he assured her he was amply provided for. He looked for Katya but she had left early for her kitchen work in the house on the hill. He was glad she had spared him a leave-taking. Spared herself, too, he imagined, for all words were dangerous between them. He would think about her on the journey back to Vosrov, for he could depend on Dr Lvov's silence. And indeed the doctor said very little during the journey. Once he offered comment that the Countess Tatiana had taken to her bed, prostrate with grief, and Ivan remarked that his mother could not enjoy the luxury of lying abed though her sorrow was none the less. That seemed to put an end to the conversation, and no more words were exchanged until Dr Lvov put him down at the printer's shop.

'My regards to Chernov,' he said.

Ivan went straight to Pavlenkov's machine.

'Back so soon?' Pavlenkov said. 'You gave me no time to miss you.' Then he laughed and embraced him, and the village and its Katya slipped entirely from Ivan's mind.

That night they didn't go to the tavern. And there was no meeting. Golikov, Pavlenkov told him, had gone on business to St Petersburg. So they stayed in their room, and played chess together.

'Let black be the Tsar,' Pavlenkov said. 'The colour of his soul. And because I love you, I volunteer to play on the side of evil. You shall be white and we shall see who wins.'

When, a couple of hours later, Ivan mated, he asked, 'Was it a true victory, or did you allow it?'

'I have to admit', Pavlenkov said, 'that my principles won. Consider it as a rehearsal for the Revolution.' He put the pieces back into the box, then he whispered in Ivan's ear.

'It's close, Ivan. Closer than we dared to hope.'

4

It wasn't that close, but certainly the revolutionaries had reason for hope. The year of 1904 was not happy for the Tsar. The war was going badly. Those 'little short-tailed monkeys' were giving the Russians a very hard time. In February of that year the Japanese fleet sank two Russian warships at Chemulpo in Korea and torpedoed the main Russian force in Port Arthur. The annihilation of the Russian fleet was a gross humiliation, and that it was engineered by an underdeveloped nation was the unkindest cut of all. And on top of all this, the Tsar was having trouble at home. The workers were on the march, and for the first time in the long terrible years of Tsarist oppression there was the smell of mutiny in the streets. Workers were marching in protest against their miserable conditions. The following year saw 'Bloody Sunday' in St Petersburg, where, in a peaceful demonstration outside the Winter Palace, a hundred people were mown down by the palace guards. Their gift was a hundred martyrs to the Revolution. The Tsar was distinctly uncomfortable. He strengthened his secret police force, the Okhrana, and gave them licence to arrest and summarily dispatch those with subversive intent.

It was during this period that Chernov's little print shop in Vosrov was called upon to utilise all its resources. The presses turned all day and most of the night. Meetings of the cell were irregular, and discussions were heated, while Smirnov's hand cramped with his note-taking. Then came the taverns, and what little was left of the night, for sleep, but not before Pavlenkov and Ivan had re-capped on their day and organised the next stage of the

Revolution. During this time, Golikov, the leader of their cell, was shuttling back and forth to St Petersburg. It was on his return from one of these journeys, shortly after the Bloody Sunday massacre, that he brought an order to the print shop for five thousand leaflets. They were to contain a single word, centred, and in heavy black. STRIKE.

The presses began to turn, and all the men believed that at last they were witnessing the birth of the Revolution.

The job would take about a week, considering it had to be camouflaged by the more legitimate orders of invitations, concert programmes and the like. On the third day, the men assembled for work and it was noted that Smirnov was missing. It was assumed that he was ill, but Bazarov, his room-mate, reported that he had not slept in his bed and was probably dead drunk on a tavern floor, his notebook clutched in his hand.

'He'll turn up sooner or later,' Bazarov said. 'I'll start up his machine.'

But Pavlenkov was uneasy. Smirnov was not a drinker and in any case, drunkenness beyond control was strictly prohibited. Drunk or not, somehow or other, Smirnov, as a reliable comrade, would have found his way home.

'I think he may have been picked up,' Pavlenkov said. 'We must not print the leaflets today. And we must hide those we've already done.'

The men groaned at the extra chore. But what Pavlenkov had said made sense, so they set about their cover-up. Then froze. Caught red- and leaflet-handed. At the door, no longer hinged or bolted, its wood shattered on the floor, stood Gribov, known and avoided by all. Gribov, the local head of the Okhrana. Pavlenkov had been right, they all thought. Smirnov had been taken, together with his notebook, and under their torture, had spilt the beans.

At first they did not notice the posse of men behind him. The large figure of Gribov seemed ample enough to carry out whatever he had in mind without support. It was when he shouted an order that they saw them, six secret policemen bursting into the print shop to search and destroy. The workers shivered in fear. They knew all about the Okhrana. Each of them knew of a comrade who

53

had walked with them and had never been seen again, and each of them thought of those they loved, and forced themselves to believe that they loved the Revolution more. But Ivan did not think of Katya, nor of his mother or father. He thought of little Sasha, and with some envy, for he knew with absolute certainty that he would inherit the Revolution.

More men arrived and man-handled the workers into a police wagon that waited outside. Pavlenkov was the first to enter. He was surprised to find Chernov there, patiently waiting, accepting his fate. He smiled.

'We did our best,' he said. 'All of us.'

The wagon took off with a jerk. The guards sat between them. Even if escape had been possible, the men were too stunned by their capture to move. Sleep was still in their eyes, and the breakfast bread in the cracks of their teeth. Some of them prayed, but strictly to themselves, for to advertise their prayer would have betokened a loss of faith in their Cause. The wagon was covered, but they knew the streets of Vosrov by heart. They knew each turning, right and left, and every alley where the wagon stumbled. They knew each tavern that they passed, and the location of their meeting cells. And all of them stiffened as they neared the police station. When they would be bundled out of the wagon, each man promised himself a last look at the sky.

But the guards threw blankets over their heads, blankets that smelt of other doomed men, and it was within that acrid darkness that they entered what all of them assumed to be their last shelter in this life. They were thrown together in one cell. The blankets were removed from their heads and tossed onto the floor.

'Your bedding,' one of the guards said. Then laughed and left the room.

The men took a short time to adjust their eyes to the light, though there was little of it. High on one wall was a barred window and they were anxious to see what it overlooked. A few trees perhaps, or a children's playground, a hopeful reminder of growth and life that they might well forfeit. Bazarov, the strongest amongst them, offered his shoulders to Pavlenkov, the lightest in weight, to share with others what he would see. Bazarov squatted down, and Pav-

54

lenkov took off his shoes. Then gently he balanced himself on the strong man's shoulders. Slowly Bazarov rose to his full height and settled Pavlenkov at window level. Almost immediately Pavlenkov turned his face away. Its colour was ashen and tears welled in his eyes.

'Our Cause is just,' he whispered, and the men knew that their cell overlooked the gallows.

They huddled on the floor, close to each other for comfort. They shivered and made no attempt to hide their fear.

'We could do with a chess set,' Pavlenkov said.

'And who would play black?' Ivan asked him.

'That would indeed be a problem,' Pavlenkov laughed.

He would never laugh again.

They heard scuffles outside the cell and a jangle of keys. And all of them froze in fear.

'That is the last of them,' they heard a warder say.

The cell door was opened, and a body covered with a blanket was thrown inside. The door was quickly locked and the men stared at the hump on the floor, crouched like a giant insect, and they were fearful of touching it. Then it suddenly moved and they heard it groan. The face was caked in blood and bruising. Two teeth, offensively white, framed a row of bleeding and empty sockets, and the lower lip was swollen and blue. But out of that ravaged crater, Golikov managed to smile. Pavlenkov took him in his arms, cradling his pain.

'I told them nothing,' he whispered. 'They knew it all already.'

'Who did this to you?' Ivan screamed.

Golikov managed another smile. 'Smirnov,' he said. 'In his Okhrana uniform.'

Then they knew why Smirnov had not slept in his bed. Then they knew the purpose of his notebook and his constant scribbling. Their anger was sublime, but it was directed at themselves for having been so grossly deceived. It was then that Ivan made the decision to escape. By whatever means. He had to survive if only to kill Smirnov.

'Don't talk any more,' Pavlenkov said. 'Try to sleep a little. I'll hold you.'

55

The men fell silent once more. After a while, a murmuring was heard from the corner. One amongst the men was not ashamed to pray. Chernov. And in a strange tongue that the men could not connect with their own Orthodox Church. Yet they knew it was prayer by its pleading tone of lamentation.

'Chernov's a Yid,' Bazarov said. None of them had known, and all of them, fed from birth with time-honoured Jew-hatred, now wondered how they had been able to love him.

'What difference?' Golikov said. 'We're all going to die anyway.' Then he himself went about his prayers; the others joined with him. But Pavlenkov and Ivan held a common silence. For both of them, prayer would have been abdication.

'Our cause is just,' Pavlenkov said again, but to himself for reassurance. The Cause could compete with any faith and conquer them all. He would not sully it with prayer. He heard a clock chime, and he counted the hours. Only ten. It was still early in the day, yet the nightmare had seemed an eternity. He was suddenly hungry and he was angry that facing death he could still be assailed by mortal longings. He thought of Natasha, his wife, conjuring her face and her body from a long and distant past, her plaintive and bewildered face as he slowly convinced her that she was less important than the Cause. 'Our cause is just,' he said to himself again. He looked down on Golikov's face, and was glad that he was sleeping. Did Golikov have a wife, he wondered. Children? They had been friends for many years, but he knew none of these things. They hadn't seemed to matter. But now, for some reason, nothing else in the world mattered more. He had to know. 'Golikov,' he whispered.

His friend opened a bruised eye.

'Do you have children? A wife?' Pavlenkov begged him.

'I'm thinking of them,' Golikov said. 'And for the first time in many years. Comrade,' he whispered, 'did we do the right kind of loving?'

'Go to sleep,' Pavlenkov said. His heart turned over. There were other causes, he thought, and they were equally as just.

Ivan crawled over to his side. 'It's nothing,' he said. 'I just want to hold your hand.'

What's happening to all of us, Pavlenkov wondered. We've marched for a million men that we don't know. It was so much easier than marching for just one whom we knew and loved.

He clutched at Ivan's hand. 'Is there anybody that you love, Volynin?' he asked.

'My mother, my father, my brothers,' he said. But he too expected death, and there was no longer any point in suppression. 'And Katya too,' he almost shouted.

'If you live,' Pavlenkov said, 'look after them. Look after that love.'

There were heavy footsteps outside the cell. A warder opened the door, and suddenly in its frame stood Smirnov. Ivan made an instinctive move towards him, but Pavlenkov held him back. 'He's not worth it,' he whispered. He wondered whether Smirnov had a wife and children.

Smirnov stood looking at them. He appeared strange without his notebook. Undressed, almost, despite the shameful uniform that he wore. The prayers ceased. The men would not give Smirnov that satisfaction.

'Pavlenkov,' he shouted. He addressed him as a stranger. How could he have forgotten, Ivan thought, the nights and days they had spent together, the drinking, the laughing and singing, all that so terrible comradeship that they had enjoyed.

Pavlenkov eased Golikov off his lap. He stood up. He trembled with fear and could not stop himself from praying. For a moment, he looked forward to seeing the sky.

'Golikov,' Smirnov called. 'And quickly.'

'But he's sleeping,' Ivan said.

'He will sleep soon enough,' Smirnov said.

The men helped Golikov to his feet. All were fearful of the next name on the roll call.

'That's the lot,' Smirnov said, and they sighed with a relief of which they were ashamed.

'Quickly,' Smirnov ordered again.

The two men linked arms. The others crowded around them. Ivan fell on Pavlenkov's neck and embraced him. His tears drenched his mentor's cheek and mingled with Pavlenkov's own. He hadn't meant to cry. He had meant to go with dignity, to shake hands with each of his comrades and to assure them that their Cause was just. But his heart wasn't in it any more. So he wept for his loss of faith, and he thought of his wife. 'I'm sorry,' he muttered. 'I'm so terribly sorry.'

The door clanged shut after them, and its echo muffled their departing steps. The men in the cell looked at each other, and then at the floor. Then Chernov began to pray aloud. Kadish, the Jewish prayer for the dead. Ivan touched Bazarov's arm and led him to the window. There the strong man squatted while Ivan mounted his shoulders. Bazarov rose. When Ivan's eyes met the window-ledge, they shut of their own accord, as if fearful that the scene outside the bars would blind them. But Ivan forced himself to look. He could see the back of Pavlenkov's head, and resting on his shoulder, Golikov's, his broken and tortured body already halfway to heaven. The two men seemed soldered together, as if they had it in mind to die as one. But as they mounted the steps, a guard roughly separated them. Golikov staggered, his steps as unable as they were unwilling. He was shoved onto the platform, and held there by a guard's distant and disdainful arm. Then they were turned, facing Ivan, their sole audience. He put his fingers through the bars, waving them in trickling farewell. He thought Pavlenkov smiled at him. He watched the noose as it laced Pavlenkov's neck. He saw how he opened his mouth to speak. And then a cry came from lips struggling through the throes of death, the shrill of a birth-pang.

'Natasha,' he called. And again, 'Natasha.' No reference to a cause that was just, no paean to the Revolution. Just a simple cry of love and life that echoed around the death yard like a contrapuntal passing bell. Then his body dropped from view while the echoes of his love resounded like a requiem.

Ivan could look no longer. He signalled to Bazarov to let him down. Then he sat on the floor of his cell and mourned his friend aloud.

In the silence the men listened for the thud of the second drop and when it came, they uttered a unison, 'Amen.' Then silence again, for remembrance.

After a while the cell door opened. 'You're to be moved,' the warder said. 'Line up, all of you.' No one dared to ask where they were going. They all surmised that it was better not to know. Chernov had difficulty in getting to his feet. His face was ashen but for a sickly yellowish tinge. Ivan helped him rise, and stood behind him in the line. They were halfway down the corridor that led to the open front door of the station, when Chernov stumbled and fell.

'Get up.' One of the guards kicked his prone body.

Ivan knelt beside him. A drop of spittle slithered down Chernov's chin, and a prayer dribbled from his lips.

'I think he's dying,' Ivan said.

The guard knelt by Chernov's side, and shortly he was joined by his partner. The men, aware of some disturbance, stood still and, cowed into obedience, waited for orders. But not Ivan. All he saw was the guardless open door to freedom. He recalled Pavlenkov's farewell smile, and the shameful treachery of Smirnov's uniform. Two very good reasons why he should survive. He had nothing to lose now, and risked only a shot in the back. He sidled down to the front of the line. And then ran. Ran for his life and his Smirnov revenge. He thought of poor Chernov. The Yids were always making trouble. Now he was grateful for their disturbance. He wished Chernov well – he had been good to him – but he wondered whether in the circumstances the old man would not be better off dead. He ran. He was making for the fields. In the streets his speed would be conspicuous. Yet he ran, fear in his heels and hatred in his heart. He knew Vosrov street by cobbled street and he made for its outskirts, where the fields would shelter him and he would have time for that promised look at the sky. But now he concentrated on the cobbles and slunk into an alley to catch his breath. He wondered whether he had yet been missed, and that thought drove him on, his knees melting in fear. He did not stop again until he came to the open country. Then he flung himself under a tree, and took his pledged look at the sky. But all he saw was Pavlenkov's head as it slithered out of the clouds. And he heard again that passionate call to Natasha, and he knew that wherever she was, she must have heard its echo.

In the distance he heard the barking of a dog, and he took to his heels once more. But the dog must have been a lone farmer's and after a while he heard nothing. He rested again. He reckoned he was about two versts from his village. But he couldn't stay there. Once his escape had been discovered, Larionovka was the first place they would search. He would go home for food and clothes, and for a sight of his family. Then somehow or other he would find his way to St Petersburg and lose himself in its ample anonymity. He ran. Fear still gripped him, but now hunger fuelled his speed. After his mortal encounter, he was assailed by a crude and almost offensive appetite for life. He had to live for Pavlenkov and Golikov too. And perhaps now, even Chernov, Yid though he was. He ran, and after a while his loping legs assumed their own rhythm, and he moved like an automaton, so that the effort of stopping would have been so strenuous, it was hardly worth his while. So he ran. Mindlessly, insensible, numbed by the irresistible rhythm of his steps.

He must have run for over an hour, he thought, when he saw the spire of his village church. At first, listless as he was, he thought it was a mirage, and he forced his legs to wind down, so that he could stop and consider it. The pain of stopping was excruciating, and he flexed his knees to accommodate it. He looked at the spire, and studied it for a long time. And it did not go away. He dared to let out a cry of joy. Now his knees, unused to stillness, began to tremble, and he set off once more though at a slower pace. He thought it must be past midday. It had begun to rain and he was glad of it, for it meant that his family had left the fields. He crept to the hedge that skirted the road to his village. He would walk, he thought, at a measured pace. Then he would draw no one's attention. At most, a greeting perhaps from a neighbour, who would show no surprise at his presence, for he was a village native after all. Nor would they guess at the sorrow and fear in his heart, for how were they to know he was a mourning fugitive? Nevertheless he hoped that he would meet nobody, lest they sniff the runaway on his person. He walked down the cobbled street. He could see the cluster of huts where he lived. There was no one about and he was tempted to run once more. But he wanted to give himself time to anticipate their greetings, to savour them, for he knew that they would be fleeting. In time he reached his hut. He waited outside a while, steeling himself against their joy, their anger, and their concern. Then he went inside. They were at table, all of them. His father, his mother, little Sasha and Katya. They stared at him, and knew that he was a fugitive.

'What happened?' Maria whispered. 'Have you come here to hide?'

He was suddenly angry. No greeting. No affectionate touch. Not even a smile. It was all rubbish about Natasha, he thought. The Cause was just and nothing could override it.

'I'm hungry,' was all he said.

Katya rose from the table and prepared him a plate of food. He sat down. He wondered how much he should tell them. He was aware that knowledge would endanger them. The Okhrana would come to the village soon enough.

'What's happened to you?' Maria asked.

'I can't tell you everything,' he said. 'Just that I must get away. And quickly.'

'Where will you go?' This from Vassily, who was trembling.

'St Petersburg,' he said. Such information was harmless. The Okhrana in any case would assume that he had gone to the capital to lose himself there.

'How are you, my son?' Maria said at last. She crossed over to him and folded him in her arms.

'I am alive,' he said, for that was the most and the least he was.

Then Sasha climbed onto his knee and clung to him. 'We miss you, Ivan,' he said.

Then Ivan rose and, knowing his father's reticence, went to embrace him. And all joined in that silent embrace, forsaking all words, for they knew that all of them were explosive. But Katya stood on one side. She wanted to be alone with Ivan. She could bear the burden of his love no longer. She had to declare it to him once and for all.

'What news of Pyotr?' Ivan asked.

Then Katya spoke. Pyotr, after all, was her domain. 'I had a letter yesterday,' she said. 'He is well. He's somewhere in Kamchatka.'

'But Count Nicolai has been wounded,' Maria said. 'He's in hospital. They don't think he will fight again.'

'Such a waste,' Ivan said. 'Such a terrible, terrible waste.'

'Let's not speak of it,' Vassily said.

They resumed their meal in silence. It was Katya who broke it. 'I shall give you a dress, Ivan,' she said. 'You can wear it to St Petersburg. That way, they'll never find you.'

It was such an obvious disguise. Yet it was preposterous and Sasha laughed aloud. 'Ivan in a dress,' he shrieked. Ivan took him on his lap.

'Sasha,' he said, 'the dress is a secret. You must never never tell anybody about it. Or they will catch me, and I shall never see you again.'

That possibility would seal his lips for ever, and he hung on to Ivan's neck. 'Promise, promise, promise,' he said.

So it was arranged. A train to St Petersburg was due to call at the little station in Larionovka at eight o'clock that evening. But he knew he would not wait in the house all day. He would effect his disguise and go to the station and hide there until the train arrived. Maria gave him what little food they could spare. He took Katya's dress and kerchief into the side-room, and there he made himself into a woman. There was no mirror so he had to depend on the others' assessment of his authenticity. His exposure was greeted with a mixture of gasp and giggle.

'I wouldn't know you myself,' Maria said.

Then came the farewells. They feared they would never see Ivan again. So they were loath to say goodbye, a farewell that would in some way sanction his absence for all time.

'No goodbyes,' Maria said. 'Just kisses.' She held him close, unruffled by his strange womanness. 'Take care, my son,' she said, 'and send word when you can.'

Then Vassily's turn. His father, who could say nothing, but who could leave a tear on Ivan's cheek.

'I won't say anything, I promise,' Sasha said, 'so you'll come home again.'

Ivan lifted him in his arms. He thought perhaps that he might miss Sasha most of all. He turned to Katya, and noticed with some surprise that she was crying.

'No tears, Katya,' Ivan said gently. He took her hand and kissed it. And allowed the echo of 'Natasha' to ring in his ears.

They took him to the door of the hut and watched and listened as his skirts swung and rustled out of sight. Then, wordless, they returned inside and wondered whether his short visit had been a dream.

Ivan crossed the village streets. Occasionally he encountered those he knew, but none of them showed signs of recognition or even surprise. He grew confident, and felt entitled to assume a woman's gait. So his progress through the village was slow and assured. When he reached the railway station, he climbed down to the bank, to a copse below, and there he hid in the bushes waiting for darkness to fall. As he sat there he fingered the folds of his dress, as Katya might have done, and he longed for her. He wondered whether he would ever see her again.

Towards nightfall, he heard the approach of carriages. He was not frightened. He knew the harsh sounds of the Okhrana wagons, but these were the hooves of gentle horses, leisurely in their approach. He assumed that those others travelling to the capital had arrived to await the train. He judged that it would be safe enough to join them. He climbed to the top of the bank, and edged his way slowly to the end of the platform. There he composed himself, smoothed down his dress, and waited. A bunch of travellers stood at the other end of the platform. In the waning light he discerned two children, and he assumed that the gathering was a family. He felt suddenly lonely. Since that morning the Cause had ceased to be a companion. But he refused to be deserted. In time he would relish its company once more. He heard a noise behind him, and turning, he saw the figure of a woman approach. He could not see her face in the darkness, but her gait was familiar and filled him with longing. He knew it was Katya long before she reached him. He held out his arms. She walked slowly into his embrace. She did not need to declare her love. Nor he, his. For it was known between them. He held her for a while, listening to the throbbing of her heart. Or perhaps it was his own. He cradled her face in his hands, then he kissed her.

'Will you come to me in St Petersburg?' he said.

'Where shall I find you?'

He loosened his hold, and took a paper and pen from his pocket. On it, he wrote an address. 'I was told about him in Vosrov,' he said. 'He is a friend. You can trust him. He will tell you how to find me.'

He kissed her again, and they heard the distant rumble of the train.

'Come soon,' he said. He held her close, as the rumbling grew louder behind him. Then he detached himself.

'I long for you,' he said. 'I always have.' Then he turned and boarded the train. 'Come soon,' he called softly.

She smiled that distant, bewildered smile of hers, which didn't fade even when the train was out of sight.

Ivan was relieved to find an empty carriage. In his woman's attire, he feared to risk his voice in company. Despite his lawless escape, all fear had drained out of him. Except the one fear that the Cause could be overridden.

5

Ivan was fortunate enough to travel the whole journey to St Petersburg without company. He had trembled at every stop in fear of
fellow travellers. Or in worse fear of the Okhrana, who were wont
to inspect trains at random. From time to time he had practised a
woman's voice to himself, but he had to confess he had not found
its tone convincing. He studied the map he had hidden in his skirts
and immediately recalled Pavlenkov and a chess game they had
played a few evenings before their arrest. Perhaps Pavlenkov had
had a premonition of what was to come. Or perhaps it was just
that he was always on his guard.

'Ivan,' he had said between moves, 'we may one day be separated. We may be caught and we may be able to escape. The best
place to run is St Petersburg. You can lose yourself there, and they
can lose you. I have a friend there. A comrade. You can trust him.
Here is his name, and his address. And a map showing you how
to get there. Never never ask directions of a stranger.' He had
handed Ivan a folded paper, bearing the name, address and a
detailed map. Clearly Pavlenkov had prepared for such an eventuality. 'Try to learn it all by heart. Then destroy it,' he'd said. Then
they had finished their game, but Ivan couldn't remember who had
mated.

Now he studied that piece of paper until he knew it by heart.
Then, as they reached the capital, he tore it into many pieces, and
threw them at intervals out of the window.

When the train arrived at the capital, he alighted and assumed
a woman's gait. The map was vivid in his mind and he looked for

the landmarks that Pavlenkov had drawn to guide him. On each sight of them, a church, a bridge, a clock tower, he uttered a small cry of delight, like a child finding clues on a treasure hunt. At last he turned into the street where Ilya Martov lived. Pavlenkov's map had been exact to the last detail. He found the number and knocked on the door. He heard footsteps inside. Then a loud voice. 'Who is it?'

Ivan tried a woman's voice. He thought it would be safer. 'I'm a friend of Pavlenkov,' he squeaked.

The door opened immediately. A large man stood there, a smile prepared on his face, but not quite ready to be released. It needed more proof.

'How do you know Pavlenkov?'

Ivan dropped his voice disguise and took off his kerchief. 'My name is Ivan Volynin. I worked with him in a print shop in Vosrov.'

Then the smile made its debut, large and welcoming.

'Come in,' the man said. 'Do you know my name?'

'Ilya Martov,' Ivan said.

Ivan followed him into a large room. Furnished in the weighty classic Russian style, it was neat and ordered, with not a book in sight. A samovar steamed on the table.

'Sit,' Ilya said, as he poured him a glass of tea. 'Tell me all about my friend. It's weeks since I heard from him.'

Ivan was silent for a while, and Ilya thought he might have been duped, that this man was no friend of Pavlenkov, and had probably never even met him. He feared yet another Okhrana disguise, and his feet itched for flight. 'Tell me!' he shouted.

Slowly Ivan unfolded his story. As he told it he realised the enormity of his personal loss. He told the story in the greatest detail, more for his own sake than his companion's. He particularly stressed Pavlenkov's last words to Natasha, crooning his quietus with her name. 'Did you know Natasha?' Ivan asked.

'She was my sister,' Ilya said. 'She died a year ago.' He paused. Then, after a while, 'He never knew,' he said.

Now there was silence between them. Each of them remembering. Ivan thought of Katya, and wondered whether, in the fullness of time, he would call her name with the same heartbreaking regret and longing.

'You loved him,' Ilya said after a while. 'So be my friend.'

He stretched out his arms and they embraced. Then in endless teas and talk the day passed. Talk of the Cause and its progress. And talk of Pavlenkov, and the part he had played. But Natasha's name was never mentioned again. By the end of the day, Ivan was settled with a room in Ilya's house, and a job in the print shop where he worked. Together with the promise of friends and comradeship.

His work in the presses was similar to that which he had practised in Vosrov. And its routine was the same. Subversive matter camouflaged by the printing of legitimate orders. Ivan settled in quickly and within a few weeks he had been enrolled as a member of Lenin's group, the Social Democratic Workers' Party. As in Vosrov, there were cell meetings that ended in taverns and heated discussion. But always there was the fear of the Okhrana, whose activities had intensified since the Bloody Sunday of that year. Ivan kept Katya's dress hidden in his closet. Occasionally he tried it on, together with his woman's voice, and each time he longed for its owner.

Then one evening, on his return from a meeting, he found her in Ilya's kitchen, sharing his samovar. Suddenly he realised that he hadn't thought of her for many weeks, but he was overjoyed to see her, and longed to be alone with her. Ilya claimed he had a meeting, and winked at Ivan as he left the room. 'We must fix her up with a job,' he said. He had assumed that there would be no need to find her somewhere to live.

Ivan was nervous. The full realisation of her presence and what it would entail frightened him. Katya was a married woman, and his sister-in-law to boot. Moreover, she was a peasant, literate, it's true, but still lumbered with peasant expectations and obedience. He had to confess to himself that, here in the capital, she simply did not fit, that in time she might even become a nuisance. She must have read his thoughts.

'I've been reading,' she said. 'Dr Lvov told me I should prepare myself. He gave me books and pamphlets. I can work with you,' she pleaded. Then gave him her smile. He took her in his arms, then to his room, and for a while the Cause was forgotten as, tenderly and awkwardly, he offered her the gift of his virgin love.

The first time Katya went to a Party meeting she was taken there blindfolded, even as Ivan had been initiated in Vosrov. She noticed that there were other women in the cellar, and she was glad of it, for she was shy in a man's world. One of them was Ilyenka. By day she worked in a cigarette factory. Her nights she devoted to the Party. Over the next few weeks she and Katya became close friends, and Ivan was glad of it, for it gave him relief from his compulsive yet irritating appetite for love.

In the work at the presses, Ivan was printing a journal called the *Spark*. Its articles called the attention of the workers to their miserable conditions, and the wretched inequality of the society in which they lived. It called on them to strike, and those in industry to sabotage their machines. It promised them that the Revolution was near. It was the women's job to distribute those journals, to leave them in secret inconspicuous places, to slip them under doors at night. Ilyenka and Katya often went on those night sorties. Other women joined them, and Katya tasted once more that sweet sisterhood that she had known in the kitchens of the Larionov estate.

She told Ilyenka that she was pregnant even before she told Ivan. Such news, she thought, was women's business. Besides, she was nervous of telling Ivan. She sensed he would not welcome such an encumbrance. And there was Pyotr. He would find it hard to accept that their marriage was over, but the baby would be forcible proof. She rarely thought of him, but she knew that he would soon return to Larionovka. The war was ignominiously over, and the men, what was left of them, were making their defeated and demoralised ways home. She dared not dwell on how Pyotr would view her absence. With anger, she was certain, a rage that would no doubt fuel his steps towards St Petersburg. Maria knew Ivan was there, and she would not deny her eldest son an avenue of reconciliation. It was all too much for Katya. She would not think about it. She would be like Ivan. She would immerse herself in her work and try to believe that nothing else mattered.

She even managed to put the baby out of her mind, and when morning sickness assailed her, she told Ivan that it was something she had eaten, and even managed to convince herself that it was so. In her third month, Ivan complained that she was getting fat and she promised to go on a diet to please him. One night, after a meeting, she refused to drink at the tavern. In any case, she had little appetite for it. She was feeling unwell, and she knew that she couldn't keep her secret much longer. She asked Ivan to take her home. He did so grudgingly, because he always enjoyed their post-meeting tavern discussions. They walked home in silence. She would tell him that evening, she decided. She felt too tired to worry about the consequences.

As they put their key in the door, they were surprised to hear Ilya's voice. Ilya was a night owl, and rarely came home until the early hours. Ivan was glad – he would have someone to talk to – but less glad when he recognised Ilya's companion. Pyotr. Ilya left the room immediately, pleading an appointment. He knew from what Pyotr had already told him that there was likely to be trouble. And that trouble was private.

'I'll see you tomorrow,' he shouted.

'Pyotr,' Ivan said, stretching out his arms to embrace him. Whatever had happened, they were still brothers. But Pyotr moved out of his reach and looked at him with hatred.

'Katya,' he said, and with little gentleness, for his love for her was breaking him, 'I've come to take you home.'

Katya shook her head. 'I don't want to go back to Larionovka,' she said wearily.

'You'll do as you're told,' Pyotr said. 'I'm your husband. Or have you forgotten?'

The reminder injected her with a little strength. 'I refuse to be a servant for the rest of my life.'

'You talk like him,' Pyotr said, with a withering look at Ivan. 'You talk like him, and you think like him.'

'That's because he's right,' Katya said. 'We're fighting for a new world. A better world. People are homeless. Children die from hunger. We have to fight, Pyotr.'

69

'I don't want to know,' Pyotr shouted. 'All I know is that you're my wife and you're coming back with me.'

Katya shook her head. 'No,' she said. 'I can't.'

Pyotr grabbed her wrist. 'Get your things,' he hissed at her, 'or I shall have to force you.'

'Let her alone,' Ivan said. He tried to come between them, but Pyotr felled him with one blow. He staggered to his feet, helpless.

Katya felt faint, and she welcomed it. 'I'm pregnant,' she said. 'I'm carrying Ivan's child.' Then she fell as Ivan caught her on his bewildered arm. In her dim consciousness, she experienced a sense of relief that she would not have to face the consequences. She was half-conscious of being carried to her bed, of water on her lips, of a hand on her forehead, and of a long forgiving sleep. When she awoke, Ivan was by her side. And Pyotr was gone.

'Is it really true?' Ivan said.

She was glad he was smiling. 'Yes,' she said. 'In another six months.'

He held her in his arms. 'Why were you frightened to tell me?' he asked. He had answered his own question. 'We will have to find a bigger place to live, just the three of us. Does anyone else know?'

'No,' she lied. There was no point in hurting him.

Thereafter, he grew more loving. He insisted that she stop working and attend the clinic regularly. 'First you'll have our baby,' he told her, 'and afterwards you can see to the Revolution.' He thought then of Pavlenkov, and it comforted him.

For the next few months, Ivan carried the Revolution alone. With Ilya's help he had found a neighbouring apartment, and Katya was happy to nest in their first home. She was close to her time when a letter came for Ivan from Larionovka. It was from Maria. Vassily had had a stroke, she wrote – or rather Dr Lvov had written for her. He was not expected to live. He had asked for Ivan and she begged him to return. There was no mention of Katya.

Ivan was torn. He wanted desperately to see his father, though he knew that returning to his village would endanger him. Moreover, he didn't want to leave Katya. But Katya insisted. She would ask Ilyenka to come and stay with her. And he could wear her dress again to go back to the village. But Ivan drew a line at that. His father wanted to say farewell to a son, and he would not comfort his dying father in woman's attire. He would take his chances. He might get away with it. Ilya had provided him with forged papers. As long as he was not recognised, he could be lucky.

But he found it hard to leave Katya. After Pyotr's unhappy visit, he had grown to love her with greater caring, and it pleased him for he did not want to die with Pavlenkov's regrets. He went himself to Ilyenka, and moved her into their apartment, urging her to look after Katya well. Then he took his anxious leave.

The train was crowded. He found himself sitting next to a young woman who seemed anxious for conversation. She asked him where he was going and why, and what he did in St Petersburg. Ivan was wary. People were not to be trusted. Or perhaps, she was asking him questions in order to pre-empt his questioning of her. It was a common ploy.

'We have met,' she suddenly whispered. 'I'm Maria, a friend of Ilya's.'

Ivan looked into her face. It was vaguely familiar. He smiled, and felt more at ease. So he talked to her, avoiding any reference to the Cause. He told her about Katya, and their baby that would come soon. And about his father who was dying.

'I'm sorry,' she said.

Suddenly the train came to a stop. Ivan stood and peered out of the window. Then he slunk back into his seat in some agitation.

'Okhrana,' he whispered.

She sensed his fear. 'D'you have papers?' she asked.

'Of a kind,' he said.

'Give them to me. Put your head on my shoulder, and pretend to sleep.'

They heard heavy footsteps in the corridor. Then Maria's sight of the hated uniform. The officer entered their carriage, demanding the travellers' papers. When he reached Maria, she handed him the two documents. She smiled at him, that smile reserved for emergencies and that had nothing to do with pleasure. 'We're getting married,' she said.

'My congratulations.' He handed back the documents, and Maria put her smile away.

Down the corridor there was a sudden sound of screaming. The officer darted out of the carriage. Ivan peered out of the window and saw a figure of a man jumping for his life from the train – or for what was left of his life. As he scuttled across the fields, his body arched into the shot, its curve astonished. Then fell into stillness, his Cause, for him, in vain. There was laughter then as the three Okhrana officers alighted from the train, their duty done. As the train passed them by on its way, they actually raised their hands and waved.

The carriage was silent for the rest of the journey. Maria alighted some stations before Larionovka. Ivan missed her company, and he felt less safe. He urged the train forward to his village.

He arrived at nightfall, and was glad of it. In the village and the open spaces, he felt safer in the dark, unlike in St Petersburg, where even the parks at night were threatening, and the rustling not always from the leaves on the trees. But here there was almost a spring in his step, modulated by the thought of the sadness that awaited him.

Outside his hut, he listened for voices. He heard whispers punctuating the silence. He waited for his heartbeat to settle. Then he opened the door.

Vassily lay on the marriage bed with Maria sitting at his side. Avdotya squatted on the floor. Pyotr and Sasha sat together at the table. Both had their backs to him. They had not heard his entry.

'Ivan,' Maria called. Then they turned.

Sasha ran into Ivan's arms. 'He won't die now,' he said. 'Not now that you've come.'

'Papa is only waiting for him,' Pyotr said. Then he turned and faced Ivan. Their last meeting had been so full of hate and bitterness, but now, in their father's dying presence, all the anger drained out of them both. Pyotr took his brother in his arms without words. But Sasha sobbed into their silence. He could not accept that Ivan was not the saviour. Then Ivan went to his father's side. He leaned over his mother. He stroked her cheek, already bereaved. Then he took his father's hand. It was limp in his grasp, and cold. His face was ashen, and Ivan listened in fear to his shallow breathing, each limp breath apologetically delaying his last.

'Papa,' Ivan whispered.

Avdotya rose from the floor. She put her arm on Ivan's shoulders. 'He knows you're here,' she said. 'He was waiting.'

Then Vassily opened his eyes. He smiled with them, those only senses that were left to him. 'You came,' he said. Then he closed his eyes again. He was ready. Just three more words that had done for him throughout his taciturn life. All that he had learned to say. All that his own silent and loving father had taught him. 'Good luck, son,' he murmured. Now nothing more could keep him.

'He's gone,' Avdotya said.

Vassily Volynin was buried in the village churchyard where his own parents lay. It was a sad and silent gathering. As they lowered his coffin into the earth, Ivan wept for his loss. Not for his own, but for his father's. For his grinding poverty, for his eternal strife, for his desperate failure and frustration. His father had paid the price for all that was rotten in what he called his Mother Russia. Its cruelty, its indifference, its wrongs. He wept not only for his father's loss, but for the millions like him. Now his Cause had become a revenge, and his tears seethed with his anger, and his cheeks were afire.

A few days later, a letter came from Katya. He was the father of a beautiful boy, she wrote. And she longed for his return.

The news lightened all their hearts. Even Pyotr quietly rejoiced. It was as if their father's spirit had not entirely given up his ghost, for the child would be named Vassily.

PART TWO

6

The century was twelve years old. And so were the milk-children. Over the years, Sasha and Anna had seen each other seldom, but on each occasion the memory of their shared infancy was a magnet that drew them together. Pyotr would often take Sasha to the big house, and though he didn't like horses, he would go with Pyotr in the hope of catching a glimpse of Anna. And Pyotr noticed how often Anna would pass by the stables and pretend that it was on her way to wherever she was going. Pyotr had taken a new wife, Nina, the kitchen-maid who had taken Katya's place. She could neither read nor write, and she knew her station. Pyotr had found happiness with her. But more than that: he had acquired land of his own. After the war, and the terrible humiliation of Russia's defeat, the unrest and agitation in the cities had spread to rural areas. Tenants burnt down their landlords' houses and set fire to the crops. The rioting had not as yet reached Larionovka, and Count Dmitri cunningly decided to pre-empt it. So out of his estates, he gave ownership to a plot of land to each returning soldier and his family. Thus Pyotr became a farmer with a holding slightly larger than his dwelling. But withal it was ownership of a kind, and it blunted the edge of peasant discontent. For to attack private ownership would have been tantamount to attacking themselves.

But change was inevitable. Count Dmitri was aware of its certainty. And he would accept it; however, for the time being, he would do his best to postpone it. But Nicolai, his son, found the prospect of change offensive in the extreme. In that respect he was like his grandfather, though, unlike his grandfather, he was determined to fight it. It was Andrei, without the status in the family of first- or last-born, who assumed the logical role of outsider. He resembled neither his father nor the faint-hearted Count Fyodor. In his heart he was a revolutionary, but he kept his thoughts strictly to himself. When he was given a post in the Ministry of Internal Affairs in St Petersburg, he knew it was due to his father's influence, and his family's proven lifetime loyalty to the Tsar. The thought sickened him, but he knew better than to refuse the posting. With such a legitimate cover, there was no end to the support he would give the Cause without risk of discovery. He trembled at the thought of the secrets he was keeping from his family. And not only those political. For there was something else that he dared not own to them, nor even to himself. An untellable secret, filled with as much longing as fear. He would be glad to get to the capital. There his secrets could be revealed behind locked doors, amongst others of his kind.

Nicolai saw him go with envy and bitterness. His war wound had sorely incapacitated him. He walked slowly and with a lumbering gait. His stick was the closest this born soldier would ever again come to a sword. He was angry, too, because he would miss Andrei. Anna was still too young for company, and his father was getting old. Getting soft, too, he thought. Sometimes he treated his serfs as equals, and he would never forgive him for his foolish gifts of land.

'In time, I'll join you,' he told his brother. 'Don't worry, there's still some fight in me.'

But on the wrong side, Andrei thought. And the losing one.

Andrei's apartments in St Petersburg were lavish, and for the first time in his life he felt free. Unencumbered by the strict and watchful eye of his family, he felt free to be himself, to choose his own friends, perhaps amongst them one who shared his secrets. He found that the department in which he worked concerned itself with the world of the Okhrana, a supervision of those hated supervisors. Their work and their methods disgusted him, especially their cruel and summary dispatch of suspects. Others in his department admired their methods and he too feigned approval, but with each file that found its way to his desk, he searched for ways to subvert their tactics. At first he laid low. He was nervous. He had, as yet, found no one with whom to share his secrets. Those with whom he worked talked like his brother, Nicolai, with the same arrogance and aversion to change.

Then one day, he was given a new assistant. On arrival at his office Andrei found him standing at his desk, a file in his hand. He was young, and clearly nervous. Yet there was a certain arrogance about him. A lock of fair hair fell over one eye. And he made no attempt to remove it. There was a hint of a smile about his lips, as if freely given, yet he puckered his brow in serious fashion, the one look to offset the other, in case either were unacceptable.

'What's your name?' Andrei asked. He noticed that his voice trembled.

'Pavel,' the boy said.

'What have you got there?'

'From the Okhrana,' Pavel said. 'Tomorrow's lot.' He put the file on the desk. Then added almost under his breath but audible enough, 'Poor buggers.'

Andrei trembled. Was that a comment, one that would have come from any of his colleagues, a remark made simply for the sake of having something to say? Or was it an opinion, a judgement, even? The difference between the two was a difference in ideology. Dare he hope that the boy was expressing a perilous point of view? He decided to take the risk. 'Will you have supper with me tonight?' he asked.

Pavel unknitted his brow and freed his smile into his entire face. 'I'd like that, sir,' he said.

As it turned out, Andrei had taken no risk at all, and over the next few weeks, slowly and with infinite tenderness, he shared his secrets with Pavel.

Some months later another list, Okhrana doomed, landed on Andrei's desk. Such lists, almost weekly now, depressed him, not only for themselves, but for the fact that he could do little about them. He ran his finger down the condemned list, and stopped short and with stuttered heartbeat, when he came to a familiar name. Volynin, Ivan. This was a man to whom he owed his life. He recalled that moment, years ago, that drenched near-death moment in the river, when he had hung on to Ivan's life-saving neck and clung there for a while in sworn brotherhood. He had no doubt in his mind. He owed, and he would find pleasure in settling such a debt. He read the details of the Okhrana mission. A warehouse was to be raided and its contents destroyed. Those on the list were accused of writing and printing a publication called *Pravda*, a pamphlet of scurrilous subversion. The location of the warehouse was given together with the separate addresses of the accused. No exact date was given for the raid, but Andrei knew he had to act immediately. He would go to Ivan's house that evening. He would say nothing to Pavel. Although he trusted him implicitly, he did not want to put him at risk. He told him he had a meeting, and not to wait supper for him.

He waited until it was dark. Then left his office. He was nervous, but excited too. Excited at the prospect of seeing Ivan once more. And Katya too. It was many years since he had seen either of them, and he hoped that they would trust him.

He found their apartment without difficulty. It was in a silent and empty quarter of the city. It was unlikely that he was seen. He knocked quietly on the door. He heard scuffling inside. And whispering. He knew that people such as Ivan lived in constant fear of arrest, and he wondered whether he should give his name to allay that fear. But he sensed that the sound of Andrei Larionov through the wooden door was not guaranteed to inspire much confidence. So he called, 'Ivan', and then, 'Katya', hoping that his familiarity would ease them. It was Katya who opened the door. A little boy stood by her side. She recognised Andrei immediately and she paled. The Larionov connection was not good news for Ivan.

'Count Andrei,' she said. She found herself curtseying, astonished that old habits died so hard. And sickened too by that hangover of obedience. She wanted to ask him what he wanted, but that too would be to overstep her station. She stared at him.

'I want to see Ivan,' he said. 'Can I come in? It's urgent.'

Then she opened the door wide. 'This is Vassily,' she said, pointing to the child at her side. 'Our son.' Then to Vassily, 'Shake hands with Count Andrei.'

'Andrei will do.' He smiled at her, and followed her inside. She left him in the living-room and went to fetch Ivan. 'It's Count Andrei,' she whispered. 'He says it's urgent. What can he want?'

'I heard he's working in one of the ministries. Did you tell him I was here?'

'He knows.'

Ivan was nervous. Yet excited too. Like Andrei, he had not forgotten that hovering moment of brotherhood. 'Be ready to move, Katya,' he said. 'Just in case.'

He went into the living-room. Vassily was playing in a corner, ignoring their guest. Andrei stood at the table, expectant. When he saw Ivan, he stretched out his arms. Ivan was reminded of that same gesture in the river so many years ago, but he had a sense that this time, it was Andrei who was the saviour. They embraced.

'I owe you,' Andrei said.

Ivan laughed. 'Will you have supper with us?'

'I can't stay,' Andrei said, 'and it would be dangerous for me to be seen here. But you're in trouble. That's why I'm here.'

He told him of the nature of his job at the Ministry. 'I'm not on their side,' he whispered. 'I can be of help to your Cause. I *want* to be of help, but you have to trust me. You're surprised,' he said.

'Of course,' Ivan whispered. 'With your background —'

'There are many like us,' Andrei said. 'You will see. But first, you're in danger. You are on the Okhrana list for arrests. They know the warehouse and they know what you're printing. They intend to raid it, destroy it, and arrest all of you.'

'When?' Ivan was trembling.

'That I don't know. It could be any time. Probably soon. But you must run immediately. You must go into hiding.'

'I can't,' Ivan said. 'Not before I warn the others. Oh, you are good, Andrei.' He embraced him once more. 'I never regarded the river as a debt, and now you have more than paid it.'

'I'm anxious that you should go,' Andrei said.

'I'll get to the warehouse early in the morning. I'll warn them all. By noon we'll be gone.'

'I hope you're in time,' Andrei said. 'Now I must go.' He stood

81

up. 'I shall be in touch with you. But don't contact me. Ever. You must promise that.'

Ivan gripped his hand. 'We're brothers,' he said.

After Andrei had left, Katya and Ivan marvelled at their surprising new recruit. But Katya was anxious. 'Where will you go?' she said.

'The usual place. I'll contact you when I can. Don't worry.'

She didn't know where the 'usual place' was, and it was in the interest of her own safety that Ivan didn't tell her.

He got up very early the next morning and went straight to the warehouse. But they were waiting for him. Four of them. Two of them grabbed him on each side, and held him in a painful grip. Then out of the shadows came Gribov. Ivan recognised him from his first arrest in the Vosrov print shop. Ivan knew that this time there was no escape. But he would not be taken timidly.

'So you've been promoted, Gribov,' he sneered.

Gribov approached him. His answer was a slap across the cheek with a stinging leather glove. Ivan felt an offended trickle of blood.

'We should have hanged you in Vosrov,' Gribov said. 'Take him away.'

They bundled him into the police wagon. As he was led away, he noticed a posse of Okhrana looming in the shadows of the warehouse. They were waiting for his friends. And there was nothing that he could do about it.

There was darkness inside the wagon. And silence. Ivan was grateful for both. They seemed to be travelling for a long while. Ivan assumed that they had left the city, and that he was probably being taken to the prison that lay on the outskirts. He had heard of that prison. Few people ever left there. It was known to have the busiest gallows in Russia. He was frightened. Not of death but of torture. For the prison was known to be a specialist in that too. But greater than his fear was his anger that he had been given such little time to serve the Cause.

Soon the wagon lurched to a halt. It was already dark. Ivan feared he would never see daylight again. And his fears were well grounded. For it was over two years before he saw the sun again.

During that time, though he had no notion of its duration, he was kept in solitary confinement. All day and every day, he crouched in his cell and waited for the hangman to come. Sometimes he would have welcomed him. He knew that time was passing, but he could not count it in days or weeks. He was kept in darkness for most of the time, so he could not reckon each sunrise. Sometimes he was taken to eat with the other prisoners. At first he was eager for news of the outside world, but all communication was forbidden. He might as well have eaten in his cell. He thought often of Katya and his son. And longed for them both. But in time that longing faded, and all thought of them. He thought now only of Gribov, and of Smirnov, who had betrayed them all, nourishing thoughts to feed his anger. For rage was the only feeling that was alive in him. His heart had drained itself of all loving in order to house the fury that engulfed him. And when, more than two years later, he saw the sun again, all that was left of Ivan Volynin was his body of rage.

They had come for him early in the morning, throwing his breakfast on the floor of his cell. 'You're being moved,' one of them said. 'Get yourself ready.'

Ready? What was ready? He had nothing with which to ready himself. Nothing to pack. No clothes. No papers. Nothing to take with him to God knows where. Only his rage, and that was already packed. It was a dressing suitable for any setting. Even the gallows.

He ate. Then he was taken. A swift look at the sky and then the darkness once more. But always the rage comforted him, and clothed him through the long days and nights of journeying. Then a train took him, with different guards. But there he was not confined. Only handcuffed. And he saw others. Soldiers. And heard rumours of war. Once he caught a glimpse of a traveller's newspaper. He craned his neck to see the date. October 1915. Then, for the first time, he realised how long he had been incarcerated. And it stunned him. He reckoned on his son's age. The last birthday he had celebrated was Vassily's seventh. Now he was nine and already two years orphaned. His rage simmered. For two years he had been given life, but he had been denied living. He wanted to talk to someone to find out what had happened in those years. Who had died, and who, if anyone, had fallen from power? And all those soldiers, where were they all going?

83

He dared to question one of his guards. He started with the soldiers, because they were visible. 'Why are there so many soldiers?' he asked.

The guard did not ignore him. He too perhaps was bored by his own silence.

'There's a war on,' he said.

And so their conversation began. In its course Ivan learned that Russia was at war with Germany, that St Petersburg had been renamed Petrograd, thus ridding it of its German derivation. And that the Tsar still ruled in his palace.

'You want to ask about your little Revolution, don't you?' the guard said. Then, without waiting for a reply, he added, 'It's over. The leaders are all dead. Or in prison. You'll be joining them.'

'Where are you taking me?'

'All in good time. You'll see.'

The latter stages of Ivan's journey were by dogsleigh in a landscape of eternal snow. Their destination was the village of Kareika in the exiled heart of Siberia. They arrived at nightfall. The sky was black and starless yet its darkness was overcome by the blinding whiteness of the snow's expanse. So Ivan was able to decipher the outlines of his exile, a row of prison huts, a dozen or more. As the sleigh pulled into the clearing, a handful of men emerged from the huts. They stood by silently, watching the newcomer. One of Ivan's guards unlocked his handcuffs, and the other threw his belongings into the snow. Then, without a word, they drove off, leaving him stranded, as mere carrion, perhaps, or, hopefully, fellow prisoner. Ivan picked up his bag. He felt frightened, deserted. He looked around him, and didn't know what to do. The men were staring at him, casing him, it seemed. He realised it must be an event in such as was their lives to view a different face, so he forgave them their staring. But he was afraid to move. Frightened too that they would move towards him. He shivered. Then one of the men took a step forward, and the others followed. They lined themselves up, facing him. There was no malice in their eyes. Merely curiosity. One of them even smiled.

'Welcome to our exile,' he said, or rather whispered, for the snowscape seemed to dictate silence.

'Thank you,' Ivan whispered in return. He put out his hand. 'My name is –'

'No names here,' the man interrupted him sharply. 'No real names, that is. You must give us another. My other name is Lebedev.' He put out his hand.

Ivan grasped it. 'And mine is Pavlenkov,' he said. The name of his dead friend leapt to his mind. He gave it as a memorial.

The other men introduced themselves with their own chosen fictions. One of them picked up Ivan's bag. 'Come,' he said, 'we'll show you where you'll live.'

Ivan was glad to ease himself into their friendship. He was anxious to know what had happened in the world during his long incarceration, though he feared that in these remote wastes, they were as ignorant as he.

His hut was sparsely furnished. A narrow bed, a shelf, a cupboard and a paraffin lamp. It reminded him of the room he had shared with Pavlenkov, now his namesake, in Vosrov. It had the same basic bareness that only thoughts and shared ideas could furnish. But this room was his own. Private without being solitary, and for the first time in many years a rusted yet warm feeling of happiness overcame him. Even if his entire future lay in this barren exile, he wanted suddenly to live. He stretched himself out on the bed, and availed each part of his body to that wish.

'Are you married, Pavlenkov?' Lebedev asked.

'Yes. My wife's name is Natasha.' Thus he honoured them both. And for the first time in years, he thought of Katya and his son. But without longing. Such a feeling was so sorely out of practice, he knew it was for ever beyond rehearsal.

'Don't make yourself too comfortable,' another man said, who answered to the name of Leonid. 'You have to be interviewed.'

Ivan sat up quickly. That word curdled his brain. In the past it had been a prelude to torture. 'Who by?' he asked. 'The police? The Okhrana?'

'By Koba,' Leonid said.

'Who is he?' Ivan asked.

'He's like all of us,' Lebedev said. 'No one knows his name.'

They accompanied him to the last prison hut in the row. It

85

seemed larger than the others, and Ivan suspected that it would be more comfortable. As indeed it was. On entering, he trod a thick carpet on the floor. There was a door on one wall, slightly ajar, and behind it Ivan caught sight of a large brass bedstead. On the table in the living quarters was a bottle of cognac with some glasses. Yet the man seated at the table was dressed like the rest of them, in prisoner's garb. He was clearly one of them, though just as clearly in view of his privileges, a cut above the rest. A self-appointed leader, perhaps. He motioned to the other men to leave. Ivan looked into the man's face. It was pointed, its purpose, interference. The eyes were small but with cunning rather than apology, and the skin was pockmarked. A large moustache drooped down each side of his chin. His sharp nose sniffed with suspicion. This is not a man to be trusted, Ivan thought. Rather to be feared. It would be well to keep on his right side.

'I'm Koba,' he said, or rather shouted. He was the only man amongst them who did not respect the silence of the snow. 'Sit down. When did you last taste cognac?'

'Never,' Ivan said.

'Then start living.' Koba poured two glasses. 'What shall we drink to?' he said.

It was a test question, possibly a trap. So he said, 'To the future.' Such a toast could be proposed by anybody, whatever his political cover.

'As you wish,' Koba said. He had time. 'To the future. Ours.' He raised his glass and downed the drink in one gulp. Then poured another for both of them. But Ivan refrained. He feared a loose tongue. The man could well have been a prisoner like the rest of them. But he could also be an Okhrana spy. He'd not forgotten Smirnov, with his notebook and his friendship.

'You'll have to learn to drink here,' Koba said. 'It's one way of keeping warm. Tell me,' he said, 'is the Tsar still cleaning his toenails?' He roared with laughter. Another test question, Ivan thought. So he joined in the laughter and said nothing.

'D'you know what I've heard?' Koba went on. 'Every day in this war, ten thousand men have died. That's good, you know. The more we lose, the greater the discontent. The greater the discontent, the nearer the Revolution.'

They could have been Ivan's own words. He had actually used them himself during the war with Japan. Yet still he didn't trust Koba. He would find out about him from other men. But could he trust any of them, he wondered, and was saddened at the thought of the suspicious and mistrusting person he had become.

'We shall meet again,' Koba said. 'But meanwhile, welcome. You will find good friends here.'

Ivan went back to his hut. He stretched out on his bed, covering himself with the blankets. He was desperately tired, and the cognac had accentuated his fatigue. Very soon he was asleep. His last thought was of Pavlenkov, and his new identity.

He woke feeling refreshed. Excited, almost, by the prospect of a new and very different life. He stood outside his hut and greeted the other men. He noticed that there was no sign of Koba. Shortly they heard the sleighs in the distance and the barking of the dogs.

'They come every day,' Lebedev said. 'They bring the food. We heat it ourselves in the dining-room. There's a stove there. Books too. And cards. D'you play?'

'No,' Ivan said. 'But I'm ready to learn.' But he was more interested in the books. Perhaps they would give him a clue. He would examine them after breakfast. He helped off-load the sleighs, and carry the food to the mess-room. It was warm in there. There were tables, even a few armchairs and rugs on the floor. It was like a club-room, which it probably was, a meeting place for the exiles to read and re-read the few-and-far-between letters they got from home. As one of them was doing now, sitting near the stove poring over a much-thumbed piece of paper, the contents of which he knew by heart.

Ivan was excited. 'Can we write home from here?' he asked.

'Once a month,' the man said. 'They bring you paper. But you have to be here a month first,' he added.

'How long have you been here?' Ivan dared to ask.

'I haven't seen a woman for fifteen years,' he said. In such manner he counted his years of exile.

'What do you all do here?' Ivan asked.

'We live. We work, we read. We carve wood. Or we paint. We make music sometimes. The years pass.' He went back to his letter-reading. Ivan went over the bookshelves. What he saw delighted him. He could have been looking at his own collection.

The men sat down for breakfast, and still Koba had not put in an appearance.

'Doesn't Koba eat?' Ivan asked his neighbour.

'Not with us. He eats in his own quarters.'

'Why?'

'He's our leader. That's why.'

There was a tone of finality in the man's voice. Ivan could question no further.

For the next few days, Ivan joined a working party in the forest. They were felling trees and sorting the wood that would be shipped to the timberyards. Two guards accompanied them on each sortie, but Ivan noticed that they were not overvigilant. Indeed they seemed quite friendly with their prisoners, many of whom they had come to know intimately over the long years. On the fifth day, when he'd returned from the forest, Ivan was summoned to Koba's hut. He had not seen him since his arrival at the camp. In that interval he had gathered little information about the man, but it was clear that he enjoyed everyone's trust and respect. Why, some of the men even loved him. So on this visit he was less afraid.

Koba was drinking when he entered the hut. And again there was an extra glass on the table.

'Sit down,' Koba said.

It sounded like an order, and Ivan did what he was told.

'Settling in, are you?'

'Yes,' Ivan said. 'I'm settling.'

'Well, don't get too settled,' Koba said. 'You're leaving soon.'

'But where? And why? I – I'm not unhappy here.'

'You'd be happier in Petrograd, though, wouldn't you? With Katya? With Vassily?'

'How d'you know all this?' Again Ivan doubted him.

'Have a glass and I'll tell you.' Koba poured him a glass.

Again it sounded like an order and Ivan took the glass, but with little appetite.

88

'Today I had a letter about you. From somebody who knows you well, and whom I know well enough. No name. He is reliable. He gives you a good testimonial. Obedient, he says. Doesn't question orders. You'll do for what I have in mind.'

Ivan was afraid to ask exactly what that was. In any case he was supposed not to ask questions. He was aware of a flutter of excitement in his heart. That he would see St Petersburg again, and learn to call it Petrograd. But above all, that he would see Katya and his son.

'How am I going to escape?' he asked. He was entitled to know that.

'I have a certain influence here,' Koba said. 'Everything is arranged. There are guards and guards, you know.' He smiled with a certain cunning.

'Then why are you still here? And the other men?'

'We will all go when the time is ripe. But not yet. Your mission is urgent. There's no time to lose. Have you a good memory?'

'I think so,' Ivan said.

'I have written down my instructions. You will learn them by heart. Then you will throw them away.' He handed Ivan a slip of paper, and a sheaf of documents. 'Read them in your hut tonight.'

'When am I leaving?'

'Tomorrow. Before the guards arrive.'

Ivan shivered with a mixture of fear and excitement. 'Where am I going?' he asked. He was suddenly bold.

'It's all written,' Koba said. 'But I shall tell you. It will help you remember. You're going to Georgia, Pavlenkov.' He paused. 'Now *there* was a good man, Volynin, and you were very clever to take his name.'

Ivan smiled. Koba seemed to know everything. He was tempted to ask what name lay hidden under Koba. But he refrained. He sensed that in time he would know the name well enough.

'To Georgia,' Koba said again. 'To a little village called Gori. It's where I was born. You'll collect a package there. The address is on the sheet of paper.'

'And then?' Ivan whispered.

89

'You will take that package to Petrograd.'

'But I'm a wanted man. Petrograd is the last place for me to be.'

'You will be protected,' Koba said. 'Trust me.' He gave that smile of his again, a smile that inspired anything in the world except trust. 'We have to protect you. We need printers. All those speeches and manifestoes. All that shit.'

Ivan looked at him in horror.

'Don't be surprised,' Koba said. 'Many of us think that way. We don't like writers and speech makers. All those artists and intellectuals. They talk a lot and write a lot and they don't know how to wipe their own arseholes. One day I'll show them.'

Ivan said nothing. But he winced at the man's crudity. He wondered if it were true that there were many like him.

'But whatever you print, a revolution needs printers,' Koba went on. 'But let's get back to the package. You will hand it over in Petrograd to the name and address that is written. It will then be taken to Lenin in Zurich.'

'Lenin?' Ivan whispered. It was a holy word amongst those who worked for the Cause.

'Yes, Lenin,' Koba said. 'I'm only following orders.' He smiled his smile again and did not care to hide its cunning. 'Go now,' he said, rising. 'You will need sleep. Say goodbye to no one. Just leave at first light.'

They shook hands. 'Good luck,' Koba said. 'We shall meet again in Petrograd.'

Ivan could not sleep. He spent the night reading his instructions and learning them by heart. At dawn he was to take a prescribed route through the forest. At the end of an avenue of fir trees, a troika would be waiting. The driver would be waving his lantern, to guide him to the carriage. Then he read the instructions for the rest of his journey. And last of all, the names and addresses of his contacts. These he repeated to himself over and over again. He designed them visually, so that they would be imprinted on his memory. By first light, he felt confident that he would never forget them. He crept out of bed and wrapped a blanket about himself. Then he stole out of his hut and walked silently out of the camp.

As he passed Koba's hut, he thought he saw a shadow behind the windowpane. When he reached the forest, he took the sheet of paper from under the blanket, and scanned it one more time. Then he ate it, and continued on his way.

7

Ivan journeyed for many long days and nights. From time to time they stopped to change the horses and to buy food and drink. He and the coachman took it in turns to sleep and to drive. They travelled nonstop as if they were being followed. Occasionally Ivan repeated the names and addresses that he had learned, especially when he was holding the reins and he could sing the names and the numbers to the rhythm of the horses' hooves. By the time they reached the borders of Georgia, Koba's page had become a mantra. Ivan was excited. He was anxious to visit the village where Koba was born. For some reason, that man's birthplace seemed of historical significance. He didn't know why. He had no reason to suppose that Koba was any more than a regular revolutionary, who obeyed orders like any of his kind. Yet there was something about the man that smelt of future leadership and Ivan was not sure that that smell was to everyone's taste. Perhaps at the address he had been given he would meet his family, and knowing them would give him a clue to that enigma in the Siberian wastes. But the address that he had been given turned out to be a small café on the road that led to the village. Clearly no family abode. An anonymous station of conspiracy. He looked around to check that he was not being followed. Apart from some field workers and hedgers, there was no one in sight. He slunk into the café and took a seat by the window. There were three other men inside, each at separate tables. They eyed him suspiciously. Ivan was nervous. He signalled the woman at the counter and ordered some lemon tea. She turned to the samovar behind her, and shortly put a full glass on the counter.

One of the men rose, and collected it, and took it over to Ivan's table.

'Pavlenkov?' he asked.

Ivan nodded.

The man signalled to the other men at the tables. They rose and joined Ivan. Then the three of them sat down and stared at him.

'No names,' the first man said.

Ivan shrugged his shoulders. He was content to know as little about them as possible. Their hands were calloused, but with cruelty rather than toil. They slurped their tea as they stared at him.

'Where's the package?'

The first man laughed with a certain contempt, and his companions joined in with the pity of it.

'Don't you know *anything*?' the man said. 'We have to get it.'

'Where is it?'

'In Petrograd. In a bank.' He laughed again.

'What's so funny?' Ivan said. He was beginning to be weary of these men. He wondered whether they were Koba's friends.

'You're so green,' the man said. 'That's what's funny.' He leaned over the table and whispered, 'We're going to rob a bank.'

Ivan shivered. It was not exactly the mission he had expected.

'Don't worry,' the man said. 'All you have to do is sit in the drive-away cart, and whistle.' He stared at Ivan with little confidence. 'You can whistle, can't you?'

Ivan thought of his father. Long ago, in the fields of Larionovka, Vassily had taught him to whistle. It was the only useful legacy he had left him, and after some practice, Ivan was acknowledged as the best whistler in the village. He had not whistled for a long time. He had had no cause. He had not wished to draw anyone's attention, nor had he experienced any joy to celebrate. He pursed his lips and prayed for the old skills to return. The men waited expectantly. Ivan took a deep breath, then pursed his lips once more. He blew. And reddened with shame. For out of his mouth came a thin and reedy wheeze, barely sibilant.

'It's clear you're not a Georgian,' one of the men said with disdain. 'Give the poor bugger a whistle.'

93

Their leader took a child's whistle out of his pocket. He stuck it roughly in Ivan's mouth. 'Perhaps you can manage that,' he said.

Ivan blew. And a sound emerged that shipped him right back to the Larionovka fields and his hungry childhood.

'Here comes the Revolution,' one of the men sneered.

'Let's be serious,' the leader said. 'Everything has been arranged. We leave for Petrograd today. The train goes at noon. Here are your papers.' He handed Ivan a document. 'We will travel in separate compartments and we meet tomorrow night at the address you've been given. Now go,' he said. 'And for God's sake, don't lose your whistle.'

Ivan was glad to be rid of them. It was still early morning, but he made his way to the station, preferring to wait there rather than remain in their company.

He did not see them get on the train. Perhaps they were waiting for the last minute. But he did not look for them either. He preferred to be alone and to wonder at this mission of his that was so alien to his nature. He fastened onto his belief that the money was for the Cause. That revolutions had to be financed and from what better source than a bank, that symbol of corrupt capitalism. He thought of his mother and was glad that she didn't know where he was or what he was doing. He slept most of the way to the capital. Only once was he asked for his documents, and they were scantily reviewed. For a while he had eavesdropped on the talk of his fellow travellers. He was hungry for news. But fatigue overcame him. Since leaving Siberia, he realised, he had not spent one untroubled night. He comforted himself with thoughts of Katya and his son. Koba had promised that he would see them, but he wondered whether he could trust him. The thought crossed his mind that he might refuse the mission, that he should lose himself in the streets of Petrograd, and take his luck where he could. But that would mean an end to his role in the Revolution to come, and without that, there would be no point in living. He arrived in Petrograd in a mood of deep depression, barely lifted by the thought that he was in the same city as Katya. He was tempted to go straight to their old apartment, but he knew that was dangerous. And besides, Koba had not allowed for it. So he went straight to the address of the conspiracy.

The robbery was to take place on the outskirts of the city. Ivan's job was to drive the drive-away wagon. He was glad that he would not be involved in greater violence. He was to be the lookout man too, and give warning by means of his whistle. Early in the morning the men dragged themselves into the wagon. They were bleary eyed and probably, Ivan thought, still drunk from their wassailed night before. He had a terrible fear that their enterprise would fail and he would end up on the gallows, not as a martyr, but as a common criminal. He whipped up the horses and drove according to their directions. They circled the bank twice, then stopped at the corner of the street and waited for it to open. Ivan did not join them in the wagon. His lookout duties had begun. There were a number of people about even at that early hour. They were on their way to work. Some had gathered outside the bank waiting for the doors to open. There were no policemen to be seen. Ivan patted his pocket to make sure of his whistle. He hoped he would never have to use it. He had noticed that his companions were armed, and had not even tried to conceal the fact. The thought crossed his mind that perhaps one of the bullets was for him after the job had been accomplished. And another missionary would deliver the package. Everyone was expendable. His namesake had taught him that in Vosrov, though it was clear that on the gallows his friend had had second thoughts. Again Ivan thought of running, but of the consequences too. So he stayed shivering in the wagon.

He saw the bank door open, and he gave the arranged tapping signal to the men in the cart. He felt them alight behind him, and watched them cross the street, their bags and arms hidden. They suddenly seemed sober and professional as if they'd done this sort of thing before. They had told him to keep an eye out for the police, his hand on his whistle. They promised that they would accomplish the theft within five minutes. He was shivering, as much from fear as from cold. Though he was grateful for it, he couldn't understand why there were no policemen around. Perhaps Koba had arranged that too. He fell to wondering about Koba and the power and organisation that he seemed to exert from such a distance. Koba

95

had known his namesake, it was clear, but Pavlenkov had never mentioned Koba. Perhaps that was part of his power too. The terrible pseudonym lingering in the Siberian wastes, waiting for his time to come.

A long time seemed to have passed and he grew restive. He was waiting for a single shot in the air. That would be his signal to drive the cart across the street, ready for a swift getaway.

And then he heard it. Dimly. It seemed the snow could soft-pedal even gunfire. He whipped the wagon across the street in time to greet his fellow bandits as they streaked out of the bank, their loot held high over their heads. Then they dived laughing into the back of the wagon, rolling about in the sudden speed of their takeoff. Ivan lashed the horses. He heard screams from people in the street. He assumed a crowd had gathered outside the bank but he daren't look behind him. He heard the bell of the police wagon, and his knees melted in fear. But he'd had a good start and he knew the route that he was to take. The false trails, the double backs, and then the shelter of the forest. After a while the bells ceased, and all he heard at his back was the echo of the horses' hooves in flight. He wondered whether those in the police wagon were Koba's men too. But he did not slow the horses. As he turned into a new trail one of the men poked his head out of the wagon.

'You can slow down a bit, Whistler,' he said. 'Have pity on the horses.'

Ivan drew in the reins and they carried on at a trot. He heard the men laughing again and the clink of bottles. He knew there was a place that he had to stop. Somewhere in the forest. But he had been told to wait for a signal from the men. He had reached the forest now and he began to be afraid. It was dark amongst the trees, and without witness. When the signal came from the back of the wagon, the reins fell from his trembling fingers. He heard the men alight beside him.

'Get down,' their leader said.

Ivan slithered down his seat. 'Did you get it?' he asked. He knew that the raid had been successful, but he wanted to make conversation.

The two men went behind a tree to relieve themselves and this

96

move seemed ominous. It was as if they were absenting themselves
to let their leader get on with the business of dispatch.

'If you want to pee, do it now,' the man said.

There was a measure of hope in his suggestion, for what did it
matter if one went to one's death with a full or an empty bladder.

'You won't be able to pee for quite a while,' he said.

Ivan did not know how to interpret this rider. It could have
meant anything. So he went towards the trees, his back tingling.
He did what he had to do, then returned to the wagon. Whatever
was to become of him, he wanted it over and done with.

'Get in,' the man said. 'And strip.'

It did not augur well. Without clothes, and in that temperature,
there was little hope of a future. But he did what he was told. He
was bare when the leader joined him in the wagon.

'Skinny little thing, aren't you, Whistler?' the man said.

Ivan thought he heard a tone of affection in the man's voice. He
tried not to give himself hope. He watched as the man bent down
towards the bags. He drew out the notes, packaged in bundles and
strung out in the form of a belt. It was a skilful piece of packaging,
Ivan thought, and assumed that they had fashioned it during their
getaway. He put the sash of money round Ivan's waist. 'There's
your package, Whistler,' he said. 'Now dress. Then walk to the
edge of the wood. A coach will be waiting.'

Ivan dressed and stepped down from the wagon. He felt a little
safer. There would have been little point in dressing him for a kill.
Much less point when dressed in roubles.

'Come back to Georgia one day,' one of the men said. 'We'll
teach you Russians how to whistle.'

Ivan ran to embrace them, not out of affection, but in relief and
gratitude for this life.

One of them took out a bottle. He handed it to Ivan. 'For the
road,' he said.

'Drink with me before I go.'

They took out their own bottles. 'To the Revolution,' one of them
whispered. They were drinkers beyond any need of toast, but they
felt that the farewell called for some formality.

He left them, drinking and singing. Then heard their dying

laughter as the wagon wheels took them away. He went on his way with confidence. He did not doubt that there would be a coach waiting for him. Koba had managed to organise everything. The delivery of the package was the last stage of the plan, and though less perilous, certainly more important. He began to trust that he would see Katya again. And his son. 'Natasha' thoughts, as he called them, but he felt he could indulge them for a while. As he walked, he pursed his lips, and unaware, he started to whistle. The sound that issued from his lips was pure and shrill, with that birdlike timbre of his childhood. He could out-whistle any Georgian, he thought, and he was sorry that the men were no longer there to hear him. He found himself whistling the first tune he had rehearsed with his father, a children's song, in the form of a two-part round. He missed his father's descant, and tried to hear it in his inner ear. And thought he did. Very clearly. So clear and so shrill that he slowly understood it was not in his ear at all, but in the forest somewhere. And not as an echo from the trees, but as a fugue in its own right. He stood still, and was silent. And the descant persisted. He pinpointed the sound. It came from the clearing at the edge of the forest and he ran with joy to its source. At the end of the clearing he saw a troika with its open inviting door. He stopped himself a little distance before it, listening to the song. Then he ran towards it. A hand grasped his arm as he entered. Then shut the door as the troika drove off. The sudden light of the clearing after the darkness of the forest, and now in the troika the darkness again, had left Ivan slightly unfocused, and it was a little while before he could adjust his sight to view his companion. Then he heard his voice.

'Ivan. Welcome to Petrograd, comrade.'

Andrei's voice, and then, in the light, Andrei's person. They embraced.

Ivan was startled and surprised. Surprised by Andrei's sheer presence, but startled by the sound of his own name. It had been a long time since anyone had called him Ivan. In prison it had been a gruff 'Volynin'; in Siberia it had been a more gentle 'Pavlenkov'. The 'Ivan' in him had faded, and for a moment he wondered whom Andrei was talking to. It disturbed him, this easy loss of identity, and he wondered what other aspects of himself had been lost together with his name.

'Andrei,' he said, and again, 'Andrei.' That name at least was known.

'You're safe, Ivan,' Andrei said.

Ivan embraced him once more. There were so many questions he needed to ask. About Katya, Vassily, the Cause, and what Andrei was doing in this troika in the first place, but for the moment, the embrace was all that he wanted, all that mattered. That touch of gentleness and friendship, that solid proof of his Ivanness of which he had been starved for so long. So for a while they embraced in silence. It was Ivan who broke it, though he clung to Andrei as he spoke.

'Do you know Koba?' he asked.

'No names. No questions,' Andrei said. 'I still work at the Ministry.'

Then he did know Koba, Ivan thought, and by now was pretty well entrenched in the Cause. They loosened their embrace, looked at each other smiling.

'Now tell me everything. Everything,' Ivan said.

'Where shall I begin?'

'Katya,' Ivan said. He surprised himself with the priority he had chosen. But it did not displease him, though he knew that that priority belonged more to 'Pavlenkov' than to 'Ivan'.

'She's well,' Andrei said. 'And so is Vassily. You will see them both soon.'

'How soon?' Ivan could barely contain his excitement.

'Some hours yet. We've a few versts to travel. Be patient.'

In a way, Ivan was glad of the respite. After such a long absence, he was nervous of meeting Katya. He was nervous of his anticipation. It was too high, too expectant. He thought if he talked about other things, the Cause, for instance, he could divert his excitement.

'Tell me what's happened, Andrei. It's nearly three years, and I know nothing. I haven't even asked questions, because I have learned to trust nobody. First tell me about Larionovka. D'you ever go back home?'

'Sometimes. Your mother is well. She misses you.'

99

'And Pyotr?'

'He misses you too. Believe me. He's happy with Nina and his plot of land.'

'And little Sasha?' He heard a break in his voice and he realised he had missed him more than anyone.

'Not so little any more. But still beautiful. He's a bit of a dreamer. Looks like a poet.' He smiled. 'The Revolution could do with a poet.'

Ivan recalled Koba's words in his prison hut, and how he had spat with vitriol on 'artists and intellectuals'. 'How d'you feel about intellectuals, Andrei?' Ivan asked.

'We're short of them as leaders,' Andrei said.

Then he couldn't have been a friend of Koba's after all. Ivan thought of Katya again. They had not travelled far, and he knew there was still some time before he would see her. So he asked for news of the Cause.

'Everything looks good,' Andrei said. 'The war is going badly. Our men are sent into battle without guns, without ammunition. The casualties don't bear thinking about.'

'And the Tsar, curse him. How much longer can he last?'

'Ask his wife, that German bitch. It's she who rules him. But there's work to be done. We have a print shop. It's safe. We're still printing *Pravda*.'

Ivan smiled. *Pravda* was the last newspaper he had held in his hand, and it had cost him his freedom.

They were silent now, but Ivan's thoughts did not return to Katya. The mention of the printing press and *Pravda* recalled his heart to the Cause. He looked at his companion. He trusted him utterly but he couldn't understand his allegiance.

'Tell me about you, Andrei,' he said. 'You're so different from your brother. And your parents. What happened that made you so different?'

'I don't know,' Andrei said. 'I always felt an outsider. I didn't know what was wrong, but I had a sense that things were unfair. You remember that book I gave you? I wanted to know what you were reading. So I read it myself later on. It made some things clear to me. That was the beginning, I suppose.'

'I didn't save your life in vain,' Ivan laughed.

There was silence again, and Ivan could not help but think of Katya once more.

'I'm nervous of seeing her, Andrei,' he said. 'It's been so long.'

'It's been long for her too,' Andrei said. 'Take it slowly. Vassily will help. You'll be a family again.' He wanted to tell Ivan about his own happiness. He needed simply to sing Pavel's name. But caution stilled his tongue. He knew about peasant morality and he could in no way rely on Ivan's understanding.

'Are you married yet?' Ivan asked.

Andrei was startled by Ivan's timing. 'No,' he laughed. 'I haven't found the right woman.' He was weary of that phrase. He had used it in so many drawing-rooms and he hated the lie in himself. So often did he repeat it, that at times he even wondered that it might be true, that, should the 'right woman' come along, he would embrace her. He wondered whether there would ever come a time in his life when he could fully declare himself.

It grew dark outside. Andrei put his hand on Ivan's arm. 'We're almost there,' he said. 'When the troika stops, get out and just walk straight ahead. A lantern will signal you the way. There's a dacha there. A man will be waiting to take your package. Then your mission is over.'

'And Katya?'

'She will be waiting too.'

The troika stopped and they embraced once more. 'You have done well, Ivan,' Andrei said. 'I shall be in touch with you soon.'

Ivan stepped down from the carriage. He followed the path that Andrei had shown him. As yet he saw no sign of habitation. He heard himself whistling again but it was a nervous sound. So he sang softly to himself for company. After a while he saw a shadowed silhouette of a distant cluster of dachas. Or they seemed to his eye to be a cluster, but as he neared them he saw their distinct separation, almost fields apart. Now he looked out for the lantern that would identify his point of arrival. When he saw it swinging in the window, he stopped. All was dark around him. And silent. He wanted to savour the moment, to create for it a prelude of sorts, a calm preparation for his Katya encounter. He stared at the lantern, hypnotised by its pendulum movement. Then he walked towards it as if in a dream. The door was opened as he approached. It was semi-dark inside. Through the half-light he deciphered the salient silhouette of a printing machine, a shadow that above all else spelt home.

'Ivan,' a voice said.

Katya stepped out of the shadows. 'Close the door, so that I can light the lantern.'

Her voice had not changed, and he knew it was smiling. He watched how the light grew, first in the corners, then stretching lazily to the ceiling, and faintly on the back of her as she hung the lamp on its hook. Then she turned, smiling. He went towards her and held her close, holding all the words that they had lost between them, all the loving and quarrelling time that they had been denied. And would have held her there for ever had not a gruff voice boomed from the inner door.

'Where's the package?' the voice said. 'I have to leave before dawn. You can do all the loving later.'

The man came into the light, and Ivan discerned a figure of thuggish and rough appearance who might well have been a friend of Koba and the whistlers from Georgia. Ivan detached himself from the embrace.

'I have it,' he said. 'It's strapped to my body. I have to undress.' But for that he needed privacy, not from this man, this final courier, for he was a passing stranger, but from Katya, of whom he was suddenly shy. She understood, and led him to an inner room. She said nothing. Just smiled, and left him. He disrobed quickly, glad to be unburdened at last of his mission. Then, dressed once more, he returned to the living-room and handed over the package.

'A safe journey,' Ivan said.

The man didn't even thank him. He picked up a kitbag, and went to the door. There he turned. 'Now you can get on with it,' he said. He slammed the door after him, leaving the 'it' that he had referred to hanging in the air. Then Katya broke the silence.

'I told Vassily I'd wake him when you came,' she said. 'I promised him.'

He was relieved. He supposed that his son would be more

comfortable to deal with and he followed her into a back room, leaving the darkness behind her as she carried the lamp. She hung it on a hook beside Vassily's bed, and she motioned Ivan to join her. He looked down on his son and was startled by the likeness to himself. Before his arrest, he remembered that he had looked like Katya. It was as if, in his absence, he had assumed his father's part, and his features had obliged that role.

'Vassily,' Katya whispered. 'Papa's here.' She nudged him gently on the shoulder.

He turned and opened his eyes. Ivan sat on the bed and held him, tongue-tied once more as he held that loss of fatherhood, the praise and chastising times that he had been denied. Then he clasped Katya into the embrace and together they held the silence that stood for all the words that none of them could say. All those words, so often rehearsed and now so seemingly redundant.

It took a little while. Over the next few weeks, words came slowly between them, and at first they were spoken to the floor or to the middle distance without targeting. Gradually they were addressed, and face looked into face and it was as if there had never been absence or silence.

In any case there was little time for talk. The sheer business of living took up most of their waking hours. Food was in very short supply and Katya's day was wholly devoted to foraging. Sometimes she travelled to Petrograd, where bread was available, and she joined the long lines of women waiting hopefully outside the shops. She sensed a feeling of deep unrest amongst them. She even heard a few muttered curses against the Tsar, and not so muttered against the war, and for the thousands of sons who would never come home. One day she saw a man hurl a brick into the window of a baker's shop, where doors had been closed against him after an hour's waiting. She rushed home to tell Ivan. The growing dissent gladdened his heart. All day he worked on the presses. He was alone but it did not disturb him. His years of solitary confinement had robbed him of what small social graces he had had. He was still very uneasy in company. Except for Katya and Vassily. And Andrei, who was an occasional visitor. Over the next few months, others came to the dacha bringing speeches and pamphlets for the presses, and later came for their collection, but few words passed between them. In the afternoons Vassily would come home from school and help his father. Those were the best times for Ivan, when the silences passed unnoticed.

After his homecoming, he grew a moustache and a beard. Andrei had advised it, and had procured for him a set of false papers to match. Now he was reasonably safe. Even so, he kept himself indoors most of the time.

One day Andrei came to the dacha in a state of high excitement. At great risk to himself he had intercepted a message from the Okhrana. It was addressed to the Minister of Internal Affairs and it appraised him of the mood in Petrograd, opining that it was extremely dangerous. People were talking openly of doing away with the Tsar and his hated Tsarina. There was undisguised talk of revolution.

'That's wonderful,' Ivan said. 'I'll print hundreds and hundreds of copies.'

'No,' Andrei said. 'Just one. Only one. It must be taken to Zurich. Lenin must return immediately.'

'Will he come, d'you think?' Katya asked. Tears were in her eyes. Lenin was a god for her.

'He'll judge whether or not the time is ripe,' Andrei said.

Some months later, the courier called once more, that same 'package' courier, and Ivan noticed that he was wearing Swiss snowboots.

Christmas was not far away. It would be bleak for the whole of Russia. Andrei suggested that they should all go back to visit Larionovka. In his posting, he had access to limitless food. He had no doubt his father had the same access, but the Volynins would welcome the wherewithal to celebrate. Ivan had a sudden longing for his village and his family. He wanted to show it all to his son. Katya was wary of the visit. She was shy of meeting again with Pyotr. But Andrei reassured her. They would all travel together, he said, but once in the village, for all their sakes, he must be Count Andrei once more.

'We must all guard our secrets,' he said. 'The secrets that we share.' Except one, he thought. Unshareable.

8

It was the third Christmas of the war and there was both fear and hope that it would be the last of the old regime. But whatever the hopes and fears, there was little to celebrate. The war was taking its toll. Both towns and villages suffered a dire shortage of food and from both was heard the long and melancholy sigh of bereavement.

Larionovka had its share of scars. It had responded to the calls not only for men's wounds but for their recovery and rehabilitation. The great house on the hill had voluntarily turned itself into a hospital and all those in the village who did not tend the crops volunteered their services as orderlies, cleaners, and general assistants. Thus the painful division between the rich and poor was less in evidence. Social barriers were no longer easily defined. The Countess Tatiana depended entirely on her servants for the maintenance of her charitable work, and, what's more, she was daily in their company. Officers and other ranks attended at the same bedside. A patient's recovery, or otherwise, was a great leveller, and was as much due to his surgeon as to the woman who emptied his bedpan. Thus the Volynin family, like their neighbours, spent much of the day beneath the glittering chandeliers. Subterfuge and excuse were no longer needed for the now almost daily meetings between Sasha and Anna. At the turn of the year, both would be seventeen, and in all their years, neither had been able to ignore that gravitational pull between them that had sprung from their babyhood. It was a magnet beyond class, wealth, and station, and would not be denied. But both were shy of each other, and neither would make an approach. Yet the need to declare themselves was urgent enough, for in the New Year, Anna, like all gentlewomen of her class, would go to finishing school in Petrograd. Each day Sasha promised himself to speak to her, and each day Anna resolved to allow herself to be spoken to. So the hovering days passed, until, under the legitimate cloak of work, their paths one day crossed in the gardens. Both were waiting for chair-bound patients, in order to perambulate across the lawns. He smiled at her, his knees melting, and she at him.

'You're going away soon,' he said.

She nodded.

'I'll miss you,' he said. He was horrified at his audacity, but relieved too, that he had in some way declared himself.

'I'll miss you as well,' she whispered.

Then they were called to their charges, and both were relieved, for neither of them could have accommodated the silence that would have ensued. But it was a beginning, they thought. The first and most difficult hurdle was cleared.

It was Count Nicolai who called them. The Count was in total charge of the hospital, and in his lame condition, it was the nearest he would ever again come to command. And, indeed, he ran the establishment like an army base. In this role he was assisted by one Fedya, who had served as cook on Nicolai's ship during the war with Japan. Nicolai had been wounded in the shelling, and it was Fedya who had dragged him to the life raft. In the hospital Fedya acted as go-between from patient and staff to management, for Nicolai kept a cool distance, suitable to his rank. Yet, for all his power, provincial though it was, his frustration was acute. His fingers itched for the sword and battle, but his legs refused combat. His sense of thwarted career was accentuated by Andrei's Christmas visit, and by his tales of bustle and activity in Petrograd. He told of the unrest in the city, of the occasional strikes and riots, and Nicolai was incensed. His beloved Tsar was in danger. And more than the Tsar. Mother Russia herself was trembling. He informed Andrei that in the New Year he would join him in Petrograd. Andrei feigned delight, though in his heart he was uneasy. His brother's presence in the capital would hamper his subversive activities. And his dear Pavel would have to be kept strictly out of the way. He prayed to God that Nicolai would not choose to stay in his apartment.

The Countess Tatiana was appalled on hearing of Nicolai's decision. 'I shall have no children beside me,' she wept. 'And who will look after the hospital?'

'There are other officers,' Nicolai said. 'They will do as well as I. Besides,' he added, 'I shall be able to keep an eye on Anna.'

This last mollified the Countess a little, and she allowed herself to be comforted.

Having made his decision, Nicolai's heart lightened and he planned his Petrograd future. He would present himself at Naval Headquarters. There he would demand a commission. Fedya would accompany him. Together they would teach the rabble a thing or two. His zeal and his confidence in victory was equal to that of his brother's, though he had no notion that Andrei was part of the 'rabble' that he would overcome. On Christmas Eve he placed himself by his father's side at the table, and received his blessing. Then he raised his glass as his father gave a toast to the Tsar.

Andrei swallowed his own treachery, smiling the while. As he drank, he caught Anna's eye.

'To the Tsar,' she said, smiling too, and Andrei wondered whether her toast was as deceptive as his own. And deceptive it was, for like Andrei, who toasted Pavel, she too had a secret love, a love almost as calamitous and as forbidden as her brother's.

That afternoon, they had spent a while together. Their meeting had been accidental. Anna had been sent to the garden to gather ferns for the Christmas table and Sasha's errand was to collect wood for the fires. As Sasha was returning to the house, his arms laden, he saw her. Her back was towards him, and he stared at her for a while, willing her to turn. But she was intent on her picking, and he knew that he must go to her, for such an opportunity so rarely presented itself. He was nervous. He reminded himself of his first declaration, and that lent him courage. He put his load of logs on the ground and went towards her. On his way he saw a lone and late rose in the bushes. He plucked it. It would ease their encounter. He did not want to startle her, so he called her name. She turned and smiled at him with surprise and delight. Thus encouraged, he went towards her, the rose outstretched like an offering. As she took it, she touched his hand, blushing at her boldness, and to share that audacity and thus to spare her, he took both her hands in his and with heroic terror, he put them to his lips. 'Anna,' he whispered.

She gave him his name in return, and with equal trembling.

'I have loved you for many years,' Sasha said.

'And I you,' she said. 'We cannot help ourselves.'

He took her in his arms, and she had to cling to him to control their mutual trembling. He held her close until she was still, then very gently he kissed her. He knew that never again in his life would he feel so happy.

'It's dangerous,' Anna said. 'If Nicolai finds out, he will kill you.'

'He won't find out,' Sasha said. 'It's our secret.'

'It will be so long before I see you again.' Anna's eyes were bleared with tears, with that rapturous sadness that is love's eternal shadow.

'I shall come to Petrograd,' Sasha said. 'I cannot stay here without you.' He kissed her again. 'When can I see you?' he asked.

'Tomorrow. In the conservatory. Before breakfast. No one will miss me then.'

Now, at their Christmas table, Anna relived every syllable of their exchange. Her toasts and smiles were for Sasha, as were Andrei's for Pavel. Both inexorably forbidden.

In the Volynin hut, Sasha was doing likewise. He was no longer 'little Sasha', and Ivan, who had not seen him for so many years, had difficulty in accommodating his new big brother. He wondered what would become of him. He was not like himself or Pyotr. He was a dreamer. Unfathomable. He looked around the table, so heavily laden with Andrei's purloined hamper, the meats and the wines and the large bottle of vodka that had inadvertently been placed in that setting where his father once sat. And though that space was now taken by Pyotr, Ivan still saw its shrieking vacuum. He missed his father terribly. And daily. For if there were no other reason on earth for a revolution, the person of Vassily Volynin would have sufficed. His father's frustration would have merited an earthquake. He looked at Pyotr, who filled that paternal void that was still defiantly there. Unfillable.

Pyotr had done well. Vassily, for want of anything on earth to say, had wished his son good luck, and Pyotr had obliged. He was happy. He had land, a wife and two children, and the Katya episode seemed comfortably accommodated. Indeed she sat now by his side, and they were smiling at each other like strangers. As Ivan looked at Katya, he wondered whether he still loved her, and it disturbed him that he had to wonder. He knew he would never love anyone as much as she, but he could not help but think of Pavlenkov, and his regretted Natasha neglect. He looked at his son, who sat next to her. That was a different kind of loving, a more natural one, less nourished, less fed by wily technique. A self-love, almost, that no cause could override. Next to him, and so close to that first grandchild of hers, sat Maria. She looked well. Age became her, together with the easing of her work and Pyotr's faint prosperity. No doubt she still loved the Tsar, but the Tsar was not a Cause, and could with ease be overtaken by family. And beside her, Avdotya, the village retainer, its bush telegraph, its deliverer. Now, between village babies, she worked at the hospital, as did all of them around the table. He was glad that he had come home, and he marvelled at the pull of family, and was relieved that he was still available to its magnet.

While he was at home, he never went up to the manor. Neither did Katya. They were wary of meeting with Andrei in such alien surroundings. Besides, Count Nicolai, with his rabid loyalty to the Tsar, might well have informed on him. So they kept to themselves, at times with Maria, and at others with Avdotya. Very occasionally Sasha would stay with them, but reluctantly, it seemed, for his pull for the manor was irresistible.

'Why d'you like the manor so much?' Ivan asked him.

'There's a lot to be done there,' he said.

'I think there's something more,' Ivan teased.

Sasha smiled. 'It's a secret.'

'Anna?'

'Don't say anything,' Sasha said. He was relieved that he could share it. 'Ivan —' he was little Sasha again — 'I don't know what to do.'

'Does she love you?'

'She says so. But she's going to Petrograd on our birthday. I shan't see her again.'

'Of course you will. You can write to each other, and she'll come home sometimes.' He knew it was of little consolation. He was aware too of the total impossibility of a marriage between them. Even a revolution could not crash through such barriers. They were too deeply embedded in the soil of privilege and wealth. Ivan felt sorry for his younger brother. He thought he might change the subject. 'Promise me you won't join the army, Sasha,' he said.

Sasha laughed. 'The army's not for me,' he said.

'What *is* for you?'

'I write,' he whispered, as if it was audacious to say it even to himself. Then, in a greater whisper, 'I want to be a writer.'

Ivan was astonished. They were both born of a mother who had few words, mostly tailored for God and the Tsar, and of a father who had no words at all. Where could Sasha's words come from?

'What do you write?' Ivan asked.

'Stories. Poems.' He blushed his confession.

'The Revolution could do with a poet,' Ivan said. It's what Andrei had said. But not Koba. Koba would have spat on Sasha. Ivan didn't know what to think, but his filial loyalty put him on Sasha's side. 'You must write about the changes,' he said. 'They're coming. And soon. The days of the Tsar are over. The people will need a voice. Someone who will express their needs, their sufferings.'

'If the Tsar is overthrown,' Sasha said, 'what will happen to people like Anna and her family?' If it meant their deaths, he would stand by the Tsar, whatever the principle.

'They will have to join us,' Ivan said. 'Many are already on our side. D'you talk politics with Anna?' he asked.

Sasha laughed. In the seventeen years of their intimacy the words that had passed between them could be numbered in those days when they did not think of each other. Barely countable. Neither had need for words. That time-honoured magnet between them was

110

a dictionary in every tongue. So silence dictated their communion, broken only by words of love. 'No,' he answered. 'Not yet. Later perhaps.'

That meant never, Ivan thought. Anna was doomed. And all her kind. He put his arm on his brother's shoulder with appalled tenderness.

Sasha awoke on Christmas morning, trembling. He sensed that he had been trembling all night with the thought of his morning rendezvous. He was nervous. His exchange with Ivan had disturbed him. He had talked himself into believing that when Anna left for Petrograd, he would never see her again. That she would pay the price of Ivan's Cause. For a moment he disliked his brother. He wanted nothing to change. And if revolution there must be, it must confine itself solely to the union between him and the object of his love.

The Christmas bells began to chime as he left the hut, and made his way to the house on the hill. He wondered what he should say to her but his words were for writing, with the pen between his thumb and forefinger, that very first gesture of creation known to man. His pen was the carrier of thought. His lips refused that porterage. So he knew he could say very little to her, and theirs would be a meeting of looks and smiles and kisses. He reached the conservatory and crept inside. He sat himself on an upturned barrel, and waited. He heard the bells chiming, and wished they would stop, for they would muffle her approach. He needed to prepare himself, though for what, he dare not imagine. He peered through the windows, curtained with foliage. He could see the house directly above him. Despite its Christmas decorations, the frontage looked bare, gaunt and austere. He had never considered it anything but a portal to paradise. Now he saw it doomed, because of all that it had ever stood for. He kept his eyes on the grand steps that led to the entrance. He did not expect her to come brazenly out of the front door, but it was enough for him to view the façade that housed her. He thought he saw a shadow behind the curtains, and presumed it was a nurse or an orderly. He waited, his ear cocked for the rustling of her skirt, and cursing the bells that almost deafened him. Then he saw her suddenly, creeping around the side of the house. He felt her trembling, and he knew that she was rehearsing the words she couldn't say. He watched her intently, breathing each step she took towards him. As she neared the conservatory, he turned his back. He did not wish to expose his feverish suspense. His back was towards her, and he faced the door where she would enter, so that for a moment he blindly sensed her approach. Neither did he see the stunned figure of Count Nicolai hobbling down the steps of the manor, his lame foot electrified in a spasm of suspicion. But all that was behind him. He saw the door open and rose to greet her, his arms outstretched, his words liquefied. She glided into his embrace, gently planting her lips on his, their breaths held in wonder. And thus they stayed, soldered together. And thus they were discovered.

Count Nicolai stood at the conservatory door. Before him he saw a total and absolute breakdown of the natural order, more total and more absolute than any bloody revolution. His good leg trembled, and he was unable to move. So he let out a shriek of such revulsion and such bile that the windows trembled behind the foliage. Sasha saw him first, for Nicolai was in direct line of vision. He had no words for this eventuality, but fear needs no rehearsal. He knew that he was the sole target of Nicolai's wrath, but he feared too for Anna. So he did not relinquish his hold. Instead he held her closer, cradling the back of her head with his hand so that she could not turn and cower at his rage. He stared at the Count, more out of terror than defiance.

'Animal! Barbarian!' Nicolai screamed. At last his rage propelled him, and he staggered towards Sasha, cursing his disablement, cursing, too, all the deprivation that his injury had entailed, and armed with his stick and his explosive frustration, he lashed out at Sasha's head. Sasha's ears stung with the pain, yet he managed to unclasp Anna and to distance her from her brother's rage. He tried to dodge the weapon and to escape, but Nicolai was blocking the door. Besides, there was little room for evasion. So helpless, and unarmed, he cowered under the blows, shielding his face, and praying for Nicolai to swiftly vent his spleen. But the punishment seemed endless. He heard Anna sobbing, and her cries enraged him. He knew that somehow he had to resist. He stood erect, taking a stinging blow on his cheek as he did so. He tasted blood on his lip. His whole body was throbbing with pain. It is enough, he thought. Not the pain he suffered, but the sheer and overweening arrogance of the man who inflicted it. Sasha's fury was sublime, and overrode his pain. He lunged at Nicolai, snatching his stick from his hand. He suffered a split moment of scruple that he was disarming a cripple, and in that moment, he threw the stick to the ground. Then he pushed Nicolai roughly aside and watched him land painfully and sprawling among the potted plants. He looked at him for a moment with total contempt. And assured that he could not rise again without assistance, he took Anna in his arms and comforted her. 'Nobody will ever stop me loving you.'

She fumbled in her skirt, and ascertaining that Nicolai could not see her, she thrust a piece of paper into Sasha's hand. 'I love you,' she whispered. 'I always have. I always will.'

He looked into her face. He saw that she had smudged her cheek with blood. He made no attempt to remove it. It was undeniable proof that they were sworn to each other. He slipped the paper into his pocket, picked up Nicolai's stick, and helped him to his feet. Then he ran, his body throbbing with pain at every step and his heart halfway to heaven.

In the conservatory Anna looked at her brother with contempt. Sasha's declaration of love had given her courage. 'You deserved it,' she said. 'And you're lucky to get off so lightly. And it's only because Sasha Volynin is a gentleman.' It was salt in his wound.

'How dare you,' Nicolai spluttered.

'I never want to see you again,' she said. She passed by him, trembling a little, stunned by her own bravery. She rushed back to the house, and to her room in the private wing. Once there, she did not have to be brave any longer. Neither did she have to be an adult. She could cry like a child, and with those tears of fathomless despair which the passing years had learned to control and understand. When Marfa, having heard the sobs, came into her room, Anna crawled into her arms as she had done as a child.

Marfa's role as nanny in the Larionov household was now redundant. A Miss Cameron, a governess, had taken her place. But Marfa was kept on the estate in the manner of an old retainer. She worked when she could in the hospital, but her health was failing. She had become mellow with the years, and the memory of her lost love was no longer laced with bitterness. But the pain never left her, a dull thudding ache in her very bones. Anna need say nothing to her. She knew the source of her sorrow. She had not been ignorant of her charge's love for Sasha. She had watched it flower since she was a child. And flower despite her awareness of impediment. It had all started, Marfa knew, when she had reluctantly taken the newborn Anna to the Volynin hut as the bells were pealing the century's turn. She knew even then that no good would come of it. She rocked Anna in her arms.

'You must try and forget him,' she said wearily, hearing the absurdity and hollowness of her advice. The loves of middle age can, with little difficulty, be put aside, but those of one's youth are for ever immovable. So she rocked and cradled her, the only comfort she could give. In time, Anna fell asleep in her arms, and Marfa knew it was not from fatigue, but from a desperate need for oblivion.

In the Volynin hut, Avdotya was tending Sasha's wounds. He had pretended he had fallen amongst the brambles, but his cuts were more severe than briars, and she had forced the truth out of him, and for Sasha it was something of a relief to reveal it. Maria immediately fell before the icon, prostrating herself in pleas for forgiveness for her wayward son, who now paid so dearly for his ideas above his station.

'I love her,' Sasha shouted, 'and that's nothing to do with station. I shall marry her, and I don't care what Nicolai says.'

It was blasphemy, and Maria shrieked her despair. Avdotya went to the floor to comfort her. She turned to Sasha. 'You should pray for your salvation,' she said.

Sasha left the hut. Unlike Anna, he had no place for privacy, yet he was desperate to be alone. He daren't show his face in the manor and he wondered when, if ever, he would see her again. Then he remembered the note she had thrust into his hand. He pulled it out of his pocket. *Countess Anna Larionova*, he read. *Finishing School for Young Ladies. Smolny Institute, Petrograd.* He smiled for the first time since leaving her. She wanted him to write to her. Or perhaps, he dared to think, to follow her to the capital. He folded the paper gently, then put it away, although he already knew it by heart. He regarded it as his first love letter. He would reply to her with a poem. He crossed into a field to find his solitude. And all those words that were not fashioned for speaking fell from his pencil and singed the page with their longing.

Christmas was over, and Ivan and Katya were preparing to leave the village. At the house on the hill, preparations were afoot for another leave-taking and Sasha watched the manor from a lookout on a rise, and his heart faltered at the signs of departure. The carriage was waiting at the door, the four grey horses immaculately still. He saw Pyotr and a footman load the luggage onto the carriage. Four large trunks. In his eyes the sheer bulk of it spelt out a long absence. His poem burnt in his pocket. Yet he could see no way of giving it to her. But at least he would see her, a fleeting glance perhaps of her skirt, as it looped the carriage door. He waited. The luggage was strapped down, and Pyotr disappeared into the house while the footman took his stand at the carriage door. All was inexorably ready. There was nothing else left now but her departure. Inside he heard himself weeping. But for the footman and the carriage, the façade of the house was bare. Its nakedness and silence seemed a prelude to an event, one of noise and multitude. Then Count Dmitri appeared at the door, with Tatiana on his arm. And after them, the travellers. Count Nicolai was first, with Fedya at his side. Resplendent in his naval uniform, he looked, even from Sasha's distance, very pleased with himself. He kissed his mother, who wept on his arm. Andrei joined them and said his farewells. Then both men walked down the steps, and waited there.

It seemed an eternity before Anna appeared, Marfa and Miss Cameron at her sides. Her leave-taking with her parents was formal to the point of indifference. Clearly Nicolai had told them his story. But Anna kissed Marfa, and held her close. It seemed that she would miss nobody from that stern fortress except her old nanny and comforter. Then slowly she walked down the steps. Halfway she stopped and looked around her. She scanned the gardens that fronted the house, then stood on tiptoe to view the conservatory. Perhaps she hoped to find Sasha there. He was tempted to signal

115

to her, but he was afraid of drawing attention to himself, and that, as a consequence, she would be the victim. So he put his hands in his pockets, his fists clenched hard. He watched as Andrei and Nicolai took steps towards her to lead her to the carriage. He watched as she openly refused Nicolai's proffered arm, and took Andrei's with both of hers. He lost sight of her then as she entered the carriage, but he stood there for a long while, long after the carriage had moved out of sight, staring at the space on the steps that she had once filled. Then, full of tears, he walked back to his dwelling.

Ivan and Katya were leaving on the night train. For a moment he thought he might entrust Ivan with his poem and Anna's address. But his was a private grief and a private joy, and both were too precious to share.

The family leave-taking, unlike that at the manor, was tender and tearful. Maria knew that there was danger in the capital, and possibly soon in the whole country and she knew, too, that Ivan and Katya were part of that peril. She wondered if she would ever see them again.

In the New Year, Maria found a note that Sasha had left on her pillow. *Dearest Mama*, she read, or rather Avdotya read it for her, *I cannot bear to be without her. I have gone to Petrograd.*

'You still have Pyotr and Nina and the children,' Avdotya comforted her.

But Maria could not stem her tears. For now, more than ever, it was Vassily whom she needed by her side.

PART THREE

9

As their carriage drove through the streets of Petrograd, Nicolai looked discreetly out of the window, and was horrified by what he saw. There were long queues outside the food shops, and those who waited were not patient. They were shouting in chorus: 'We want bread.' The corners of each street thronged with idle striking workmen, and at one of them an orator stood on a box haranguing the crowd. As the carriage approached him, Nicolai could hear his words.

'Down with the tyrant,' the man shouted, and in case he hadn't made himself clear, 'Down with the Tsar.'

Nicolai shrank back into his seat. He was mortified. 'My God,' he said. 'Why doesn't somebody *do* something? We should execute their leaders, bite off the head of the snake. That would put a stop to this anarchy.'

'You're right,' Andrei said solemnly, though his heart soared at those many signs of discontent. 'You're right, Nicolai,' he said again. 'They should all be rounded up and shot.'

Anna, who sat between them, was silent. What Nicolai had said did not surprise her. It was totally in character. But she was disturbed by Andrei's agreement. She had hoped that, concerning Sasha, she could win Andrei to her side. Now she suspected that in his social priorities, he was no better than Nicolai. She despaired of allies. She knew that Katya and Ivan were somewhere in the capital. They would surely be her friends, but she had no means of finding where they lived. And she dared not ask of anybody, for she knew that the name Volynin spelt treason. She had heard stories of Ivan's crimes murmured with disgust at their table. 'A shame to Larionovka,' Nicolai had said, and all around the table had agreed. She was desperately unhappy. Over and over again, she relived her rare meetings with Sasha, but the memory of his smiles and kisses was soured by the recall of their conservatory encounter. She looked at Nicolai with abject hatred.

The carriage came to a halt. Andrei drew the curtain on the window. Through it Anna saw that they had stopped outside a large building, with the legend 'Smolny Institute' sculpted into its frieze. It looked like a prison. Andrei opened the carriage door, and Anna was escorted inside. Fedya followed with her luggage. She turned around to look at the sky. She sensed that she would not see it again for a long while.

The headmistress of the establishment was waiting in the hall. She was a large woman, dressed entirely in black, as stern and as forbidding as the building that housed her.

'You are welcome, Countess Anna,' she said. There was no smile of welcome, but there was a curtsey, and Nicolai was gratified that there remained in Mother Russia at least one class that had not entirely lost its senses.

'You leave your sister in good hands.' She addressed Nicolai, and for him there was a smile. It could have been in recognition of his rank, or perhaps mere pity for his injury. 'Like all our new girls,' she went on, 'Countess Anna will be confined to the school for one month. During that time there will be no visitors. But parcels and letters may be delivered. Now come along, Countess,' she bristled. 'Say goodbye to your brothers.'

Anna would have been happy to forgo the leave-taking, but the woman was looming over her, waiting. Andrei put his arm around her shoulder. Then whispered in her ear, 'Don't worry, I'm your friend.' He smiled and distanced her. She could make of it what she would.

His remark gave her heart enough to turn and look at Nicolai. But she would not kiss him and she shunned the move he made towards her. 'Goodbye,' she said, turned again, and allowed herself to be led away.

Nicolai feigned indifference, but he was deeply hurt by her slight.

He resolved that over the next month he would woo her with gifts. He must not alienate her. She was impressionable, and he feared that in the present perilous climate of his country, she would be seduced by Volynin ideas. He had a month in which to cleanse her soul. He had arranged to rent an apartment on the outskirts of the city. Or rather, Andrei had arranged it to pre-empt any suggestion of sharing his own. Nicolai had agreed, on condition that they would meet regularly. 'I shall be needing all your co-operation,' he said. 'It's useful to have a friend in high places.'

It was, Andrei thought, and he ached to get back to Pavel and their subversive exchange.

'I'll do all I can,' he said, and meant it. But what he would do was not for Nicolai and his like. He settled them in their apartment and went on his way.

Nicolai lost no time. As soon as Fedya had unpacked, he went shopping. Perfume for Anna, silk handkerchiefs and scarfs. And a box of rose chocolates, which he knew to be her favourites. These he sent with Fedya with strict instructions that he should specify the sender. Not Andrei, nor anyone else, but he who wished her happiness more than anyone.

When Fedya returned from his errand, he grilled him on the reception of his gifts.

'Did you tell her they were from me?'

'Of course,' Fedya lied.

'And did she smile? Was she happy?'

Fedya nodded, lying again, as he had lied to Anna. For in truth, when Anna had seen the gifts she had to ascertain that they were not from Nicolai before she would accept them. The good Fedya had lied that they were from Andrei, and in that name, Anna had received them. But without a smile.

'Fedya,' she had said, 'I hate it here. And as soon as I can, I shall run away.'

'Where will you go?' he had asked her.

'Somewhere where my family cannot find me.'

This news Fedya could hardly relate to her brother. So he lied about her smiles and happiness. But he sympathised with Anna. From what he had seen of the school, it was indeed a prison.

For the next few weeks, Nicolai acquainted himself with the city. And on each sortie he returned disheartened. Anarchy openly prevailed. He'd actually seen defacement on a statue of his beloved Tsar. His sole consolation was his occasional visit to Andrei where he met people who were sympathetic to his views.

He had called at Naval Headquarters and had been horrified at his reception. He had offered his services and in any capacity.

'You're crazy,' the officer had told him. 'What's there for you to do? What's there for any of us to do? There are rumours that they are forming a provisional government. Our days are over.'

'To hell with the provisional government,' Nicolai had told him. 'What about our loyalty to the Tsar? I'm an experienced officer. Surely I can be of some use.'

The officer had acquiesced. And wearily. 'If that's what you want,' he had said, 'die in your uniform. Die with the rest of us.'

And so Nicolai had been reluctantly enrolled. They said they would be in touch. But three weeks had passed and still he had not been called. He called for Fedya, and they hailed a carriage and ordered the driver to take them to the Naval Headquarters. He would not look out of the windows. He could hear the rabble outside. Some of them actually banged on the carriage doors, shouting, 'Down with the Tsar. Death to the tyrant.' Nicolai was apoplectic with rage. He tapped on the driver's window, urging him to hurry. But suddenly the coach came to a complete halt, and the noise outside was deafening.

'What is it, driver?' Nicolai shouted.

There was no answer. He drew the curtain of the coachman's window, and he saw that his seat was empty. Then the carriage started to rock.

'Quick, sir,' Fedya said. He opened the door, and helped his master down the steps. Then they rushed through the crowd and turning, saw the carriage splinter on the cobbles. And all around them was chaos.

Who knows when the Russian Revolution started. It had throbbed for many terrible Tsarist years. It had fed itself on hunger, poverty and frustration. It was spoken of in whispers, or screamed aloud from a thousand gallows when there was nothing more to lose. But if the Revolution could ever claim a birthday and a place of birth, it was on the cold morning of Monday, 27 February 1917, and its place was the gates of the Tauride Palace, seat of the government. Thousands of workers, soldiers amongst them, Cossacks even, those dreaded enemies of the people who had joined the masses sniffing the winning side, countless tramping thunderous feet marched on the Palace to demand an end to Romanov rule. And likewise in Moscow, in Odessa, in villages and hamlets across the land, for the Revolution was a multibirth of many sites and many days. And multiheaded too. For it reared itself into the very heart of the establishment. Army units weary of the war, mutinied. Generals were summarily shot. Those who have been so long oppressed find little difficulty in assuming the role of oppressor. They have been tutored well, if not wisely, and the whole country seeped with blood and savagery. A provisional government was formed. The Tsar's gruesome days were at an end.

In the countryside, in Ivan and Katya's dacha, the printing press turned on an astonishing headline. 'The tyrant abdicates.' Ivan and Katya danced with joy, and made plans to return immediately to the capital.

It was about this time that Sasha arrived in Petrograd. Never in his life had he seen so many people, and people it seemed, in a state of continual excitement. He did not think of going to Ivan's. His purpose in the capital was to meet with Anna, and to take her away and marry her. He had no other thought. From the station, he went directly to the Smolny Institute. He was given short shrift at reception. No visitors were allowed, he was told. Only close relatives. He was tempted to announce himself as the Countess Anna's husband, as indeed he felt himself to be, but he knew that they would resist such a declaration.

'When do they come out?' he asked. 'They must go out sometimes.'

The receptionist looked at him with pity. 'For the moment, with all these disturbances, our ladies are confined to the Institute,' he said.

'For how long?' Sasha asked.

'That I cannot tell you.'

But he would wait. However long it took. He took up his stand outside the building, leaning against a pillar, or sometimes sitting at its base. When it grew dark he roamed the streets, bought what food was available, and mingled with the crowds. For the city never seemed to sleep. Sometimes he lay down with other homeless in doorways, but always at first light, he was back at the Institute, leaning against his pillar. For four days he kept such vigil, and on the fifth, he saw a familiar figure outside the building. It was Fedya. He did not hesitate to approach him. They had had occasional and friendly encounters at the manor house during their orderly duties.

'Fedya,' he said.

'Sasha. What are you doing here?' Though he knew well, having heard the story from Count Nicolai.

'I'm waiting for Anna,' he said simply. 'Are you going to her?'

'I'm taking her a parcel. You must go away, Sasha. There's too much trouble and no good can come of it.'

'Fedya,' Sasha said, 'you're not like them. I know you're not. I must see her. Let me take the packet to her.'

'Look, Sasha,' Fedya said, 'I'd like to help you. But if there's one man in the world Count Nicolai hates, it's you. If he ever found out, he'd cut me in two with his sword.'

'He'll never know,' Sasha pleaded. 'Let me take it. I'll say I'm his messenger.'

Fedya hesitated. Sasha was right. He was one of them. He had no business siding with the gentry. In any case, it seemed that they would not be gentry for long.

'Never breathe a word to anybody,' he said. 'You must promise me that.'

'On my own and Anna's life,' Sasha said. He took the packet from Fedya's trembling hand. 'Go home and tell him you have delivered it.' He couldn't bring himself to pronounce Nicolai's name. 'Tell him she thanked him.'

'I always do,' Fedya muttered. 'But I tell her the packets are from Andrei. So must you. Otherwise she won't accept them.' Then swearing him once more to secrecy, he trembled on his way.

Sasha was nervous. He ran the risk of meeting that same receptionist who had given him such short shrift a few days ago. He prayed that another had taken his place. But he needn't have worried. When he entered the building, he could see that the place was in turmoil. Porters were crossing and recrossing the hall carrying luggage, and depositing the trunks close to the door. Women were bustling around giving orders. He noticed two burly men removing a large bust of the Tsar from its plinth in the centre of the hall. Sasha smiled. For some reason, that gesture spelt Anna's freedom. A man was at the desk, but barely in control. He was sorting papers and most of them he tore into pieces, fear in his trembling hands. 'Have you got my trunk?' he shouted, between his frantic shredding. He clearly would have wished to be anywhere but where he was. Sasha approached the desk.

'I have a package for Countess Anna Larionova,' he said between the shreds. 'Where can I find her?'

'A fine time to bring a package,' the man said. 'Who is it from?'

'Her brother Count Nicolai Larionov.' The name sickened him.

'Well, at least that will save me another messenger. Will you please tell the Count to have a carriage here at eight o'clock tomorrow morning. The school is closing down. The ladies have not yet been told. There will be a roll call shortly.'

Sasha tried to hide his pleasure. He thanked God and even the Tsar for the Revolution, that it had offered him the simple possibility of elopement. He would take Anna to Ivan's. They would be safe there.

'Where can I find her?' he asked again.

'Fourth floor. Room six.'

Sasha took it slowly. He was a simple errand boy, and he did not want anyone to think otherwise. He even paused at the Tsar removers. 'Want a hand?' he asked.

'No,' one of them said. 'This is our pleasure.'

He took the stairs at his leisure. He heard his heartbeat triple his steps. He was not worried about the words he would give her. Most of them would be concerned with practical arrangements. He drummed his fingers idly along the banisters, but when he reached the fourth floor, his nonchalance deserted him. He began to tremble. The figure six beckoned him from the end of the corridor. It seemed to waver and then to blur, and he felt tears running down his cheeks. He did not trust his feet to reach her door. He wiped his cheeks on his sleeve, and tried to steady himself. He told himself that he was a mere errand boy with a package to deliver, but whatever he thought, he could not stop his tears. He wiped them again on his sleeve and forced his steps to the door. Now the number six looked like no number at all.

It floated amoeba-like on the wooden panel. Without thinking, he knocked, and then very much wanted to run away.

'Come in,' he heard. The voice was like a stranger's. He wondered whether he had the right room. He hoped that he had made a mistake, for that would give him breathing space. He opened the door. A girl lay on the bed, her face turned to the wall, her shoulders heaving with sobs. He knew it was Anna, not by her dress, or the back of her head, or the small shoeless feet, but by a simple presence in the room.

'Anna,' he whispered. Knowing his voice, she jumped startled from the bed, then ran into his arms.

'Why are you crying?' he asked her between kisses.

'I so hate it here, Sasha,' she said. 'I thought I'd never see you again.'

'I'm here,' he said softly. 'And I'm never going to leave you.'

'That's impossible,' she whispered.

'No. I have news.' He took her to the bed, and he sat by her side, and slowly he told her the strange turn of events.

'D'you know about the Revolution?' he asked her.

'This morning, in prayers,' she said solemnly, 'they told us not to pray for His Imperial Majesty. We had to pray for the Provisional Government instead. What is the Provisional Government, Sasha?'

'I'm not sure. All I know is that the Tsar is finished.'

'Then what will happen to me?' she asked. 'All my family?'

'You're my family now,' he said, 'and tomorrow I shall take you away. The school is closing down. I have to tell your brother to call for you early in the morning.'

She shuddered. 'I won't go with Nicolai,' she said.

'You don't have to.' Then he told her how he had persuaded Fedya to let him deliver the package, and how the porter had ordered him to give instructions to Nicolai. And how they need never find out, and that he himself would take her in the morning, and never let her go again.

'Where shall we go?' she asked.

'To Ivan and Katya. We shall be safe there.' He knew that he had to leave. He didn't want to arouse any suspicion downstairs.

'I shall have a carriage outside at eight o'clock,' he said. 'I shall say that Nicolai was at Naval Headquarters. He probably will be anyway,' he said.

She clung to his neck. She did not want to let him go. 'Only a few more hours,' he said. 'Dry your tears. You need never cry again.' He gave her the packet.

'Thank Andrei for me,' she said. 'I would like to see him, but I never want to see Nicolai again.'

'He will change,' Sasha said. 'He will have to. He cannot fight a changing world.' He kissed her again, and had to tear himself away. He did not look around, but dashed down the stairway until he reached the first landing. There he composed himself and once more assumed a nonchalant air. In this manner, he passed through the hall. Outside the Institute the two Tsar breakers were sweeping away the shattered pieces of tyranny.

He took Ivan's address out of his pocket, together with the map that his brother had provided, and he made his way through the crowds. What he saw appalled him. Bodies dangled from lampposts, some still twitching in their last agony. A child lay dead in the gutter, its mouth still open with its last heartbreaking cry. It had not been a peaceful revolution. The mob, aided by soldiers who had broken their allegiance to the Tsar, had rampaged through the city, shooting down all those who clung to the old regime and had the temerity to be on the streets. Sasha leaned against one of the lampposts that overnight had become a gallows, and found himself weeping. He thought of Larionovka and of his family and friends and he wondered whether the Revolution had yet reached that tiny outpost, and of the measure of its scars. He bent down to the gutter and picked up the child's body and cradled it in his arms. He carried it to a low wall, and laid it gently on the top, out of the way of further mutilation by indifferent carriages and people. He kissed the child's forehead. The innocent victim of an oppres-

sor's downfall, whose tyranny he could never have practised nor
even understood. He walked sadly away while a poem festered in
his mind. So intense was his concentration, and so turbulent his
thought, that his pace inevitably slowed and it was almost dark by
the time he reached Ivan's house. During that time he had not
once thought of Anna, and when she occurred to him as he knocked
on Ivan's door, it was as if he recalled a stranger. There are other
causes besides revolution. The making of poetry is one of them.

He heard a scuffle behind the door. And Katya's voice.

'Who is it?'

'Sasha.'

The door opened wide. 'Ivan,' she called, 'it's Sasha.'

'Sashenka,' Ivan called from the back of the apartment. He
rushed to the door and embraced him. 'Welcome,' he said. 'Welcome to Petrograd and freedom.' The image of the dead child
seared Sasha's retina. What use was freedom to him? He followed
them inside. Food was put on the table, and they plied him with
questions about the family and the village gossip, and, though they
both knew, about what he was doing in Petrograd.

He unfolded his story, detailing the days and nights he had spent
in the city. But Ivan interrupted him, before he could tell them
about Anna. 'You must write it all down,' Ivan said. 'A revolution
needs its witnesses. There's so much work to be done, Sasha.
Pamphlets to be written, speeches. We are short of people who
can do that. You must stay here with us, and work with us. Oh,
Sashenka, I'm so glad to see you.' He embraced him once more.

Then Sasha told them about Anna, and his plans to take her
away.

'Can she stay here with me?' he asked.

They marvelled at his audacious piece of planning, and they
laughed.

'Of course,' Ivan said. 'We will find room for you both.'

But Katya was cautious. 'I can't wait on her here like I did in
Larionovka,' she said. 'We all work here. Vassily too. She will have
to do her share.'

'Of course,' Sasha said. 'She'll do whatever she has to. She's not
like Nicolai or Andrei.'

Ivan smiled. Sasha would be surprised at how like Andrei she was. So it was arranged. Katya was nervous, but Sasha reassured her. Vassily, who had never smelt the manor house, who had been fed and weaned on and temporarily orphaned by the Revolution, couldn't understand what all the fuss was about. 'At last I won't have to do the washing-up,' he said.

'We will all share in everything,' Katya said sternly.

They gave Sasha a room at the top of the house, one that was used for storage of papers. That evening, they set to clearing it, and to make it fit for the loving that it would house. That night, Sasha did not sleep. But it was not the thought of Anna that disturbed him, but the poem that was almost ripe in his mind.

He was up early in the morning, eager to be on his way to the Smolny Institute. He walked in order to save what little money he had. When he neared the school, he ordered a carriage, and sat inside it until the clock struck eight. Then he went inside with the purpose of having Anna called, and to give the excuses of Count Nicolai who had a previous engagement. But all was chaos inside the foyer. No one was at the reception desk. The hall was milling with schoolgirls and teachers, and all with one purpose. To get out of Petrograd as quickly as possible. He looked round the hall and dared to call her name. Then he saw her rushing towards him. She was intent on throwing herself on his neck, but he warned her against any public display of their happiness.

'It doesn't matter any more,' she said. 'It's all changed.'

'Tell that to Nicolai,' Sasha laughed. He took her luggage and she followed him to the carriage. Once they were settled inside, he gave the driver Ivan's address. Then he leaned back and took her in his arms.

'This is the beginning,' he said, 'and it will never end.'

'Will it be all right at Ivan's?' Anna asked tentatively. 'Will they accept me?'

'Will you accept *them*?' he asked. Then he told her about the work that Ivan was doing, and had been doing for many years. 'We will join them, Anna,' he said. 'We will help them. There are many others of your class who are on our side.'

'I know nothing,' Anna said helplessly. 'I've never talked to

129

anybody about any of these things. In my society women aren't supposed to think.'

'Then you must talk to Katya. You will learn from her.'

It was Katya who answered the door to them. Sasha noticed her involuntary curtsey. But Ivan who joined her, who had long outgrown the forelock tradition, said, 'You are welcome, Anna.'

Katya gasped at the sudden loss of title. 'Come in, Countess Anna,' she whispered.

'No more of that,' Ivan said. 'We are all equal here.'

'Of course,' Anna said, though she was as flummoxed by her changed status as was Katya. She smiled at them. 'You're very kind to have us,' she said.

They all shuffled inside. Awkward. Ivan pressed Anna to some food. He tended to overdo his welcome. He had decided that there was nothing different about the Countess, and she bloody well would have to learn to be like anybody else. So there was a tinge of hostility in his welcome, which was not lost on Anna. At the moment she preferred Katya's reticence. They were both learning, and it would take time.

After they had eaten, Katya rose to clear the table. Anna followed suit. Ivan smirked a little.

'No, please,' Katya said. 'I'll do it.'

'Let me help you,' Anna insisted, and she followed Katya into the kitchen. They were silent together, exchanging the occasional smile. In time it will work, both of them thought, both marvelling at the precarious bridges that could be crossed. Later Sasha and Anna went to their room, and for the rest of that day dwelt in an Eden closed to the spoken or the written word.

But there was an Eden of a kind down below. Word had come through that Lenin was coming to Petrograd. Katya and Ivan subdued their celebrations in deference to the lovers above, but they hugged each other, and even opened a precious bottle of wine, for both of them knew that, with the arrival of their leader, the Revolution was a certainty.

They set to work immediately, according to their instructions. There were leaflets to be printed, and a group of helpers recruited to distribute them.

130

'The first job for Anna and Sasha,' Ivan said.

So they went to the presses. 'Lenin arrives tomorrow. Meet him,' they printed and printed in thousands.

'We will take Vassily with us to the station,' Katya said. 'At last you're safe, Ivan. Nobody can take you now.'

Towards evening the lovers reappeared, and were sent immediately on their first mission. They were excited, an excitement heightened by the expectancy of the street crowds. They deposited their fliers in shops, letterboxes and outstretched hands. Sasha noticed that the lampposts were lampposts once again, denuded of their hanging tinsel, and as he passed the wall where he had lain the child to rest, he noticed that it too was bare. He prayed that its mother would have found it, and closed its young mouth on its bewilderment.

Already the crowds were making for the station where they would spend the night in joyful anticipation. Sasha and Anna followed them. As the morning light broke, the crowds intensified. Somewhere amongst them were Katya, Ivan and Vassily.

'I'm sure of one thing,' Anna said. 'Nicolai and Andrei are not in this crowd. I'm safe here.' Then she wondered if they had yet discovered her disappearance. She would not want them to worry. Perhaps she could find a way of getting word to Andrei. She cared not how Nicolai was disturbed.

But Nicolai was disturbed enough. And not on account of Anna. As yet neither he nor Andrei had heard of the closure of the school. His disturbance centred around the face of him whom he had worshipped, the pillar and support of his Mother Russia. At that moment, a little time before Lenin's train would arrive at the station, he was attending a meeting in Andrei's office with some service officers who had remained loyal to their leader.

'Our main concern', Nicolai was saying, 'is to be prepared to take up arms in the case of any further insurrection. Our ultimate aim is to restore the monarchy. We all have men at our command. Loyal men and true.'

'I'll drink to that,' one of the officers said. He poured vodka for them all.

'Andrei,' Nicolai said, 'you will keep us informed of all new developments. You have the ear of those who still matter.'

'You can rely on me,' Andrei said. He raised his glass.

'To the monarchy,' Nicolai declared.

But it was all too late. As they toasted their beloved Tsar, Lenin's train arrived at the station, and his tumultuous welcome could be heard all over the city. It echoed through the open window of Andrei's office. The men's glasses were halfway to their lips, and there they hovered an instant at this reminder of the futility of the toast. The glasses were returned to the table. Andrei was relieved of yet another deception. Of late he had had difficulty in even pronouncing the tyrant's name.

'Our time will come,' Nicolai said, as the tears rolled down his cheeks.

10

But Lenin did not stay long in Petrograd. In the years of growing rebellion against the Tsar, many factions had developed within the opposition. Bolsheviks, Mensheviks, and straightforward socialists, all jockeying for power. The main contention between them centred around the issues regarding the war. Russia was suffering probably more than any other of the allies who were aligned against Germany. Their casualties on the battlefronts were uncountable. But if they were told, they were told in millions. It is no wonder that many Russians wanted to see an end to it. Lenin was one of these. He wished to make peace with Germany and start to mend his shattered homeland. The Bolsheviks, on the other hand, were in favour of continuing the war. Moreover, Koba and his fellow exiles had returned from the Siberian wastes. Not for nothing had they rotted away their years on those frozen plains. Their time, too, had come. Koba's especially. He would bide his time for the high office that he sought, and until that time, he would still answer to the name of Koba. In the meantime, he satisfied himself by taking over the editorship of *Pravda*.

The war was not the only bone of contention. Another fundamental issue was the way in which the Revolution should proceed. The Bolsheviks believed that the working class should unite with peasants and fight against the entire bourgeois class, the Mensheviks took the opposite view, and the Kadets, a more liberal party, favoured a constitutional monarchy. Kerensky belonged to this latter faction. He was Minister-President of the Provisional Government, and Lenin's most bitter and formidable opponent.

He accused Lenin of preaching counter-revolution, and he issued a warrant for his arrest. Lenin went into hiding in Finland. From there he sent his instructions. Through his many connections Ivan was privy to all contentious argument in the Provisional Government. Andrei was still his prime source of information. On one of his clandestine visits, Ivan told him about Anna. At the time she was in the streets with Sasha distributing leaflets. Andrei was anxious to see her, and relieved too that she was well. Moreover he was delighted that she had strayed from her class.

'I must tell Nicolai,' he said. 'He is very anxious about her. But I won't mention Sasha. I'll let him believe he's still in Larionovka. But I must see her.' He arranged with Ivan that he would meet Anna in the City Art Gallery. Their viewing of paintings would be a good cover for conversation.

They met a few days later. Both were delighted to see each other. He took her arm as they toured the pictures.

I'm glad you're one of us,' Andrei said.

'Does it surprise you?'

'Yes and no. After all, I have been one of them for a long time.'

'That surprised *me*,' Anna said.

'But they're right, you know, Anna. It was impossible to perpetuate the old ways.'

'Are you happy here, Andrei?'

Suddenly he wanted to tell her about Pavel. To share him with her. Her liaison with Sasha was after all, almost as illegal as his own. But she interrupted his thoughts.

'Have you found yourself a beautiful mistress?' she giggled.

He shook his head. Now he couldn't tell her. Her assumptions were too deeply rooted to be shaken.

'You are so handsome, Andrei,' she said flirtatiously. 'I shall make it my business to find a beautiful wife for you.'

Andrei laughed. It was the only response he could give. They circled the gallery. 'I have a message for Ivan,' he said. 'Listen carefully.' He steered her to another wall where the pictures were smaller and required closer viewing. 'Tell him I have to lie low for a while. They are watching me. Not only me. Everybody. They are desperately nervous. Tell him that Kerensky has now taken over the Foreign Ministry as well. He seems to be running the whole show. I saw a memo on his desk. They know Lenin is coming back. They know his plans. That painting's from the Suprematist School,' he said loudly, as a couple passed behind them.

'I'll tell him,' Anna said. 'Though it's not good news.'

'No. But he must know it.'

They had come to the exit of the gallery. He embraced and kissed her before they parted.

'I have a message for you from Nicolai,' he said.

She distanced herself from his embrace. 'Goodbye, Andrei,' she said. 'It was lovely seeing you.' And she was gone.

Andrei looked after her, Nicolai's greetings and love still hovering on his lips. He understood now that she would never forgive him.

The months that followed the Revolution were dire in the extreme. The changeover from tyranny to a comparative freedom was swift and unprepared and in many ways and in many places, the results were anarchic. Soldiers deserted from the army in their thousands. What guns they had they turned on their officers and proved to be torturers equal in skill to their former tormentors. They held up trains and hijacked them to their villages. Once there, they burned down the manors of their former landlords, and put their masters to the sword. A programme of pillage, looting, rape and arson spread from village to hamlet, and from hamlet to city. Kerensky and his Provisional Government were clearly out of control. The Bolsheviks waited for Lenin to give the word.

It was during this terrible summer of 1917 that Sasha found his voice as a poet. The body of the dead child, which he had witnessed in his early days in Petrograd, had fed his anger, his shame, his compassion. Between his errands for Ivan, and often late into the night, he wrote like one obsessed. Many poems he discarded because of their untempered rage. They throbbed with an anger more suitable to a politician than a poet. A poet's fury does not boil. It simmers. His tears do not fall. They trickle. His compassion does not overwhelm. It pervades. Sasha's poems learnt themselves by heart, and stayed in the memory long after an orator's harangue and, though initially inspired by the Revolution, were applicable to universal suffering. By the end of that summer, Sasha had

135

completed a collection of poems, which he called *Days of Love and Hope*, and he dedicated it to Anna.

It was Anna who saw to its publication. Sasha was nervous and shy, and wary of promoting himself. So Anna took it upon herself to manage him. She took the manuscript to Yakovlev, one of the most prestigious publishing houses in the city, publishers in fact of Mayakovsky, the unofficial laureate of the Revolution. She demanded to see the great Yakovlev himself, a man not known for his accessibility, but doubtless Anna's beauty facilitated their meeting. She left the manuscript in his hands and told him she would return in a week. But before the week was out, Yakovlev himself arrived on their doorstep, a contract in his hand.

'Where is the great Alexander Volynin?' he asked.

It was Sasha who opened the door. He was frightened. He thought the man had come to arrest him. Alexander was the name he used only for official documents.

'I am Sasha Volynin,' he said, giving himself a faint loophole if such were necessary.

'Then you are my new discovery,' Yakovlev said. 'Our people are hungry for poetry. They will take you to their hearts.'

Sasha trembled with excitement. He was alone in the house at the time, and though he would have welcomed company, someone with whom to share his success, at the same time he was glad that he was alone for he was faintly ashamed of his accomplishment, and he resolved that he wouldn't tell anybody. Except perhaps Anna, whom he would swear to secrecy.

But as it turned out, *Days of Love and Hope* could not be kept hidden. Within weeks of its acceptance, Sasha's slim volume of verse appeared in bookstalls all around the city. People queued to buy it, for they had heard it would confirm all their sadness, their fears and uncertainties, and above all, their hopes. Overnight Sasha became the people's poet, and the name Alexander Volynin a household word.

Sasha tried to ignore the acclaim. He wanted to get away from it all. He longed for his village and his family. And circumstances obliged him, albeit unhappy ones.

At the height of his fame a letter came from Larionovka. It was from Dr Lvov and informed Ivan and Sasha that their mother was ill, and that she was pining for her sons. It warned them about the dangers and discomfort of travel in those times, and advised Katya and Vassily against travelling. He clearly knew nothing about Anna. When Ivan read the letter his face betrayed a slight disturbance, but his reaction was bold and immediate.

'You will have to go alone, Sasha,' he said. 'I cannot leave Petrograd. Not at this time. I have important work to do here.'

Sasha was silent for a moment. His brother's priorities horrified him. He marvelled that they came from the same parentage.

'Important work?' Sasha asked. 'What are you talking about? How important can work be, any work, when Mama is ill. Dying perhaps.'

'I can't go, Sasha,' Ivan said. He was adamant. 'The personal life has to take second place.'

Sasha knew that Ivan could not be argued with. He knew, too, that his poems, even if he read them, would mean nothing to him, and that hurt him more than anything.

'Let me come with you,' Anna begged. 'It's time I made my peace with my parents.'

'No.' Now Sasha was adamant. 'You've read what Dr Lvov writes. It's dangerous. I won't have you put at risk.'

'What about you?' she said. 'And your risk.'

'I can look after myself,' Sasha said. 'Besides, it's easier for a man.' He turned once more to Ivan. 'Please come,' he said.

Now it was Katya's turn. 'He cannot leave now, Sashenka,' she said. 'He has work to do.'

Sasha noted a faint lack of conviction in her voice. She sounded like Ivan's echo. No more. No less. No questioning, no explanation, no rider. Just a simple confirmation. Somehow he felt sorry for her.

Anna accompanied him to the station. She had insisted on coming that far. Their parting was a tearful one. In the few months that they had been together, they had earned a kind of happiness that neither had thought possible, and could not even understand. Anna feared that in his absence, Sasha would forget her and this fear chilled her bones.

'Write to me, Sasha,' she said. 'Every day. Promise.'

137

'I cannot promise,' he said, with utmost truth. 'If it is possible and if there is time, of course I will,' he said. 'But I shall think of you every moment.'

She clung to him, loath to let him take his place on the train. When the whistle blew, he unfolded her, and boarded. He shut the door and held her hand through the open window. As the train moved he loosened his grasp and she ran along the platform to its end.

'I love you,' she called, and she saw him mouth those same words, but the sounds and the shapes of their farewells faded in the whistle and the steam of the train.

The carriage was crowded. There were only two coaches in all. The others had been requisitioned by the government. Although there were few travellers in those times – people were frightened of the risks that travel entailed – there were still enough people who of necessity had to move from place to place, possibly like Sasha, to visit a sick relative or to ascertain that that relative was still alive. With such spare accommodation, the coaches were full to danger point. Those who had seats took children and cases on their laps. But more, like Sasha, stood than sat, and jostled for room amongst themselves. In such crowded conditions there was little room for conversation. All energy was spent in accommodating their bodies into a modicum of comfort, so there was continual movement, with the occasional giggle and much crying from the children. Thus they travelled for the first hour of their journey and had achieved a mood of acceptance and resignation. And then the train suddenly stopped. They heard the brakes screech and the children started screaming. Sasha was standing near a window. He managed to lower it and look outside. He saw a large mob of soldiers stumbling along the track towards the engine. Some, clearly wounded, were supported by comrades, their uniforms torn and ragged. All of them seemed overarmed. Their leader fired a shot into the air. Behind him, Sasha heard the panic in the carriage. 'Deserters,' they were whispering. 'They will put us off the train and kill us.'

Sasha looked to the front of the train, and saw the driver climb down from his cab. The leader of the men approached him, and what seemed like angry words were exchanged. Then he saw the leader push the driver aside and he strode down the train firing his gun in the air. Sasha wondered why the train had stopped at all. Then he saw the reason for the sudden braking. The soldiers were dragging a tree-trunk off the track, which they had obviously placed there for that purpose.

When their leader reached the first carriage he began to shout, 'Out, out. Everybody out. Everybody leave the train.'

Then the soldiers joined him and started to open the carriage doors. The coaches were so packed, that those passengers near the doors practically fell onto the tracks. The women were screaming, and the children crying. But the men were timid, doing exactly what they were told. This was no time to make trouble. Obedience might secure their survival. Sasha handed down the luggage, and as he did so, he thought he recognised some of the soldiers. Their faces were familiar, village familiar, and he thought they might be going to Larionovka. But this was no time to declare neighbour-hood, and he got down with the rest of them.

The passengers did not know what to do. They were afraid to run. Escape might provoke violence. In any case, fear rooted them where they stood and they watched, trembling, as the soldiers boar-ded the train. Sasha could now observe them more closely. Yes, they were indeed from his village, and he now dreaded what he would find on his arrival. Their leader was the last to board, but before doing so, he signalled the astonished and terrified driver to get the train on the move. Then the train slowly chugged along the track. The soldiers hung triumphantly out of the windows, and the displaced passengers, with the overwhelming relief of survival, actually waved to them as they passed by.

The passengers struggled to the road that ran alongside the tracks. For a while they stayed close to each other, as victims will in the first trauma of survival. Slowly their gratitude ebbed and anger took its place, a rage that could not be dealt with in a crowd. So they straggled into little groups and some, like Sasha, walked alone. In time he distanced himself from them and he was aware of the silence around him and of a creeping melancholy. The absence of Anna was not its cause, nor anxiety about his mother, though both were sorrows of a kind. Rather it was the sadness that comes with the awareness of change. That a certain way of life is gone for ever and with it, one's childhood and innocence.

He was approaching a village. There was no one about though it was still early in the day. He had the impression that the villagers were in hiding, and this was confirmed when he saw what was left of the manor house on top of the hill. It stood there, skeletal, blackened by smoke, its windows shattered, and its grounds in offensive disarray. The village street was silent, and all the doors to the houses were shut. Yet he saw furtive shadows behind the windows and overall was a pervading smell of fear. But more than fear, for as he crossed a field he saw a trench that had been recently dug, and in it, a dozen or so bodies, two of them children. From their stylish clothes, it was clear that once they had lived in the manor house on the hill. He turned away sickened. He thought of Ivan, and knew what he would have said: 'The Cause is greater than the people' – and this thought sickened him most of all. He reached the road once more, and heard behind him the distant rumbling of a cart. He waited and in time it came into view. A haycart full of people. As it neared him, the driver slowed, and Sasha could see that they were passengers from the train.

'Where are you going?' the driver called.

'Larionovka.'

'Climb aboard,' he said. 'They'll make room for you.'

They helped him onto the wagon. No one said a word, and Sasha had the feeling that they had been silent for a long while. They too must have seen the sights he had seen, and that same melancholy clothed them. The cart took off again, and the only sound was the grinding turning of its wheels.

It grew dark. During the whole journey they had seen few people, and each passing village told the same story. A burnt-out manor house, hayricks still afire, and doors closed against the fear. They were nearing Larionovka and Sasha dreaded his arrival. He asked to be put down a little way before his village. Whatever he was going to see, he wanted to see alone. He watched the cart out of sight, and he prayed that his family was still alive. Still he was loath to arrive so he made a detour so that he would enter his village from the top of the hill, on a level with the manor house, and from there he could view the houses and the fields, and sniff the air for their fear. But when he saw the manor, he knew that his village was no different from any other, despite its benign master, and his rare liberality. The manor had been set alight, but recently it seemed, for smoke still curled from its ruins. In the darkness he saw the silhouettes of men, running from their quarry, carrying off its treasures in their arms. He waited. He was afraid of being discovered. But he wanted desperately to go inside, and there to learn the story he would have to take back to Anna. No one had come out of the house for a long while, and he thought it safe to enter. But he did not need to go into the house. The sight that met his eyes on the marble steps was enough for a million stories for Anna's ears, yet too many even for one. The bodies were draped elegantly on the stone steps of the portal. Count Dmitri, an axe embedded in his heart, the blood still flowing through the silk ruffles of his shirt. Close by his side, in a position she could never have assumed while living, lay Marfa or what was left of her hacked body, a look of terror, surprise and sheer bewilderment still etched on her face. And a little lower down, her head at Marfa's feet, Miss Cameron, stern daughter of duty, her black governess's uniform humanised with blood. Sasha knelt down beside them. These were people he knew. People with whom he had shared his childhood. People who had nurtured his great love. He thought of Ivan again, and wondered what he meant by 'the people'. He knelt beside the bodies and prayed. Then he heard a cry, a whimpering, a sound of life. He looked around him, and wondered for the first time what fate had overtaken the Countess Tatiana. The cry came again. It was a woman's voice and it came from below, from the clump of bushes beneath the balustrade. He rushed towards the sound, seeking its source. And there on a grass mound he found the Countess, her legs spread-eagled, the blood trickling down her silk petticoat, her bodice torn, whimpering her violation. He covered her as best he could. And he stroked her brow.

'It's Sasha,' he whispered. 'Sasha Volynin. I'll take care of you. Everything's all right now,' though he knew that nothing in her lifetime would ever be all right again.

'All dead,' she sobbed. 'Where is my little Anna?'

'Anna's well,' he told her. 'She's in Petrograd, with Nicolai and Andrei. All safe,' he said helplessly.

'All dead,' she said again. 'All dead. Even the dead are dead. Dead now for ever.'

He wondered what she meant, and assumed that she was in delirium. He lifted her in his arms, and shielded her eyes from the carnage on the steps, and carried her towards the stables where he hoped they had spared a horse and a cart. On his way he passed by the Larionov mausoleum. The door was off its hinges open to night and death. A half-hearted fire had charred the many coffins of Larionov lineage. Now he understood what the Countess had meant. They had murdered the dead as well.

He found a horse and cart in the stables, the only one remaining. Gently he lay Tatiana in the wagon. Then he mounted the cart and drove down the hillside. He saw shadows of the soldiers in the fields and the flames of their torches. A haystack was on fire in the distance, and the sounds of drunken laughter appalled him. Tatiana whimpered behind him. He dared not think of what torment she had suffered. And he tried not to think of Anna, for how could he comfort her sorrow? He guided the horse as gently as he could, not wishing to make too much noise.

In time he arrived at his house. The door was shut, and he sensed that it was bolted from inside. But he saw the dim light of a lamp through the window and he was hopeful of finding life inside. He got down from the cart, and knocked softly on the door. He was loath to make a sound of any kind. The air was of mourning, it seemed, and dictated silence. To break it would have been blasphemy.

'Who is it?' It was Pyotr's voice. Trembling.

'It's Sasha.'

He heard a cry of joy from inside. He dared to hope it was his mother's voice. He heard the bolts quickly unbarred, and there suddenly was Pyotr before him, his arms outstretched.

'Thank God you've come,' he said. 'Where is Ivan?'

'I'll explain later,' Sasha said. 'But first, I have the Countess Tatiana in the cart. I'll explain that too. She must stay here. There is nowhere for her to go.'

'She *survived?*' Pyotr said.

'If you can call it that. How is Mama?'

'She's waiting for you,' Pyotr said.

They crossed each other on the threshold, Pyotr to the cart, and Sasha to his mother's bedside.

Maria fell into his arms. Avdotya and Nina, who were sitting with her, moved from the bedside.

'Thank God,' Avdotya said as she watched the embrace. 'Thank you, Mother of God, Jesus Christ, thank you. She was waiting for you to come,' she told Sasha. 'Now she will get better.'

'What's wrong with her?' Sasha asked.

'She worries about you and Ivan. That's what's wrong with her.'

'Where is Ivan?' Maria asked.

'He's very busy,' Sasha said. 'But he will come as soon as he can. They send their love, Ivan, Katya and Vassily.'

The smile faded from Maria's face, and once again, Sasha found it hard to love his Cause-riddled brother. 'Mama,' he said, 'Countess Tatiana is here. I brought her from the manor.'

At that moment the door opened. Pyotr entered, his arm around the Countess, as he led her into the room. Avdotya and Nina stood immediately to attention and gave automatic curtseys though they hardly recognised their former mistress. Even Maria, frail as she was, rose from her bed and did her obeisance. Though all of them knew, from the gunfire and the arson, that that time was gone and that the curtseying was over.

'Countess,' Avdotya said, horrified at her appearance, yet still mindful of the station she once held. She took her in her arms. In her frailty, she was a simple woman, and in that gender, when the chips were down, as prone to exploitation and abuse as the rest of them. She settled her down in a chair.

'I'll make you some soup, my lady,' she said.

Tatiana stared after her. She was beyond speech, and mercifully beyond feeling.

'What's happening?' Maria asked as Sasha helped her back into bed. He whispered his story into her ear. Tears welled in Maria's eyes.

'Can you keep her here, Mama?' he asked. 'She will be safe here.'

143

'We will look after her,' Maria said. 'Avdotya, Nina, Pyotr. She was good to all of us. What has happened to our country, Sashenka?'

He could not begin to tell her. 'Sleep, Mama,' he urged her. 'I shall lie by your side.'

Within seconds she was asleep in his arms. Sasha rose from the bed and went to the table where Pyotr sat with Nina.

'Where are the children?' he asked.

'They're with Nina's mother,' Pyotr said. 'They're safer there. That village has already been ransacked. There is nothing left there to destroy. Tell me, Sashenka, is all this Ivan's doing?'

Sasha was horrified. Horrified because Pyotr was not entirely wrong. Yet for some reason, he felt he had to defend Ivan even though his heart was not in it.

'No, Pyotr. You mustn't think that. This is not what was meant to be. Freedom is a dangerous possession, especially for those who have never experienced it. It was all too sudden and the people have gone mad. It seems that everything is out of control.'

'The Larionovs were good people,' Pyotr said. 'They harmed nobody. They knew their place, and we knew ours. It was peaceful here. Is it true that Count Dmitri is dead?'

'I saw his body,' Sasha said. 'And Marfa's. And the governess. All dead. The dead are dead too. They set fire to the mausoleum.'

'Then Russia is dead,' Pyotr said.

Sasha held him in his arms. If only Pyotr could read, he thought. He more than anyone else would understand his poetry.

Avdotya was spooning soup into Tatiana's mouth. She swallowed it, but it was clear that she had no notion of its taste. She was simply doing what she was told to do. She had regressed into her childhood where everything was more simple and her body's pain could be soothed with loving care. And for that care Avdotya would do, and for that protection the Volynin hut was as adequate as any manor. She was sipping the soup like a child, dribbling onto the napkin that Avdotya had placed on her bodice. She was back in her high chair in the nursery, back in her simple uneventful past, because the present was a nightmare, and unconfrontable. Avdotya sat with her throughout the night and lullabied her into oblivion.

144

Nina pleaded fatigue. She kissed the brothers good night. 'Tomorrow we will give our room to the Countess, Pyotr,' she said.

He nodded his agreement. 'I'll stay up with Sasha a while,' he said.

Sasha was glad to be with him. Pyotr was like their father, entirely without ambition and wanting peace at any price. Yet his soul was of gold.

'How is Katya?' Pyotr whispered.

Sasha heard the loving in his voice, that quality of loving that would never, never fade.

'She's well,' he said. 'And so is Vassily.' He would not mention Ivan.

'But is she happy?' Pyotr insisted.

How can anyone be happy with Ivan, Sasha thought. Because in truth Ivan was with nobody except Ivan, and ever more would be so.

'I think so,' Sasha said. Which was the truth. But he did not add that Katya had fashioned her measure of happiness according to that which she was entitled to expect. And only that. And for that she would settle.

'Dr Lvov says you're famous,' Pyotr said. 'All Petrograd is talking about you. Is that true?'

'I suppose so,' Sasha said. 'I was lucky. I was published at the right time.'

'I'm sure it's more than luck,' Pyotr said. 'I wish I could read them.'

'I'll read them to you if you like,' Sasha said. He pulled the book out of his case and gave it to Pyotr. Pyotr held it gently, stroking its binding, marvelling that he should hold such treasure in his hand. 'My brother, a poet,' he whispered.

Sasha opened the book and shared its holding with Pyotr, so that he could see the printed word and know that it was real. He flicked the pages over, seeking a suitable poem.

'Start at the beginning,' Pyotr said. 'I want to hear them all.'

So Sasha did as Pyotr wished, and through the night he poured out his songs of love, rage, pity and hope. Occasionally Pyotr interrupted and begged him to repeat a verse that had particularly impressed him. Many he wished to learn by heart. It was growing light as the recital drew to its close. It was Pyotr who turned over the last page, a gesture that fed his belief that he had read them himself. Then he threw his arms around Sasha's neck. 'I wish Papa were alive,' he said. 'He would have loved them too.'

Sasha wondered whether, out of all the Volynins, Pyotr was the only true revolutionary.

In the morning Avdotya announced that Maria was much better. But she would stay with her and look after the Countess.

'Dr Lvov tells me you are famous,' Maria said, as he sat beside her.

Sasha opened his attaché case and brought out a few volumes of his work. 'One of these is for you, Mama,' he said. 'Look, I have written inside it. *For my mother, from her loving Sasha.*'

'I'm proud of you,' she said. 'Of all my sons. You are all so very different. But I love you all. Easily.' In this way she told Sasha that she had forgiven Ivan for not coming home.

'How is Countess Anna?' she dared to ask. 'Are you with her?'

'We're together, Mama,' Sasha said. 'I want to marry her.'

'Everything is changing,' Maria said. 'Go find your happiness.'

A few days later, they buried Count Dmitri, Marfa and Miss Cameron. Or at least Sasha buried them with Pyotr's help. As the Larionov mausoleum had been destroyed, the Count had to lie with his servants in the graveyard of the village church. No gravedigger could be found. None of the villagers wanted any part in it for fear of reprisals. Even the priest was loath to conduct the funeral service, and finally agreed, with the proviso that he would bless only Marfa and Miss Cameron. It was more than his life was worth, he said, to ease Count Dmitri's path to heaven. But as it turned out, there was no need for proviso. Nobody attended the funeral, but for Sasha and Pyotr, who had shared the gravedigging between them. Even so, the priest did not mention Count Dmitri's name, not even in a whisper. Sasha snatched the missal from his hand, and there and then he intoned that service to which all mankind has title. The priest slunk back into his church, while Sasha and Pyotr refilled the graves, blessed each one with a named marker, and strewed them with flowers.

Back in the Volynin dwelling, the Countess had been installed in Pyotr's and Nina's bed. Though a baby's crib would have been more suitable. Babyhood was Tatiana's only safe haven. She sat up in bed, humming and smiling and occasionally sucking her thumb. Avdotya at her side gave her caresses and baby talk, settling her back into her infancy.

'What will happen to her?' Sasha asked.

'Some grow old to die,' Avdotya said. 'And others grow young. But the end is the same.'

But those words would not do for Anna. Nor any words at all, and Sasha wondered in what language or gesture he could transfer what he had seen. There could be no instalment in his telling. He could not first offer that her father was a little bit dead, or that her mother was slightly raped. Death and rape have no gradation. He would have to give her the absolutes, and hold her to contain her pain. He longed to see Anna, but he dreaded his return.

I I

All lines of communication had broken down between the cities and the rural areas. People crowded onto railway stations, their eyes skinned for a puff of steam on the horizon. Sasha went every day to Larionov station, which hadn't seen a train since the hijack of Sasha's journey. He was not unhappy to remain with his family, and though he missed Anna, he was glad to postpone the news he would have to bring her.

But Anna had news for him as well. News that gladdened her heart, but frightened her too. She desperately needed Sasha at her side. She had not been feeling well for a while, and she ascribed her malaise to Sasha's absence. But when one morning, she vomited into her basin, she worried that something might be wrong. She said nothing to Katya, but that morning, on the pretence of distributing leaflets she went to see a doctor. After hearing her symptoms, he examined her, and shortly gave his verdict.

'What a time to bring a baby into the world,' he said.

'A baby?'

'Yes, my dear. You're going to have a baby. In about six months. Will your husband be pleased?'

'Oh – oh yes,' Anna stuttered, realising for the first time that she didn't have a husband nor even, at this time, a man by her side.

'Come and see me again,' he said. 'Bring your husband with you. Then we can make plans for hospital attendance.'

She walked home slowly. She knew that she was happy, but until she could tell Sasha, she knew too that she must curb her joy. She needed desperately to share her news, but she would tell nobody before Sasha. On her way she passed a church. Through the open door she heard the singing. She went inside. Some old men and women were praying there. She crossed herself and stared at the icon. Then kneeling, she prayed that Sasha would come back soon.

Every morning when rising, she was quietly sick in her room, then went about her work with Katya. They were both helping in a soup kitchen, which had been set up in the city to cater for those impoverished by the upheavals. Over the last few weeks she had grown close to Katya. And Katya to her. The initial embarrassment between them caused by class discrepancy had been overcome. In their working and living together, they had come to respect each other, and the common denominator of gender had overridden all other differences. As they ladled the soup, in that shared gesture of giving, Anna was often tempted to tell her secret to Katya, but every day she postponed it, hoping that Sasha would have found some way of returning to Petrograd.

But it seemed unlikely. Chaos was growing in the city. Lenin had returned and given orders to overthrow the Provisional Government. The Bolsheviks attacked and captured the telephone exchange, that hub of power. Their final coup was their assault on the Winter Palace, seat of the Provisional Government. It was 26 October in the early afternoon, when three hundred or so Bolsheviks entered the Malachite Chamber of the Palace. There they arrested all members of the Provisional Government and took them to the Fortress of Peter and Paul. But Kerensky had already fled. The assault was a comparatively bloodless one, recording only six casualties. Lenin was installed as leader of the new Russia.

In Katya and Ivan's apartment, the celebrations continued throughout the night. Towards midnight Andrei arrived with Pavel. It was the first time that he had dared Pavel in a social gathering. He was introduced as a colleague, and in such benign role he was accepted, for it would never have occurred to anybody at the gathering that Pavel was something more than a friend. Andrei was glad of his acceptance but he longed to undeceive them, and to declare Pavel's true role in his life. But such a declaration in such company was unthinkable.

149

'You're late, Andrei,' Ivan said. 'You have to catch up on the drinking.'

'I was with Nicolai,' Andrei said. 'I came clean with him. It was time.' But not clean about Pavel. There would never be a time for that.

'What did he say?' Katya asked.

'He regarded it as yet another betrayal. He swore never to speak to me again.'

'Poor Nicolai,' Anna said. Despite her antagonism to her brother, she felt the natural pity for a loser.

But not so Ivan. 'He has had his turn,' Ivan said coldly. 'And for long enough too. Now it is ours, and let's drink to that.'

Anna took Andrei aside. 'What is Nicolai going to do now?' she whispered. She was anxious for his safety.

'They have sent the Tsar and his family to Siberia. Nicolai and his friends intend to follow him and bring him back to power. Not much chance of that,' he said.

'Is there news from Larionovka?' she asked. 'Will they be safe there?'

'I've heard nothing,' Andrei said, 'but no news can get through from anywhere. I'm not worried though. Father has always had a good relationship with his peasants. Mother too, and her hospital. I'm trying to secure a car. I still have useful contacts. As soon as I can, I shall drive there. Would you come with me, Anna?'

'Please, Andrei, please. There's nothing I want more. Sasha's still there. I've not heard from him for weeks.' She had made up her mind. She would go to Larionovka and have her baby there. With her mother, Marfa and Miss Cameron. And Sasha by her side. 'Try your best, Andrei,' she said. 'I could go as soon as you wish.' She felt relieved having made that decision. In some strange way, it eased the burden of bearing her secret alone. She joined in the revelry, but took care to take no alcohol. She was a sober participant, as was Pavel who rarely touched spirits. He joined her in the corner of the room.

'It's very pleasant for me to meet one of Andrei's family,' he said. 'He speaks often of you.'

'And Nicolai?' Anna asked.

'Nicolai is the outsider, it seems. But he will adjust. He will come to terms with it all.'

'And if not?' Anna knew he was headstrong and she feared for him. She feared too for her parents. They would adjust, she did not doubt that. But it took two parties to adjust, and would the Bolsheviks be as accommodating? She was anxious to go home.

'If he doesn't,' Pavel was saying, 'he will be very much alone.'

'A toast.' Ivan silenced the revellers and raised his glass.

'Long live the Revolution!' he shouted. They all echoed his cry as glasses were refilled.

'To Lenin,' someone shouted. And, 'To our leader,' another. Toast after toast was consumed, and as a finale Ivan shouted, 'An end to those who put their boots on our necks!' This occasioned the greatest cheer of them all. Anna looked at Andrei, and she noted that he did not raise his glass. Like Anna, he was wondering about their parents. Had his father ever put his boot on the peasants' necks? It was an act difficult to imagine. And there must be others like him, many others, scattered throughout the country. But Andrei knew, and sadly acknowledged that Bolsheviks did not pause to ask for credentials. To have been a master was enough. Too bad if he was an exception. He would go the same way as the rest of his class, and Andrei trembled in fear for his family. Tomorrow he would try again to secure a car.

The Smolny Institute, which had once housed the daughters of the aristocracy, was now the offices of the new government. In the foyer a bust of Lenin had replaced that of the Tsar, and its pedestal was draped with the flag of the hammer and sickle. The building housed all departments of government, including that of the secret police. What was once called the Okhrana, was newly baptised. It took the name of Cheka, but its functions were the same. Its leader was one Felix Dzerzhinsky, and he was every bit as ruthless and tyrannical as his predecessors. In time the word Cheka would generate the same fear as Okhrana had in its time. The fear of torture, enforced confession, and finally death. For in the region of terrorism, the means are the same, whatever the end.

It was from this unenviable government department that Ivan received an official letter. It required him to report to the Smolny on a certain day and to keep that appointment confidential. Ivan was excited. He had no idea of the nature of the summons, but he suspected that it was to offer him a position of rather greater importance than a mere printer of *Pravda*. He speculated on what it might be, daydreaming himself into power. And why not, he thought. I have deserved it. I have paid my dues. He noted that the summons was confidential. That heightened its importance. He was not even tempted to share the invitation with Katya. Orders from the party were orders, and he would obey them to the letter. He could barely contain his excitement, and he counted the hours till his appointed time.

When it came, he presented himself at the Institute. He noticed that on entering he had assumed a military gait, and that seemed to him to be right and proper. He paused for a moment before the Lenin statue in the hall, and bowed his head in obeisance. He asked the porter for directions to the Cheka offices and he thought the man backed away a little, either in awe or fear, before he gave his directions in a whisper. He must have assumed that Ivan was a man of importance, for he bowed slightly and led Ivan a little part of the way.

'Up the stairs, comrade,' he whispered, 'and then to your right.' He bowed again before leaving him, and then he returned to his counter.

Ivan took the steps slowly. Dignity he felt was called for. At the appointed door, he paused, straightening himself. But he was trembling, and his nervousness irritated him profoundly. 'I have deserved this,' he kept saying to himself, but each time with less conviction, and when they called, 'Come in,' in answer to his knock, his knees melted and he entered rather as a victim than a potential victimiser.

The chief himself received him. He was tall, bearded, and undeniably impressive. There were other men in the room, about a dozen in all, seated around the table. Ivan was directed to a seat amongst them. He recognised nobody. In his eyes they all looked the same.

'I think we are all here now,' Dzerzhinsky said. 'I am the Controller of this section and my name is Dzerzhinsky.' He thrust the name into the group of men like a weapon, which befitted its daggerlike sound. He paused for a moment to let it sink in. 'Each one of you here', he went on, 'has been chosen for an important task. Each one of you has been recommended by a senior member of the Party.'

Ivan wondered who could have recommended him. He knew no one in high office and he feared a mistake might have been made. He thought he might dare to enquire when the meeting was over.

'We're forming a Special Commission,' Dzerzhinsky went on. 'Its aims are to investigate and liquidate all attempts at counter-revolution. The Cheka will have its eagle eye everywhere. We stand for organised terror. This we frankly admit. We will track down all our enemies, saboteurs, speculators, and political traitors. Even if they are to be found amongst your friends, and I go further, amongst your own families. We will show no mercy. We shall judge quickly, and our sentences shall be carried out immediately. You will begin special training straightaway. You will proceed now to room 14 along the corridor where you will be given further instructions.'

The men sat for a moment, faintly stunned by their leader's address. Eventually they stood, mindful of the responsibilities they were to shoulder, their eyes shining with missionary zeal. Ivan waited for them to leave, then he approached Dzerzhinsky's desk.

'Excuse me, comrade,' he said, 'but I don't think I know any senior members of the government. Can I be told who recommended me?'

Dzerzhinsky consulted a paper on his desk, running his finger down a list of names. When he partnered Volynin with his sponsor a look of mild surprise spread over his face. 'Joseph Stalin,' he said.

'I don't know him.' Ivan was bewildered.

'Koba?' Dzerzhinsky asked. 'Does that name mean anything to you?' He was smiling. 'You spent time together in Siberia. He's Comrade Stalin now. And very important. He says you're a good man. You do as you're told. You'll meet him again one day.'

So it was Koba. Ivan recalled how in Siberia he had speculated that Koba, or whatever name it concealed, was a man whom the future would have to reckon with. He congratulated himself on his foresight. He made his way to room 14 for further instructions.

Some days later Andrei arrived at Ivan's apartment, with the exciting news that he had managed to commandeer a car. It had once belonged to a colleague at the Ministry, who, on Lenin's return to Petrograd, knew better than to wait for the consequences and had fled the city on horseback. His car was still parked outside the building, miraculously spared from the looting and the pillage.

'I have it outside,' Andrei said. 'Are you ready to come, Anna?'

Anna was more than ready. 'My bags are upstairs,' she said.

'I'll get them.' This came from Vassily who bounded up the stairs.

'I've room for Vassily, too,' Andrei said to Katya, 'if you'd like to send him. And for you. And Ivan too.'

'We can't leave,' Katya said. 'Ivan is too busy. And so am I.' There was no regret in her voice. It seemed that she could happily live out the rest of her days without seeing Larionovka again. And it was probably the same for Ivan. So the two of them set off, brother and sister, happy in the thought of sitting once again at their parents' table, and regaling them with tales of the big city and the Revolution.

'Shall I tell them about Sasha, Andrei?' Anna asked. 'That we're living together?'

'I think that will be too abrupt,' Andrei said. 'The most you can say is that you see him often in Petrograd. Then after a few days, you can tell them that you love him. If you can clear that hurdle,' he laughed, 'you can gently break the news that you want to get married. It's not going to be easy, but I'll back you all the way.'

She snuggled up to him. 'I love you, Andrei,' she said. They travelled in silence for a while, then Anna said, 'And what about Pavel?'

Andrei started. 'What about Pavel?' he said.

'Will you tell them about you and Pavel?'

He stopped the car. He did not trust himself to drive.

'How did you know?' he said.

'I watched you both at Ivan's party. I know the signs of loving. I exchange them with Sasha.'

'Did it not upset you? Tell me the truth.'

'It did at first. It seemed – not right. But then, it was *you*. My brother. And it was loving. That's all that matters. I'm happy for you, Andrei. And for Pavel.'

He kissed her on the cheek. How different she was from Nicolai and the others – from Ivan and Katya and most of the comrades that he knew. She had no cause that obsessed her and dictated her morality. She was simply good, kind, tolerant and caring.

'But I don't think you should tell Papa,' Anna said. 'And certainly not Mama,' she laughed. 'Mama would not understand it at all.'

He started the car again. He felt suddenly a new lease of life, unburdened, understood.

They were driving through the countryside. It was terrain unknown to both of them, since, apart from their train journey to Petrograd, they had rarely travelled outside the confines of Larionovka. So they didn't know that they were passing through a village that was no longer there, and the broken huts and burnt out barns were proof of no habitation. But these same signs multiplied as they drove deeper into the countryside. For here there were villages which were clearly inhabited. Men and women were working in the fields, mending shattered barns, and even dowsing the fires on hayricks. But worst of all, the graves in the village cemetery had been violated and their headstones smashed to pieces. Women were kneeling beside the open graves, covering them with handfuls of earth.

'What's happened?' Anna said. Though she knew. She had heard rumours of it. And Andrei knew too. And both trembled at the thought of Larionovka, though neither said a word. Village after village told the same story, and now Andrei was gathering speed on the road as if intent on rescue. At last Anna broke the silence. One of them had to articulate their fears.

'They wouldn't do it to Larionovka,' she said. 'Papa was never a cruel master. And Mama gave the house for a hospital. They wouldn't do it, would they, Andrei?'

What could he answer her, he thought. He drove even faster. The thought that his parents need never know about Sasha or Pavel turned his heart over. They must be there, they *have* to be there, he told himself. From time to time, they encountered road blocks, a fallen tree, or an overturned cart, and they had to make long detours, so that it was dark by the time they reached the outskirts of Larionovka. There were few people about, and Anna was tempted to ask one of them for news from her village, but she was frightened of their answers. So they drove, slowly now, for they knew that rescue, even if not required, was in any case too late, and their speed slowed even further in dread of their arrival. They saw their church spire loom in the distance. Its continued proud presence gave them hope, and as they passed the graveyard, they turned their eyes away so they did not notice a lone horseman, galloping a path through the dark and in the opposite direction. And even if they had noticed, it would have been too dark to recognise the rider as Sasha, who, tired of train-waiting, had found a good horse that looked as if it might take him to Petrograd. So Anna passed Sasha in the silent night, each one en route to seek the other.

Andrei and Anna drove slowly through the village. It was mercifully dark, so that the random wreckage of the village was not easily discernible and could be construed as shadows in the deceptive night. But they could see the outline of the house on the hill. It was there, without doubt, and they dared to hope that all might be well. Though neither remarked on the total darkness of the house, that not a single lantern shone through the windows.

'There's nobody there,' Andrei said. 'They must have gone somewhere for safety.'

'Of course they're there,' Anna insisted, though her voice trembled. 'They're all in bed.'

'But there's always a lantern on the steps,' Andrei said. He already feared the worst and he wanted to prepare her.

'Let's go there,' Anna insisted. 'We must go. We must see for ourselves.'

Andrei steered the car slowly up the hill. In his terror he felt that the car was stationary, and that the house was moving towards them like a ghost from a distant past. The car stuttered along the gravelled driveway, and came to a reluctant rest at the portals of the house. Anna made to get out.

156

'You stay here,' Andrei said. 'I'll go and see.'

'I'm coming with you,' Anna said.

A lantern lay at the foot of the steps, wrested from its pedestal. One pane of glass was broken, but otherwise it seemed functional. He lit it with a match, but turned its light away from the house.

'It's destroyed,' he said to Anna. The broken, unattended lantern had told him all.

'I want to go inside,' Anna said. She was adamant. She took Andrei's hand and led him up the steps. At the entrance, he raised the lamp. The great wooden doors had been torn away, offering no pause for preparation, no interval for a sigh, and the scene before them assaulted their sight with savage immediacy. The floor was littered with a chandelier, its anchorage still stubborn and pathetic on the ceiling. The balustrade of the grand staircase leaned apologetically on its few remaining struts.

'Mama!' Anna screamed.

Andrei held her close as the echo of her cry bounced through the hollow hall, and came back empty-handed.

She ran up the stairs and Andrei followed. From one wrecked room to another. Then to the nursery and the most heartbreaking carnage of all. For that was the site of the rape of all their childhood. But they did not climb to the attic. Neither of them dared that floor. That floor had housed its own counter-revolution many years ago. Nothing could touch it further.

They heard footsteps below and turning, saw the light of a lamp.

'Count Andrei?' a voice called.

'Who is it?'

'Pyotr. Pyotr Volynin. I heard the car. I thought it might be you or Count Nicolai.'

They descended what was left of the stairs.

'What happened?' Andrei asked. 'What's happened to us all? Where has everybody gone?' He was almost in tears.

Pyotr shifted from one foot to another. He cursed himself for having to be the bearer of such dire news. 'You must prepare yourself,' he said gently. He would tell it as quickly as he could, and without elaboration. In any case, he had no words for adornment. 'Some soldiers came,' he said. 'Deserters. They burnt the crops and then they came to the manor. They killed your father and Marfa and Miss Cameron.' He had to pause, because he himself was crying.

'And Mama?' Anna said. Her voice was strangely strong. There would be time enough for weeping.

'She hid,' Pyotr said. 'She's safe. She's staying with us. We're looking after her. I'll take you to her.' He would spare them the rape, he decided. They would learn soon enough from the sight of her.

'Who found her?' Andrei asked.

'Sasha.'

The name struck Anna's ear as that of a stranger. 'Where is he now?' she asked tonelessly.

'He left tonight for Petrograd. He couldn't wait any longer for the trains that didn't come. He missed you so much, Countess Anna.'

Then she did cry, long and loud, and not only for Sasha but for the loss of everything she had loved in her life and for fear of the child inside her.

'Come,' Andrei said. 'We shall go and see Mama. We must comfort her.'

He helped her down the broken steps. Neither looked behind them. They refused confirmation of what they both feared, preferring to view it as a nightmare from which, in the benign light of morning, they would waken.

They drove slowly down the hill. Now there were three of them reluctant to arrive. Pyotr dreaded their first sight of their mother. He got down first from the car, wishing to give warning of their visitors, but Andrei and Anna were close behind him, and again there was no time for preparation. He opened the door of the hut. Tatiana sat in full view of the entrance. Her hair was loose and suddenly grey, her silks were torn, and on her face was a vacant smile, directed at nobody, a cold mask of a smile, dumb and blind, as if its wearer had seen and heard everything that this world had had to offer, and that there was nothing more to record. Anna fell on her knees before her.

'Mama,' she wept. And again, 'Mama.' She took her hand, kissing it, warming it with her tears.

Avdotya took Tatiana's other hand and placed it on Anna's head. 'It's little Anna, Countess,' she said.

'It's me, Mama,' Anna said desperately. 'It's me, Anna, and look, here is Andrei.'

Andrei had not moved from the door. The sight of his mother had chilled his step. He stood there, rooted, unable to move. He stretched out his hands towards her. Pyotr took his hand and led him to Tatiana's chair. He motioned to Nina and Maria to go into the other room with the children. Then he took Avdotya by the hand and went with her, leaving what was left of the Larionovs to mourn their loss.

In the bedroom they talked in whispers. Maria's concern was where everybody could sleep, and at the same time maintain a little privacy.

'They won't want to sleep,' Pyotr said. 'They won't be able to sleep. They will sit with each other all night and give each other comfort.'

And so the night passed, in weeping and in whispers, and in the morning Tatiana's smile was gone. Gone with the mask and all her defences. Her children had brought her back into the real and terrible world so that she might mend again. 'Look, Avdotya,' she said. 'My dress is torn. And my hair is uncombed. Are there clothes still in the manor?'

'I'll go and fetch them, Countess,' Nina said with a little bow.

Avdotya crowed with delight. 'We will make you beautiful again,' she said.

'I want to take my children to visit their father's grave,' Tatiana said.

So Tatiana was duly dressed and combed. She had lost none of her beauty. Indeed, it was enhanced by her pallor and her melancholy. They walked to the churchyard. On their way they met the astonished and bewildered looks of the villagers, many of whom curtsied at their approach. There was both courage and sorrow in their step, a pride without defiance, and no die-hard Bolshevik would have dared to touch them. They walked through the grave-

159

yard, littered with broken headstones. Yet they did not remark on them.

'They told me he lies near the church door,' Tatiana said. They made their way there, silently. Then, close to the entrance, were three newly dug graves. Their markings had been left intact. 'Miss Cameron', 'Marfa', and 'Count Dmitri'. All three then knelt at the Count's graveside.

'He was a good man,' Tatiana said. 'A good husband, a good father. And a good landlord.' This last memory she said with a certain defiance. Then she gathered pebbles, and shared them with her children, and together they strewed them on the earth that covered him. They said their farewells, and gave prayers, pebbles and adieux to the two graves by his side. Then they made their way back through the village and noted that the villagers had lined the road in homage.

Avdotya decided that Maria was now well enough to look after herself. She would return to her own home, and take the Countess and her children with her.

'Will you stay with me a while, little Anna?' Tatiana asked. 'I know that Andrei is busy, but perhaps you can stay a while.'

'Yes, Mama, dearest Mama,' Anna said. She would not leave her. Sasha would return from Petrograd, and she could have her baby in Larionovka. There would come a time when she could tell her mother.

But it was a secret she couldn't keep much longer, and she didn't know how soon Sasha would return. She thought she might confide in Maria. Maria was gentle and without judgement. But perhaps she should tell Andrei as well and on his return to the city he could tell Sasha. Yet she was loath to let Sasha hear it from another's lips. She would tell Maria and in time, Avdotya would deliver her baby.

A few days later, Andrei returned to Petrograd. He promised to come again soon, and to bring Nicolai. Nicolai, he was sure, would overlook their quarrel in view of their common bereavement. And he would come back with Sasha too. Whatever Nicolai would say. His farewell was not tearful. In those few days he had spent with his mother, he had felt closer to her than at any time in his life.

She had always been a shadowy figure in his childhood, a floating angel. But now she had become real, capable of tears and touch. He had never loved her so much. So he would return, and with Pavel. She would learn to touch him too.

When he was gone, Anna went to the Volynin hut. She wanted to thank Maria for looking after her mother, and when that was done, she would share her secret.

Maria was alone. Pyotr was working his field with Nina and the children.

'I knew you would come,' Maria said.

'I've come to thank you for looking after my mother.'

'It was an honour,' Maria said.

There was a silence between them then.

'I hope you are better,' Anna said.

'I get stronger every day. You love my Sashenka, don't you?'

Anna nodded.

'I know,' Maria went on. 'And he loves you.'

Again a nod.

'And you're carrying his baby.'

'How did you know?' Anna was startled.

'I've carried babies myself. I know the look. And Avdotya knows it better than anybody,' she laughed.

'Does Avdotya know?'

'We both knew it together.' Maria laughed again, and took Anna's hand. 'You'll have the baby here and we'll look after you. And Sasha will come home.'

She took Anna in her arms. 'The world is changing,' she said. 'And some people are changing too.'

PART FOUR

12

When Sasha had left Larionovka he had intended to ride through the night. But he grew fearful of the dark and it was clear to him that his horse was uneasy. So he rode into a forest and found a clearing. He tethered the horse to a tree. The excitement of meeting again with Anna kept him awake for some time, but eventually towards dawn he fell asleep.

But not for long. He was awoken by a sharp blow on the shoulder. He squinted and saw a man standing over him.

'Anna is waiting,' Sasha said. He was clutching the tail end of a dream.

'Anna will have to wait a long time,' the man said. 'Get up.' The knife in his hand gleamed in the sun.

Sasha got painfully to his feet. He opened his eyes wide, and blinking with terror, he saw that the clearing was filled with a ragged army of men. What passed for uniform were remnants of the insignia of the Tsar's army. He trembled. Amongst the men, one was prominent. His uniform was less ragged than the others, and his jacket sported an array of medals, which Sasha suspected had been stolen. He was laughing with delight at this new quarry, and he strode towards Sasha to examine him more closely, touching his body, part by part. At first he stroked Sasha's cheek. It was a caress almost, and was reason, Sasha believed, for a faint ray of hope. But the man's touch on his shoulders was rather less than gentle. Sasha's stomach merited an out-and-out punch. The thighs were next and with equal violence, then his crude fat fingers crept like an infant's to Sasha's crotch. He steeled himself against what he knew would be the final torture so he was surprised and obscenely grateful when the man, ripping Sasha's trousers, gently cupped his genitals in his hand, holding them like a rose.

'I can smell it,' he said. 'You're a Bolshevik. I know you by your stink.' He took his hand away and wiped it down his torn trouser leg. 'D'you know who I am?' he shouted.

Sasha summoned enough energy to shake his head.

'I am General Ranjevsky,' he said. 'Commander-in-Chief of the White Army. And do you know what I hate most?'

Sasha didn't know, but it was not hard to guess.

'Bolsheviks, that's what. And you're a bloody Bolshevik. You stink of it.'

'No, sir, you are wrong,' Sasha stammered. He knew he was pleading for his life.

'My nose is never wrong,' Ranjevsky said. 'And that case of yours. That stinks too. What have you got in there? *Pravda?*' He roared with laughter, and turned to his men, and they, as if obeying an order, laughed too.

'Bring it to me.' He addressed the soldier who stood guard over Sasha.

The soldier picked up the attaché case from the ground, and stretched it out to the General. He would not leave Sasha's side. He couldn't understand why he couldn't knife him there and then and be done with it. All through their forays in the last month they had given their enemies far shorter shrift than this one. The General tore the clasp apart, and emptied the contents of the case onto the ground. There were some clothes, a pair of shoes and three copies of Sasha's poems. These he picked up, a glint in his eyes. He was clearly puzzled by the fact that they were all the same, the same binding, the same poems, the same author. 'What are you for God's sake,' he shouted, 'a Bolshevik bookseller?' He laughed again, and again turned to his men who chorused his laughter. He clearly thought he was very funny indeed. Then he opened one of the books and studied it more closely. His face was suddenly serious.

'D'you know, you Bolshie scumbag,' he said, 'I have one weakness. Just one. *Only* one. And don't you forget it. I love poetry. So if you don't mind, you can leave me these in your Will. I'll take them anyway.' He laughed again and Sasha trembled. 'Good, good,' he muttered as he read. 'Who is this Alexander Volynin? No bloody Bolshevik, I'll tell you that for nothing.'

'You're right,' Sasha dared. 'I am Alexander Volynin.'

'And I'm the Empress of Russia,' Ranjevsky said. This time he was apoplectic with laughter. 'Put him away,' he said to the guard, 'so I can read in peace.'

The guard raised his knife with pleasure. 'About bloody time,' he muttered.

'Please, please, I am Volynin. Test me, please. I know every poem by heart. I wrote them. There are three books. My publisher gave them to me. They are presents.'

'Sit down,' Ranjevsky said. 'I like tests. But if you fail on one syllable, I'll give you one minute to say your prayers. Though what a turd of a Bolshevik prays to I can't imagine. Lenin, perhaps, Trotsky. All those slabs of shit.' He opened the book at random, and read out a line. 'Follow that, you Bolshie bastard.'

Sasha recited the following line, and on and on until he was stopped. Then Ranjevsky read another random line, and Sasha obliged with its cadence. And so the testing continued, and soon became a game, and later on a pleasure as Sasha declaimed his lines with increasing passion. At last the General came towards him, and clasped him in a bearlike hug.

'God help me, but I wouldn't have slept again if I had killed a poet. Volynin,' he boomed, 'you are now the official poet of the White Army. Here is your medal.' He unpinned the single medal from the guard's tunic, and attached it to Sasha's lapel. 'I give you the Tsar's blessing,' he said. 'We will save Russia from the Red Army scum, and you will celebrate our victory in poetry.'

That night when they bedded down beneath the trees, Ranjevsky crept to Sasha's side. 'Go to sleep now, poet,' he said, 'and dream of glory.' He stood up and gave a salute to nobody in particular, then he knelt again by Sasha's side. 'Don't you try and escape, Volynin,' he said, 'because if you do, I shall personally castrate you.' Then he went off enveloped in the roar of his own laughter. Thus Sasha was shanghaied into the White Army, in a ragged regiment of thugs, led, or rather coagulated by, a raving lunatic.

167

But Sasha's was not the only regiment. The White Army was strong and not always ragged. Moreover, they were well supplied with arms and ammunition from foreign powers, none of whom would have welcomed a Red Army swarming over Europe. The civil war in Russia lasted for almost three years, and the suffering of its citizens was grinding and merciless. For this the Cheka was largely to blame, for any citizen or group on the merest suspicion of sabotage was tortured and put to death. In the terror even the most loyal Bolsheviks held their paralysed tongues but often their silence was equated with conspiracy, and they met with the same fate as those who had dared to speak aloud. Nobody was safe. Even the Tsar and his family, tucked away in the Urals, totally without any power, still represented the symbol of the old regime, and as such, impotent as they were, had to be put to death. On 16 July 1918, when the civil war was in its ruthless infancy, Tsar Nicholas the Second, his hated Empress, and their five children were murdered by their guards in Ekaterinburg, and there were many thousands in Russia who drew down their blinds and mourned in secret. Amongst them Count Nicolai, who had, with many of his kind, remained steadfastly loyal to the old regime. But his frustration was sublime. Unable to join the navy, he had to satisfy himself with meetings with his military colleagues, helping to devise war strategy. But at times his thwarted ambition drove him to despair. On one such evening he secured a pot of blue paint, and he limped his way to the monument of Peter the Great, and there he vented his seething spleen onto the pedestal. 'Long live the spirit of the Tsar,' he painted and stood back to admire his work. But not for long. One brutal Cheka hand grabbed his shoulder and another, his arm. Count Nicolai could recall very little after that, until he woke up, bleeding, in a dark cell.

When his master did not return at midnight, Fedya knew that he was in trouble. First he rang round the hospitals to ascertain whether or not the Count had met with an accident. After a general and negative response, Fedya assumed the worst. But he had contacts. He knew somebody who knew somebody else who was a friend of a guard at the Peter and Paul Fortress. If his master was in trouble, that is where he would have landed. He took what money he could find, and a precious icon that the Countess Tatiana had given to her son, and thus, loaded with bribery, he set off to deliver his master.

His first port of call, and his first rouble drop was at a bar not far from the prison. The barman there, Sergei, was a close friend. A word in his ear, and a scratch of his palm ensured Fedya of a further contact. This was not far away in another bar, and once there, Fedya peddled the same whisper and a larger bribe, in consideration of the fact that he was nearer to his target.

'Leonid's a friend of mine,' the barman said. 'I'll take you there. He's on night duty. But he's expensive. You'll have to give him more than you've given me.'

'*If* the Count is in prison,' Fedya stressed, 'and *if* this Leonid is a guard, and *if* he can deliver the prisoner, he will be well paid for his pains.' He fingered the icon in his pocket. If the Countess knew, she would approve, he thought. His master was her favourite son.

When they reached the prison, Fedya's companion took his arm. 'I often drop in to see Leonid,' he said. 'They know me here.' And indeed it seemed that they did, for they passed through without hindrance.

Shortly, they reached the guardroom. There were two guards inside reading a newspaper. Fedya's companion tapped at the window. Leonid looked up and motioned that he would come outside. When he stood, Fedya noticed how tall he was. Everything about Leonid was big and gross. His head was bull-like and, without benefit of neck, sat squarely on massive shoulders. His feet were surprisingly small, dainty almost, and Fedya marvelled that they could bear such an offensive weight. But his hands matched the rest of his vast girth. Their size was considerable, their colour a rough red, and their texture sandpaper. This latter was confirmed when Leonid took Fedya's hand in greeting, covering it with his itching palm. They walked a little down the corridor, and Fedya listened to the menacing echo of their steps. His companion put Leonid in the picture.

'We have him here. I put him in myself an hour ago. He's on the list to be shot tomorrow. So it will cost plenty.' He turned to Fedya. 'What have you got for me?'

Fedya slipped the icon out of his pocket. Leonid was clearly impressed, but tried to hide his enthusiasm.

'Is that all?' he asked.

'It's worth thousands of roubles. You know that,' Fedya said.

So a deal was struck. They were to wait outside the prison, and within the hour a black van would drive slowly past, stop for a moment and make the delivery. Fedya handed over the icon. He would have preferred to hold on to it until the promise had been fulfilled, but Leonid insisted on immediate payment, leaving Fedya with little choice.

'Now go,' Leonid said. 'You can depend on me.'

The two men left the prison.

'Where must we wait?' Fedya asked.

'On that far corner,' his companion said.

'How do you know?'

'Leonid has done me favours before.'

Fedya was much relieved. The loss of the icon and the possibility of no payoff had begun to worry him. If his master were really to die in the morning, he would of course never discover its loss, but Fedya cursed himself for such a thought. He cursed himself too for his ambivalent nature. In his heart he was with the Bolsheviks, but his sense of duty and time-honoured slavery kept him by his master's side. So he cursed both sides and prayed that they would leave him out of their struggle.

They reached the corner and waited. In silence. Then after a while, his companion said, 'Why are you so eager to free a traitor?'

'He's a friend,' Fedya said. He hoped it would satisfy him.

And so it seemed, for he was silent once more. In those days when two strangers met, politics could be the only subject of conversation. Now that was barred between them. They had no friends in common to discuss, or relatives to ask after. Only the weather was left to them and neither man thought it worth a syllable. So they waited in silence. After a while Fedya got restless. 'It must be almost an hour,' he said. 'Are you sure we can depend on him?'

'He'll be here. Be patient.'

A distant clock chimed the hour. Slowly, it seemed to Fedya, as if it were deliberately holding back time. In the striking of the hour and its reverberation, he could not hear the rumbling of the approaching van. He saw it only when it slowed down at the corner. Then he saw the back doors open, and a sack was thrown on to the cobbles. Then the van moved quickly away. For a long moment Fedya stared at the sack, convinced that Leonid had delivered a corpse. But then the sack was seen to wriggle, and through it Fedya heard a cry. He rushed towards it, and slit it open with a knife, then tore it apart with frenzied hands. Nicolai lay in front of him, shivering and terrified.

'Master, Master, God bless you,' Fedya said, gathering him to his feet.

'God bless *you*,' Nicolai stammered. 'How did you know where I was?'

'Let us go home,' Fedya said. 'You will eat, drink, and sleep and then I will tell you the story.' He looked around for his companion, but there was no sign of him. 'Come, we'll find a carriage.'

In the morning, the list of condemned men was placed on Ivan's desk. It was mere routine. Every morning brought a different list and occasionally Ivan would go to the prison to supervise the kill. He gave the list a cursory glance. He stopped short at the name of Nicolai Larionov. And he smiled. But not for long. For the smile quickly vanished when news was brought to him that Larionov had escaped during the night and was nowhere to be found.

'Forget him,' Ivan told his men.

They were astonished at their leader's sudden leniency. But they did not question it. He must have his reasons. Which indeed he did. Andrei had served them well. He did not wish to endanger him. He looked at his list again, more carefully this time. If Larionov had been taken, there might well be others who could implicate Andrei. He knew Nicolai's associates, and knew too their bitter enmity towards Andrei, the rogue Larionov. But none of the names were familiar. However, there was one that caused him to pause, and his finger trembled. Smirnov. The name shipped him back to the print shop in Vosrov so many years ago. But he couldn't remember the man's face. All he recalled was his notebook and his eternally scribbling hand. And the hate and craving for revenge that had simmered in his heart for so many years now craved its resolution.

171

He picked up his phone and connected himself to the prison.

'Volynin here,' he said. He heard a tremor in his voice, a tremor akin to ecstasy. 'I am coming to the prison,' he said. 'I need to talk to Smirnov before he is shot.'

He sent a message to his driver and within minutes he was on his way. He stiffened in the back of the car. His body was tense with blinding recall. He remembered his escape from the prison in Vosrov, and his desperate need to survive if only to take his revenge on Smirnov. Then, for the first time in many years, he thought of Pavlenkov, and he berated himself for having almost forgotten him. And not only the man himself, but that infinitely kind father figure he had stood for. And then, inevitably, he heard the echo of his last desperate cry from the gallows. 'Natasha,' he had called. Thirteen years had passed since that time, and that name had been shrouded in their mists, but now its echo reverberated like a clap of thunder. And with the name, that entire Natasha syndrome, that oh-so-irritable disturbance to his dedication to the Cause. Only in the beginning had it bothered him, but over the years all 'Natasha' thoughts had conveniently faded. But now they came to disturb him once more. He thought of Katya. He still loved her, he thought, but she was inseparable from the Cause, and so required no special pleading. But there was Sasha and Pyotr and his mother, outsiders in their own way. If ever he were to hang like Pavlenkov, would he call their names from the gallows? Ivan did not relish such thoughts, and he tried to console himself with the thought of his Smirnov revenge. He wished he could remember what he looked like and wondered why faces faded with more compulsion than names.

They were nearing the prison. He was not prepared to confront his old enemy, but he was glad that the passing years had in no way diluted his appetite for revenge.

The prisoners on that morning's killing rota were gathered in one cell. Ivan looked into the spyhole. The group of men were huddled on the floor. None of them made a sound, as if they were rehearsing for the eternal silence to come. He wondered whether, so many years ago, he and his comrades had looked the same to Smirnov's triumphant eye. Then he recalled how different it had all been. He heard the cries of defiance, punctuated by the keening chant of Chernov's prayers. He and his comrades would not have gone gently to the gallows. Not like this lot, this cowering defeated scum of the earth. He ordered Smirnov to be taken to another cell. Then he himself went there to wait for him. After a while a guard shoved Smirnov inside. The prisoner's head was bowed, and Ivan could not immediately seek recognition. He asked the guard to stay. He was Alexis, an old comrade, and a known and skilled torturer. Ivan might well need his services.

'Look at me,' Ivan ordered.

Smirnov's head remained bowed, but Alexis cupped his fist under the prisoner's chin, and thrust his head upright. Ivan studied the face carefully, and wondered how he had ever forgotten it. On Smirnov's face was an immediate pallor of recognition, and his bowels melted in fear where he stood.

Ivan smiled. 'You remember me then,' he said. 'Now it seems it is *my* turn.'

Smirnov would fain have dropped his head again, but Alexis's fist was an immovable prop.

'Have you anything to say?' Ivan asked.

'I'm sorry,' Smirnov said.

Ivan spat at him in disgust. 'You rotten cringing coward,' he hissed. 'Do you hope to gain mercy with your repentance? You would have impressed me more with defiance. You're sorry? Why should you be sorry? Did you not believe in your cause? Do you not still believe in it? Our comrades have never been sorry. Never. D'you remember Pavlenkov? Golikov? They went to their deaths with no apology. Because they *believed*. And they *died* believing.' He turned away. He had nothing more to say. He had meant to ask questions. He had wanted to know the 'why' of all those years ago. But it didn't seem to matter any more. 'You should be happy, Smirnov,' he said. 'Soon you'll be joining your beloved Tsar.' He went to the door of the cell, then turned to Alexis. 'Before you lead him out,' he said, 'burn his balls. He won't be needing them where he's going.' Then he left the cell, and lingered outside for a while until he heard the screaming. Then satisfied, he went into the prison yard to await the executions.

The men were brought outside and tied, each one to a post. They were trembling. One of them asked for a blindfold. Ivan couldn't help but smile. He might as well have asked for a trial. The last post in the line was untenanted, waiting for Smirnov. The firing squad shuffled from foot to foot, impatient. Then finally the last of the quarry appeared, or what Alexis had left of him. Smirnov was a sorry sight. He was trouserless and could barely place one naked foot in front of another, a pathetic gait indeed for one's last journey on earth. Alexis dragged him along and settled him against the post, holding him upright while another guard secured him with ropes. When it was done, Alexis stepped back to view his handiwork. No doubt it pleased him. Then he leant forward, and tenderly moved a lock of Smirnov's hair which hung over his eye. He wanted everything to be nice and tidy. Then he turned and joined Ivan at the spectator's stand. The commander gave the order to take aim. In the deathly silence, Ivan listened for a voice. A single voice would have done, and a single name. A wife, a sister, a mother, a sweetheart, but all those left, were left unsung. But neither was the name of the Tsar called upon, nor any name that might have symbolised their cause. As the bullets struck, the men fell in silence. Ivan turned away. The Natasha syndrome had clearly never bothered any of them, for neither their love for the general nor their love for the particular, neither of these had been unconquerable.

Ivan returned to his office. For some reason he was deeply depressed. His revenge, justified as it was, had given him no pleasure. Perhaps, he thought, he was becoming immune to all feeling. Every day he ordered the torture and the shootings of hundreds of men. The Cause dictated it. He obeyed its order without scruple. Yet it disturbed him that his feelings had so atrophied. Once again he thought of Pavlenkov. He too was immune. He too had smothered his intrinsic nature in the name of the Cause. And he had had to achieve the gallows before he could utter one human and heartbreaking cry. Ivan shivered in the back of the car. He was angry. He would not have his indifference ruffled. 'Bugger Natasha,' he said aloud.

His depression persisted the whole day, and was in no way lifted when news came through late that afternoon that an attempt had been made on Lenin's life. He was apparently coming out of a meeting, when a woman approached him. She complained of the shortage of food. Then she had shot him, wounding him in the neck. Her name was Fanny Kaplan, and she was a young socialist of a kind. An unlikely suspect for an assassination attempt on her leader. Perhaps she was deranged. She had spent eleven years in prison for the attempt on the life of a Tsarist official, hardly a way of life conducive to a sound mind. Whatever, she was given short shrift, and three days later she was executed at the Lubyanka. The fact that she was Jewish did not pass unnoticed, and there followed a wave of arrests and executions, 512 in Petrograd alone, and amongst them there were many whose only crime was of sharing the faith with Fanny Kaplan.

The civil war was going badly for the Bolsheviks. The White Army, helped by the British and the Czechs, held Siberia, the Urals, and most of the Volga territory. They were pushing towards Moscow. Against them, Trotsky and his Red Army. On both sides the casualties were legion. In the towns and villages famine threatened. At times, even those die-hard revolutionaries wondered whether the prize was worth the price. But not Ivan Volynin. His eye was only on the prize for the price was only people.

13

It was in the spring of that year, 1918, that Anna Larionova gave birth to a boy. Avdotya delivered the baby with the help of Tatiana and Maria. They called the child Dmitri after Anna's father. It should have been a happy occasion, but Sasha's absence, and worse, his whereabouts unknown, cast a blight on the event. Anna had written to Katya, and in her reply she wrote that Sasha had never returned to Petrograd. All her enquiries had come to naught. Andrei, too, had had no success. Lately he had written that he was leaving for Moscow. In the same Ministry of Internal Affairs, but under different management. Though sometimes, he had added in his letter, the new was very similar to the old. He had enclosed his address. *If you can find a train on its way to Moscow, be sure you're on it*, he had written. But in all his letters, and they were frequent, there was never any news of Sasha.

And so the months went by. Maria looked after the baby while Anna helped Pyotr and Nina in the fields. Pyotr was proud of his smallholding, and what it grew sustained the family and warded off hunger. Privately Pyotr thought that Sasha was dead, that on his way to Petrograd he had been captured by the Whites and killed. The landscape was trench-riddled with bodies. All over the country those thousands of 'missing' were eventually mourned. Pyotr had done his weeping, in the late evenings when he could walk alone. Behind him in the hut he left the acrid smell of hope, and it suffocated him. Even Nina smelt of it but it was more for the sake of sisterhood than logic, for sometimes in the fields when she thought she was unseen, he caught her crying.

The tide was turning for the Bolsheviks. Towards the end of the year the White Army was on the run. And in their humiliating defeats, they wreaked their vengeance. As they pulled back from the villages they raped and looted where they could, then razed the crops to the ground with their torches. The earth was scorched in their passing, and cropless fields brought famine in their wake. Ranjevsky's army was even more ragged than before, sullen, resentful and suspicious. They no longer dreamt of victory; their sole concern was to make the best of what life they had left. To this end they hid themselves in forest clearings and out of their booty drank themselves into a stupor. Occasionally, ragged remnants of other units would join them in their retreat. In those days they kept Sasha close by them. Ranjevsky especially kept a watchful eye on him. He was their poet, the poet of the counter-revolution, and in Ranjevsky's eyes such a presence legitimised their campaign. Over the months of his enrolment, Sasha had written many poems in praise of their cause. He had written of freedom, love and a world without pain. As he penned them he realised with a certain bewilderment that they would have done for either side of the conflict. At night Ranjevsky would read the poems aloud, in a raucous vodka-laced voice, and for a time, he could still assume the role of conqueror.

On one of these wassailing evenings, in a field of hayricks still intact, they were joined by another straggling group of retreating Whites. They were laden with chests of booty. One Grigorev was in charge, and Sasha noted the greeting between the two leaders. They embraced with the affection of long-lost friends.

'You're sober, my old friend,' Ranjevsky croaked. 'You smell like one defeated. Come drink, and then we can talk of old times.' He plied him with vodka, and the rest of the troop were happy to drink themselves into the stupor that surrounded them. After a while Grigorev's head rested on Ranjevsky's chest.

'I've brought you a present my friend,' Grigorev said. 'You still love books, Ranjevsky? Well, I thought of you, comrade. The other men took silver and gold, and if they had time, the wine. But I took the books. Not many books in villages, my friend. D'you still love books, Ranjevsky?' His voice was very slurred, and it was unlikely that he would be awake much longer. But he managed to crawl over to a sack and drag it to Ranjevsky's feet.

'Do I like books?' Ranjevsky said. 'Why, I have my own poet. My very own. He travels with me. He rhymes in my ear. He whispers of love and freedom, and every syllable of his belongs to me. Volynin,' he shouted, 'come over here and make yourself known to my friend. But give him no poems, not a single rhyme. Or I shall kill you with my bare hands.' He was by now so drunk that he too threatened sleep, and he motioned Sasha to untie the sack. Sasha rarely joined in the revelry, and that night, he had drunk nothing at all. He was as sober as the two guards who kept watch over the camp. He opened the sack with steady fingers, and emptied the contents onto the ground. It was a long time since he had seen a book other than his own, and the sight pleased him. He sifted through the meagre pile. Most of the books were bibles and missals. There was a manual on dairy farming and a book of knitting patterns. The library of a simple God-fearing peasant. Then his heart stopped as his eye caught the familiar binding, and that title that nowadays he could hardly equate with himself. *Days of Love and Hope* by Alexander Volynin. He opened the book, and tears started in his eyes, as he read that inscription that he seemed to have written another world ago. *For my mother, from her loving Sasha.* He read it over and over again, until the words blurred into the blackness of a shroud.

'Where did this book come from?' Sasha shouted. He ran in panic from man to man, screaming the question. But most of the men were asleep. One of them however was still drinking, humming softly to himself. Sasha gripped his shoulder. 'Where does this book come from?' he shouted.

'How should I know?' the man said. 'And why should I care?' he added with spite. 'You can't eat books, and I'm starving.'

'Where were you before you came here?' Sasha tried again.

'All villages look the same to me,' the man said. 'And their women. You rape them, and they're all the same.' He took another swig of his vodka.

'Did you by any chance go to a village called Larionovka?' Sasha had to know and he prepared himself for the worst.

'Larionovka?' the man said. 'A small bell rings. Perhaps we were. Who knows. Anyway, if we were, there's not much left of it now.' He gave a little laugh, then his head fell sideways, and he joined his companions in their merciful oblivion.

Sasha was trembling. He knew he had to escape. He looked around him. Everybody was asleep, except for the two guards on the perimeter of the field. He noticed that the campfire was still smouldering, its embers giving out a last dying light. But it was enough. He pulled what was left of a log out of the fire bowl and, surreptitiously, he edged himself backwards towards a hayrick. He blew the embers on the wood until they glowed with willing life, then he threw the log onto the rick. The combustion was immediate.

'Fire! Fire!' he shouted. The men stirred in the billowing smoke, and the guards came running towards the camp. In the panic that ensued, Sasha withdrew, untied a whinnying horse from its moorings, and galloped away, heedless of the noise of the horse's hooves, drowned as they were by the raging fire. He raced at full speed, and the horse obliged, grateful for its deliverance. He rode for a long time, before he thought it safe to slow his pace, but even at a light trot, his heart galloped still. He would not stop to rest. He had no idea where he was, but he knew he had to use the night for his cover.

As dawn broke, he recognised the church of a village very near Larionovka, and he dismounted, and got down on his knees and gave thanks to God. Then he rode slowly through the deserted village, praying all the while, pleading with God that Larionovka had by some miracle, been bypassed, that it had escaped the destruction that he saw all around him, the scorched fields, and the ditches filled with bodies on the sides of the road.

'Dear God, dear God, dear God,' he prayed and the horse's pace echoed the rhythm of his prayer.

As he drew nearer to his village, he slowed his pace. He feared he did not have the courage to arrive. He was climbing the hill that overlooked Larionovka. From its summit he knew he could view the whole village, and in that moment he would know everything there was to know. He stopped on the incline. He wished he had a messenger who could run on ahead to bring him back a picture of the scene from the top of the hill, somebody who could share the burden of a terrible discovery. He braced himself and rode to the summit. The church was still there. He would concentrate on what was positive, but when he sought out other landmarks there was none to be seen. No sign of the school, nor of the tavern. No row of shops. One chimney sported a wisp of smoke, a ribbon of incense, a frail wrapping for the ruins below. Yet it was a sign of habitation. The village, though destroyed, could not be entirely deserted. As he rode down the hill, he deciphered more smoke, but not from living chimneys, but from dead and smouldering dwellings. As he entered the village streets he saw those same signs of devastation, the burnt-out fields, the ditch of corpses, the sullied visiting card of both armies, Red and White. He would not look in the ditches. He feared he would know the faces. He wanted no sudden proof of bereavement. He wanted clues, hints, keys to possible doors of hope, a trail that could lead him to life, or possibly the final proof that all was lost. He would risk that proof, but he needed it in instalments, hope alternating with despair, and hope again, until the trail would resolve itself in tears of rejoicing. He kept his eyes firmly in front of him. From a distance he could see that the curl of smoke could possibly be rising from his own chimney, and that gave him enough hope to increase his pace a little.

And indeed by some miracle, the Volynin hut was the only dwelling that showed signs of life. He dismounted and tethered his horse. He wiped his feet before entering the house. It was an old habit from his childhood. His mother insisted on it, and with reason, for she was house-proud and, however mean their dwelling place, it was always clean and tidy. But now, as he viewed the interior from the threshold, he could see that it was filthier than the street outside, and as broken and as wounded as the village itself. He tiptoed across the floor. It was strewn with wreckage. Broken pots, cups, bowls, chairs. The clues were too sudden, too abrupt, and he wanted to go away from there and make detours on the trail, stop-overs even, anything to delay the message screaming from the wreckage of his home. But the most terrible bulletin of all stood propped in the corner. A broken wicker cradle of appalling emptiness. He knew instinctively that Anna had rocked that cradle and

180

that once it had held his child. He gave out a scream of despair that rebounded through the emptiness of the village and reverberated in the hut, and the cradle rocked, astonished.

'Don't move,' a voice ordered from somewhere in the wreckage. Sasha heard fear in the voice and a hint of familiarity.

'Pyotr?' he called.

Pyotr appeared suddenly in the space between the two rooms. He levelled a gun at Sasha's head. Sasha noted tears on his cheeks, and on his face the desperate weariness of loss.

'Who are you?' Pyotr said.

Then Sasha realised how much his appearance must have changed. He had not seen himself for many months, but he felt he had a beard and that his hair was very long.

The gun was trembling in Pyotr's hand as a slow glimpse of recognition passed over his face. 'Sashenka?' he whispered.

They fell into each other's arms. 'What happened? Where is Anna? Where is everybody?'

'They're safe,' Pyotr said.

'Then why are you crying?'

'All safe, but Mama,' Pyotr said. 'We had warning that they were coming, the Whites. So we decided that the old people and the women and children should leave. But Mama wouldn't go. She absolutely refused. She was ill, she was tired. Or perhaps she'd had enough. I don't know. She wouldn't move from the house. I've just come back from the hills.' He started to sob uncontrollably. 'I found her,' he whispered. 'She's in there.' He turned his head towards the other room. Sasha made a step towards where she lay.

'Don't go,' Pyotr said. 'It's not a pretty sight.'

'I must see her,' Sasha said.

'I can't go with you,' Pyotr said. 'I've seen enough.'

He crumpled to the floor, racked with weeping. He heard Sasha's scream of horror. Maria, or the pieces of her, lay neatly on the crumpled bed, as if she had been tidied by her tormentor. The head was severed, but placed neatly at her shoulder. She was naked, but her clothes had been carefully piled, each fold aligned with another. Her thighs were bloodied, and he covered them quickly for the sake of his own shame as well as for hers. He had never seen his mother's body nor even thought of it, and now its torture and violation had robbed him of any belief that at one time it must have been beautiful. He dared to glance at her face. A look of bewilderment was etched into its vigour as if she couldn't understand why they thought her an enemy. Had she not loved the Tsar? Had she not mourned his passing? But she had never been prepared to die for him. He took no precedence over her home and her children.

Gently Sasha placed the head on her shoulders, and covered her body with her clothes. He went to where Pyotr sat. 'Let us bury her,' he said. Together, and in silence, they wrapped her in a sheet, and between them, carried the body to the church. They made for Vassily's grave. The headstone had been broken, and fallen onto the earth beside it, where Maria was to lay. In silence the brothers cleared the plot and dug a grave, and without a word, they laid her down. No language could express the horrors they had seen, no words could report them. Only silence could cover them, in its dismal pall. But walking back to the village the silence began to jar; it fed resignation and lack of hope. They had to return in words to the living.

'How is Anna?' Sasha asked. 'And that cradle?'

'Your son,' Pyotr said. 'Dmitri. He's a beautiful baby. Avdotya and Mama looked after him. Anna helped me in the fields. She's different from the others,' Pyotr said. 'She works hard. We all love her.'

'When will they come back?'

'Tomorrow. Or the next day. You'll see. They'll come back.' For a moment Sasha was happy. And then ashamed, that he was smiling on his way back from his mother's grave. They passed the death ditches along the road.

'We must bury them,' Sasha said.

So for the rest of that day, and most of the night, the brothers buried the dead. Most of the faces were known to them, peasants all of them and all had died, untutored, each one of them a stranger to causes. As they buried them, in families where they could, the silence fell again between them, and when they had finished, they knelt and prayed for the village that was no more.

The following day, they waited for the women to return. It was nightfall before they heard the first rumblings of the carts. Then they saw them, coming over the hill.

Sasha started to run. 'Anna,' he called. 'Anna.' The name echoed up the hill and along the line of stragglers, and riders, all weary, all indifferent, all bereft. He ran alongside them, ashamed of his speed and excitement, in the face of their torpor, calling 'Anna' along the line.

'Yes? Yes?' one of them said, and, 'I'm Anna,' another.

A common enough name in Russia at the time. And what did it matter any more how one was called? One was alive and any appellation would do. Even a man amongst them answered to the name, but only as an echo. Perhaps he was mourning a wife or daughter who was no more.

'Anna Larionova,' Sasha called, in an attempt to narrow the field, and he measured his steps to its rhythm as he moved along the line. At last he deciphered Avdotya's cart. It was the last in the line. It was moving slowly, in stops and starts, as if there was no point in return. Avdotya was holding the reins. He ran to the cart, and jumped to sit beside her. She did not look at him, but he scanned the cartload for Anna's face. It was full of children who would never see their fathers again.

'Where's Anna?' he screamed.

'She's alive. And the baby.' Avdotya's voice was flat. Uninvolved. She had seen too much to care ever again.

'But where is she?' Sasha knew he had to be patient with her. He put his arm around her shoulder.

'You weren't here,' she said. 'You should have been here.' She was clearly angry with him. But he would not take the time to explain his absence. He needed to know about Anna. 'Tell me, Avdotya,' he pleaded. 'Where is she?'

But Avdotya was going to take her time. Anna had waited long enough for news of Sasha. Now it was his turn to wait. She spoke slowly and every syllable bypassed feeling.

'We went to Vosrov,' she said. 'We slept in the railway station. Hundreds of us, from all the villages around. Then this morning a train came in. Your Anna got up, took Dmitri from me, and

183

grabbed her mother's hand. And they got on it. Just like that.'

'Why didn't you stop her, Avdotya?' Sasha said.

'*You* try stopping her,' Advotya shouted at him. 'She left me with no one on earth to care for.' Then mercifully she gave way to tears. Sasha dared not tell her about his mother. But she asked, as if reading his thoughts. He shook his head, and she understood. 'My best friend in the world,' she said. The cart rumbled forward, and Sasha allowed a silence.

Then, after a while, 'Where was the train going, Avdotya?' he asked.

'Who knows?' She turned to him and started to shout again. 'Perhaps it was going to Moscow. Perhaps to Petrograd. Perhaps to Siberia. It was a train. It was moving. It was going *somewhere*. She went to look for you.' Now Avdotya was exhausted. She handed Sasha the reins. 'You drive,' she said. 'What have I got to go home to?'

'Many orphans,' Sasha said. 'They will need looking after.'

They heard the sighs and the moans and the screamings of the first arrivals, and the sounds of mourning grew louder as they approached what was left of their homes. Sasha stopped the cart at Avdotya's home. It lay on the outskirts of the village, and perhaps for that reason, it was untouched, as were the dwellings alongside it. He helped her down from the cart. She looked at the children behind. 'Which one of you is alone?' she asked.

Three children timidly put up their hands.

'Come,' she said. She lifted them out, one by one, took their hands, and let them into her house. Then she turned to Sasha, and gave him her first smile. 'Say goodbye to me before you go,' she said.

He drove the cart into the village, and listened to the weeping behind him. He stopped outside the church, and helped them to alight. Then he left them to their own sorrows.

Between them, during the day, Pyotr and Sasha had put their dwelling into some kind of living order. A fire was burning in the grate, and Nina and the children were seated at the table. He greeted them with heartfelt gratitude. Pyotr was possibly one of the few in the village who had been left with his family almost intact.

From somewhere he had foraged food, and even a bottle of wine. So they drank a toast to the living, while remembering the dead.

In the morning Sasha made preparation to leave. It seemed to him that most of his life had been spent looking for Anna, finding her and losing her again.

'Where will you go?' Pyotr asked.

'To Petrograd first. Then, if she's not there, to Moscow. Ivan will help me find her.'

Pyotr was shaving away Sasha's beard. He paused with the strop. 'Be careful of Ivan,' he said.

'Why d'you say that?' Sasha asked. 'He's our brother.'

'I hear terrible stories about him,' Pyotr said.

'What sort of stories?'

'Torture.' Pyotr was not a man of many words, but he invested those few with the intensity of the inarticulate.

'He's high up in the Cheka. That's their business,' Sasha said. 'I've heard them too, and I try not to believe them. He's very different from us, Pyotr. He always was.'

'How is Katya?' Pyotr asked. He could still pronounce her name with love. 'Are they happy together?'

'So long as she works with him, they'll be happy. He has no love for anything except the Cause.'

'God help her,' Pyotr whispered.

By now, Sasha was clean-shaven.

'You're beginning to look like Sashenka again,' Pyotr said. 'Now I must cut your hair. I'll cut it in one piece. It's long enough for a plait. Nina will find some use for it.'

'She's lovely, your Nina,' Sasha said.

'I think so too.'

So Sasha's hair was cut, and the plait handed over.

'I'm surprised you were fighting the Whites, Pyotr. I thought you'd be on their side.'

'I'm on my side, Sashenka,' Pyotr said. 'Me and mine. I'm a farmer. That's all I know how to do. When all this is over, I'll start farming again. That's all I want. To be left in peace to lead my own life.'

Sasha embraced him. 'Thank you for looking after them all,' he said. 'You've been a good son, the best of us all. And it was hardest for you, I know. When it's all over, let's be together. The family, I mean. What's left of us.'

'Ivan will be too grand,' Pyotr said. 'He would never put the family above the Cause.'

'One day he might have to,' Sasha said. He started to pack his bag. Pyotr removed the Red Star badge on his cap. 'Take this,' he said. 'I found it. You may find it useful, depending on whom you meet. If they're Reds, say you were separated from your unit. If Whites, show them the cap you were wearing.'

Pyotr rode with his brother to the outskirts of the village. On the way, they stopped at Avdotya's house. Inside, the three orphans were sitting at the table eating a simple meal. Avdotya was on her way to the village. 'A baby is coming,' she said to them. She was returning to living with a vengeance.

Sasha said his farewells. 'When you come back, Sashenka,' she said, 'you'll come with Anna and the baby. And you will stay here,' she ordered, 'and I shall deliver a sister for Dmitri.' Then she was gone to bring life into the village of the dead.

The brothers rode for a while.

'Have you been making any more poems?' Pyotr asked.

Sasha laughed. 'I was Poet Laureate of the Whites,' he said. 'I've never stopped, and I hope I never will. My next book is for you, Pyotr.'

'Poems?' Pyotr was grinning with gratitude.

'No. A novel. I'm going to call it *The Banner Falls.*'

'What's it about?'

'Have you time?' Sasha asked.

'I'll ride with you till you've finished,' Pyotr said.

So Sasha told him the story of Ranjevsky, of their days and nights together, of his cruelty and his poetry, of his curses and blessings, and how, despite his ideas and philosophy, Sasha had somehow loved him.

'Is he still alive?' Pyotr asked.

'I hope so,' Sasha said. 'Though I would not wish to run into him again.'

They parted some way out of the village.

'Be careful,' Pyotr said. 'And good luck.'

They embraced. In the days that they had spent together, in their mourning and their weeping, both men had kindled a love for each other, that had long been dormant.

'I shall miss you,' Pyotr said.

'We shall both miss each other.' Then Sasha embraced him once more, and clutching his white and red insignia, both at the ready, he took the road to Petrograd.

14

Sasha reached Petrograd with no interference. He tried to still his heart as he approached the city, having had lessons in expectation before. If Anna's train was destined for Petrograd, he would find her at Katya and Ivan's. If she were not there, he would go to Moscow and enlist the help of Andrei. And if not Moscow, then he would travel to every railway terminus in the whole of Russia until he found her. Even if it took his lifetime.

Petrograd looked much the same as when he had left it. The long queues for bread, the idleness that hugged the corners of the streets, the beggars, the ruins, and the smell of despair. What had it all been for, he wondered. All those crops destroyed, all those children in ditches, all that causeless blood that had been spilt. He prayed that wherever Anna was, she had food enough for herself and Dmitri.

He knew that Ivan would be surprised to see him. Like Pyotr, he had probably assumed his younger brother was dead. So he knocked gently at the door and hoped he would be welcome.

It was Katya who answered. She threw her arms around him. 'Sashenka,' he cried, 'you're alive!'

'Is Anna here?' It was all he wanted to know.

She shook her head, and called Ivan.

He wanted to leave at once. To go and look for Anna. There seemed to him to be no point in dallying in an Anna-less place. 'Where is she? Have you heard?' Katya shook her head again. Then Ivan was at the door, and Sasha found himself in his brother's embrace.

'We thought you were dead,' Ivan said.

Sasha noted that Ivan was actually weeping. There was hope for him still, he thought. 'I have to find Anna,' he said. The name had begun to obsess him. Instead of her face, he saw her name, the single letters of it. He couldn't remember what she looked like. Her face was blurred by calligraphy.

'Come in, come in,' Katya said. 'You must eat. You must sleep.'

They dragged him inside. 'Have you any news of Larionovka?' Ivan said.

'I was there. I have just come from there. Mama's dead.'

He knew that his abruptness was cruel, but he wanted to curb their delight in seeing him. He wanted them to be as miserable as he.

'How did she die?' Ivan whispered.

'How does anybody die nowadays?' Sasha raised his voice. 'Who dies from nature any more? There's only one death nowadays,' he said bitterly. 'Death by rape, torture, the knife. You know it, Ivan, as well as I.' Then he regretted his outburst, and put his hand on his brother's shoulder.

'They're barbarians,' Ivan said. 'Savages.'

Sasha wanted to remind him of the barbarians and savages who had swept through the Larionov manor on the hill. But he held his tongue.

'Come let's eat,' Katya tried again. She called Vassily and together they prepared a meal. As they waited, Sasha told Ivan of his conscription into the White Army. But he did not mention Ranjevsky. That name was for Pyotr's ear alone. He told him of the escape and his sojourn in Larionovka. He spared him his mother's rape. 'I think she died of fear,' he said, 'but at least it was in her own bed.' He did not mention the state of that bed nor the two separate parts of their mother that lay on it. But the recollection sickened him, and he mourned once more with his brother. They sat at the table with little appetite.

'Where did Anna go?' Katya asked.

'They went to hide in Vosrov,' Sasha said. 'Avdotya was with them. A train came, and Anna got on it with the baby and her mother. Avdotya didn't know where the train was going.'

189

'She could be anywhere,' Vassily said.

'I have to find her,' said Sasha. 'I have to. I have a child I've never seen. You have to help me, Ivan.'

Ivan straightened in his chair. 'I have to be careful,' he said. 'At the moment the Larionov name may be a hindrance. Enquiries about Anna will have to be made with extreme caution.'

Sasha stared at him in disbelief. His brother was back at his Cheka desk talking like a bureaucrat. 'What does all that mean?' he shouted. 'The Larionov name?'

It was Katya who told him about Nicolai's arrest and escape. 'Ivan's right,' she said. 'We have to be careful.'

'I want to help you, Sasha,' Ivan said, his brother once more. 'But you must let me do it in my own way. I'll talk to Andrei in Moscow. Perhaps he has news. Come to the office tomorrow and I'll see what I can do.'

Suddenly Sasha didn't trust him. He recalled Pyotr's warning. 'Be careful of Ivan,' he had said. But he had no one else to turn to. He would have to trust him.

Ivan had told him to arrive mid-morning, so that he would have time to make discreet enquiries. When Sasha arrived at the Cheka offices, he had to wait. He was alone in a long corridor. Officers walked up and down carrying files. Sasha felt they were all looking at him, as if the file-carrying was a simple cover to take a look at their superior's brother. He was uneasy, and by the time he was called he had lost all hope of Ivan's support.

He was shown into Ivan's office. It was clearly the superior's headquarters. The number of telephones was impressive, together with the two secretaries at adjacent desks. Ivan told them to leave, which they did promptly.

'Sit down,' he said when they had left.

'Have you any news?' Sasha could contain himself no longer.

'Yes,' Ivan said, 'and it's not good. I spoke to Andrei this morning in Moscow. They're not there, and he has no news of them. He thought they were still in Larionovka. But I did make further enquiries, Sashenka,' he said, using the affectionate diminutive to offset the shock of the news he had to tell. The 'Sashenka' told Sasha that it was all over, and he began to tremble. 'I checked on the trains,' Ivan went on. 'There was only one possible train from Vosrov at about the time you've given me. There weren't too many trains, so it was easy to identify. The train was ambushed by Whites. We have no information as to survivors. In fact we doubt that there were any.'

Sasha crumbled in his chair. He refused to believe it, yet he had no reason to suppose that it wasn't true.

'Try to forget the past,' Ivan was saying. 'Start again. Make a new life.'

Sasha could have struck him. 'Anna *is* my life,' he said. 'Anyway, you have no proof. It's just rumour.'

'We'll continue to make enquiries,' Ivan said, sheltering behind his bureaucracy. 'But please, don't be too hopeful.'

'I can't give up hope. I've nothing else to live for.'

'You have your writing,' Ivan said, though with little confidence. He found it difficult to take writers seriously. 'Work,' he said. 'It will take your mind off things.'

He had a point, Sasha thought. Work would help and it would be good to see Yakovlev, his publisher, again. But to see *anybody* would mean losing time in looking for Anna. That was his only purpose in life. Yet she couldn't be in Petrograd or she would have gone to her friends. But wherever she was wandering, she would know that he would be in the capital. In time she would make her way to their meeting. He would wait, and meanwhile he would work.

He was still trembling when he left Ivan's office. But he refused to give way to weeping. Tears would have acknowledged loss and the need for mourning. He walked along the street whistling softly, as if this were just another day like any other, but when he reached Yakovlev's office, he was still trembling. He collapsed on Yakovlev's couch.

Yakovlev had not seen Sasha for over two years, and he had no idea of what had happened to him. But he could see that he was in trouble now. He sat beside him on the settee.

'D'you want to talk about it?' he said.

'I've lost Anna,' Sasha said, then quickly amended his statement, because it was too final. 'I cannot find her,' he said.

'Tell me,' Yakovlev said. 'I have time.'

It was a relief to talk to somebody. About his feelings. About his fears. Neither Katya nor Ivan would have bothered to understand them. He missed Pyotr, that strong and silent reliance. He told Yakovlev everything. And when he came to relate Ivan's latest information, he tossed it off lightly as if it were a joke.

'You mustn't give up hope, Sasha,' Yakovlev said when his tale was told. 'But meanwhile you must work. In that respect your brother is right. There's work for you here. Reading. Editing. And when we're not too busy, you can get on with your own. It's time for a second volume of poetry. And I think you must move out of Ivan's apartment. It will be good for both of you. I have room in my apartment. We can talk about books together. We can give politics a rest. What d'you think, Sasha?'

'You're a friend,' Sasha said. 'And, my God, I need a friend.'

'We can't give in,' Yakovlev said. 'We can't just become cogs in a machine. Like your brother, for instance. We have to survive as people, as individuals. People with voices and dreams. We have a right to believe in ourselves. Read Chekhov. He says it all.'

That night Sasha told Ivan he was going to share a flat with Yakovlev.

'The publisher?' Ivan said. 'The man who published your poems?'

'Yes. Why?'

Ivan did not answer for a moment. And when he did, he dodged the question. 'You can stay here you know. You're no trouble. This apartment must be bigger than Yakovlev's.'

'Of course it is,' Sasha said. 'Yakovlev's not a party official.'

'Please yourself,' Ivan said. 'But I'd rather you didn't.'

'Why?'

'Let's just leave it at that.'

Sasha felt uneasy. He wanted very much to stay with Yakovlev. He was more comfortable in his company. Ivan and Katya talked of nothing but the Party. They had no other interests. Besides, although he had his own room, for Ivan's apartment was spacious, he found it difficult to write there. It was as if every word he wrote was subversive and the shadow of the censor's pencil fell on the page. It was easier to write for Ranjevsky. At least he was aware of his own hypocrisy.

'I'm going anyway,' Sasha said.

Katya tried to persuade him to stay, but she too gave no reason. 'We're family, Sashenka,' she said.

He wondered about that. In many ways Yakovlev was more like family. 'I'll come and see you often,' he said. Still he was hesitant – not about leaving his brother, but in joining Yakovlev. There had been a tone of warning in his brother's voice and he couldn't understand why. But it was not long after he had moved in with Yakovlev and started work in the publishing house, that Ivan's misgivings became clear.

Each morning when they left for work, both Sasha and Yakovlev noted two men dawdling on the pavement opposite the house. The same two men every morning and the same idling behaviour. They made no attempt to conceal themselves and in time their faces grew familiar enough to greet. 'Good morning,' Yakovlev would say, but they never replied. As far as they were concerned, their role was to remain strangers. They were there in the evenings too, when Yakovlev and Sasha returned from work, and it was possible that they had idled there all day. Once during the night, when Sasha happened to look out of the window, there were two other men on the pavement, apparently the night shift, and Sasha became nervous.

'D'you think I ought to report them to Ivan?' he asked Yakovlev.

'Your brother probably sends them,' Yakovlev laughed. 'All Cheka men look the same. Anonymous. They daren't look like anything resembling a person. They are a Party, and the Party, as your brother no doubt has told you often enough, takes precedence over the people. Ignore them. They'll tire soon enough.'

But Yakovlev was wrong. They had the persistence of robots. Then one evening when Sasha and Yakovlev returned from work, they noted that the men had gone.

'Didn't I tell you?' Yakovlev said. 'They had enough and they're doing their dawdling elsewhere.'

But on entry to their apartment it was clear that the men had gone because their purpose had been achieved. The flat was in a shambles. Books were strewn on the floor, the mattresses had been knifed, and clumps of straw were neatly laid out on the tables and chairs. The desk had been rifled and the wardrobe. Trouser pockets were ripped. Not even the shoes had escaped investigation. Their uppers had been slashed from the soles.

'Cheka's work,' Yakovlev said with disgust.

'My brother can't have known.' Sasha was deeply ashamed.

'There's not much your brother doesn't know in that department. Anyway, you don't have to apologise for him. Or for your being here. They're not after you. It's me they want.'

'But why?'

'Who knows? They don't need reasons. Any trumped-up charge will do. We have to discover what's missing. That might give us a clue.' Yakovlev went through the rifled drawers of his desk. 'I can't see anything's gone,' he said after a while. Then he went through the books that were strewn on the floor. He stacked them in neat piles, and Sasha replaced them on the shelves.

'My Chekhov's gone. All my Chekhovs,' Yakovlev said. 'I must say, that scum had got pretty good taste. My Pushkins too, would you believe.'

'But why Chekhov? Why Pushkin?' Sasha asked.

'Ask them,' Yakovlev said. 'Ask your brother. I'm sure he's read every line of both of them. Come, Sasha, they're not going to get me depressed. That way, they win. We'll go out and get drunk. Both of us. And bugger them.'

They took themselves to the nearest tavern, and in vodka after vodka, raced each other into oblivion. Then after midnight, they staggered home, each holding the other's reeling self like a lover. There was nowhere to sleep, so they curled up on chairs, dreading the shambled sight of the morning and its monumental thirst.

Yakovlev was up early. He was making a strong pot of coffee and humming softly to himself. He moved about with a dogged determination. He would not be cowed into submission, though he suspected that such an alternative would not be allowed him. When the coffee was ready, he woke Sasha.

'Come,' he said. 'Quench your thirst, then we'll go to the offices and see what they've left of our publishing house.'

Sasha woke in a state of deep depression, which his hangover did little to alleviate. He had slept fitfully, and in sleeping had dreamt of Anna and he woke without hope, and a despairing sense of the nightmare his country had become. He drank his coffee silently.

Yakovlev put his arm around Sasha's shoulder. 'Things will get better,' he said. Though he didn't believe it. He had no reason to suppose that they wouldn't get worse. They were cheered a little on arriving at the publishing house to find that everything was in order. Samarin, Yakovlev's assistant editor, was at his desk, reading.

'Samarin,' Yakovlev said, 'do we still have that list of banned authors, or did I put it in the waste-paper basket where it belonged?'

'I have a copy somewhere,' Samarin said. He rummaged through the papers on the top of his desk, but Sasha noticed that the rummaging was a pretence, for the list was right in front of him, loud and clear under his nose. He wondered then if Samarin was a friend of Ivan's.

'Here it is,' Samarin said. 'Why do you want it?'

'My place was raided last night. They took my Chekhovs.' He scanned the paper that Samarin had given him, and laughed aloud. 'He's top of the list. Look, Sasha. "List of suspect authors: Not to be published. Anton Pavlovich Chekhov." Now I've seen everything.'

Then Samarin spoke, but to his desk, as if he was afraid to look Yakovlev in the eye. 'All authors, past and present, have to be re-evaluated, Yakovlev. You know that.'

At that moment Sasha knew that Samarin worked for Ivan. He saw the rage on Yakovlev's face.

'Re-evaluated? Chekhov?' he shouted. 'One of the greatest writers in the world? Who the hell are we to re-evaluate him?'

'Cool down, comrade,' Samarin said. 'All art is political. No one is exempt from that truth. Not even your great Chekhov.' There was a hint of contempt in his voice that was not lost on Yakovlev.

'I'm a socialist, comrade, not a censor,' Yakovlev shouted. 'Who are we to tell the people what they can or cannot read? We promised the people freedom. Since when does freedom mean censorship?

We're no better than the Tsars.' He took the list in his assistant's hand and tore it into shreds. 'It's all shit, that's what it is. Shit. All of it.' Then he left the room, trembling with fury.

Samarin did not turn around. He simply went on shuffling his papers. Then again to his desk he said, 'If you've got any sense, Comrade Volynin, you'll move out of Yakovlev's apartment.'

'Why don't you look at me?' Sasha shouted.

There was no reply. So Sasha went over to the desk and stood behind him. 'You rotten treacherous rat,' he hissed into his ear. Still he didn't turn around, and Sasha was about to strike him, when he heard a scuffle outside. He turned and recognised the two loiterers standing at the door.

'Where's Yakovlev?' one of them shouted.

'In the small office,' Samarin said.

But Yakovlev obliged them with an appearance. 'I'm not hiding,' he said. He was calm. 'What do you want?'

'You're under arrest,' one of the men said.

'What's the charge?'

'You are charged with being an enemy of the Revolution,' the other said. They clearly wanted to share the honour of the arrest.

Yakovlev laughed. Very few expressions were legal any more in Russia, but laughter was one of them. Derision, tears, and suffering, and that more or less summed up the charter of freedom. They grabbed him on each arm and dragged him to the door.

'Write about it, Sashenka,' he shouted. 'That's all we can do. And publish abroad. People have to know what's happening to us.'

The men clapped their hands over his mouth, and pushed him outside. Sasha stood helpless, and looked after him. He whispered a farewell, for he knew he would never see his friend again.

'Well, now that's over,' he heard Samarin say, 'you can get back to your work, Volynin.'

Then Sasha remembered how he had meant to strike him, and how Yakovlev's arrest had interrupted his fury. Now was the time, he decided. He went over to Samarin's desk. 'Get up,' he shouted.

Samarin did not move, but he could not hide his fearful shivering. Sasha pulled him up by his collar and kicked the chair away behind him. 'Now look at me, you piece of shit,' he said. 'Look me in the eye if you can.'

Samarin had to oblige, but he was blinking with fear. His lower lip trembled and tears smarted from his eyes. Sasha looked at him with contempt. He wasn't worth laying a finger on. So he simply shoved him on the floor, and spat at him. Then without another word, he left the room.

He went back to Yakovlev's apartment. The door was open but he was not surprised. Nothing was private any more. But what did surprise him was the presence of Ivan. He was sitting on one of the few unbroken chairs waiting for him.

'What do you want?' Sasha said. He was not pleased to see his brother. Indeed he would have been happy never to see him again. 'What have you done with Yakovlev?'

'He will be charged.'

'You mean he'll have a trial?' Sasha sneered. 'Things *are* looking up, aren't they?'

'Look, Sasha,' Ivan said. 'Sit down. I need to talk to you.'

'Say what you have to say, and go.'

'Sasha, listen to me,' Ivan insisted. 'You're in trouble. All Yakovlev's associates are in trouble. There's only one way out. You must join the Party.'

'Writers don't join parties,' Sasha said with disdain. 'If no one else can speak the truth, then writers have to. And publishers must publish. People like Yakovlev. Yes,' he insisted, 'my friend Yakovlev.'

Ivan rose. 'I cannot help you,' he said. 'You're too stubborn. And you don't listen. You're in trouble, Sasha. Don't think that because I'm your brother that you're safe. You're not. Because nothing matters to me except the Revolution.'

'What happened to you, Ivan?' Sasha said. 'You used to be so gentle. You used to believe in decency, in dignity, in equality. Those are the things you fought for. But now they don't matter to you any more. People don't matter to you. The flesh and blood doesn't matter. All that matters to you is the blood-stained plague of the Party.'

Ivan went to the door. 'Don't try me, Sasha,' he warned.

197

'I want to see Yakovlev,' Sasha said. 'Where are you keeping him?'

'You're too late,' Ivan said, and there was a certain pleasure in his voice. 'They shot him straightaway.' Then he was gone.

Sasha crumpled on to a chair, and gave way to the tears that he had been storing ever since Yakovlev's arrest. They were tears of hate as well as sorrow, and he knew he would have to leave Petrograd if only to be rid of his brother. If it weren't for Anna and his son he would leave the country for ever. And never never come back. Except to see Pyotr, he thought, his only tie of love left in his heart. He thought he might go back to his village, but he was not a farmer, and there was no one there with whom he could talk about his writings. He would go to Moscow, he decided. There he could meet with Andrei. Perhaps Andrei had not given up hope of Anna. They could share their hopes together. He straightened Yakovlev's room as well as he could. Then he packed his valise and went to the station to wait for a train.

He waited a whole day and a night. He expected that at any time one of Ivan's men would come to collect him. There would be some trumped-up charge, and a summary shooting at the back of the station. But he didn't care any more. Yakovlev's grossly unjust dispatch had left him entirely disenchanted. Even the thought of Anna and his son could not raise his spirits, for they too were now clouded with his disenchantment, and he felt he no longer had any right to envisage seeing them again. His life seemed to him to be entirely without purpose, and as he boarded the train at last he almost regretted that they had not come to fetch him.

It was early morning when he reached Moscow. The sight of a new city kindled a small excitement in him, and once again he thought of Anna with hope. He asked directions to the Internal Ministry where he had been told Andrei was employed. He walked through the streets with the curious insatiable eye of a stranger. In many ways, he thought, he could still have been in Petrograd. There were the same long lines of people waiting for bread, the same idleness on corners, the same beggars, many children amongst them, and the same anonymous loiterers of Ivan's domain. The whole of Russia had become a sewer, he thought, ruled by the faceless faces of cloned Ivans, and Sasha felt that his entire lineage was stained.

He walked, sickened, and in time he reached the Internal Ministry. People were beginning to emerge from the building and he decided to wait outside hoping that Andrei would appear. He idled on the pavement opposite, then worried that he might be mistaken for one of Ivan's men, so he walked briskly to and fro, keeping his eye on the building all the time. Eventually, he caught sight of Andrei, and the joy he felt surprised him. In looking at Anna's brother, he felt close to finding her. He would have crossed the street to join him straightaway, but Andrei was in the company of a number of colleagues and in animated conversation as they walked. So Sasha kept to his side of the street and followed them. One by one, his colleagues went their own ways, but Andrei was still accompanied by two others. And remained so until he came to a large building, where he stopped and bade farewell to his friends. Then he walked slowly up the steps and disappeared through the entrance doors. Sasha followed him. When he came to the building, he looked at its portal to see the legend. 'Institute for the Infirm and the Insane', it read. Or blazoned rather. Unashamed. Sasha was puzzled. Perhaps Andrei was visiting a friend, and he should not disturb him. But he was anxious. So he followed him inside.

There seemed to be no receptionist in the foyer. Nurses and porters crossed and recrossed it. Visitors too, some carrying flowers or boxes of fruit. He was assumed to be a visitor, so nobody questioned him. The flight of stairs to the upper storey was barred by a gate, with the notice 'Private. Staff only.' He was relieved that there was only one floor to explore. He walked along a corridor. He heard screams and muffled cries, and two porters appeared, carrying a struggling patient between them. As he reached the end of the corridor, a group of women turned to look at him. They each wore uniform dressing-gowns, and on their faces were uniform grins, which they pointed in Sasha's direction. Sasha was a little afraid. And ashamed of his fear. He walked past them steadily and came to the entrance of a large ward. The doors were open, and along the walls were rows of beds. Some were occupied, others uninhabited, but both for some reason looked empty, for those who lay or sat staring between the sheets seemed not to be there at all. Then suddenly he saw Andrei. His back was towards Sasha, and he was holding the hand of a woman who sat between the sheets, but who looked suspended between heaven and earth, racked with indecision as to which to choose, but with little appetite for either. Sasha stared at her. Andrei was sitting to one side, so he had a full view of her face. He found himself trembling. The face was painfully familiar. It spoke of his childhood, of a world that was no more. It spoke of terror and torture, but above all, it spoke of love, and it was this last contradiction that proclaimed itself as the strongest clue to her identity. And at once, in a fever of bewildered recognition, he knew her for Anna's mother. Then there had been no ambush of a train from Vosrov after all. His legs began to tremble, and he felt himself sinking to the floor. The lino was cold on his back, he saw a circle of grinning faces above him, and heard the cackle of their laughter. Then the laughter faded and he saw and heard no more.

The women stared at him, grinning the while. No one of them thought to help. Here at their feet was an event, a rare enough occurrence in their monotonous, repetitive lives, and they were going to relish it, to milk it for all its entertainment value. Here was one of them who was not one of them, but, when the crunch came, was one of them all the same. So they danced in a circle around him, shrieking their delight that their own frailty could be so triumphantly contagious.

Their commotion quickly called the attention of a nurse who doused Sasha's face with a douche of cold water. He opened his eyes. The nurse lifted him to his unsteady feet and sat him on a chair. Then she left him, taking his tormentors with her. Now he had an uninterrupted view of the Countess Tatiana. It had been no dream. The Countess was alive, albeit ailing. Then Anna and the child had survived too. Ivan had lied to him, and so, in conspiracy, had Andrei. He rose and walked down the corridor. He would sit in the foyer of the hospital and wait for him.

He did not have to wait long. He heard the hospital bell, which must have signalled the end of visiting hours, for many people began to pass through the foyer, now flower- and giftless, some weeping, others with a look of profound relief of guilt that was partially assuaged. When Andrei appeared, he looked simply bereaved, helpless and melancholy. It would be hard to upbraid him.

'Andrei,' Sasha called.

Andrei looked around for the source of the voice, and on finding it, was seen to blush, and to tremble both from excitement and from the fear of discovery. But his pleasure on seeing Sasha overrode his fears and he ran towards him, and embraced him.

'How did you find me here, Sashenka?' he asked.

'I followed you from the Ministry. I saw you with your mother. Where is Anna? I want no more lies. Tell me where I can find her.'

'I'll tell you what I know. Come. We'll have supper together. Give me a space of silence for a while. You are entitled to explanations. We'll sit down, and I'll tell you everything.'

Sasha respected that need. He could see that Andrei was deeply troubled, and he loved him enough to give him time. The promise of news of Anna at last would try his patience only a little longer. Andrei led him to the restaurant in silence.

It was a vast place, and practically empty. There were many more waiters than clients. A string quartet played with little appetite at the far end of the room. They took a table in the corner. Andrei was clearly a regular client, and the waiters served him with deference. They placed a basket of black bread before him, a bowl of caviare and a bottle of vodka. Clearly his usual order. Then they left the table, and patience and silence were no longer called for.

'Tell me where she is,' Sasha said.

'Let me start at the beginning,' Andrei said. 'There's so much to tell you.'

'I only want to know one thing. The explanations can come later. Where is Anna?' His voice had risen. His patience was clearly exhausted.

Andrei knew he had to respond immediately. 'I don't know,' he said. 'It's as simple as that. Listen. I'll tell you everything I know. I saw her last only a short time before Ivan telephoned me and I learnt you are alive. She is well and you have a beautiful son. They had been staying with me for a few weeks. I was trying to get her a travel permit. She wanted, like thousands of us, to leave this godforsaken country.'

'But where is she now?' Sasha could hardly contain himself.

'Listen to me,' Andrei said. 'I don't know, and that's the truth of it. She wanted to leave. Anywhere, she said. As long as she got out of the country. You see, she thought you were dead. We all did. Nobody had heard word of you for so long. She had begun to mourn you.'

'But where is she? Where did she go?' Sasha asked again.

'I don't know, and that's the truth of it. I managed to get her a special travel permit.'

'But where to? What country?'

'In these days,' Andrei said patiently, 'people only plan their departures. That's a big enough hurdle. Their destinations are irrelevant. They simply want to get out. She could have gone anywhere. France, Germany, Finland.'

'Help me to get out, Andrei. I've got to find her. I'll travel the world. But I've got to find her.'

'If that's what you want,' Andrei said, 'I'll do what I can. But I fear it will be a hopeless search.'

'But you'll get me papers? Promise, Andrei.'

'I promise,' he said. He spooned some caviare onto a piece of bread and handed it to Sasha. Then he did the same for himself, and poured vodka for them both. He needed to fortify himself. The most uncomfortable explanation was to come. His collusion with Ivan in the deception.

Sasha downed his vodka. He too needed to brace himself. He didn't want to lose Andrei as a friend. And more than that, for he considered him as a brother. But he had to know why he had deceived him.

'Why did you do it Andrei? Why?' It was as much a question as an expression of his own disbelief.

'Because I'm a moral coward,' Andrei said. 'It's as simple as that. When Ivan called me, he gave me orders. One knows better than to disobey orders from the Cheka. He told me to confirm that the train was ambushed. That I had never seen Anna, or Dmitri or my mother.'

'But why was it all so necessary?'

'Self-protection. That's why. Nicolai had been arrested. He'd escaped. You know that. He's an enemy of the State. The name Larionov is a dangerous name. Any linkage between that name and Ivan would land him in serious trouble. Guilt by association, it's called.'

'But what about you. You're even closer.'

'That's why I must show even greater loyalty. Ivan will protect me as long as I collude. I said I was a moral coward. That's the long and the short of it. Does he know you're here?' There was fear in Andrei's voice. 'He didn't warn me you were coming.'

'He doesn't know where I am. Not yet.'

'Then you must leave the country as soon as possible. I'll make arrangements. You had better not stay with me. I shall arrange a safe hotel.' He downed his vodka. The worst was over. 'Let's make a toast,' he said. 'To the Sasha and Anna reunion.'

Sasha was glad to drink to that. Now he felt more at ease. His life had a mission and he would not rest until he had found her.

Over supper, he asked about Andrei's mother. 'With Anna so determined to leave,' Andrei said, 'I could no longer look after her. So I put her in the home where you found me. She is ailing, both in mind and body. She is a casualty of our Revolution. One of millions. Sometimes I wonder whether it was worth it. I pray sometimes that she will die soon. In many ways she has already left this earth. She talks to my father and Marfa all the time. Her spirit has gone, but her flesh is offensively alive.'

'I'm sorry,' was all Sasha could say. He raised his glass to her. 'Let her go soon in peace,' he said.

A few days later Andrei came to Sasha's hotel and handed over his travelling papers. 'Go as soon as you can,' he said. 'Ivan is after you. And not as a brother. It's a Cheka pursuit. He rang me this morning. I said I hadn't heard from you.'

Sasha embraced him. 'You are more my brother,' he said. 'This is no farewell. I know we shall meet again. My peace and my love to your mother,' he said.

That evening Sasha set out on his travels. He was excited. His journey promised adventure, but above all, it had a purpose, and if it took him to the ends of the earth, he would not yield until he had found Anna. He would have few regrets leaving his motherland. It had become a slaughterhouse. Ivan was dead for him, but he would miss Pyotr. And Andrei. These two men were his little family, and the only people who would call on his nostalgia. He took the train to Odessa, the port of departure.

And so had hundreds of others. Amongst them, Anna and Dmitri. When Sasha arrived at the port, she had already been waiting there for many days, huddled on the quayside with Dmitri in her arms. There was sound of gunfire, menacingly close. A tramp steamer was tied up at the quay, and people, in their panic to get away, were stampeding the companionway. Sasha found himself amongst them. In the surge of the mob behind him, his feet had left the ground and he was propelled onto the steamer by forces other than his own. Once aboard, he managed to find a place at the rail. Looking down he saw the seething, screaming mob of would-be emigrants who could not wait to see the back of their hated land. The hooters sounded, and sailors fought to raise the companionway. Men, women and children were roughly pushed aside. Some fell into the filthy water and scrambled to the dockside for safety. Others simply gave up the struggle and returned meekly to the quay. But Anna had not left her place. She would not risk Dmitri's life in the stampede. She rose and moved away from the quayside, along with many others who now accepted their lifelong sentence to hate and oppression. Sasha viewed their abdication and wept for them. The ship set sail from the harbour, orchestrated by the sound of the approaching guns, his country's disgusted farewell to its many traitors. May you all rot and sink, the guns seemed to say. But not one of the passengers regarded his sailing as a triumph, for though safe now for a while, their hearts were still with their tormented motherland.

PART FIVE

15

When Anna turned away from the quayside in Odessa, she turned her back on hope. She felt utterly defeated, and her decision to return to Petrograd simply confirmed that she was on the losing side. But she would not give way to despair. She scratched in her mind for the bonuses that could be reaped from her return to the capital. Katya and Ivan were there and she could stay with them until she found work and then she would rent her own apartment. For though she loved Katya dearly, she had never ceased to be uncomfortable with Ivan, who despite everything, still considered her an enemy. Perhaps he had mellowed a little. Andrei had told her that Katya had had another child, a little boy called Viktor. His name commemorated the triumph of the Revolution. Viktor and Dmitri could play together. But the strongest pull of the Volynins was their link with Sasha, and concerning Sasha, Anna would never give up hope. Now she refused to believe that he was dead, and she berated herself for once having given credence to such a thought. She would go back to Petrograd and wait for him. One day he would come home.

But Russia had ceased to be home for Sasha. Home was where Anna was and his son, and Andrei had made it clear that she had left the country. He would find her. Wherever she might be.

The Odessa steamer docked at Hamburg, and from there Sasha made his way to Berlin. The year was 1920 and Sasha was as old as the century. Post-war Berlin was making up for the war years with the vengeance of the defeated. Berlin was a pocket of out-and-out hedonism. Bars, cabarets, and clubs proliferated. Cabaret was daring, satiric, and performed by artists of unspecified gender. It was in one such nightclub that Sasha found work. He was responsible for raising and lowering the curtain between one grotesque act and another. At first his German was threadbare, but his curtain job required no linguistic skills. Every night he sat on his stool, his hands on the pulleys and said not a word. Occasionally an artist would smile at him but that was the limit of the communication. He felt isolated and desperately homesick. He wished he could find Russian émigrés like himself. Even if politically they were unsympathetic, at least they would have a language in common, and it was the language that he missed most of all. As a result, he talked much to himself, and was finally driven to start putting his thoughts to paper. Sometimes he despaired of ever seeing Anna again. The world was too large for his pursuit and her possible whereabouts too infinite. To sit and write in their common language was a way of talking to her, of being by her side. In this way, he began his novel, that story that had seeded on his first sight of Ranjevsky. As he wrote it he relived every moment of his conscription into that ragged White regiment. His style of writing was thus immediate, and its effect was direct and powerful. Although he had suffered at Ranjevsky's hands, he had often enjoyed his company, relished his wit, gasped at his blasphemies, and admired his fatherliness to his men. And though he told the whole truth of the man's cruelty, he could not help but draw a sympathetic character. Because he stressed that the leaders of the Red Army were no better and no worse than he. He told of Ranjevsky's raids on villages, and the slaughter that they left behind. But he told too of those villages where the Reds had left their visiting cards, and of the same bloody and body-filled trenches in their wake. The strength of his story lay in its lack of ultimate blame, for both sides were as guilty as each other. It proclaimed that only the victims were innocent, and it rang with a plea for forgiveness and remembrance. Every day in his lodgings, in the hours before he went curtain raising, Sasha eased his nostalgia, and after many years of daylight writing, the book was complete. He gave it the title of *The Banner Falls*, and he dedicated it as he had promised, to Pyotr. Pyotr would never be able to read it, but it would be told to him as Sasha had told him his poems, and he, who had known the pain and seen the blood of both sides, would understand it better than anybody.

He parcelled the book and sent it to a leading German publisher. The house had already published a German translation of his poems, so he knew that his name would not be unknown to them. Now all he could do was to wait for their response. For the next few weeks he sat on his nightly stool and raised and lowered the curtain and received and offered the occasional smile. One night he surprised himself by thinking of Anna, and he realised that it was the first time he had done so in many months. His obsession with Ranjevsky had pushed all thought of her from his mind. Ivan and Yakovlev had told him that work would make him forget. He had never believed them, but now he had to acknowledge their truth. His neglect of Anna appalled him. He could not even remember what she looked like. He recalled scenes of their past, both in Larionovka and Petrograd, but her face was fleeting and featureless, as unknown as the son he had never seen. But what saddened him even more, was the realisation that his appetite to find her had waned, and that, unaware of himself, he had taken Ivan's advice to forget her. But he balked at that. He knew that he could love again but never in the same way that he had loved Anna. And with that thought, a small spark of Anna need returned. He would leave Berlin, he decided, as soon as he heard from the publishing house. He would go to Paris. Paris was known to be riddled with Russian émigrés. Perhaps one of them had news of Anna. It was a long shot, but it would at least put him on the trail once more.

For the next few days he thought of nothing but Anna and of his resumed search. Until the letter came from the publishing house, and Anna was once more forgotten. The letter was one of delighted acceptance and of overwhelming praise. It invited Sasha to a celebration dinner.

Sasha begged leave for one night from the cabaret. He hoped perhaps that his career as curtain-raiser had finally come to an end. Hopes that were confirmed at the dinner. One of the publishers spoke Russian, and Sasha's ear watered at the sound. He told him that the book would be published both in Russian and German. 'I think your countrymen will find it very interesting,' he said.

Then Sasha thought of Anna. The book might be a way of reaching her.

The next day, Sasha handed in his notice at the nightclub. On the advance that the publishers had given him, he could afford to give up work for a while. And to buy himself some much-needed clothing. He could even travel. But he would cool his heels in Berlin until the book was published.

But after a few days of idleness, he found himself missing the nightclub. On the stroke of midnight, his hand would pull in Pavlovian response to the chimes. He missed the laughter backstage and the occasional smile. So he went back to the club and asked for reinstatement.

They welcomed him back. One of the dancers especially, Heidi, who was a woman both on and off the stage. She offered to help him improve his German but Sasha sensed that their connection would not require language. Nevertheless, he expressed himself grateful for the offering, and every evening, before curtain up, she gave him lessons in her dressing-room. And more than lessons in language. Sasha knew that he was not in love with Heidi, nor ever would be. But he was hungry for loving, and he welcomed her warmth and comfort. In those days he dared not think of Anna at all, lest such thoughts would hint at betrayal.

He stayed with Heidi, under cover of lessons, until his book was published. And he let her share his acclaim. For he was lauded on all sides. Overnight he became famous, but he still insisted on raising and lowering the curtain. Until word came calling him to Paris for the publication of the French version of *The Banner Falls*. Heidi begged to go with him, but he knew that such a relationship would not travel well. Heidi belonged to her dressing-room and her elements of German grammar. She had taught him a vocabulary that was not all that useful in the marketplace, but would stand him in good stead as a man of the world. Sasha left Berlin in the New Year of 1924, a few days after his birthday, and took himself to Paris.

And bound for the same destination, but departing from Moscow, Andrei Larionov, sent on a trade mission by the Internal Affairs Ministry. Since Sasha had left Russia, there had been no contact between the two men. It had been Sasha's failing. Andrei's whereabouts were known to him and it was in his court to make contact. After all, it was possible that Andrei had news of Anna. But it was for this very reason that he had neglected contact. In his Berlin curtain-raising days, he could not afford Anna obsession. In any case, Heidi had somewhat diluted it. And besides there was his writing. He had to finish his novel before he could afford an Anna thought. And then his success had overtaken any other consideration, culminating in the invitation to Paris for publication. But now, on the train to the French capital, Heidi-less, and with no book-obsession, he dared to indulge in Anna thoughts. He decided that he would write to Andrei for news, and then he would continue his Anna search.

On arrival in Paris, he was met by his publisher and taken to a hotel. Monsieur Grillet was effusive in his welcome. 'All literary Paris is talking of your novel,' he said. 'And we don't publish until tomorrow. But the grapevine is quivering with excitement. Now you must rest, and this evening, I will call for you for dinner. You may bring a guest if you wish.'

'I know no one in Paris,' Sasha said.

'But I think there is someone here who knows you,' Grillet said.

'Who is that?' Sasha asked, excited.

'Let it remain a mystery. A surprise perhaps. But you must wait. You will have to learn patience.'

But Sasha needed no lessons in patience. All his young life he had waited. He had waited for the war to be over. He had waited for his freedom. But above all, he had waited for Anna. And once having found her, he had lost her, and had been patient in his search. And would be patient again, until he found her.

'I shall be patient,' he said.

When Grillet had gone, Sasha would not allow himself to ponder on the surprise that his publisher had promised. So he busied himself with his unpacking, and thought of how he should write to Andrei. Then he dwelt on the possibilities of his returning to Russia and such thoughts excited him. He revisited Larionovka and the fields of his boyhood. And so absorbed was he in his nostalgia that when a knock sounded on his door, he responded in Russian as if he had never set foot outside his village. He turned to face the door. He expected a maid perhaps, or a valet, and he quickly smoothed his hair to make himself presentable. He felt disorientated, still rooted in Larionovka yet surrounded by paraphernalia so alien to his village. But when he saw the figure at the door, he was once again joyfully at home.

'Andrushka!' he cried.

'Sashenka!'

The two men embraced. Both bewildered. And both spoke at once, pelting each other with 'Whys?' and 'Hows?' and the beginnings of ragged explanations.

Then laughing, Sasha said, 'Enough. One at a time.' Then the question that had lingered for so many years on his tongue, had to declare itself: 'Is there any news of Anna?' It was hardly a question, for he expected a negative response. It was almost a formality to ask it, as if, once expressed, they were free to talk of other things. So that, when Andrei smiled and said, 'Good news, Sasha,' Sasha had to sit down and calm himself, so unexpected was the reply. Andrei knelt by his side. 'She's in Petrograd,' he said. 'And well. So is Dmitri. She has learned to drive a tram. That's how she earns a living. She lives with Ivan and Katya.' Sasha fell into his arms. His weeping was uncontrollable. Those tears that he had stored for years, stemmed from time to time by Heidi or his work, now claimed their release, and Sasha did not deny them. But one more question insisted, and through his sobs he whispered, 'Does she think I am dead?'

'No,' Andrei said. 'She knows you're alive. She has proof, I gave it to her. Copies of your book have been smuggled into Russia. A friend gave me one. I took it straight to Petrograd.'

'What did she say?'

'She cried, like you're crying now.'

'Does she still love me, Andrushka?'

'As you love her,' Andrei said.

'Then I must go home,' Sasha said. 'Whether I shall be safe there or not.'

'You take a risk,' Andrei said. 'But in Russia we all live at risk. Even Ivan.'

Sasha did not want to talk about his brother. Ivan had lied to him about Anna. He was responsible for the death of some of his friends. And he knew he could not look to him for protection. 'I'll take my chances,' Sasha said. 'When do you leave?'

'I'm here for a few weeks,' Andrei said. 'I have work here. And Nicolai is in Paris. I want to see him. Even if he doesn't want to see me. I have to tell him that our mother has died.'

'Andrei, I'm so sorry.'

'It was a blessing. She had been broken for a long time. I brought her home from the hospital, and Anna came to Moscow. We were both with her when she died. We have mourned enough, Sasha. All of us. And now we have something to celebrate. Your book, your fame. And your reunion with Anna.' He took a bottle of vodka from his attaché case. 'I came prepared,' he laughed. 'In any case, I must prepare myself for the literary lions of Paris. I have been invited to your dinner and I am terrified.'

'How did you know my publisher?'

'When I got your book in Moscow, I rang your publishers in Berlin. They told me you had gone to Paris, and the name of your publisher. So when I arrived, I went straight to Monsieur Grillet. And the rest is history,' he laughed, then downed more vodka to give himself courage for the evening's entertainment.

That evening, and in the weeks that followed, Sasha became the toast of Paris. But he was hardly touched by his success, so anxious was he to return to Petrograd. He could think of nothing but his reunion with Anna. But he had obligations to fulfil in Paris, and besides, he would wait until Andrei's business was done.

Andrei was wary of his meeting with Nicolai. It was many years since they had spoken to each other, and those words had been angry and full of hatred. But Andrei had never been able to hate his brother. In spite of their political differences, Andrei saw no reason that they should impinge on a very natural affection. He loved Nicolai for the big and wonderful brother he had been to him in his childhood. He had worshipped him as a hero and his war wounds had broken his young heart. He understood his brother's frustrations and his sorry political allegiance, but he ascribed it to his bitterness, and forgave him. He looked forward to seeing him, though he was wary of his reception. He did not know where Nicolai lived in Paris, but he knew where he could be found.

The Imperial in Montmartre was a nightclub, and a refuge and pleasant haven for White Russian émigrés. The décor and the ambience of the club were replicas of what once had been available in the homeland in the good old Tsarist days. Even the doorman wore a uniform of an officer in the Tsar's personal guard, and he saluted Andrei as he entered the club to welcome him into their exiled fraternity. The club was dimly lit and crowded. A balalaika ensemble was playing on a raised platform, and a singer accompanied their folk music.

Andrei sat himself at a corner table from which point he could view the whole restaurant in the hope of spotting Nicolai. He scanned the menu. It was exclusively Russian fare. He ordered vodka, blinis and caviare, and settled back in his seat, feeling anything but at home. But he masked his contempt with a fixed smile on his face, so that no one could assume he was not one of them. He looked around the room. There was no sign of Nicolai, but he was not disappointed for it was still early.

But one face amongst the gathering caught his eye. The man was sitting alone. He was neither eating nor drinking. Like Andrei, he seemed in the business of waiting. And like Andrei, he had a fixed smile on his face, that seemed to Andrei as much a mask as his own. His face was familiar, and Andrei stared at him trying to recall where he had seen it before. And then in a flash he remembered, and identified him with a shiver of fear. Ivan's friend and colleague from Petrograd, whom he had once met in Ivan's apartment. He couldn't remember the man's name. It is possible that he had never been given it, but there could be no doubt about the man's business in this place, and the Cheka identity card in his pocket, or the OGPU as it was now called. Andrei began to fear for Nicolai. It was true that everyone in the nightclub was a candidate for OGPU surveillance, but Nicolai was especially marked. His escape from prison had been of particular embarrassment to the Cheka and the fact that he had not been pursued embittered many of its officers. Andrei prayed that this man at the table was not one of them. He kept his eye on him, and he half hoped that

Nicolai would not arrive. But shortly he saw him at the door of the club, with the faithful Fedya in tow.

Andrei was astonished at the change in Nicolai. He seemed to have aged greatly, though he was still handsome and bore the same proud military air. He wanted to run to embrace him, and quietly turn him away from this place and its possible peril. But he was nervous of his reception, which, if unfriendly, would only serve to draw attention to Nicolai as a possible target. So he waited until Nicolai was shown a table, and had settled himself down with vodka. Andrei noted how Fedya scanned the restaurant before taking his own seat, and how he sat opposite Nicolai, masking him from others' view. In front of Fedya was a mirror – the table was carefully chosen – and through it Fedya could observe the comings and goings, even though ostensibly off guard.

Andrei gave Nicolai time to order his meal, and then, trembling, he walked across to his table. Fedya saw him first, through the mirror, and whispering, warned Nicolai of their visitor. Nicolai looked up, surprised. But Andrei noticed there was no hint of pleasure on his face.

'Nicolai,' he said, stretching out his hand.

'What do you want?' his brother said coldly. 'Has your scum of a boss sent you to bring me home?'

'Nicolai,' Andrei said again, helplessly. 'It's so long since we saw each other. I'm in Paris on a trade mission. I just wanted to see you.' He wished they would ask him to sit down. His spine tingled and he felt like a target. He eyed the OGPU man through the mirror, but he seemed intent on his food. 'I have news from home,' he pleaded. It was as if he were begging an audience.

'Just give me the news, and then go,' Nicolai said. 'You betrayed our cause, and I have nothing to say to you.'

'If that's how you want it,' Andrei said. He was furious at his brother's dismissal. He would give him the news all right. He would punish him with it. 'Anna has a child. The father is Sasha Volynin. They've called him Dmitri, after our father.' That for starters.

Nicolai paled. He was trembling with rage. 'The name of Larionov is shamed for ever,' he said. 'A curse on her, and you too,

215

and all of your friends who have sullied our house. Get out of here! I never want to see you again.'

'And Mother is dead,' Andrei said savagely. 'She died in Anna's arms.' He hated himself for being so cruel. He held out his hands towards his brother, in the hope that, in their common grief, they might touch one another.

But, 'You killed her,' was Nicolai's only response. 'You and your kind.' Then he broke into sobs. Fedya touched his arm, but Nicolai withdrew. He was untouchable. Broken. He rose slowly from the table. In seconds he had become an old man.

Andrei's heart softened. 'We have to stay together, Nicolai,' he said. 'We have to love each other as a family.'

Nicolai turned, enraged. What Andrei had said was like a slap in the face. 'Fedya is more of a brother to me,' he said.

He made for the door, allowing Fedya to take his arm. Andrei looked after them. He was deeply saddened by the encounter. Despite everything, he loved his brother, and for the sake of his love, could well have joined him in Paris, and like him, become an émigré. For unlike Ivan, Nicolai and Andrei knew that it was family that finally mattered. Family was the true meaning of history, and the most enduring. And to ignore it was to nullify all the progress that the world had ever made. He was tempted to go after his brother, but he knew it would be futile. Perhaps when time had passed, he would try again.

Nicolai and Fedya had reached the door. As it opened, Andrei saw the doorman and his brother exchange Tsarist salutes. And then the door closed behind them. He sat down in Fedya's place at his brother's table, and downed the vodka that Nicolai had left in his glass. That sad uninvited sharing was the closest he could come to a family reunion.

But he did not sit for long. Through the mirror, he saw the OGPU man rise from his table, and an arrow of fear and foreboding pierced his heart. The man's departure was too nicely timed after Nicolai's. Andrei waited for him to turn his back, then quickly followed him out of the club. He noted the Tsarist salute he gave the club's doorman. Part of his training no doubt. Andrei followed him into the street, and to his horror he saw Nicolai and Fedya

216

waiting on the corner, presumably for a cab. He watched the man slip his hand into his side pocket and bring out a pistol. Andrei could not move, and he actually watched as the man levelled his gun in his brother's direction. He knew he had to do something. He desperately wished he knew the man's name. Then suddenly inspired he yelled across the street, 'Ivan Volynin!' In Russia it was a name that could strike terror in people's hearts, and their fleeing feet would falter in its echo. The man turned round suddenly, astonished, and slipped the gun into his outside pocket. Clearly the Volynin terror travelled well. Andrei lurched over towards him assuming a drunken gait.

'Do you not remember me, comrade?' he shouted. 'I'm a friend of Ivan's. We met at his party.'

By now he had reached the man, and he embraced him in a bearlike hug using his assumed drunkenness as a cover for his familiarity. In the course of the hug, Andrei slipped his hand into the man's pocket, and pressed the gun into his stomach. He had no words for him, nor did he pause to wonder what he should say. He needed no words for what he had to do, and he had to do it quickly. Neither did he dare think about it. Only the fleeting thought of saving his brother's life crossed his mind. Then he pulled the trigger. It was all over in seconds. The man slumped in his embrace. He dropped him gently onto the paving stones, and noted the look of abject astonishment in the man's dead and staring eyes. Then he turned and ran. Hearing the shot, a few people had gathered outside the club, but otherwise the street was empty. No doubt they would examine the corpse, discover its identity, and return to their tables to give a toast to the righteous demise of an enemy of the Tsar. And that would be the end of the story. The French police would dispose of the body and make no further investigation. A blanket of silence would cover their discovery, in order to safeguard the tourist trade and those thousands of White Russians who had found in Paris a haven and a refuge. Moscow too would share in that conspiracy of silence, for they would not want it known that their agents were on missions abroad. So Andrei did not fear arrest. His present concern was to reach his hotel room

217

without drawing too much attention to his blood-soaked jacket and shirt.

There were mercifully few people in the hotel foyer, and he had the lift to himself. Once in his room, he stripped and bathed, then naked, he sat on his bed, and realised exactly what he had done. Never in his life had he killed a man, and he was glad he'd been given no time to think about it. All he knew was that his brother was in the pistol's sights, and he had to divert the man's arm. Without doubt he had saved his brother's life, but that gave him little consolation with the thought of the possible widow and orphans he had made in Moscow. And not only the widow and her children, but possibly the man's mother as well, and his heart ached at the thought. He would tell nobody what he had done, not even Pavel. He was too ashamed to tell it even to himself. He knew he must leave Paris quickly, but he had promised to wait for Sasha, and Sasha still had his publishing obligations to fulfil. He would go with him, he decided, to his lunches and his dinners, and his signings. He needed company. He was afraid of being alone.

The week passed slowly. No word of the killing appeared in the papers and Andrei was tempted to go to the Imperial once more in a last attempt at a reconciliation with his brother. But he decided against it. After the killing Nicolai would probably give the club a wide berth, and the location for both of them was fraught with danger. So he waited impatiently until Sasha was free to leave.

Then one morning, a few days after the killing, Andrei received an urgent message to contact his Ministry in Moscow. He phoned immediately. The date was 21 January 1924, a day that for ever would be one of mourning for his homeland. The message from the Ministry was terse. 'Comrade Lenin died this morning. He is to be buried in Red Square in Moscow. Your presence is requested.'

Sasha and Andrei left Paris by the night train. By now the news was known, but until they reached the Russian border they heard no talk of it, as if Lenin's death was somebody else's bereavement. At the border the train stopped to take on water, and it was in the small waiting-room at that frontier station that Sasha and Andrei saw their first confirmation that the leader was no more. A large framed portrait of Lenin hung on the wall and around it was draped a black mournful flag.

'Are you sad?' Sasha asked Andrei.

'No,' Andrei said. 'I do not feel it as a personal loss.'

'Neither do I,' Sasha whispered. Then he knew for certain that they were close to home. The whispering had begun.

16

The train drew into Moscow station early in the morning. Lenin's interment was to take place at two o'clock. Andrei would have time for his preparations. He parted fondly with Sasha. 'I shall come to Petrograd for your wedding,' he said.

Throughout the rest of the journey, Sasha pondered on Andrei's farewell. For the first time he realised that he and Anna were not married. He had never thought of her as other than a wife, and now the mother of their child. He grew excited at the prospect of a ceremony. In his mind he drew up a guest list. Pyotr and Nina would come with their children from Larionovka, and perhaps Avdotya would come too. Then sadly he listed those from his village who would not rejoice in his wedding – his parents, his childhood friends and all those who had perished for or against the Cause. Andrei would come from Moscow, and would alas be the sole representative of Anna's family. But Katya would come, and Ivan and their children. What was left of both their families would assemble in joy.

The journey to Petrograd seemed endless, prolonged by his excitement. He tried to remember what Anna looked like, and to imagine the face of his son. But Heidi's was the only face that presented itself to him with a semblance of clarity. He remembered her with affection but she belonged to another life and another country altogether. She symbolised everything that was alien, but now he was going home.

When the train at last drew into the station, he remained in his seat. He watched all the other passengers alight and he did not move until the guard ordered him out of the carriage. He was suddenly nervous of this meeting. For so long and so often he had imagined it, it had become fixed in his mind as a daydream, and as such he had accepted it and even found it comfortable. But he never imagined that one day he would face its reality. He wanted to postpone the meeting, to give himself time for its preparation. But at the same time he had no idea how to make himself ready. From what Andrei had told him, Anna would be at work on the trams, so there was little point in going to Ivan's house. He would wander around the city, he decided, and try and calm himself.

He found himself passing his old publishing house. He thought sadly of Yakovlev and inevitably of Ivan's cruelty. He was wary of his meeting with his brother. Ivan had lied to him, and had betrayed his friends. And all in the name of the Party. He had to remind himself that Ivan was his brother, and that that relationship, and that relationship alone, dictated their loving. With Pyotr it was all so simple. He longed to see him, to give him his novel, to show him its loving dedication. He would give it to him at his wedding. And then he thought of Anna, and he made a quick detour through the back alleys of the city to avoid the trams. When he came once more to the unavoidable intersection of the main streets, he heard the cathedral clock strike the hour. Two solemn and ringing tones. And then the city suddenly fell silent. The trams stopped, and so did all the people. Many of them, Sasha noticed, were weeping, as they were across the whole country, and in that same silence of mourning, their leader was laid to rest. Then after a few minutes of memorial, the strains of the Internationale were heard amongst the crowd. At first, timorously and with infinite respect. Then slowly the choir of voices swelled and across the whole city were heard those words of hope and love. Sasha joined in with the singing. He believed in the words well enough. The words themselves in their pristine purity. But so often they were twisted to suit spurious ends, so that they came to mean the very oppposite of their intent. But his heart found some joy in the singing, in the community of hope for the future. When it was over, the people moved, and the trams went on their grooved way, as if in continuity after freeze-frame. Petrograd was going about its business, or rather Leningrad as it was henceforth to be called. That benighted city, that in its time had suffered many a change of name, now trembled in awe of its latest baptism.

He walked through the main streets. He did not look at the trams. He did not want to sight Anna accidentally. He needed a prepared meeting. So he decided to make his way to the tram depot. He had no idea of her shift hours, but eventually she would have to come off duty. He would wait for her there.

He did not have to wait long, for Anna had been at work since early morning. He watched every tram as it came into dock. He noticed that almost all the drivers were women. He looked at each one carefully. He knew that after so many years he had to allow for a change in Anna's appearance. Age would have altered her, together with motherhood. But even given the years and maturity, none of the women bore any resemblance to Anna. All of them looked surly and glum. Perhaps their looks could be ascribed to their loss of leader, Sasha thought, but it seemed that their discontent was not sudden. It was engrained in their features, etched deep in time. They contrasted almost offensively with the innate gaiety of their sisters in Paris or Berlin. He hoped that Anna had not been infected by their suffering. He smiled at some of them, simply to test their ability to respond, but they glowered at him with suspicion and mistrust. He prayed that Anna was not like them.

When the next tram docked there was no mistaking her. Sasha had the advantage, that he could view her without being seen. He felt that he was cheating, but there was no way he could give her equal advantage. From his standpoint he viewed her, feasting almost, not so much on her beauty, which was evident enough, but on the joy of having found her. Feasting on that joy, and the loss too of so many years. He wondered whether he should call her name. Or whether he should simply approach her. Both would take her by unfair surprise. So he waited, placing himself more openly, so that she could see him first, wonder at him, doubt him, wonder again, and then be reassured. He looked away from her, so that he would not be staring when she first discovered him. That would give her a small edge. He first looked at the sky, darkened with clouds, and then at the other trams and the other people, all 'otherness' giving her time to spot him. Then he felt her beside him, and heard her voice.

'Sasha?' she whispered.

He turned, startled, as if seeing her for the first time.

'Anna,' he said.

They stared at each other. Without touching.

'Sashenka?' she said again.

'Anna.'

The names were enough. And their repetition. The names bonded, confirming the love that had been between them. Confirming that love's endurance. To the exclusion of all others. Their names echoed between them. Then he touched her on the sleeve. 'We shall never again be parted.' He folded her in his arms, and held her for a long while, while the other women stopped and stared, and muttered with disdain, as if joy were illegal, especially on such an auspicious day. Sasha ignored them, holding Anna close. Bugger Lenin, he thought. People would endure far longer than Party.

The tram depot emptied as he held her.

'I'll take you to Dmitri,' she whispered.

He had not yet kissed her, and yet in that long embrace he had kissed her whole body. She wriggled out of his hold and looked at him. 'No more partings,' she said. She took his arm. 'I'm living at Katya and Ivan's. Katya looks after Dmitri while I work. She has little Viktor too.'

'I know. What's happened to Vassily?' He wanted a subject other than Ivan. That encounter would come later, and he hoped it would be a private one.

'Vassily finishes school this year. He's nearly eighteen. Then he'll work for the Party.'

'Like father, like son,' Sasha said.

'They quarrel a lot,' Anna said. 'I think little Viktor will be like Katya.'

'How are they? Together, I mean.'

'You will see,' Anna said. 'No woman can compete with the Party.'

Then he kissed her for the first time. It was his assurance that she would never have to suffer that competition.

They walked the streets slowly, arm in arm. Neither felt a stranger to the other. It was as if they had never been parted.

'Will Ivan be at home?' Sasha had to ask.

'No. He comes home late. But today may be different. There is a half-holiday for the funeral.'

'The OGPU never take holidays,' Sasha laughed.

'Well, if they do,' Anna said, 'it's not to spend them with their families.'

'Tell me about Dmitri,' Sasha said. 'From the beginning. I want to know everything.'

'First you shall see him. And then you will know,' she said.

He grew excited. He prayed that Ivan would not be at home.

Although there was a holiday, Ivan was not taking advantage of it. He sat at his desk, brooding. He had had a terrible day. Apart from his overall sadness at Lenin's death – Ivan took it as a personal loss – he had had problems with Svoboda, his superior. Svoboda had called him into his office that morning, and thrown the book at him. His brother's book. *The Banner Falls.*

'Have you seen this?' he shouted.

Ivan knew what it was. He'd heard of it, through the underground. Copies were confiscated if they were found, and their owners severely punished.

'Your brother's work, I think,' Svoboda said. 'This doesn't help your reputation, Volynin.'

'My brother is a true member of the Revolution,' Ivan protested, swearing to himself that if ever he saw him again, he would kill him.

'I respect your loyalty,' Svoboda said, 'so long as it doesn't preempt the greater loyalty you owe to the Party. You must choose your associates very carefully. I thought I'd better warn you.'

The interview had humiliated Ivan and outraged him. He sat at his desk, his anger curdling. Then shortly afterwards, he was called once again to Svoboda's office. He was convinced that this was the end of his career. He began to wonder what he could do. His whole life was the Party. He was unwilling and unfit for anything else.

But when he returned to Svoboda's office, trembling for his future, he noted that there were other officers there, and there was a measure of relief in that, for if he were to be dismissed, it would be in a private meeting. The atmosphere in the room was solemn. Svoboda's face was ashen. Far paler than was warranted by Lenin's death or the discovery of yet another copy of Sasha's book. He asked the officers to be seated.

'I have had serious news from Paris,' he said. 'Yugov, our agent there, has been assassinated. Outside the Café Imperial. Well, we all know what kind of sewer that is. Yugov's mission was to track down Nicolai Larionov, who, you may remember, escaped from the prison some years ago, the night before his scheduled execution.'

Ivan trembled. That name again. That cursed name, that had so audaciously woven itself into his whole family. Although he avoided his eye, he was sure that Svoboda was staring at him.

'No investigation will be made. The French authorities are happy to say no more about it. I adjure each one of you to total and absolute silence on this matter. His widow, who lives in Paris, will be compensated, of course, together with her children. But his name must never be mentioned again. It must be as if he never was. Let it be a lesson to you all. All agents are expendable. You may go now.'

The men rose. No one said a word. Except Svoboda. 'Volynin, could you stay a moment?'

Now is the time, Ivan thought, and he trembled.

Svoboda waited until the door had closed on the last of the officers. Then he said, 'I think you have some connection with the Larionovs. Is that not so?'

'I was born in Larionovka. It's my village.' He offered the least and most innocent connection.

'I think there is more to it than that,' Svoboda said. 'That's all I wanted to say. Think about it.' Ivan returned to his office, cursing the whole of the Larionov tribe. Even Andrei who had served him so well. And Anna. He must get rid of her. She must find her own apartment. And quickly; Katya was getting much too friendly with her. It had not been a good day for Ivan and God help his family, and especially his lodger, when he got home.

But he was mercifully not there when Sasha and Anna arrived.

'Katya,' Anna called, as she put her key in the door. 'Mitya all right?'

'Fine,' Katya called. 'You're late.'

'I have a reason,' Anna said. 'Come and see.'

Katya came quickly into the hall. 'Sashenka,' she cried. She fell on his neck, weeping. Sasha was surprised by her welcome and faintly disturbed by its intensity. But Katya was clinging to her past, to an Ivan that had once been a Volynin like Sasha, but who now was a nonperson, without traits, without lineage. 'I knew you'd come home, Sasha,' she said.

He cradled her face and kissed her. She had aged, he thought, sadness had etched lines onto her face, and her eyes were large with bewilderment. She would have been happier with Pyotr, he thought.

'Come, see the children,' she said.

She led the way into the living-room. Sasha noted the expensive furnishings of the apartment, and its spaciousness. Ivan must have been promoted in the OGPU.

'We have our own bathroom,' Katya was saying. It seemed from her tone that the private bathroom was the only advantage she had reaped from her marriage. 'Mitya,' she called, 'look who is here.'

There were two children on the floor, building a house of wooden bricks. One of them looked up, and Sasha knew at once that it was his son.

'Mama,' he cried, and ran into Anna's arms.

'And this is Viktor,' Katya said. She picked him up and presented him to Sasha. 'This is your Uncle Sasha.'

Sasha kissed him quickly, for his attention was on his son. He took his little hand. The child smiled.

'This is your Papa,' Anna said.

And immediately the little hand was withdrawn, together with the smile. And he started to cry, nestling his mother's shoulder, then gripping her cheek with his hand, unwilling to share her with another. Or perhaps, from his daily acquaintance with Ivan, he knew what fathers were, and in his six lean years, had decided that he was better off without one.

'He'll have to get used to you,' Katya said. 'Come, let's eat, and drink, and celebrate. Lenin is dead, but Alexander Volynin lives.' She was desperate for celebration.

Sasha laughed. 'Sasha's good enough for me,' he said.

'But you're famous now,' Katya said. 'And dangerous.' Her tone was suddenly flirtatious.

'He's never going to leave us again,' Anna said. That was her verdict, come what may. 'Take Mitya, Sasha,' she said. 'And Viktor. Play with them. I'll help Katya.'

As the day wore on, all tension eased. The children played happily with Sasha, and they listened wide-eyed to his stories. They ate and drank and laughed and joked, and at times they had to control their merriment lest the neighbours, mindful of the auspicious day, construed it as a mark of disrespect. But as the evening drew in, Sasha noticed a change in Katya. Her face was lined, but no longer with laughter. She suddenly had a fit of tidying the apartment, clearing the dishes, hushing the children, clearly fearful of Ivan's impending return. By the time they heard his key in the lock, all laughter had faded, and the children were silent on the floor. Ivan did not call out as he came into the apartment. He did not feel the need to announce himself. He walked straight into the living-room and at once picked out the alien figure.

'Ivan,' Sasha said, and went to embrace him. He was glad to see his brother, and saw no point any more in rancour.

Had it been on any other day, Ivan would have welcomed his brother, for in his heart there was still enough affection to overcome his Party priority. But today had been a bad day, and in every piece of bad news his brother had been implicated. So he refused Sasha's embrace. 'So you've come home,' was all he could say. And a handshake was all he would offer.

Anna was appalled. And so was Katya. But both were afraid to make any comment. Sasha was in despair.

'We're brothers,' he whispered.

'That does not protect you,' Ivan said. 'And never shall.' He turned on Katya. 'It's late,' he said. 'Why isn't Viktor in bed?'

Katya was glad of an excuse to leave the room. And Anna with her. They picked up their children and took them to their rooms.

Now the two brothers were alone. Sasha tried to be calm. 'Tomorrow Anna and I will find an apartment. I know I am an embarrassment to you,' he said.

'If you would only join the Party, you'd be safe.'

'I've told you before. Writers don't join parties.'

'Your book is causing trouble for me. So is your Larionov connection.'

'Listen, Ivan,' Sasha tried to be patient, 'there is nothing I can do about either. You have to accept that your brother is a writer and that he is going to marry Anna Larionova.'

'And in both you are a traitor,' Ivan said.

'What about Andrei Larionova? Is he a traitor too?'

'Not yet,' Ivan said.

'You trust nobody, do you?' Sasha said sadly.

'In my job, I can't afford to.'

'What kind of life is it that you live, Ivan?' Sasha said gently. 'A life without trust, without relationships, without concern for family?'

'That's my way, Sasha,' he said. 'We're different.'

'But we're brothers. You lied to me about Anna. You told me she was dead. You made Andrei lie too. You took my publisher and you shot him. All in the name of the Party. But I forgive you. Because finally you are my brother.'

'Does Nicolai forgive Andrei?' Ivan asked.

'But you're not like Nicolai, Ivan, you have a heart. Or you had one, in Larionovka, when you were my big brother.'

Sasha went to embrace him, and Ivan did not resist. But neither did he respond. Between them lay an uneasy truce. Perhaps that was all that either of them could hope for.

That night Sasha lay by Anna's side, and held her close until the morning light. When she rose early for her tram shift, he pulled her back into bed.

'You're not going to work any more,' he said. 'Today we will go out with Dmitri and find an apartment for ourselves.'

She held him close. Now she knew that he was really home.

'Will you marry me, Anna?' he whispered.

'Anna Volynina!' she cried. 'Yes, I think that will suit me very well.'

Within a week, Sasha and Anna had found their own home. Living space was scarce in Leningrad, but in a society of so-called equality, influence and money could open a few apartment doors. It's possible that the name 'Volynin' was of help, though Sasha was at pains not to stress it, for it could have fallen on the wrong ear. But it was possibly money that finally ensured them a home, and Sasha had no scruple making use of it, for it was money diligently and honestly earned.

Katya missed Anna terribly. Her life seemed empty without her. Over the years she had grown more and more distant from Ivan, or rather Ivan had distanced himself from her, so that she was stranded, unanchored, adrift. Although she still believed in the ideals of the Party, she had lost her enthusiasm. She had seen the price that Ivan had had to pay for principle, and she felt that for her it was too high. She was lonely. Vassily was grown and no longer needed her care. Moreover, he was sullen all the time. Although he worked with Ivan, he did not get on with him. Often he threatened to leave home altogether. She thanked God for little Viktor, who was company of a kind, but she longed for family, for friendship and for her village. She even longed for Pyotr and realised sadly how little she had valued him. She looked forward to Anna's wedding. Pyotr would be there, and so would Avdotya. They would bring with them the scents of Larionovka, and she could bask in them a while. At night she went to bed early, long before Ivan came home. And she slept alone. She blamed him for Anna's leaving and her own resultant loneliness. She felt that there was nothing left between them. Except for their history, and the children they had made together.

One night she waited up for him, and asked him directly if he was going to the wedding.

'It would not be in the interest of my job to be seen there,' he said.

Nowadays he spoke like a solicitor's letter, and a dictated one at that. The 'Ivan' in him that she had once known and loved no longer asserted itself. He had become a puppet of the Party.

'But Sasha's your brother,' she said. 'He wants you to be there. Pyotr will be there. He wants his whole family to be with him. Please come. For my sake, come.' Occasionally she pitied him, as she did now, and at such times, she loved him as she had done in the beginning.

He felt that love and responded at once. He too had moments when he remembered his past, and wondered where the flowers had gone. Thus they came together. For a time. Until the morning when the Party would reclaim him.

On the day of the wedding, Katya asked him again. He was on his way to the office as if it were just an ordinary day.

'I have a lot of work today,' he said. 'I'll come if I can get away.'

Then she knew that he would not be there. She was sorry as much for Sasha as she was for herself.

Most churches in Russia had been closed. In a society which propagated atheism, there was little room for God. But some small churches, mainly in the suburbs of the city, were overlooked, and those who still had the courage to believe sneaked through their open doors. It was in one such church that Anna and Sasha were to be married.

It was a muted ceremony, without the ritual of pre-Revolutionary times. But it was joyful. What was left of each family was assembled there. For Anna, there was Andrei, who had bravely brought Pavel, and for Sasha there was Pyotr, Nina and their children. But for each family there was one missing sibling. Nicolai Larionov and Ivan Volynin shared the only tactics they had in common. Their deliberate absence. But a very positive presence was that of Avdotya who stood in for the older generation, since both parties to the marriage were parentless. She was acutely mindful of her position, for to represent the Larionovs and the Volynins at one and the same time was no mean assignment. So she settled for that role to which she was, in her own right, entitled. That is, the carer of the milk-children. And in that role she wept most of the time. But wept joyfully.

Katya was crying too, but not with joy. She recalled her own wedding to Pyotr. Her only wedding, since Ivan, despite their two children, had never offered to marry her. He insisted that marriage

230

was bourgeois. She remembered the pomp and ceremony of her own nuptials, contrasting so acutely with this present union. And she remembered too how the milk-children had carried the satin cushions bearing the rings. Here there were no silks, or satins. Simply two rings in pockets, Pyotr's and Andrei's. And no marquee in a grand garden after the ceremony. Just a simple reunion in Sasha and Anna's new apartment. But oh, so much happier with the bride and groom secure in each other's love. She fought back feelings of envy and self-pity, and she wondered what would become of her. She picked up little Viktor and held him close. He was her only solace.

Sasha had appointed Pyotr as Master of Ceremonies, and the speech maker. It was an unlikely choice. Pyotr was illiterate and inarticulate, but Sasha knew of his buried feelings and his need to disinter them. Moreover he was shy, and he had to be coaxed to stand and propose the toast. Katya noticed how Nina encouraged him, how she helped him to his feet and whispered in his ear. How he smiled and blushed, and allowed himself to be coaxed to stand. Nina had made a man of Pyotr, Katya thought. She could never have done the same for Ivan. Ivan had been born a man. He had experienced no childhood from which to grow. He was fixed at birth. Stubborn, intransigent, unyielding. She wondered what would become of her.

Pyotr was standing, holding a glass in a trembling hand. 'Sash-enka has made me do this,' he said, 'and I'm not very good at it. But I want to do it. Because today I'm so happy.' The gathering applauded. Pyotr went on, encouraged. 'Sasha and Anna were childhood sweethearts,' he said. 'I remember when I used to look after the horses at the manor, they would come to the stables and play together. They used to make me sad, because I knew that they would have to drift apart. But I was wrong, which is why I am happy today.'

There was more applause. Pyotr grew more confident. 'Things have changed in Russia,' he said. 'And I think for the better. This marriage has brought two families together, which in the old days would have lived apart. But there are still some people who do not recognise the change. And that makes me sad. Anna's brother

Nicolai is not here. And neither is Sasha's brother Ivan. Perhaps we have to wait until their children will accept the change.' He raised his glass. 'Let us drink a toast to Sasha and Anna,' he said. Then he sat down exhausted, bewildered by all the words he was able to find, words locked in his heart for so many years, and his relief astonished him.

Sasha went over to embrace him, then lifted his glass for a second toast. 'I want to make a toast to Avdotya,' he said. Avdotya gave a little cry, as if suddenly accused. She didn't want to be central to anybody's attention. She was holding Dmitri on her knee, and she hid behind him. 'I want to toast Avdotya,' Sasha was saying, 'not just for herself, but for the symbol that she has become. The symbol of the older generation. Our parents. I want to toast her survival, and at the same time to toast their memory. For Avdotya was a bridge between both our families. She cared for Anna and myself when we were milk-children, and she brought my own son, Dmitri, into the world.' He raised his glass. 'To our dear Avdotya,' he said, 'the bringer of life, and to the memory of all those she survived.'

Avdotya hid her face in the back of Dmitri's jacket. It was all too much for her. All around they drank her health, and it was Katya who came to comfort her. For Katya shared her isolation and the desperate sadness of her memories.

But soon Avdotya cheered. Her presence, unlike Katya's, was full of contentment. Unlike Katya, she had weathered the changes and she could look back on a life of fulfilment, so that it was she who took Katya into her arms and comforted her, for she knew that her regrets were greater than her own.

Then it was Andrei's turn, as representative of that other family who had suffered the change. He gave a toast to simple loving, for that, as he said, was a state of no boundaries, indifferent to class and culture. And he might have added gender, for as he spoke he touched Pavel's arm, as if at last he was declaring himself. When the toasts were done with, they drank freely and with no specific target.

The day wore on while Katya still hoped that Ivan would put in an appearance. But it grew dark with her anger, and she left

232

early, unwilling to infect the company with her despair. Viktor was tired, she said, and she had to put him to bed. Anna embraced her when she left. 'I'm still your friend, Katya,' she said, 'and always will be.' It was a measure of comfort. Anna would remain her link with a past that she missed without knowing why.

So they all celebrated through the night, sleeping occasionally where they could. And in the morning came the leave-taking. Andrei and Pavel took the early train to Moscow, and Pyotr and Nina bundled Avdotya and the children into the carriage.

'Pyotr,' Sasha said, embracing him. 'Thank you for all your wonderful words. We will make a future together. All of us. A future of family and people.'

Pyotr waved to him from the carriage. Sasha looked after him with love. Their future was bound, he thought.

But he was never in his life to see Pyotr again.

17

Russia was about to enter one of the darkest periods of its history. And its sullied signature was Stalin. Or Koba, as he was called in his Siberian exile. But Stalin, his given name, was more fitting, its meaning, man of steel. Hard, punitive, unrelenting. During his reign of terror, which lasted from 1927 until his death in 1953, upwards of eight million people were sent to their deaths in purges and labour camps. The plan to collectivise farming claimed another three million, most of whom died in the resultant famine. Pyotr Volynin was one of these. And three others. His wife, Nina, and their two children.

Collectivisation was one of the early schemes of Stalin's regime. Its plan was to put an end to private farming. Peasants were to work together on state-owned land, in which they would have a share, and they would be paid according to their production. The scheme was initially voluntary, but too few peasants obliged. They were content enough with their smallholdings, which produced enough for their own mouths and those of their families. But this attitude was deemed non-Communist and they were forced to collectivise. Those who refused faced the barrel of a gun, or else were sent to labour camps where they would die anyway. They were men who were willing to die for their small plots of land, not for the vast and nebulous land of Russia, but for those holdings that fed their families. Pyotr Volynin was one of those, and doomed to pay the price of his dignity.

After the devastation of the civil war, the village of Larionovka had repaired itself. All scars had been erased, except those in men's hearts. The passing years had mended the houses and the church, tidied the graveyard and grown the rich brown soil. But they had done nothing to dilute the fear and mistrust of any uniform that walked their streets. So that one day when the soldiers' trucks rolled into Larionovka, disturbing the birdsong and the sound of spade in soil, the peasants downed their tools and cowered. Pyotr went on digging. But his two helpers, Anatoly and Fyodor, had slunk behind the shed at the approach of the trucks. Pyotr called to them.

'Come back,' he said. 'They're only soldiers.'

'Why are they here?' Anatoly shouted.

'They're passing through, I suppose,' Pyotr said.

'Then we'll wait till they've gone.'

Pyotr went over to where they hid, and he tried to reason with them, but they would not be persuaded. He saw Nina crossing the field with her basket of food for the men. 'Here's Nina with the food,' he said. They surely would come out of hiding for that. But they did not move.

'They're Red Army soldiers. They're friends,' Pyotr tried again.

'All soldiers are the same,' Fyodor said. 'Are they gone yet?'

'They've turned the corner,' Pyotr said. His voice was suddenly full of foreboding, for around that corner lay the village wealth, the storehouse for grain. The shed occupied the whole street. Except to call on the grainhouse, there was no other reason to enter it. He feared that what he had heard talked about on the village grapevine, collectivisation, had finally reached Larionovka. He was determined to hold on to his land, come what may.

'Go home, Nina,' he said. 'And take the food with you. I'll bring the men to the house. But first I must go to the grainstore.'

He set off over the field. Anatoly and Fyodor, having found a leader, took courage enough to follow him. But at a distance, in case a quick escape was called for. As he reached the road, Pyotr saw that all the trucks had turned into the alleyway, and that they were full of soldiers, with rifles at the ready. He trembled for his land and his family. He thought of Ivan. He would never want to use him for his own protection. Ivan's price was too high. Then he thought of Nina and the children and upbraided himself for his selfish thoughts. He had no right to foist his principles on others.

235

Nina would use Ivan's name, much as she disliked him, in order to save the children. And so he now realised, would he, for people were more important than principle. And the village too. The village had given enough. The Cause had filled its ditches with bodies, had unearthed the dead from their tombs, had fired the earth of its crops, and left every single dwelling with wounds unhealable. It was enough. There had never not been a Larionovka, and he would fight for its historic entitlement.

The whole village had followed the trucks to the grainstore. That shed was their lifeline, and they feared its theft. For in the whole village, because of their past experience, there was no trust in uniform of whatever colour. Pyotr arrived at the shed as the last truck turned into the alleyway. At the doors of the shed stood Vladimir – Vladimir Kurlov, an elder of the village, who had somehow survived the massacres of invading uniforms. But his whole family had disappeared, and the village cared for him. He was a proud man and they had offered him the job of guarding the grainstore. A sinecure, in fact, for no one would have thought to break into it. There he stood, all five foot of him, frail with age, but a Hercules in memory. And with that strength, he withstood them, refusing to move.

A captain stepped down from the lead truck. He was in charge of the operations. 'Move out of the way, old man,' he said, 'so that we can open the gates.'

But Vladimir stood his ground. He was clearly terrified. So terrified he could not open his mouth to speak. But his pugnacious stand made his refusal abundantly clear.

'I will ask you one more time,' the captain said.

Vladimir was aware that from such a quarter he was privileged to be given a second chance. But he knew that it would be his last. Nevertheless, he found his voice. He had to, for without it he could not articulate his last words on this earth. And wonderful words they were. 'I will not be moved,' he said. 'Never.'

The captain wasted no time. He drew his pistol and shot the old man square in the chest. Vladimir fell with the grace of a swan, trembled a moment on the cobblestones and then was still. The crowd was silent, terrified to express even in a sigh their horror, their disgust and their pain, lest they themselves receive the same treatment. But silence is conspiracy. Silence is collusion. And Pyotr could not hold his tongue.

'Murderer!' he cried.

The captain turned, seeking the source of the protest. And from that moment Pyotr was a marked man.

'Take the body away,' the captain ordered.

Pyotr ran to where Vladimir lay, and before the soldiers could interfere, he picked up the old man in his arms. 'He belongs to our village,' he said to the captain. 'He is ours, and we will bury him.' He looked around for some support, but not one of the villagers had courage enough to come forward. So he carried Vladimir alone, out of the alley, and into his own street and dwelling, where he laid him out on his own bed and prayed over him. He was saddened by the villagers' indifference, but he ascribed it to their fear. Nina sat with him, praying, then she washed the body, and out of old cloth, she sewed a shroud.

'I'll fetch the priest,' she said. 'And tell the gravediggers.'

The field workers' food was still packed on the table, but Pyotr was no longer hungry. He was concerned with getting the body out of the house, away from the sight of the children. He asked Vladimir for forgiveness for his quick dispatch. He decided he would take the body straight to the church. He laid it gently on the back of his cart and drove to the churchyard. There were few people about. Most of the village had assembled at the grainhouse. When he reached the church Nina was waiting for him.

'The priest won't bury him,' she said. 'He's afraid.'

'And the gravediggers?'

'They're at the grainhouse,' Nina said. 'We must bury him ourselves.'

So they took shovels and set about digging, praying for forgiveness all the time. The digging took time, and after a while, they saw the villagers straggling back to their houses. But there was no sign of the soldiers. They had clearly come to Larionovka to stay. The villagers passed by with eyes averted, frightened and ashamed of their fear. Even when the gravediggers returned, they went quickly into the church and hid themselves in self-reproach. At last

237

the grave was ready, and Nina and Pyotr laid Vladimir inside. Then covered him, and walked silently away. Pyotr recalled how peaceful the village had been early that morning, and his joy in working his own fields. Now that peace had been shattered and possibly for ever.

With his departure from the grainstore, Pyotr had missed the orders that the captain had issued. Orders direct, he had said, from Comrade Stalin himself. But he was soon to learn what those orders were, for all the peasants were talking about them with fears for their future. It seemed that the soldiers had occupied the grain-house. Its contents now belonged to the State. They would be taken to Moscow and there distributed. The great Red Army had to be fed. In future a percentage of all the village produce must go this way. And a high percentage, leaving barely enough for subsistence. Moreover, the village had been given a quota. A minimum yield for the following year. A bleak future. The peasants could not help thinking of the past, when the manor was bright on the hill, and they wondered why everyone thought the Revolution was so wonderful. But there had been no mention by the State of private holdings. His fields still belonged to Pyotr, but he wondered for how long.

During that year, the peasants worked with frenzy. They were already feeling the effects of the denuded grainstore and hunger was rife in the village. At the end of the year, the soldiers returned with a demand for their due. The same captain accompanied them. Larionovka was now his village, and he treated it with offensive familiarity, as if he personally owned every cobblestone and field. The villagers trembled. They knew that their quota had not been fulfilled. They flocked to the grainstore and witnessed the loading. And they noticed with horror how little was left for their own consumption. This Comrade Stalin, whoever he was, was clearly a man without a heart.

When the loading was done, the captain addressed the villagers. Pyotr was amongst them. He made no attempt to conceal himself, even though he might have been recognised as the troublemaker of a year ago. Indeed, he stood in the front row, ready to defend their year's hard labours, and if necessary, the rights to his own land.

The captain stood on a raised makeshift platform and looked down on what he regarded as his rightful serfs. 'You have not achieved the quota set down by Comrade Stalin,' he said. 'You have failed and it is a mark of shame. But you are beginners, and I shall make allowances for that.'

The villagers shifted their weight from foot to foot. They were silent and angry. They had worked slavishly all the year round. And on stomachs that were rarely filled. And what did this town-dweller know about crops? What did he know about the changes in weather that for days on end rendered fields unworkable? Perhaps Comrade Stalin could control the climate too. Then their quota would have been more than filled. But all were too frightened to say a word.

'Next year you will do better,' the captain said. 'You will have to, because Comrade Stalin in his wisdom has raised the quota.'

Pyotr could no longer hold his tongue. 'That's impossible,' he dared to say. 'If you take all our grain to feed the army and the workers in the cities, what are we going to eat?' It was an audacious interruption and though the villagers agreed with Pyotr, they resented him as a troublemaker.

'Whoever heard of a farmer going hungry?' the captain said with disdain. 'As I remember,' he added, 'you were an agitator last time. We will have to teach you a lesson.'

But Pyotr would not be silenced. 'Most of this year we've all gone hungry,' he said.

'I don't believe you,' the captain said. He was fast losing patience. He turned to the rest of the villagers. 'Is this man telling the truth?' he asked. 'Does he speak for all of you?' But terror had stilled their tongues. They wanted to survive, even if it meant starvation.

'I am speaking for myself,' Pyotr said. 'I know what yield I can expect from my land.'

The captain pounced immediately. '*Your* land? Did I hear you correctly?'

'Yes,' Pyotr insisted. '*My* land. Given to me by deed by the Count Larionov.'

The captain laughed. 'You're talking of another time, you poor peasant. You're talking of another country. Those days are gone, and gone, thank God, for ever.'

'It's *my* land,' Pyotr insisted.

'Now listen to me,' the captain said, or whispered almost, his voice atingle with threat. 'The land, its produce, its livestock, its yield, everything, and I mean everything, belongs to the State. The days of the private farmer are over, and all those who made themselves rich by the sweat of the poor.' He held out his arm to the villagers in general. 'You and your sons, you fought, and many of them died to win your freedom. Are you going to give it back now to a wealthy parasite, who feeds off your life's blood?'

He's talking about me, Pyotr thought, and could not repress a smile. 'What freedom are you talking about?' Pyotr said. 'We're not free. We're enslaved to the government. To Comrade Stalin. We're not free. We just have a different slave-master.'

The crowd gasped at the blasphemy. And trembled, for it was as if Pyotr were signing his own death warrant.

The captain signalled to the soldiers at his side. 'Arrest him,' he said, and didn't even bother to lower his voice. The soldiers sprang on Pyotr as if they expected resistance, if not from the man himself, then from his friends. But nobody moved to protect him. When force is threatened, friendship quickly evaporates.

'Tell Nina,' Pyotr managed to say to his neighbour, as he was taken away. 'Tell her to report to Ivan. Ivan Volynin,' he shouted hoping that the name might strike a fearful chord in the captain's ear. But he saw no reaction on the man's face. Perhaps Ivan had already been demoted.

They took him to the prison on the outskirts of the village, threw him into a solitary cell, and left him there, while they waited for orders from the captain.

When Nina was told of Pyotr's arrest, she packed what little food she could spare, and went straight to the prison. Larionovka prison served all the outlying villages. In the old days, in the Count Larionov days, it had been run by two officers with a handful of guards. But now it had been taken over by the military, and had to be viewed far more seriously. There was a line of women waiting outside the guard-room at the entrance to the prison. Nina recognised none of them. She assumed they were from other villages, and it was a relief to know that her husband was not the only dissenter. She stood at the end of the line. She would have wished for conversation with the woman in front of her, or the women who shortly came and stood behind. She wanted to know about conditions in the prison, what the prisoners did, and how long they stayed. And were some of them just common criminals? But the line was silent, each woman still and brooding, their common anxiety unshareable.

The line moved very slowly. After about an hour's waiting, Nina was close to the entrance of the prison. Then a guard came outside and announced that there would be no more visitors that day. 'Come back tomorrow,' he told them. The women shifted warily but held their ground. Nina was incensed.

'How do I know I can get in tomorrow?' she asked the guard.

'You must take your chances,' he said.

'He's right,' one woman whispered to her. 'Don't make trouble. It's not good for your man. They say that every day. You have to be lucky.'

'But why do they do it?' Nina said.

'I think it's their idea of fun,' the woman said, then she went quickly away, and Nina was left on her own, the isolated trouble-maker.

She went the next day and the next, and on the third day she was lucky. She was the last in the line to be admitted, and behind her she heard the guard announce his daily shutdown. Inside the waiting-room the women seemed to relax a little, and there was sporadic and whispered conversation. Some of them had brought their children with them, and from one of them she recognised the mother who was holding her hand. Irina Lomonov, the dressmaker who lived opposite the church. Her husband was the village post-man, an unassuming, timid man, who could have been guilty of nothing. Nina went to sit by her side.

'Why is your husband here?' she asked.

'One day, they took away his letters. The soldiers just ripped open his bag. And they started to read them. He snatched them away. As many as he could. Then they arrested him. You don't have to do much to be arrested these days.'

'How long has he been here?'

'Nearly a month. I come every day, but I've only seen him three times.' She did not ask Nina why Pyotr was inside. She had probably already heard it on the grapevine.

'How do they treat them?' Nina asked.

'They don't get enough to eat. But then neither does anybody. He'll be glad of your basket though.'

Then Nina was called.

'Best of luck,' Irina said.

She was led into the guard-room. A captain was sitting behind the desk. 'Name?' he shouted.

'Nina Volynina,' she whispered.

'Not yours,' he said impatiently. 'The prisoner's.'

'Pyotr Vassilyevich Volynin.'

The captain did not hesitate. 'He isn't here,' he shouted. He said it with such finality and conviction that Nina feared that the 'here' referred not only to the prison but to the whole surface of the globe. She started to cry. 'Come back tomorrow,' the captain said, giving her a margin of hope.

'If my husband's not here,' Nina sobbed, 'why should I come back tomorrow?'

'It's worth a try,' the captain said. 'You can leave your basket anyway.'

She suspected he wanted the food for himself. But she had to keep in his favour. She had to trust him. She put the basket on the desk. 'I'll come back tomorrow,' she said.

'That's a good girl.' He rose and patted her on the bottom as she went to the door. She was tempted to hit him, but she would not jeopardise Pyotr's safety. And in that name she actually smiled at him, but in her heart wished him a slow and infinitely painful death.

On her way out, she paused to speak with Irina. 'You didn't see him?' Irina said.

'No. They told me to come tomorrow. Though they said he wasn't there. But they took my basket.'

'That's a good sign,' Irina said. Though without any logic. But she had to say something.

'I hope you see your man today,' Nina said. She tried to hold back her tears. She was anxious to get away. She needed to be alone to cry herself out. 'I must get the children,' she said.

She left the prison and walked past the line of stubbornly patient women. She made her way to the school. Her children would be waiting for her there. The school had become a waiting-place. It no longer concerned itself with education. The teachers were too hungry to teach, and the children too hungry to learn. Too hungry even to play. So they waited there, while their parents foraged for food, scrambling roots from the earth, or nettles from the woods. Sergei and Maria were waiting for her there, staring vacantly, and when they saw her, they smiled with hope, although she was clearly empty-handed. Then her anger overtook her distress, and she gathered them up and took them to the grainstore. Sometimes, after a grain-loading, there would be spillage on the cobblestones, enough, with patient gathering, for a loaf of bread perhaps. But others had the same idea, and when she reached the grainhouse, a gathering of women were crawling the cobblestones like foraging beetles. She got down on her knees with the children. Children were good at grain-picking. They were nimble and had eager eyes, and hunger impelled them. Sometimes two women's hands grabbed at the same grain, and there was quarrelling and even fighting amongst them. For hunger robs one of dignity and compassion. And the children took advantage of these interruptions and harvested where they could, though after an hour's picking, there was barely enough for one bread roll. But rumour spread that that evening the trucks would be reloaded for grain transport to the city. During a loading, the pickings were more profitable. The whole village would turn out for crumbs from Comrade Stalin's table. Nina took the children home. They would have to rest before the night's hunting.

When she reached their dwelling she noticed that the door was slightly ajar and she rushed towards it, full of hope that Pyotr had come home. She called his name even before she reached it, and the children echoed with, 'Papa, Papa.' But there was no answer. She pushed the door, but there was some resistance behind it.

243

Instinctively she knew that the children must not go inside, so she told them to play in the street for a while. They obeyed her listlessly and she watched them out of sight. Then screwing her courage, she pushed at the door. Slowly it opened wide enough for her to enter.

All down the street the children and the village heard her screaming. Sergei and Maria ran back to the house, and men and women came out of their houses to follow them. The screaming did not cease, not even to take breath. It was an animal cry of unending pain. One woman pulled the children aside to shield them for she had caught sight of Pyotr's body in the doorway. It was carelessly wrapped in a sack that seeped with blood. The sack was loosely tied at the neck, as if to give the head an obscene chance to breathe, and they had not even bothered to lay hands on his eyes to close them. So Pyotr stared at the villagers who crowded in on him, bewildered at his welcome. One of the women took care of Nina, while the children who could no longer be protected, stared at their father, unbelieving, and wondering what he was doing in a sack. But the blood told them, and they had to believe it.

'Papa's dead,' Sergei said to his little sister.

'Another papa dead,' Maria said. She was adding to her tally of orphans, but it would be a little while before she accepted that she was one of them.

By now the whole village had assembled outside Pyotr's hut and the story of his killing had spread. And it aroused as much anger as sorrow. Anger at themselves that not one of them had raised his voice in Pyotr's defence, although in their hearts they had agreed with him. But it was not too late for loyalty. They would ensure that his death would not have been in vain.

'To the grainhouse,' one of them shouted. 'And bring your pots and pans. We're going to take what is our due.'

'To the grainhouse,' the others echoed.

'I'm coming with you,' Nina managed to say. 'We must all go. And our children.' Her screams had subsided. She was even dry-eyed. Grief would come later, for her anger was sublime. She gathered pots and pans and gave one each to the children. 'We're collecting for Papa,' she said. As she followed her children out of the door she turned her face away from the sack. She could not

244

look at Pyotr. Although she knew he was dead, she was not yet ready to believe it. Only when she had filled her pots with his funeral feast, would she bury him, and tell herself over and over again, that she was a widow.

The main street of the village was now awash with protest. As the villagers marched they beat rhythmically on their pots and pans. It was their war cry. Nothing less. They had had enough. Pyotr's brutal killing had spurred them into action, and they had no doubt that they would return to their homes, full of bread. They marched but they did not sing. They would sing a song of victory on their return. Nina banged her drum louder than them all. Her anger compelled her, else she would have detonated. Maria and Sergei held on to her skirts. 'Papa, Papa,' they shouted to the rhythm of the pots. It was the only lyric permissible.

When they reached the grainhouse, the first truck was already loaded. The soldiers were tying down the back flap.

'It shall not pass,' one of the peasants said. It was a war cry of a kind, and dictated immediate action.

But a more compelling call came from one of the children in the crowd. 'Mama, I'm hungry,' a little boy said. It was a cry to arms. Undeniable.

The women crowded around the truck, so that, barring slaughter, it was impossible to drive forward.

'Drive on,' the captain shouted. 'What are you waiting for? They'll get out of your way quickly enough.' The driver revved the engine, but it was the most that he could do. He refused to put it into gear.

'Get him out of there,' the captain yelled.

Some soldiers dragged the young driver out of the truck, and the captain himself got into the driver's cabin, put the engine in gear, and eased the truck forward. But the men and women did not move, though they sent their children to stand against a wall, for they were mindful of the danger.

The captain leaned out of the window, and called to a group of soldiers who stood by.

'Clear them all from the truck,' he shouted.

At first the soldiers were reluctant, since most of those barring the truck's progress, were women. But one of them took the lead, and they all followed. And were brutal. Since the job had to be done, they would do it properly. They burst into the group of women, and pushed them aside, jabbing the more stubborn ones with the butts of their rifles. But this attack only served to augment the peasants' rage, and they rushed in a mob to the back of the truck, and tore the flap open. The grain poured over the cobble-stones and there was a cry of victory from the children against the wall. Now they joined their parents in their harvesting, filling their pots and pans and pockets with the precious grain.

'For Pyotr, for Pyotr,' they shouted in unison. And then for the benefit of the soldiers who were not native to their village, 'For Pyotr Volynin. Volynin.'

The captain ordered his men to fire their weapons into the air. At the sound of the gunfire the peasants paused for a moment, and looking round, saw that nobody was wounded, so they ignored the firing, and continued to help themselves to what in any case was theirs. Then the captain leaned out of his truck and gave his final order. 'Shoot them,' he shouted. 'Shoot them all.'

The soldiers fired into the crowd. A group of peasants incensed by the carnage, opened the door of the truck and pulled the captain to the ground. He lay there helpless, and as he tried to reach for his gun, one of the men trod on his hand. Then they looked down on him and spat in his face. They thought that would have been enough, but they saw their women fall and they heard the children screaming, so they trod on him, mashing his face and body into a bloody pulp. The captain's death was slow and infinitely painful, the only small measure of justice that day. But they could not savour it for long. Two soldiers approached the men as they stood looking down on what was left of the tyrant. And in close pistol range, they shot them. One by astonished one. Some women who had been out of range of the fire now returned to the grain and their harvesting. Amongst them Nina and her children.

'For Pyotr,' she said as she gathered another handful of grain.

'For Papa,' the children echoed.

But the grain slid through their fingers like sand, as did their lifeblood from their bodies, as the bullets found their marks. Nina fell first onto the soft mountain of grain that she had died for, and then her children by her side. With her last frail gesture, she rested her arms across their bodies, protecting them in death as she had done in life.

The soldiers finished off the carnage. The first killing had been the hardest. Now it was simply a matter of routine. A mopping-up operation to ensure that there would be no more trouble. Then they heaped the bodies into a pile. It was easy while there were so many of them. A package of dead did not disturb. It was only when the soldiers saw a child's body, lying alone against the wall, that they turned away and threw their hearts up.

Larionovka died that night. Few were left to revive its spirit. Just old men and women, too tired and too hungry to dare the streets. But no children. Some perhaps were hiding in the forest beyond the village, while their mothers foraged for food. They would survive out of a rabid and resentful rage. Else Larionovka would not live again.

Pyotr Volynin was never buried. He rotted where he lay and the funeral bread rotted with him.

PART SIX

18

Life came cheap in Stalin's time. Other people's lives, that is, and the news of the Larionovka massacre took its leisurely time to reach Leningrad. When it arrived, it landed in the form of a cold memo on bureaucratic desks, where it was noted, filed and merited barely a sigh. But in the offices of the Internal Police, Ivan lingered over the memo for a while. The word 'massacre' was common enough and ubiquitous. But the appendage of Larionovka narrowed the field a little. He read the note carefully. Every word of it spelt out the assault on the landmarks of his childhood, and made it clear that there was nothing left in that place to prove that it had ever been. Only the name of it was left, but a dead name now, a name of ghosts and history. But as he read it, Ivan felt nothing. One massacre was very like another, and even the name of Larionovka did not unduly stir him. The end justified the means, however terrible that means, and wherever it took place. But one name caused Ivan to pause. His own name, Volynin, but as it applied itself to his brother, Pyotr. And despite all his Party conditioning, and his brainwashed heart, Ivan acknowledged the lump in his throat, and the offensive tears in his eyes. As a child, he had loved his elder brother. Even after he had robbed him of Katya, he did not cease to love him, despite the hurdles of guilt. Despite too, Pyotr's indifference to change and his apathy towards the Revolution. He read the memo once more, and realised how radically Pyotr had changed. He had died protesting. For the first time in his life, he had claimed those rights he thought he was entitled to. In the memo, he was billed as ringleader. 'The leader of the rebels was one Pyotr Volynin,' Ivan read. No further details were given. No explanation was required for a massacre. One single dissenter was enough, and the audacious protesting voice of Pyotr Volynin had been enough to annihilate a whole village.

Ivan locked his office door. He did not want to be caught weeping, especially for one who had been called a rebel. But broken as he was, he felt no anger. He did not for one moment blame those agents that had killed him. He simply mourned the loss of a brother who had died before his natural time. He would have to tell Sasha. He saw little of his younger brother nowadays. Sasha's name was not one to be associated with, and in the present climate of suspicion, he was not likely to be free for long. Ivan had done his best to warn him, to persuade him that joining the Party was his only guarantee of freedom. But Sasha remained adamant. As a writer he was an outsider he said, and as an outsider, he was prepared to pay the price, and Ivan feared that soon enough Sasha would be called upon. In view of that imminent danger, he wondered whether he should protect his younger brother from the pain of bereavement. Sasha loved Pyotr, Ivan knew, and the news of his death would rouse him to an anger that was sublime, and that his words would scream from countless pages, each syllable pronouncing blame. Stalin would stand an ignominious trial, in phrases of undisguised contempt, and Sasha would consciously risk the danger of that dissent. Ivan had to protect him from that. He decided that he would not share his news with Sasha, and he prayed that he would not hear it through other channels.

He dried his tears, and unlocked his door. He was determined to put the event out of his mind. He would not even tell Katya. He took the memo, and filed it in its proper place along with all the other massacres that were the means to the glorious end. Then he settled at his desk and resumed his work. When later in the day, his secretary handed him a memo ordering him to authorise the arrest of the writer Alexander Volynin, he received it with a strange measure of relief. Now there would be no point in telling Sasha about Pyotr. He would have his own dissent to pay for, and Ivan prayed that the price would not be as high as it was for his elder brother.

252

Ivan decided to go to Sasha's apartment himself. He could have sent his men, and kept his own hands deceptively clean. But he wanted to see Sasha. He wanted to embrace him and to say farewell. But he could not go alone. It was protocol that two other officers would accompany him. But he would tell them to wait outside, while he apprised his brother of his arrest. He would have to wait until the middle of the night. That too was protocol. He decided he would not go home, but stay in his office until the time came. He wanted very much to know what they would do with his brother. But it would have been dangerous for him to enquire. Sasha's fate belonged to another department and to a different set of memos. He wondered whether Pyotr's rebellion and Sasha's arrest were in any way connected, and he had to conclude that the timing of both was more than accidental. The name Volynin was now as suspect as Larionov, and Ivan began to fear that its reverberations would in time rebound in memo form onto his own desk. He busied himself with work until well into the night, so that he would not have to think of either of his brothers.

Nearby, the church clock struck three, that knock-on-the-door time. He called his assistants, and directed the driver to Sasha's apartment. The arresting wagon followed close behind. He told his assistants to wait. He tapped gently on the door. Not according to the rules. The book instructed that the door should be hammered on, thus waking all the neighbours and leading to public humiliation, and serving as a warning to all. But it seemed to Ivan that at three o'clock in the morning, a gentle knock would be rousing enough, and of sufficient alarm. As brother to brother, he would dispense with the public shame.

He heard Sasha's voice. 'Who is it?' he whispered.

'Ivan.'

The door opened immediately. It did not occur to Sasha that it was anyone but his brother who called, and as his brother, Ivan was welcome at any time. The thought that he had come on official business did not enter Sasha's mind. Knowing the dire nature of his call, Ivan was disturbed at Sasha's effusive and innocent welcome. As he opened the door, though bleary-eyed with sleep he stretched out his arms and hugged him. Ivan folded himself into the embrace.

'Sashenka,' he said. It was the kindest word he could give him. He rested his head on his shoulder, then noticed a positive stiffening in Sasha's hold. Then he knew that his two officers stood behind him, and offensively in Sasha's sleep-blurred view.

'What's this?' Sasha said as he loosened his hold.

'I'm only obeying orders,' Ivan said.

In the whole history of mankind, in all its sad chaptering, the execution of every single atrocity has been prefaced by such a phrase. 'I'm only obeying orders.' Orders from what authority? And from whom did that authority take direction? And back through the labyrinth of evil to its very core. But Ivan knew that those who are only obeying orders are themselves giving those orders. In the execution of torture the buck cannot and must not be passed, and even as Ivan spoke those coward's words he knew that he and he alone was responsible, for evil does not use messengers. Yet he said it again, cowering in the shame of it. 'I'm only obeying orders.' Then he caught sight of Anna at the end of the hall, with little Dmitri at her side.

'Pack a bag,' Ivan said. 'Just a few clothes.'

'Where are you taking him?' Anna screamed, then held her hand over her mouth as Dmitri took up her screaming.

'Papa, Papa,' he shouted, but clung still to Anna, as if afraid to enter that area of danger and alarm. Sasha went to him, and held him in his arms.

'I shall be back, Dmitri,' he said. Then he folded Anna into his embrace.

'Hurry up. Get your bag,' one of the agents shouted. He could see that his superior was deeply affected by his brother's arrest, and he wanted to curtail the agony. 'The wagon's waiting,' he said.

'What shall I pack, Ivan?' Sasha asked. Was he to pack for life or death? If life, was it wear for work or pleasure? And if death, why pack at all? But certainly he must take his work. His new unfinished novel. For without that, whether for life or death, neither was tenable. 'Come,' he said to Anna, and he guided her into the bedroom. 'I won't keep you long,' he said, to no one in particular. He saw his captors as an anonymous authority, and Ivan was part of that anonymity. In the bedroom, he packed some everyday clothes, which he used as wrapping for his manuscript. Then when it was done, he said his farewells.

'I shall be back,' he said. 'I shall certainly come back. Do I not always come back? Don't cry, Anna. When I leave I want to see you smiling. Dmitri too. When I think of you both, I don't want to remember your tears.' He held them close. 'I shall come back,' he said again. 'Be in touch with Andrei. Perhaps he will have news of me.'

'Hurry up,' one of the officers shouted. Then he himself appeared in the bedroom doorway. He grabbed Sasha roughly, by the arm.

'There's no need for that,' Sasha said. 'I'm coming.' He kissed Anna and Dmitri again. 'Have patience,' he said. 'And strength. Our love will give you both.'

The officer then pushed him through the apartment. Sasha noted that Ivan had left. His shame must have overwhelmed him.

But it was not so much shame, as an unbearable sadness that had prompted Ivan's swift departure. Pyotr's death, that untold secret, gnawed at his heart, and together with his passing, he mourned his mother and father. All dead now. The sight of the captive Sasha had finally broken him, for he had no doubt that his younger brother was going to his death. And leaving him the sole surviving Volynin. There were his own children, of course, and he loved them in his own way. But Vassily and Viktor did not threaten his own mortality. It was the death of his parents and brothers that would pronounce him a survivor. Only Sasha was left, and if he were to be killed, as Ivan believed, that survivor label would hang on him as distinctly as a leper's bell. He wished he knew what fate they had in mind for his brother. He was afraid to enquire in fear of being accused of nepotism. In any case, Volynin was no longer an unsullied name, and he had to look to his own future. All he could do was to keep his ears open, and be ready to turn them deafly away, should the news render him the sole Volynin survivor. He wondered what he should do. It was four o'clock in the morning. Katya would be asleep. In the old days she would wait up for him,

255

whatever time he came home. But nowadays she went to her own bed as if she didn't care whether he came home at all. Things had soured between them. Over the last few years, her devotion to the Cause had waned. Not only had she lost her enthusiasm, but sometimes she even dared to question its principles. And in public too. In Ivan's eyes, such questioning was close to treachery. A good Party member did not allow himself the luxury of doubt; he toed the line, wherever and whatever that line might be. The Cause and their faith in it had been the bond between them, as good as any marriage vow, and it was Katya who had broken it. He wondered if he loved her still, whether in his Cause-riddled eyes she was even lovable. He began to feel anger towards her. Why, her doubts might even cost him his job. He would go home and roughly wake her, and with little pity, break the news of Pyotr's death. In any case, he needed somebody to share it with, even if his motive was one of revenge.

He did not put his key gently in the lock. He would waken Katya with far less love than he had roused his younger brother such a short time ago. And he made a point of slamming the apartment door behind him, so that she would be well and truly awake by the time he reached her room. Her bedroom door was closed, and he was rough with its handle. But even that did not waken her. Katya was in that profound sleep of depression that mercifully and for a short time obliterates reality. So he shook her, gripping her shoulder, so that she started in her sleep, and woke suddenly with a scream. She stared at him.

'Ivan?' she said. She was not questioning his person, it was his name she was scenting, for it had been deleted in her sleep. 'What is it?' she said.

'Pyotr is dead.'

Katya sat up in bed and looked at him. Her eyes held the icy stare of accusation, though she said not a word. Instead she began to keen with heart-rending cries of mourning, shedding those hot tears of regret and self-admonishment that she had never valued that profound love that Pyotr had once offered her. She wept for the loss of the years that had separated them, and above all for the unhappy choice she had made in his stead.

256

'Nina too. And the children,' Ivan shouted above her wailing. He twisted the knife in her wound, almost relishing her sorrow. But at the mention of Nina and the children, the wailing ceased. More than tears had to be shed. Much more. Words had to be spilled. And like the tears, in torrents. But only one word dropped from her lips, though its force was that of a flood. 'Murderer!' she screamed at him. For she knew how they had died. And possibly the whole village. If one family had been wiped out, it was usually part of a massacre, and of those lately, she had heard enough. And always by the same authorised assassins. And always for the same reason. The Cause, that blood-stained slaughtering Cause.

'Murderer!' she shouted at him again. Then rose from her bed, and beat his chest in an agony of despair. He let her vent her spleen. He deserved it. Not for the matter of the story, but for its telling. So he stood while she beat her fists against his chest, and released his own tears. He put his hands on her shoulder. 'Katya,' he said, 'he was my own brother. Let me weep for him too.' She dropped her hands, and leaned her head on his shoulder. 'What has become of us, Ivan?' she said. It was the first time in many months that she had spoken gently to him.

He took her in his arms. For a moment the Cause was put aside. 'These are difficult times,' was all he could say. It was the closest he could come to any human commitment, but at least it left the door open on a possible future they might have together. He would not tell her about Sasha's arrest, for it was possible his younger brother would have no future at all.

19

But Sasha was still alive, though many might have disputed whether a life such as his was worth living at all. He had been found guilty of being an 'enemy of the state', a label that was conveniently attached to any troublemaker. Who or which authority had found him guilty could not be ascertained, since there had been no trial. But for such a crime the sentence was mandatory. A spell in a forced labour camp. In Sasha's case, twelve years.

He was transported to a coal mine in the Eastern Soviet Union. The landscape was bleak and desolate and even in the summer season, it was for ever winter. His first view of his fellow prisoners told Sasha that he was likely to go hungry for the duration of his sentence. That he was likely, too, to age quickly, and even, by the sight of some of them, to go out of his mind. He consoled himself with the thought that some of the prisoners must be troublemakers like himself, and that, though everything else might be in short supply, friendship could be at hand.

A newcomer is always welcome in a prison. The smell of freedom is still upon him, and it must be savoured before it fades. Besides, he has news of the outside world, and when Sasha arrived he was besieged by most of the prisoners for details of that life elsewhere. He noticed that some of the men did not bother to question him. They huddled in the hut like men apart, their indifference and apathy sublime. Later Sasha learned that these men had been in the camp for twenty years or more, prisoners of the Tsar, who had missed out on the Revolution and had been forgotten. Imprisoned without trial, they had no recourse to appeal. The coal dust from the mine had settled on their faces like a second skin, sealing their melancholy and immunising them from further pain. Sasha viewed them with despair, seeing in their faces a vision of what he himself might become. He thought of Anna and Dmitri. He had promised them he would return, and return he would, but unchanged, but for the twelve natural years that would age him. He shuddered at the thought that his son would be twenty-four years old before he would see him again. Dmitri's childhood would have been largely fatherless. This thought filled him with anger, an anger that invigorated him, and he knew that he must hold on to that rage for the length of his sentence so that it would feed his will to survive. Else he would decline into a fatal resignation, like those old-timers huddled together in the hut, shrouded in abdication of which the coal-dust second skin was signature.

He told the men about Anna and Dmitri and in exchange they gave him their families. Their wives and children, and the younger ones gave their parents. Each called every remembered one by name, and repeated that name so that others would remember it too. For they knew that the major hazard to survival was forgetfulness, and that amnesia, though often so tempting, was simply a way of dying. Sasha answered all their questions. Some had not heard of Lenin's death, and the name of Stalin meant little to some of them. Sasha did his best to spell out its meaning and in no way could he make it a hopeful tale.

'Our poor motherland,' one of them said, and he seemed to be speaking for them all.

On his first day of work in the mine, Sasha's new friends took care of him. They warned him that he must fulfil his quota for the day, and that he must pull his equal weight with the others lest all suffer punishment. They warned him of Volkov, the group leader, who, although a prisoner himself, enjoyed certain privileges, and could be as cruel as any of the guards.

The mine was low, and the men had to crouch in the narrow tunnels. They worked in pairs, but on this first day Sasha was assigned to an already well-established partnership in order to learn the ropes. Krasotkin had worked with Devushkin for many years, but it had never been a happy union. Krasotkin was already an old man when he had arrived at the camp, and Devushkin was many years his junior. Tempers frayed between them, because the separate rhythms of their work barely synchronised. That day, Sasha's first, Krasotkin was looking particularly frail, and Sasha feared that their quota would not be filled. Devushkin was the cutter. With his axe he cut the coal from the coalface. It was Krasotkin's job to load that coal onto the cart. But the pieces were large and too heavy for the old man to lift. Sasha did what he could to help him, but he could not match Devushkin's cutting speed. As a result, the pieces of coal piled up in the tunnel and impeded the passage of the carts.

'What the hell are you doing? Or not doing?' Devushkin shouted. He was not an unkind man; like all of them, he dreaded the 'cold box', that dire and torturing punishment for quota shortfall.

But Krasotkin could not answer. He dropped the lump of coal he was vainly trying to lift, and he fell against the coalface. Devushkin sprang forward and caught him, and laid him gently on his back.

'What's going on here?' Volkov had arrived in the tunnel. He looked at Krasotkin, who clearly could not work any more. 'Get the old fool out of here,' he said. 'You, Volynin, take his place.'

Sasha moved to where the old man lay and knelt by his side. Shortly he was joined by Dorokhov, a skeleton of a man, who knelt beside him. He held Krasotkin's hand. 'He's dying,' he said.

'Well, tell him goodbye, for Christ's sake,' Volkov yelled, 'and pull him out of there. Or we'll all end up in the cold box.'

But Dorokhov made no move to shift him. 'Let him make his death in his own way,' he said.

Krasotkin's lips were seen to move, and Dorokhov put his ear to the old man's mouth.

'No more pain,' he heard. 'Free. I'm free.' It was the sad testimony of a man to whom life had spelt captivity, and for whom death was the only freedom. The men around him watched as life took its merciful leave. Then Dorokhov gently closed Krasotkin's staring and bewildered eyes. He crossed himself, and those around him did likewise, knowing that in their motherland men had been hanged for less. But in that moment of Krasotkin's passing, death had become the only freedom that was within God's gift and there was every reason to court it. So they knelt and they prayed together. Together they celebrated that the grass withereth and the flower fadeth. Even Volkov, standing to one side, murmured with them, for despite his paltry privileges he wanted to be included in that freedom. But Sasha, though he knelt, held his tongue. He was too young to embrace death, at whatever cost. He looked around at the other men, and hoped that for them this was just a passing moment of abdication, and that, when the prayers were over, they would return to life and judge it a freedom.

They laid Krasotkin's body on a cart, already half loaded with coal. It was a burial of a kind. The pit pony would haul the cart to the surface of the mine. The old man's body, without ceremony, would be returned to the earth that had claimed him and the coal would be weighed against the daily quota and be found perilously wanting. But down in the tunnels, the men would not be thwarted. They worked as they had never worked before, and between them they more than made up for Krasotkin's share. Prayer seemed to have fortified them, an illegal stimulant. The men were aware of it, and each in their subversive way, considered an addiction to faith, for it seemed a useful component of their survival kit. That night in the hut, Dorokhov, with stubborn gentleness, called the men to prayer, and exhausted as they were, they knelt in a circle around him. In his days of freedom, Dorokhov had been a priest. And still was, and felt himself to be. He led them in prayers for the peace of Krasotkin's soul and for their own strength to live and overcome evil. The men slept easily that night, with the contented sleep of conquerors.

Thus ended Sasha's first day in the labour camp. The old man's death had stunned him, but he was told it was a daily occurrence. He steeled himself never to get used to it. Never to assume its normality. Death in such a place was an outrage, a monstrous offence against nature. He must learn to mourn each death as if it were the only one, for a man's quietus was as unique as his life. He felt in that first day that he had acquired an old man's wisdom, and before sleeping, he examined his body for signs of age. But it was flawless. It even strangely proclaimed a greater youth. He was careful to sponge it thoroughly, so that not a particle of dust remained. He would in no way nurture that mask of death and abdication he had seen on the faces of the old corner-huddling men.

As the months passed, the men came to respect Sasha. They admired his stubbornness, his unwillingness to give up hope, and his readiness to shoulder the work of others in the mine if sickness was upon them. Some of them had heard about his writings. One of them even knew one of his poems by heart, and sometimes in the evenings, huddled around their fire, Sasha would tell them the story of Ranjevsky and his own grotesque participation in the civil war.

'You must write about us,' Dorokhov said. 'Our pain, our desolation and above all, our hope. You must write the story of man's hell on God's good earth. You are our witness. We must never be forgotten.'

But Sasha had already begun to write. On the evening of his first day in the camp, he had written Krasotkin's epitaph. For this camp was a death camp. Forced labour was a delusion. It was but a euphemism for a long life's dying. On Sundays, when the men were freed from work, Dorokhov would lead them in collective prayer, and then Sasha would read them what he had written. Some Sundays, especially in the winter when it was very cold, and Sasha could hardly hold a pen in his hand, there was very little to read, and the story limped along painfully and slowly until an astonished sun proclaimed the end of the snows. Then Sasha would sit easily at his table – the men had constructed a makeshift desk for him – and the story would once again lurch from one catastrophe to another, punctuated by laughter and the survival humour of ridicule. The writing numbed him from thoughts of Anna and Dmitri, and he was reminded of his curtain-raising days in Berlin, in another exile, though a more comfortable one. He remembered how in the writing of his novel, all thoughts of Anna had slipped from his mind, and that when he did recall her, it was with guilt and fear. Now in this exile, his occasional thoughts of Anna were consoling and without guilt, for he knew that writing was his cause, as much as the Party was Ivan's, and it was that cause that would light his way to freedom. Chapter by chapter, he would fight his way back to Anna and Dmitri.

But unknown to Sasha, there would be another child. After he had left, Anna had found herself pregnant once more. Like Dmitri, her child would be born fatherless, and like Dmitri's, that father would come home. So her pregnancy gave her hope of Sasha's return. She had gone back to work on the trams. In Sasha's absence she had no income. She was glad in any case not to be alone. In the mornings before going to the depot, she would deliver Dmitri at school, and when she came off duty, Dmitri would be waiting for her. He had celebrated his twelfth birthday a few days after his father's arrest, and overnight he had grown into a man. He had accepted a state of independence because he had been offered no alternative, and in the course of time he knew it as his natural spirit. But the child still lingered in him, and at times, in crises, he wished for his mother's arms. But he would deny that wish because now he was the man in the house. But one day, getting off her tram at the end of her shift, Anna saw him waiting, and the undeniable child in his stance. He was leaning against a pillar, vainly trying to hold back his tears. She rushed towards him and made to take him in her arms. But he quickly withdrew. He would not allow a maternal embrace that would confirm his young years and his inalienable right to tears.

'What's the matter?' Anna said. She kept her distance, sensing his distaste for public display. She refrained from any mention of his tears.

'Why didn't you tell me Papa's a spy, and that's why he was arrested?'

'He's not a spy.' Anna was angry. 'Who dared call your Papa a spy?'

'In school. They made me stand up in front of the class . . .'

The recall of his public humiliation throbbed sobbing through his small boy's frame. 'They made me call him traitor, an enemy . . .' He could say no more. He slipped his face into Anna's swollen skirt, not so much for maternal comfort as to hide it from those onlookers in the depot.

Anna made to fondle the back of his head. But refrained in deference to that craving of his for independence. 'He's not a traitor, Mitya,' she said. 'There were certain things Papa wouldn't do.

Wrong things. You wouldn't want him to do wrong things, would you?'

There was no answer from her skirts, and she saw him rub his eyes with the cotton folds.

'What do they call "wrong"?' Dmitri whispered.

'He wrote the truth in his books. And they didn't like it.'

'I want him to come home,' he sobbed. Then he lifted his head from her skirts. 'Papa's dead, isn't he?' he said.

'No, no,' Anna whispered. 'If he were dead, I'd know. My heart would stop.'

'They made me say it, Mama,' he said. 'You won't tell him, will you? If he comes back.'

'There's no "if",' Anna said. 'He's coming back. Remember that, Dmitri, he's coming back.' She said it as much for her own reassurance as for her son's, for at times, in the still, small hours of the night, she wondered if she would for ever sleep alone. She held Dmitri close, and those around them gave them space as if skirting their anguish that they pitied but did not understand. In time the two of them walked away.

'Can I go and play with Viktor?' Dmitri asked. 'I haven't seen him for ages.'

'Come home and play with me,' Anna said. 'I don't have anyone to play with.' She knew she was a poor substitute, but she knew too that Katya had been forbidden to allow Viktor to play with her son. Ivan did not want to underline the connection between them. But she could not explain all that to Dmitri.

But the boy was insistent. 'Why can't I play with Viktor?' he asked.

'He's probably doing his homework. You know Uncle Ivan is very strict about that.' This was true. Ivan was ambitious for his younger son. He pushed him to study, as he had pushed Vassily. Vassily had tolerated it until he was seventeen, and then, on the point of entering the Military Academy, he had rebelled and left home. In the last two years they had heard no word of him. Not even Ivan, with all his connections. But Ivan had not learned his lesson. Now he was pushing Viktor with the same discipline that he had forced on his elder son.

264

'I don't like Uncle Ivan very much,' Dmitri said.

'Why?' Anna asked.

'Because he doesn't like me.'

'Nonsense, Mitya,' Anna said. 'He's very fond of you.' She had to deny it, though she knew that her son was speaking the truth. 'Come,' she said, 'I'll buy you some liquorice.'

They went to the shop and as she waited at the counter, a swift pain shot through her body, and looking down she saw a small pool of water at her feet.

'My baby's coming,' she said to the woman at the counter. 'Can you please telephone for an ambulance?'

'What's the matter, Mama?' Dmitri tugged at her skirt angrily. He saw her sudden pallor and it terrified him. 'Are you going to die?' he said.

'No, my darling,' She held him close. 'The baby is getting ready to be born. Soon you will have a little brother or sister.'

'I bet you'd like a little sister, wouldn't you?' a woman at the counter said to him.

'I don't want anything,' Dmitri said. 'I just want my Papa.'

The woman looked at Anna with pity, assuming her widowhood. 'You'll be all right, dear,' she said.

But Anna was worried. The baby was not due for another two months. She had made no arrangements for Dmitri's care while she was in hospital. She had to telephone Katya. She would get someone to do it from the hospital.

'They're coming at once,' the shopkeeper said. She lifted a chair over the counter. 'Sit down until they come.'

Then Anna remembered the liquorice. She took some kopeks from her purse and gave them to Dmitri. She did not speak. She did not trust her voice. Her labour had begun.

Shortly, they heard the ambulance bell. She walked towards the door taking Dmitri's hand. Two ambulance men helped her inside and motioned her to lie down on the stretcher. But she preferred to sit and continue to hold on to him. It was Dmitri who urged her to lie down, ordered her almost, sensing that, for better or worse, he was now the man in the house. He put his liquorice in his pocket. Such a prop was not suitable for his present role. He enjoyed the ambulance ride and its frantic bell, but he feigned indifference. Ambulances and fire engines were child's play. When they reached the hospital, he took his mother's arm and helped her step down from the van. He could see that she was in pain, and he couldn't hold back his tears. He couldn't understand what was going on. He'd heard stories in school about babies, but they were grotesque and unbelievable. Now he was forced to give them some credence. He hurried along by her side. Some nurses approached with a stretcher and helped his mother to mount it.

'Give me a kiss, Mitya,' Anna managed to say. 'I'll see you soon with your little sister or brother.'

The nurse put her arm around him. He was a child again. 'Don't let it hurt, Mama,' he said.

'Please ring this number,' Anna whispered to the nurse. 'Katya Volynina. Tell her to come for my son.' Then turning to Dmitri, she managed a smile. 'Now you can go and play with Viktor,' she said.

Then she was rolled away, while the nurse took Dmitri's hand and took him to her office and telephone.

When it rang in the Volynin apartment, Katya was startled. She could never get used to its bell. It frightened her, and she hated to pick up the receiver. It was like listening to a ghost. There were few private telephones in Leningrad at that time, and to own one was a privilege. Ivan had been promoted in the OGPU and he was entitled to such a bonus, and this unfair prerogative only served to deepen her dislike of the machine. It rarely rang when Ivan was not at home, and she wondered and feared who it might be. When the caller announced herself as speaking from the hospital, she feared that her long-lost Vassily had met with an accident. So she was relieved that it was on behalf of Anna who was there in the simple nature of things. But not so relieved when she realised that Anna was nowhere near her time.

'I'm leaving right now,' she said.

She grabbed her coat and ran to get Viktor who was playing in his room. 'Dmitri is coming to stay with us,' she said. 'We're going to fetch him.'

'Hooray.' Viktor jumped up excited. 'Can he sleep in my room, Mama?' he asked.

'Of course. But hurry.' She was frightened of what Ivan would say. The truce between them after the news of Pyotr's death, had been short-lived. Nowadays they barely spoke to each other. But on this she would defy him. Anna was her friend.

When they reached the front door, she heard Ivan's key in the lock. He would come home at any time, day or night, and despite their telephone, he would never give her notice.

'Where are you going?' he said.

'Anna's in hospital. The baby's early. I'm going to get Dmitri and bring him here.'

'What d'you think this is?' Ivan shouted. 'An orphanage?'

'I don't have time to stay and argue,' Katya said. 'Come on, Viktor.'

Ivan caught her by the arm. 'I don't care what you do,' he said, 'but Viktor's staying here.' He picked Viktor up with one arm. 'I don't want you playing with that boy, d'you hear me?'

'Yes, Papa.' Viktor was as afraid of his father as was Katya.

'I'll be back soon,' Katya said. And added, with sudden courage, 'With Dmitri.' She slammed the door after her, drowning his response.

When she reached the hospital, Anna was still in labour. Katya waited with Dmitri outside the ward and played with him. He had resorted to his liquorice having decided it was much easier under the circumstances to be a child. The labour was prolonged and Katya was worried, but a nurse reassured her that nothing was amiss. In time, in his child's time, Dmitri fell asleep, and Katya felt alone, and longed for company. She longed for talk, for diversion, anything to keep her mind away from her home and the problems she would face on her return. Just before dawn, a nurse appeared and told her that her friend was well and had given birth to a daughter.

'Is the baby all right?' Katya asked.

'Small,' the nurse laughed, 'but very beautiful.'

'Can I see her?'

'Just for a while,' the nurse said.

Katya rushed to the ward. She had to scan the line of beds before she could find Anna, who was lying at the end of the ward.

'Katya,' she shouted. Her joy at seeing her was fed by relief. And admiration too. For she knew it required courage to take a stand against Ivan concerning herself and Dmitri. They embraced tenderly.

'You're brave, Katya,' Anna whispered.

'You too,' Katya laughed. 'All us women.'

'Where is Dmitri?'

'He's asleep in the nurse's room. I'll take him home. He'll stay with us until you're ready to go home.'

'What about Ivan?'

'That's my problem,' Katya said. 'I'll deal with it.' But she had no notion how. Ivan could well turn her out of the apartment. Dmitri too. But he would hold on to Viktor. Indeed he might not even allow her to see her son again. He was more than capable of such cruelty, and in his privileged position, he would have no difficulty in manoeuvring the law for his own convenience. 'But first I must look at your daughter,' she said.

The baby was sleeping in a crib alongside the bed. She was indeed tiny. Her little face was yellowish and puckered like a shelled walnut.

'She's a little jaundiced,' Anna said. 'But she's whole.'

'What will you call her?'

'Olga. And Katya,' Anna whispered, 'I want her christened.'

'That will be impossible. We won't find anybody to do it. And it's risky even to enquire.'

'I shall find a way,' Anna said.

Then the nurse came and suggested that Anna needed to sleep a little.

'I'll come tomorrow,' Katya said. 'And I'll bring Dmitri and Viktor.'

Dmitri was asleep so Katya woke him. Then she took a taxi so that Dmitri could go back to sleep. When she gave the cab driver her address, he said, 'Volynin?'

She nodded, none too proud to admit it.

'I am very honoured,' he said.

Katya wished she herself could feel so privileged. But she took no pleasure in Ivan's rank nor the bonuses that attended it. She knew too much about the OGPU to honour it, and certainly enough to make her afraid. She hoped that Dmitri would not wake up in the taxi, and that his sleeping figure might move Ivan to a rare degree of compassion. But Ivan was not at home when she arrived. Neither was Viktor. Ivan had probably taken him to his office. Ivan believed in early initiation, even though it had failed so miserably with Vassily. She was relieved that he was out. She took Dmitri into her own bedroom, and laid him on the couch. In a few days she would move him in with Viktor. Then she herself went to bed, early as it was, but she was afraid of facing Ivan's returning wrath. But she did not sleep. She was worried about Anna. Anna would have to stop working in order to care for the baby, and she knew that without her tram earnings, she would not be able to pay the rent. Anna was too proud to ask anyone for money, and Katya thought she might write to Andrei who would certainly help his sister if he were told about the new baby. She heard Ivan's key in the door, and Viktor's voice asking for a drink. She pulled the blanket over her head and pretended to be asleep. She knew that Ivan would check on her room to see if she was home. That he would discover Dmitri, but seeing them both asleep, he would be robbed of argument. She heard him come into her room, pause and shut the door again. She would not worry about the morning. She would deal with it when it came.

But when it did, she was awakened by the slamming of the apartment door. Ivan was clearly as ill-equipped to deal with Dmitri's presence as Katya was to defend it. She rose with some relief and prepared the two boys for school. Viktor attended a special school, an establishment reserved for the children of the privileged, and as such a pupil he was called for in a government car. That morning he suggested to Katya, that they ask the driver to drop Dmitri off at his school since they would pass it on the way. But Katya refused. Ivan would be horrified at such a request and there was no point in provoking him further. So she took Dmitri to the tram, as Anna would have done, and promised him that after school they would go and see his baby sister.

When she returned home, she found a letter. It was post-marked Larionovka. The word shocked her. She had thought that it

269

belonged to a language long dead. It was a ghost word and as she read it aloud, its syllables wailed, pleading to be avenged. She pressed her fingers on the envelope. It was real and solid enough, yet she had understood that nobody was left in her childhood village, that all its souls, except the old and infirm had gone into the streets and never returned. She couldn't imagine who would be writing to her. Yet the name on the envelope was clear. Katya Volynina. Whoever had written it clearly assumed that she and Ivan were married. She tore the letter open, and turned immediately to its signature. And her heart filled with joy as she recalled so clearly the kindly face of Avdotya, that bringer of life to the village, and now that witness of its loss.

My dear Katya, she read. You will have heard that Larionovka is no more. I was lucky, if you can call it that. They did not notice my little house on the outskirts of the village. I was there alone. My orphans had gone to the grainhouse with all the other children. I never saw them again. The village is deserted now. Only a few old people survived. So there is no future here. No more children for me to bring into this world. It is so barren, there is no place for me. I want to come to Leningrad to be with your children. Or my dear Anna's. To look after them, as if they were my own family. Please write to me, dear Katya, and tell me if I can come. Your loving Avdotya.

Katya read the letter over many times. Any reminder of her village was a solace to her, even though it was now but a ghost. And Avdotya's survival was a real joy, her letter was more than well timed. Anna would welcome her into her family, and Avdotya could nurse Olga while Anna earned what she could. She sat down and replied immediately. She told her about Sasha's arrest, and Anna's new baby daughter. *Come as soon as you can,* she wrote. *We are waiting for you.* As she wrote she recalled Avdotya's little black bag that she carried with her always. And how once, in the manor kitchen, she had opened it to Katya's delight. One by one, she had extracted the tools of her trade, explaining the function of each. Then Katya remembered the little case containing a vial. 'That's holy water,' Avdotya had said. 'For baptism.'

270

So Katya wrote a postscript. *Please bring your vial of holy water, and come soon.*

Olga would be baptised after all. Anna's apartment with all its loving, was every bit as holy as a church, and Avdotya, who had seen it all so many times before, was more than equal to any parish priest.

20

Avdotya arrived in Leningrad on the day Anna came out of hospital, and within a short time she had settled in as part of the family. With Katya's help, Anna had contacted Andrei in Moscow. He was delighted with the news of the birth of his niece, but alas he still had no news of Sasha's whereabouts. With regret he had to decline the invitation to the baptism. His business, he said, kept him in Moscow.

Over the next few years, the importance of his position in the Ministry of Internal Affairs increased. He was trusted. He was privileged. He should have been happy. But in truth, Andrei was in a state of deep depression, sunk in a melancholy that was almost paralysing.

Pavel had found a new lover, and after almost thirty years of companionship, Andrei was now alone. It had been a bitter parting. Pavel was desperately in love and in such a state, bewildered by the grief he had caused.

'These things happen,' he had said. 'We've had good years together. But now it's over.' Then he had resorted to silence.

It was this silence that had led Andrei, a man of an intrinsically peaceful nature, to an act of violence. He wanted argument, he wanted explanation, he wanted at least remorse. But out of Pavel's tormenting silence, he could expect nothing. The pain of his rejection was almost physical and he writhed in his despair. 'Stay with me,' he had pleaded, ashamed of his shabby lack of pride. Pavel had turned his back on him. And in his pain, now fed by the humiliation he had brought upon himself, Andrei had picked up the nearest object to hand. It was a silver paperweight that he had once given to Pavel on his birthday. Now that gift seemed part and parcel of his rejection, and he thought that if he could discard it, it would rid him of pain. He threw it with all his force, and in his spleen, without aim. In that moment, Pavel had turned, and the weight caught him on his cheek, and the blood spurted, astonished. They stared at each other. Andrei bit his lip on an apology. For in truth he was not sorry. For a moment he wished Pavel dead, but he realised too, that in the assault, he had given him more than enough reason to leave. Of which the silent Pavel took advantage. He had simply put a handkerchief to his cheek, and left the room. Andrei sank into a chair, defeated, and gave way to his tears and his sorrow. But all the while he listened carefully to the torturing silence of Pavel's departure. The tiptoe across the bedroom floor, the apologetic creak of the wardrobe door, the sorry click of the suitcase, and again the tiptoe through the hall, to the front door. And all in the same leaking shroud of silence. Andrei had remained in his chair, unable to move, benumbed in sorrow, and there he stayed till morning, when he stirred slowly from a half-sleep, in mournful recall, and epic frailty.

His heartbreak was compounded by the fact that he could not expect any public sympathy. Over the years, his affair with Pavel had been clandestine. In the Ministry, amongst their colleagues, they had been accepted as friends and flatmates. Neither of them could afford any other interpretation. So in his work, Andrei had to feign a certain indifference, and to maintain that face of bon-homie for which he was known and admired. Moreover, Pavel's new lover worked in the same department, though on a lower level of rank and Andrei's daily encounters with Pavel and his own replacement were unavoidable and painful in the extreme. He knew he had to seek a transfer. Life in Moscow had become unbearable.

He had a certain influence in his department and his superior was a close friend. But he could not confide in him. He could simply express his wish that after so many years in Moscow, he needed a change, and that if a foreign posting became available, he would be grateful for a transfer. He knew that their man in Berlin was due for retirement soon. Berlin was a posting he would wish for.

Nicolai was there now, and although they were so bitterly different from each other, Andrei still felt for him that love and worship of a younger brother. Over the years, he had secretly enquired after Nicolai's welfare, for his brother was still considered an enemy of the State, whose life was never out of danger. Indeed he had learned some years ago that the loyal Fedya had been killed in the defence of his master, and on that same spot outside the Café Imperial where Andrei had saved his brother's life. He had learned too, that Nicolai had married, one Vera, of White Russian lineage and one of his own kind. They had a son too, he had heard, named Nicolai for his father. He would love to see him again, to embrace him in secret, to talk about Larionovka, and those happy days before the sword had divided them. But nothing of this did he mention to his superior. He simply stated his availability for transfer.

And in a few weeks, the offer came through. And as he had hoped and half expected, it was for Berlin. He said his farewells to all his colleagues, all that is, except for Pavel, for Andrei too had learned the value of the weapon of silence.

He arranged his journey to pass through Leningrad. He wanted to see Anna. Anna was part of that family that he longed for, a family that included Nicolai, kin bound by blood and history for whom, despite differences, the tribal love was inviolable. He told Anna about Pavel. She was the only one he could confide in, and there was a certain measure of relief in sharing his bereavement with another. Anna consoled him. She accepted that her brother had loved Pavel with the same passion that she shared with Sasha. And in that acceptance she envisaged the agony of its loss. She cheered him with reminiscences of their happy childhood, memories of which they could never be deprived. Stories that would not desert them, events that knew not how to betray. She told him too that she had forgiven Nicolai, and that she sent him her love, because for her too, the bond of family had been accepted as mercifully unbreakable. By the time Andrei left Leningrad for Berlin, he felt undeniably healed, and he knew that in time, his Pavel wound would close.

Before leaving, Andrei called on Ivan. He went to his office at the Smolny Institute.

'You're better off away from here,' Ivan said. 'You don't have the talent for palace intrigues. Berlin will suit you far better.'

Andrei noted the sumptuous furnishings of Ivan's office. He was clearly on his corrupted way to the top. He was saddened by the thought. He wondered what was left of the young Ivan, that boy who so many years ago, had saved his life in the freezing waters of the river.

'How's Katya?' he asked. He thought that the tone of Ivan's reply to that question might indicate a lingering of the Ivan that was.

'She goes her own way,' Ivan said coldly. Then Andrei knew that Ivan had changed irrevocably.

'Your brother's in Berlin,' Ivan said. 'D'you know that?'

'I have no contact with him,' Andrei said. 'I'm aware that it would be dangerous.'

'I have to tell you that he will not be forgiven. His escape from the prison is not forgotten. But what is worse is the murder of one of my best men in Paris. He was following your brother at the time. He was murdered by one of your brother's kind.'

More kin than kind, Andrei thought, and experienced a certain pleasure in the sight of Ivan so deceived.

'You'd best not contact him in Berlin like you did in Paris. I know about that,' Ivan said.

'He sought me out,' Andrei lied.

'I'm not asking you to betray him,' Ivan said. 'Just protect yourself.'

'Is there any news of Sasha?' Andrei asked. He threw the fraternal ball into Ivan's court.

'Nothing,' Ivan said. 'If he's still alive, he's in a labour camp somewhere. And Pyotr is dead, of course,' he added.

For the first time in their meeting, Andrei sensed a chink in Ivan's suit of mail. 'I heard about Larionovka,' he said. 'I'm terribly sorry.' He went to touch Ivan's arm, and Ivan did not recoil. Indeed he seemed to welcome his touch and responded likewise. 'We all need families,' he said. 'Even if it has to be the Party.'

It was a confession of gross emotional failure and Andrei pitied him.

'We're family, Ivan, you and I,' he said. 'We're brothers.'

Then Ivan embraced him, and his body shook with sobs. For the word 'brother' had triggered the person of Pyotr after all this time.

'Katya is family too,' Andrei said.

Ivan loosened his embrace. 'Katya's not blood,' he said. There seemed little more to say. Andrei feared for Ivan's future. For if the Party had become his family, in time he would learn that there was no greater expert in betrayal.

He made his way to the railway station, and as he settled into his sleeper, he wondered whether he would ever return.

After only a few days in Berlin, Andrei had a comfortable sense of coming home. Berlin was a city rampant with his own kind, open, unashamed and without fear. He noticed how they dressed, with a certain proud flamboyance, and he straightaway took himself to tailors and shirt-makers, to equip himself in likewise fashion. His job at the Legation entailed much socialising and nightlife. But he was warned to be on his guard. The year was 1939, and rumours of war were rife. But the Soviet Legation was not perturbed. Their country had signed a non-aggression pact with Germany. Each agreed not to wage war against the other. Let Britain, if she so wished, take up arms against Hitler. And the rest of Europe too, if Hitler gave them time. As long as the Soviet Union was left in peace. Nevertheless, caution was advised, as it was advocated in Soviet Legations all over the world. For the Soviets had learned to trust nobody.

Andrei was anxious to contact Nicolai. Unlike Paris, he did not know the gathering places of White Russians in Berlin. And he dared not make enquiries. He could only eavesdrop amongst his colleagues. He hoped that Nicolai would hear of his new posting and would himself seek him out. Though he could not be sure whether Nicolai had mellowed over the years, and the bitter greeting that he had given Andrei in Paris still haunted him. But he would wait. He dared not search for him. In any case, he had much else to do. The work at the Legation was far more loaded than in

Moscow, and sometimes he had to work late into the night. Besides, Andrei had fallen in love.

Shortly after his arrival in Berlin, he had discovered the haunts of his kind. The Kurfürstendamm at night was an avenue of pure and simple pleasure that catered for all manner of tastes. Bars proliferated, and dancing clubs. Each sported their regulars, and it was not long before Andrei found one to his taste. It was called The Black Cat. It lay slightly off the avenue as if to stress that it was exclusive. Which indeed it was. For it was expensive, and sumptuously furnished. There was a choice of rare and exotic foods and a small and discreet orchestra could be heard from the gallery. On his first entry, Andrei felt immediately at home. He was warmly greeted by the head waiter who offered him a table. But Andrei preferred to sit at the bar, since he was alone. Many men sat there, and he hoped for conversation. Among other reasons he needed to practise his German. It was already of reasonable standard, but he was rarely called upon to use it. In the Legation they spoke only Russian, and on social occasions there was always an interpreter at hand. He approached the bar nervously, both on account of its language and its nature. He placed himself at the end of the bar with a distance of three stools between him and his neighbour and he ordered a schnapps. The men eyed him warily. Then one rose and came to his side. 'You're new here,' he said. 'My name's Kurt. Why don't you join us for dinner?'

'That's very kind,' Andrei said. 'My name is Andrei.' He shook the man's proffered hand.

'You're Russian, I can hear,' Kurt said. 'But your German is very good. Come, meet my friends, and we'll get a table.' Kurt took Andrei's arm and introduced him to the other men at the bar. There was a Karl, a Peter, a Fritz and a Herman, and they were all very friendly.

'It's good to see a new face,' one of them said.

At dinner, they told him about themselves. They were all artists of a kind. Poets, musicians and painters. Andrei had rarely mixed in such company. He was tempted to ask them if they had heard of Alexander Volynin, but he was mindful of the caution that was the watchword of the Legation. And mindful of it too, when they

277

asked him about his profession. He said that he was a mere clerk at the Legation, responsible for the incoming and outgoing mail. In such a menial position, he could hardly be a source of information to anybody. The evening passed in great pleasure, and for the first time in many months Andrei felt that he might still be available to happiness. He left in the early hours of the morning, promising them to come again. And soon.

He was tempted to return the following night, but he knew it must not become a habit. Habits did not sit well with caution. Over the next few weeks he went occasionally to the club and dined with his friends. It was on his fifth visit to The Black Cat, that Andrei met Hans Elder. One look, and the very first that passed between them, predicted the perilous and blissful narrative of their future, and neither attempted to deny it. They had dinner together, along with Andrei's other friends, but it was as if they dined alone – others' talk, others' presence, were merely the background of strangers. After dinner Hans invited Andrei to his apartment for a postprandial schnapps. He alerted the head waiter to call his car, and by the time they had taken their coats and said their farewells, a chauffeured limousine was waiting at the door. Hans Elder was clearly a man of means, as was further evidenced by the apartment in which he lived. A penthouse, the walls lined with pictures by the artists of the time. Hans was an art dealer, and in the course of his career, had amassed a serious collection of his own. Some Picassos, a Modigliani, two Braques, a Matisse, and a number of banned and decadent Noldes. Hans was in his late forties, a year or so older than Andrei, but clearly a man of many more years' experience. As Andrei was later to learn, Hans's apartment was the focal point of the Berlin artistic society, and he, its most generous and amicable host. They were silent as they sipped their brandy. An occasional smile passed between them as if they had known each other for a very long time. Both knew that theirs would be no casual affair, that its tempo would begin in a slow and leisurely manner, unsure at times, and open to risk. But they would both carefully skirt that slippery perimeter in prolonged foreplay. Though the tone of their conversation, when it began, was intimate, its matter was of general concern.

They talked politics. Andrei still insisted on his menial job at the Legation, for caution was very much the style of perimeter travel. The year was 1939, approaching Christmas, and Germany was already at war. Russia clung to its neutrality confirmed by the Russo-German peace pact. Hans wondered how long that non-aggression pact would hold, and expressed his wish that their countries' friendship would last for ever, if only for the reason that he and Andrei would not be separated. It was the only hint of intimacy that intruded into their conversation that evening. Otherwise they kept to world affairs, steering very clear of family and personal details, for those would have been too familiar. When Andrei left Hans's apartment in the early hours of the morning, he felt that he had been reborn. He gave a passing thought to Pavel, but it was one of pity and contempt.

Over the months that followed, Andrei settled easily and cautiously into German society. He saw Hans almost daily, and often attended soirées at his apartment. At every party he deftly ferreted for news of Nicolai's whereabouts, turning the conversation to White Russian émigrés and feigning his disgust. But he gathered no clues. Although Germany was at war, the cultural life of the capital still flourished, and Hans and Andrei frequented the opera house and theatres, and often supped post-performance at The Black Cat.

One night at the opera house, there was a performance of *Boris Godunov*, Mussorgsky's opera, based on a Pushkin play. A thoroughly Russian evening. Andrei looked forward to it with a certain nostalgia.

They arrived early. Part of the pleasure of the evening was to view the audience as they took their seats in the auditorium. Hans's membership of the opera committee entitled him to a private box, which was a perfect vantage point for viewing. Andrei admired the women for their sheer elegance and the languor with which they displayed themselves. Suddenly his attention was drawn to a figure walking down the aisle. Not so much the figure as the limp. Although he could only see the back of the man, and his dragging gait, he knew that it was Nicolai, because his heart stuttered at the sight of him. He was tempted to call his name, then remembered

279

the official caution. Besides, Hans knew nothing about his brother, nor indeed anything about his family or their past. Though they had kept each other's company for many months, both men were still skirting the circumference of their friendship, but both knew that the time would soon come to drop their perimeter guard and to embrace an intimacy and all that that would entail. Andrei glued his eyes on the man's back, willing it to turn. He noticed that he was closely followed by a woman, and a boy about fourteen years old, whom Andrei surmised were Vera and Nicolai, their son. He grew excited, with a comfortable and warm sense of family. When the group reached their row, Vera touched her husband on his arm, and he allowed her and his son to pass by him into the row, so that he could use the aisle seat. As he turned, Andrei stared at him, and brotherhood was confirmed. They were but a short distance away from each other, and Andrei dared to raise his hand, hoping to draw a swift attention to himself. Nicolai, who was viewing the arrivals too, caught the gesture and looked in his direction. He stared for a moment, and then smiled. He moved his hand slightly to return the wave, but then thought better of it, for he too was schooled in caution. But the smile was undeniable, and Andrei took it gratefully for forgiveness.

'Somebody you know?' Hans asked, seeing Andrei's raised hand.

'Just a colleague,' Andrei said quickly, then looked at Hans, and felt his tenderness. He knew then that he could not ration his person with this man, that very soon he would have to tell him all.

'A close colleague?' Hans asked, for Andrei was still smiling.

Immediately Andrei became serious. He did not want to be misunderstood. 'No,' he said, 'just a working one.' But inside himself, Andrei was still smiling. For he realised that now that Nicolai knew he was in Berlin, he, on his own account, would seek him out. So he did not linger in the foyer when the opera was over. In any case, Hans was anxious to dine at The Black Cat, and they both hurried to their waiting limousine. Andrei was in a state of euphoria for the rest of the evening. That night, after their usual postprandial cognac in Hans's apartment, Andrei asked if he might stay. It was time for the end of caution, and the renewal of family. The following day Andrei moved into Hans's apartment and made his home there.

A few days later, as he left his office, Andrei caught sight of Nicolai on the corner of the street. He was waiting beside a car. Nicolai waved and signalled him to cross. He opened the car door and within seconds Andrei was inside, with Nicolai at the wheel. He drove quickly out of the traffic until he reached an open road. Then he pulled into a lay-by and the brothers embraced.

'You saved my life in Paris,' Nicolai said. 'Why?'

'Because you're my brother.'

'I come before the Party?' Nicolai asked.

'You always will. And thank God for that,' Andrei said. He smiled. 'Where are we going?'

'To my apartment. I want you to meet my family.'

'We have a lot to talk about,' Andrei said.

'Let's wait until we get home,' he said.

Nicolai lived in the suburbs and it was a long drive out of the city. The brothers were silent during the journey. Only once did Andrei speak. 'Anna sends you her love,' he said. He felt it was the most important news he had to tell him. It sanctioned a reunion of family.

Nicolai stopped the car suddenly. 'Is that true?' he said.

'Of course,' Andrei said. 'She made a point of it.'

Nicolai drove on, his face wreathed in smiles. 'We have so much to talk about,' he said again.

Nicolai lived well. His apartment was tastefully furnished and appointed, and Andrei assumed that Vera had brought wealth to the marriage. He studied her and was struck by her resemblance to their mother. He was glad of it for it seemed to further cement their family. The young Nicolai took after his father, and sometimes, in jest, he even assumed his limp, which seemed a symbol of the closeness between them. Nicolai had aged, but he had mellowed too, and Andrei assumed that Vera had brought him a measure of content.

Over supper, Andrei filled them in with news of the family. Anna's children, Sasha's arrest. Nicolai showed concern.

'That monstrous man of steel, as they call him, has to be destroyed,' Nicolai said.

For a moment there was a spark of the old Tsarist patriot, and in a way, Andrei welcomed it, because it hinted that his brother, even though on the wrong side, was still a fighter.

'There are thousands who think as I do,' Nicolai went on. 'All over Europe. Our time will come.'

Andrei decided not to argue with him. His was fantasy talk. Perhaps Nicolai knew it himself and as he grew older, his fighting talk would become but an expression of his nostalgia.

'Will you stay in Berlin?' Andrei asked.

'So long as there is peace with our country. But I don't trust the Germans. They will turn on us too in time.'

'But we have a non-aggression pact,' Andrei said.

'A piece of paper,' Nicolai said with contempt. 'Hitler will not stop at Russia. He has his eye on the whole of Europe. He and Stalin are exactly the same, and there's only room for one such monster on the planet. But let's not talk politics. Tell me again about Anna.'

And so the evening passed in Larionovka reminiscence. It was a happy time, and Andrei knew that the rift between them had closed. When he returned to Hans's apartment that night, he regaled him with their talk of the evening. Hans was now family to him, and he was entitled to his share of Larionovka.

Over the next few months, Andrei spent much clandestine time with Nicolai, sometimes alone, and often with his family. He had told Nicolai everything, but the names of Pavel and Hans had stuck in his throat. He did not think that Nicolai could ever accept their reverberations. And it saddened him. For without knowledge of those names, he would never be wholly known by his brother. Yet he was anxious for Nicolai to meet with Hans, and he wondered whether he dare take him to the suburbs for their next meeting.

The opportunity came shortly afterwards. It was Nicolai's birthday and he was giving himself a party. He issued Andrei's invitation and suggested that, if he wished, he could bring a friend. A friend. Under that label, Andrei thought, anyone could pass for anybody. Hans was delighted to accept, and selected a small drawing from his collection as a birthday present. Nicolai was delighted as much by its donor as the present itself. Indeed he spent much of the evening talking to Hans until Vera had to drag him away to attend his other guests. Most of them were White Russians in varying degrees of rebellion. Some talked openly of Stalin's tyranny, and the need to overthrow him. Others dispensed with that need, but dissented none the less. But a few of them were well on that road to nostalgia, the signposts of rebellion a mere formality. When they were leaving the party in the early hours of the morning, Nicolai took Andrei to one side.

'I like your friend very much,' Nicolai said. 'I like him because he loves you. And I know that you love him. I'm happy that you're happy together.' Then he embraced him. 'Come soon again. Both of you,' he said.

Andrei had spent over a year in Berlin, and he considered it the happiest time of his life. He could not envisage a life without Hans, and he prayed for peace so that they would never be separated. But there were rumours of war.

It was on New Year's Day in 1941, that Andrei was called into his superior's office at the Legation.

'You have been ordered home,' the officer said.

'But why?' Andrei had to control his voice, for it was blocked with tears for this sudden and unexplained loss of Hans and Nicolai.

'No reason has been given,' the man said. 'Orders from home.'

Andrei didn't believe him. He had the impression that his superior knew far more than he was giving away, and Andrei was frightened. Yet he could think of no reason for his recall, and could only surmise that his meetings with Nicolai had been discovered. That evening he couldn't bring himself to break the news to Hans. He didn't want to believe it himself and to speak it aloud, would only make it true. But he had to leave in three days. They had already arranged his travel. There was so little time. But he held his tongue. Hans was particularly affectionate that evening. They dined at home and afterwards listened to music as they sipped their brandy.

'How lucky we are to have found each other,' Hans said. But

still Andrei held his tongue. The thought crossed his mind that he might even leave Germany without saying a word.

But he had to see Nicolai. He didn't care if he was being followed. Whatever they knew about him could not now be withdrawn. He left it until the day before he was due to leave, and then, in broad daylight, he went to Nicolai's apartment.

Nicolai himself opened the door. He was surprised but delighted to see him.

'I've come to say goodbye,' Andrei said. 'They're sending me home.'

Nicolai's face clouded in disappointment. 'But why?' he said. 'Is it because of me?'

'I can't think of any reason. And if that *is* the reason, then you must leave here immediately. You are not safe, Nicolai. Neither is Vera or the boy.'

'Where *am* I safe?' Nicolai asked.

'You could go to France. The NKVD are not so active there. Not any more.'

'It only takes one man and one bullet,' Nicolai said.

'But there's less of a risk there,' Andrei said.

Nicolai embraced him. 'When shall I see you again?' he said sadly. 'Shall I *ever* see you again?'

Andrei couldn't answer. He could give him no words of reassurance. 'Will you promise me to leave?' he said.

'I'll do what I can. Vera has always wanted to go to France.' They embraced once more.

'Andrushka,' Nicolai said, 'I regret those years that we lost. I was stupid and hot-headed. I didn't realise then how much I loved you.'

Andrei could not stem his tears. 'I've always known that,' he sobbed, 'because I never stopped loving you, even in the worst of times.' He wondered whether his parting with Hans would be as deeply painful as this one.

'Write to Anna,' Andrei said, 'and she will tell me where you are. There will come a time when you can come home. Russia is no motherland if she cannot welcome all her sons.'

They embraced again, loath to take leave of each other. Then

Andrei turned quickly. 'Kiss Vera and Nicolai for me,' he said.

'And Anna for me.'

He was leaving the following day. He would go to the Legation and say his farewells to his colleagues and try not to notice those who avoided him. For over the last few days it was clear that some of them openly shunned his company, and their slights frightened him for he felt he carried a stain that was infectious. A man is known by the company he keeps and they clearly did not want Andrei Larionov as reference. His departure from the Legation was swift. The farewells, such as had been offered to him, had been cold, and he had no regrets in leaving. He considered that the hardest parting was over. There now remained only Hans.

Hans had arranged a dinner that evening. Andrei knew most of the guests. He had met them at The Black Cat. It was as if Hans was throwing him a farewell party of all his Berlin friends. For a moment Andrei thought that Hans might somehow have heard of his impending departure. But soon he dismissed the idea when Hans made arrangements for him to attend the opera later in the week. 'Then perhaps we can go to the country for the weekend,' he said. 'I know a lovely hotel. We both need some fresh, unpolluted air.'

The party whirled into the early hours. At one point after dinner, Andrei withdrew to his room, and started to pack. As he opened his suitcase and the wardrobe door, he was reminded of the creaking silence of Pavel's departure. But he was not leaving of his own accord, and certainly for no other loving. He was being discarded, and by a body of people who knew nothing about love. Only in so far as it referred to the Party. For a moment he shared his brother's conviction that Stalin must be eliminated.

He finished his packing and joined the party downstairs. Hans had put on his record player and the men were dancing. When he saw Andrei reappear, Hans left his partner and went towards him. Then with an exaggerated spread of his arms, he spun him into a waltz. The evening was beginning to be pervaded with a sense of finality. They had had their last supper together and now it was the last waltz. He sensed that never in his life would he see Berlin again.

After the last guest had left in the early hours, Hans made to go to bed.

'I must talk to you,' Andrei said.

'What is it, my dear? Are you not well?'

'No. I'm well enough.' He put his hand on Hans's arm. 'They're sending me back to Moscow. I leave tomorrow.'

'That's impossible.' Hans had paled. 'But why?'

'They give no reason. They don't have to. I think it was because I was seeing my brother.'

'But that's nothing. That's not a crime. They will reprimand you and then you will return.' His voice was desperate.

'I doubt that very much,' Andrei said.

Hans took his hand. 'I shall miss you so terribly,' he said.

'And I you.'

Neither of them wanted to sleep. Neither wanted the morning to take them unawares. By waiting for it, with their eyes well open, they could possibly delay its arrival, as a watched pot is slow to boil. So for the rest of the night they lay in each other's arms in the firelight, and they spoke of their love and mourned their parting. When the morning light filtered undeniably through the latticed panes, they took each other in violent and loving farewell.

It was not an easy journey. As the train neared Moscow, Andrei's fears grew. He had been ordered to report immediately to the Foreign Ministry. He was to present himself to Astakhov, his immediate superior. They were friends, or had been, in his Moscow days. He prayed that that friendship still held. When the train pulled into the station, he hurried to find a taxi. He wanted no delay. Whatever it was he had to face, he wanted it over and done with. Perhaps it was nothing at all, he tried to hope. Perhaps they were simply short of a man in Moscow. He would make the most of such a posting. He would be closer to Anna. And maybe Hans could even come to visit him. Thus he deluded himself until the taxi drew up outside the Ministry. But at the sight of its awesome façade, fear once again invaded him. But now he could not turn back. His knees buckled as he climbed the steps.

As he entered the foyer, once so familiar, he had no sense of homecoming, as if he was pre-empting the rejection he would receive. There were few people about. The porter greeted him warmly like a long-lost friend, and that greeting heartened him a little until he realised that the porter was in far too menial a position to know what was going on upstairs. Then a group of people crossed the foyer, but Andrei recognised none of them. He had been away from Moscow for over a year, and he accepted that there must have been a turnover in personnel. He started to climb the stairs. On the first landing, he saw a familiar face. The man used to be his filing clerk, but he couldn't remember his name. They had been friends, and often they'd had a drink together after work. The man started when he saw him, turned away, and quickened his pace as if he had urgent business to attend to. Andrei paused and leaned on the banister. He could hear his heart beating in fear. He was returning to Moscow as a pariah.

He dragged himself up to the next landing. And looking suddenly, he saw a figure watching him from the landing above. Quickly the observer turned his back, but in that split second of viewing, Andrei swore that it was Ivan. He was tempted to call his name, but if it were Ivan, it was clear he did not want to be recognised. To be shunned by Ivan presaged the severest sentence, and Andrei was tempted to rush down the stairs and out of the foyer and find himself somewhere to hide. He could return to Berlin, he thought, and share concealment with Nicolai. He turned and slowly made his way down the stairs. He knew he must not run, though his feet itched with a fugitive's urgency. As he reached the first landing, he saw two men coming towards him. He did not know their faces, so he thought it safe to smile. A smile was a matter of courtesy as well as the badge of the innocent. But their faces remained stony. As he neared them, they parted and took his arm on each side. Then they turned him, and guided him back up the stairs. To an observer their hold was gentle, but Andrei felt it was an iron grip. He had the feeling that he'd seen the last of the sky.

The journey back to the second storey seemed interminable, and he wondered at his escorts' slowness of pace. For his part, having

287

been trapped, he would have bounded up the stairs, and he assumed that their steady and measured tempo was punitive. At last they reached Astakhov's office. One of them knocked on the door. Then, at the response, the other turned the handle, and Andrei was shoved unceremoniously inside. His escorts withdrew, and Andrei faced Astakhov alone. He was relieved that whatever would pass between them would not be public. Then he noticed that the door of the adjoining office was ajar, and that the shadow of a figure loomed unsteadily on the jamb. He would have liked to sit down, but there was no invitation from Astakhov who sat so comfortably behind his desk.

'Welcome back to Moscow, Larionov,' his superior said. It was a hopeful beginning, and Andrei dared to ask why he had been recalled.

'It's true that we have a non-aggression pact with the Germans,' Astakhov said. 'But that doesn't mean that they can be trusted.'

'Of course,' Andrei readily agreed. 'For my part, I don't trust them at all.' He thought of Hans suddenly, and all his friends in The Black Cat, and he felt a traitor. At the same time he wondered what mistrust of German promises had to do with his visits to Nicolai, and the patent lack of connection disturbed him. He watched the shadow on the doorjamb as it undulated in its eavesdropping.

'You say you don't trust them, Larionov,' Astakhov said. There was a time, Andrei remembered, when his superior had called him by his first name, accompanied sometimes by a friendly slap on the back.

'I don't trust them at all,' Andrei repeated, though he knew that Astakhov did not believe him.

'You made certain exceptions,' Astakhov said. At last there was a smile. But it was not a smile of pleasure or friendship. Rather one of cunning and discovery. Andrei had no idea what he was talking about. What was now clear to him, however, was that his recall had nothing to do with Nicolai.

'I don't know what you mean,' he said.

'You were friendly with a certain Hans Elder,' Astakhov said. 'Very friendly, I believe.'

Andrei felt himself redden. He hoped that it might be generously read as his sexual shyness. But it could equally have betokened guilt.

'I saw him from time to time,' Andrei admitted.

'You bloody well lived with him,' Astakhov shouted.

Andrei's knees began to tremble, and his bowels threatened. 'May I sit down?' he pleaded.

Astakhov nodded, and Andrei took a chair and folded himself into what he considered an embrace, for the comfort it afforded him was such a physical relief, that he felt he could well withstand further questioning. For a moment he relished the easing of his bones. 'Thank you,' he said.

'You moved into Elder's apartment in December 1939,' Astakhov said. He referred to notes on his desk. 'You made several visits to the opera and the theatre together. And frequently you dined at The Black Cat.' One could not miss the note of contempt in Astakhov's voice as he named the club. Clearly he considered it a den of depravity. Still Andrei consoled himself, there was no crime in going to the opera or theatre, and The Black Cat was not out of bounds. And still the name of Nicolai had not been mentioned. He was bewildered by his recall. But the bombshell was about to drop, and Andrei noticed once again how the shadow salivated on the adjoining door.

'D'you know who this Hans Elder is?' Astakhov shouted.

'He's an art dealer,' Andrei said in all his innocence.

Astakhov laughed. 'You fool. You were completely taken in by his loving,' he spat the word, 'by his opera and theatre tickets, by his salons and his country retreats.'

'Who is he then?' Andrei whispered.

'He works for German Intelligence,' Astakhov said flatly. 'He knows the inside workings of our Berlin Legation better than those who work there. And he knows it, you fool, from you. "How was your day at the office, dear?" he would ask you. And every evening you told him exactly what you had done. And more than that. What the others were doing. And every fact and figure he took back to German Intelligence.'

'How do you know?' Andrei was almost weeping. Weeping for Hans's treachery as well as for his own fear.

'We have our spies too,' Astakhov said.

So it had nothing to do with Nicolai, and there was some relief in that.

'What will become of me?' he dared to ask.

'They will want to question you.'

It was the 'they' that was the death sentence, the anonymous 'they'. 'They' who asked the questions as a mere formality and 'they' who were monumentally indifferent to the replies.

'Please, please,' Andrei begged. He wanted to rise from his chair but he did not trust his shivering legs. 'Hans was only my lover,' he confessed, and his confession astounded him. It was an admission that could only be wrung from him on the pain of death. 'I'm – I'm not a spy,' he stammered. 'You know that. For God's sake, Astakhov, we worked together long enough.'

But Astakhov had lost interest. He rapped loudly on his desk. The outer door opened and the two escorts entered. At the same moment Andrei noted how the adjoining door was suddenly closed. He felt himself lifted by the elbows. As he was raised from the chair, he felt his trousers wet with fear.

'Pig,' one of the escorts said, noting the stain on the chair covering. Then they dragged him out of the room. When they had gone, Astakhov went into the adjoining office. Ivan was seated at the desk.

'Thank you for sparing me that,' Ivan said.

'It was enough that you came from Leningrad, comrade,' Colonel Astakhov said. 'Your presence will legitimise the outcome.'

'Where have they taken him?' Ivan asked.

'To the Lubyanka. He is guilty. There will be no further questioning. He will be hanged tomorrow. Those are my orders. I regret that you have to be present, but Andrei Larionov need never know.'

Andrei was thrown into a cell in the Lubyanka and he waited for the 'they' to come and question him. He had not yet fully assimilated Hans's treachery. He recalled their days and nights together and all that he had told him. But Hans had never pumped him for information. He didn't have to. Andrei had told him everything in the name of love. Yet he couldn't hate Hans. He would need time for that and he wondered in fear if that time would be given him. He started to cry, as he thought of Anna and Nicolai. He wondered if Ivan knew about his plight, but he had to conclude that Ivan was ignorant of his recall. Otherwise he would have saved him, as he had saved him from the river when he was a child. He was suddenly tired and wanted very much to sleep. But he was afraid that 'they' would come and he didn't want to be caught off guard. He was hungry too, and realised that he hadn't eaten since he had left Berlin. He was glad that he could still be assailed by those very human needs, for it meant that his body was alive and in protest. He listened for footsteps outside his door. But all was silent. Perhaps they would not question him after all. Perhaps they had put him in the Lubyanka simply to frighten him, and after a few days he would be back at his desk. He thought of Nicolai, and wanted desperately to be in touch with Anna so that he could give her her brother's love and forgiveness. It seemed to him the most important reason for his return home.

He dared to think once more of Hans. He recalled their loving together, but now he had to acknowledge that it was obscenely laced with deception, and that knowledge soured his recall. Yet still he longed for him and his depraved desire offended him. He recalled that Hans had seemed desolate at his departure. Perhaps he had really loved him, although he had so subtly engineered his fall. He hoped that Hans missed him, and in those longing moments, that he was racked with remorse. He called his name into the darkness of his cell, and it reverberated around the walls in sordid discord. His hunger now began to accentuate his fatigue. He knew that if he closed his eyes, he would fall asleep quickly, but he willed himself to stay awake in case 'they' would arrive. In time his will weakened and he lay on his cot, and indulged in the soothing thought of Nicolai.

When he was roughly awakened, he thought that 'they' had come. He noted that it was morning. A grey dawn light loitered at the window. He must have slept long for he felt refreshed, but it was a little time before he realised where he was, and why, and that the two men who stood above his cot were not the 'they' he

291

had been expecting, but those same who had escorted him some time ago. Then he began to shiver.

'It's time,' one of the escorts said. 'Get up.'

Time for what, Andrei thought. For breakfast perhaps, realising his hunger. He rose willingly, and let the men grab him by his arms. They led him out of the cell, and down a long corridor. At the end of it, through the chinks of an iron door, Andrei could see the dawn. He faltered. He had served the Cause long enough to know the meaning of dawn. That lonely latitude of twilight, without witness. Too early for breakfast, and too late for living. He smiled at the futility of it all. The escorts had to drag him the last few feet to the door, and when it was opened the grim grey light of the dawn almost blinded him. He saw the gallows, and marvelled at its simple symmetry. He thought of his parents, of Anna and Nicolai. All of them maimed in the name of the Cause. And now he himself. He noted that he had stopped shivering and he was glad that he was not afraid. There was no one about, except those who would put a swift end to his life, but he held his head high for he needed no witness to his pride. He mounted the steps and looked with love at the sky.

But there was one witness. And he stood aside. Unseen. Colonel Ivan Volynin, whose rank had merited his journey from Leningrad to legitimise his friend's despatch. His face was a pall of desolation. He was reminded of Pavlenkov, all those years ago in Vosrov, and he wondered who, if anybody, would be Andrei's Natasha. He kept his eyes on his friend, on his every movement, though he would have preferred to look away. But he knew that to witness his friend's death, and every moment of his dying, was the only loyalty he could afford him. He watched as they put the noose around Andrei's neck. Now was the time for his naming. Andrei opened his mouth to speak. In other times it could have been 'Pavel' or 'Hans', but both had betrayed him. He would utter a name of loving, and in that divine state he would go to his death. Ivan listened carefully, trembling in his sorrow. Then he heard it. Loud and clear. Andrei's Natasha.

'Nicolai.'

The name rang over the prison yard like the song of the morning lark. Ivan listened to its echo as the tears rolled down his cheeks. Nicolai. A brother. It was to Nicolai that Andrei had sent his last love, and for a moment, in his brainwashed heart, Ivan heard it as his own cry for Pyotr.

PART SEVEN

21

The non-aggression pact between Germany and the Soviet Union turned out to be no more than a holding device. Germany was biding its cunning time, and after the fall of France, it throbbed with a sense of victory. It was time to turn its attention to the Soviet Front. June 1941 saw the launch of Operation Barbarossa against a Russian army totally unprepared for attack. Ill-equipped, undermanned and untrained, the soldiers staggered against the German advance and within six months, Leningrad was under siege and the German soldiers goose-stepped the suburbs of Moscow.

But it was Leningrad that bore the initial brunt of the German onslaught. The siege lasted for almost three years, and during that time over a million people were its victims. The town was continually bombarded from the air. Fires burnt uncontrolled, and rubble littered the streets. Leningrad, like the whole of the Soviet Union, was unprepared. There were no official shelters, and people hid in their houses and prayed. And none more fervently than Anna. Not for herself, but for her family. For Olga and Avdotya, for Dmitri, serving as a medical officer in the Leningrad hospital, but above all for Sasha, whom she had not seen for almost twelve years. Olga had never known him, but from Anna she knew him intimately. And Dmitri had been a mere twelve when he had been taken in the night. And for some reason Dmitri had blamed him, and blamed him still for robbing him of fatherhood.

Anna listened to the bombers droning across the city, and through the window she could see flashes of light in the night sky. She heard Avdotya's stuttered snoring and found it comforting.

She checked that Olga was sleeping, then crossed to the window. Although it was dark the occasional flash lit the street into daylight, and in the course of one of these she thought she saw a figure cross over to the apartment block. It was the figure of a man huddling himself in the perilous spasms of light. She thought how stupid he must be to dare the streets at such a time. She watched his progress and was relieved that he managed to achieve the entrance to the building without coming to any harm.

Anna's apartment was on the ground floor, and with every bombardment she offered up thanks and pitied those who lived on the upper floors. She thought she heard a knock at the door, but dismissed it as one of those sounds of the offensive night. But the knocking continued and its tone was one of urgency. She crept to the door. Again the knocking, but this time accompanied by a cry. 'Shelter, shelter.' She opened the door at once, glad to be of assistance, and eager too for a little company. A man stood on the threshold, bearded, shivering, his head bowed.

'Come in,' Anna said and wondered whether she was being unwise to admit a stranger at this hour. Yet he was not altogether a stranger. There was something in his mien that reminded her of Larionovka and as he raised his head to smile at her, she discerned through the beard and the ingrown grime on the skin, a vision of her childhood, and the certain glow of its delight. Her heart throbbed to the rhythm of her astonished recall. She stretched out her hands.

'Sasha,' she said.

'Anna.'

Once before they had named each other, when, after years of absence, they had embraced at the tram depot. Then they had given each other their names, and the names had been enough. And once again the names bonded, confirming the love that was between them, and that love's endurance. They touched each other tentatively, a finger on the sleeve, the brush of a hand against the cheek, those trembling and teenage touches of courtship.

'Sashenka,' she said, and folded herself into his embrace, and waited for those words that he always gave her.

'We shall never again be parted,' he said. Then they both laughed, for their story seemed punctuated by such a phrase and they knew it as no guarantee, but simply a chorus for each of their reunions.

'Is that my daughter?' Sasha asked catching sight of the sleeping shape on the bed. 'And Avdotya? Is it possible?' The sight of Avdotya troubled him, for what had happened to Larionovka if Avdotya were here? And Pyotr, and Nina and their children? He was fearful of enquiry. Questions could come later, and the ensuing sorrow of their replies. But now he would greet his new daughter and find joy in family. So Olga was woken, and Avdotya stirred, sensing her charge was disturbed. Slowly they woke to their new joy and the night was spent in reunion and tales of their separate pasts. In all their laughter and recall the name of Larionovka was closeted by each one of them, and its very absence tolled a solemn bell. As the bombardment faded and the morning light confirmed survival, Anna released the name from its hiding, and she told Sasha about Pyotr. He had to mourn, she knew, as all of them had mourned, and the years that had passed since the massacre in no way would alleviate his sorrow. So she held him as he wept and comforted him with his blessings.

'Tomorrow I shall go and see Ivan,' Sasha said. 'He must know that he is not the sole Volynin survivor.'

He said it with as much anger as love, for he knew that it was in the name of Ivan's Cause that Pyotr and his family had been sacrificed.

But on enquiry the following day, Sasha was told that Ivan was in Moscow. Since Andrei's execution some months before, Ivan had been called upon to spend more and more time in Moscow. He was glad of it. For he had very little to go home for. Viktor had volunteered for the air force and he was unlikely to get home leave for some time. In any case, he was not close to his father.

Vassily's whereabouts were still unknown. That name tugged at Ivan's heartstrings, plucking at his sorrow for both his father and his elder son. He didn't know whether or not to mourn him, but alive or dead, he knew that his son was the only being who could claim his enduring love, and that if one day he should be led to the gallows, it would be Vassily's name that would fray the noose. Not Lenin, not Stalin, nor any name of revolutionary colour. Neither would he call Katya. For Vassily was his Natasha, the name of all

299

his loving and all his regrets. He recalled that day Vassily had left, heaping curses on his father's name.

'I am your son,' he had pleaded. 'I am not a vehicle for your Cause.' And he had gone. And not a word had come from him since. Katya never spoke his name aloud for it dwelt like a lump in her throat, heartbreaking, immovable. He thought of Katya, but with cold indifference. She was barely a reason for his return to Leningrad. Even when he was in the city, he was wont to put up at another apartment, one leased by the NKVD. For he and Katya had grown sadly apart. Her faith in the Cause had soured, and with it, her bonding with Ivan. She had become a stranger to him and even a threat to his status. He found it difficult to believe that she was the mother of his two sons. But had Ivan known that Leningrad housed Sasha, he would have made his way there forthwith, and in return for their loss of Pyotr, he would have gently offered Anna the loss of her own brother. And together they would mourn, the Larionovs and the Volynins, each line now bereft of one sibling. But Sasha's return was as unknown to Ivan as Andrei's death was to Anna. So Sasha would have to wait for Ivan's return.

He was anxious to see Dmitri. But nervous too. Anna had hinted at Dmitri's anger, but she felt sure that in time, as they learned to know each other again, that anger would abate. Besides, Dmitri had fallen in love. Her name was Sonya Mozhinskaya, and she worked as a nurse in the Leningrad hospital. Anna saw them both almost daily, for her tram had been converted into an ambulance to convey to hospital those wounded in the air raids. She urged Sasha to go to the hospital, to make his peace, if peace were to be made, with his son.

Sasha set out with equal excitement and trepidation. He envisaged their meeting and tried to rehearse what he would say to him. But he knew that rehearsal was futile, that he should speak from the heart and hope that Dmitri, whatever his words, would do likewise. He lingered outside the hospital, and watched the stretcher line of wounded. There were children amongst them and he turned away at the sight and was ashamed of himself that a meeting with his son should disturb him. In the face of such tragedy, his self-absorption was mere arrogance. At least his son was alive and

300

well, and he himself had survived the labour camp. He would count his blessings as Anna had advised.

He joined the end of the line of stretchers and entered the hospital. He enquired for his son and was directed to the casualty ward. The hospital seemed in chaos. Clearly it was not equipped to deal with so many hundreds of casualties. The wounded were lying on pallets on the floor of the corridors and Sasha felt ashamed to be walking whole amongst them. He would not recall his sufferings in the labour camp as a form of consolation, for he had survived them, and his survival made those deprivations irrelevant. He wondered how many of those wounded on the floor would survive as well as he.

He entered the casualty room. It was crowded. The wounded were everywhere, and doctors and nurses darted amongst them. The smell of blood and gangrene was overwhelming. He looked at the men in white coats, hoping to recognise his son amongst them. But it was twelve years since he had set eyes on him, those years in which the features took their time to change, before settling into the permanent face of their future. Sasha wanted to weep for the loss of years, for those years of fatherhood of which he had been deprived. He scanned their faces once more, this time looking for a likeness of Anna or himself, but none of the faces answered that image. He thought he might call out Dmitri's name, but he didn't want to publicise his lack of recognition. There was no room to go further into the ward to investigate, so he stood helplessly at the door, ashamed.

Then he heard a voice. Above the din and the moaning and agonised cries, he heard a sound that was well, healthy, that was free of pain. 'Papa,' he heard. He dared to hope that the word was addressed to himself, but there were many in that room who merited that call, and even more, those who cried it out. He heard it again, then moved towards the sound. And then he saw a smile that belonged to the word and the face of the boy he had held in his mind's eye every day of his sojourn in the camp. He wondered if his son had recognised him by the same token of remembrance. For in the mine, he had kept his boy's face in his mind's eye, for he could not easily let his son grow fatherless into manhood, and Dmitri had fixed his young father in his memory, because he would not accept that loss of paternal care.

301

'Mitya,' Sasha said, and quickly embraced his son, because he did not want him to see his tears. For tears in this place were appropriate enough. But not tears of joy, as were Sasha's as he greeted his son.

'Forgiven, forgiven,' he heard Dmitri say, and Sasha understood, for how could a grudge be borne in such a place between those unharmed and unthreatened.

'I'll try to forgive myself,' Sasha said. Then wondered at it. For how had he wronged? He had espoused no Cause above his children. He had simply spilt the words that were his life's blood. And not to spill them would have killed him. He could not stop writing. Nor would he. He had seen too much in the labour camp. A witness to torture must *bear* witness else his silence betrays those who succumbed. He would not let them be forgotten. He would fill his pages with their pain so that their souls could rest in peace. And if all this would cost him the love of his son, then he would have to pay that price. By forgiving him, it seemed that Dmitri had understood. He was proud of such a son, and he acknowledged that much of him was Anna's doing.

'Come and meet Sonya,' Dmitri said. He took his father's hand and manoeuvred them both between the stretchers. Sonya was cleaning the leg wound of a little girl. With the other hand she caressed the child's cheek.

'What's your name?' she asked.

'Olga,' the girl whimpered.

Dmitri squeezed his father's hand. 'Olga is everyone's child,' he said.

When Sonya had finished, Dmitri made a formal introduction. She was shy and lowered her face as she greeted him. Sasha took her hand. 'I'm glad you're Dmitri's friend,' he said.

Then she looked at him, reassured. 'Mitya has told me about you,' she said. 'And I've read your poems and your novel.'

'I'm flattered,' Sasha said. And was indeed, for there was no better compliment than being read by a further generation.

'Is there another one?' she asked.

'I wrote in the camp,' Sasha said. 'And I finished it there. I had to. Because hindsight is deceptive. That's why memories can be comfort-

302

ing. Because we can select. We omit what was painful. But in the centre of despair there is no hindsight. One can get closer to the truth.'

He realised that for the first time in his life, he was sharing his writing thoughts with another, and one who was almost a stranger. Not even with Anna did he share such thoughts, and he supposed that, in trusting in Sonya, he was really talking to his son in an effort perhaps to explain that his absence had not been entirely in vain. That his father had been a father and son to many others, never losing sight of the one whose blood he shared.

'We're busy, Papa,' Dmitri said. 'I have to get on. I'll come home when there's a lull. But God knows when that will be.' He kissed his father once more. 'Welcome home,' he whispered.

But there was never a lull. The bombardment continued. Anna was rarely off duty, and Sasha feared for her safety. Indeed for the safety of them all. After some weeks in Leningrad, he still had not seen Ivan. Nor Katya. Lately Anna had seen little of her. She lived on the other side of the city, and most people kept indoors unless their journey was absolutely necessary. Anna's tram did not serve Katya's area, but she had heard that it was no less devastated than the rest of the city. Before she could see Katya she would have to wait for a lull in the storm. As the whole of Leningrad waited. And would wait for hundreds of days.

Meanwhile the wounded were collected off the streets, and the corpses were buried, and Anna's tram ferried both the quick and the dead. The windows of the trams had been taped to prevent the splintering of glass, and the glass itself had been painted blue, and it cast a cheerless and livery pallor over the dead and not-so-dead faces. Often the trams were diverted because of uncleared rubble in the tramlines, and such delay cost many lives. Anna's was a gruelling job and her dreams were nightmares.

Sasha had found a job in the State Broadcasting Company. He was officially a producer but most of the programmes he wrote himself. His brief was to mount productions that would lift the morale of the people. Often he read his own poems, poems of man's strength and endurance, of his loving and his faith, and Sasha's voice could be heard around the city and in shop doorways where passers-by loitered to listen, and for a while forget their hunger.

303

For there was near famine in the city. Between the raids people ventured into the streets to queue for food. There were terrible rumours abroad. Corpses had been found with parts of their limbs missing. Flesh sliced neatly from legs, and arms and thighs, with a precision and nicety that no bomb could have achieved, and who knew, so the rumours spread, whether those looted bodies had not been hand-murdered in the first place. So no child was let out into the streets, and those people who walked alone, walked armed.

Since the beginning of the siege, it was clear that Leningrad was no place for children, and slowly the government began to make plans for their evacuation. It was to be voluntary, but all parents were urged to let their children go. Anna was torn. So rarely in her married life had her family been altogether. She worried about Olga. All day and every day she was cooped up in the apartment. Schools were closed and she missed her friends. But if she were to leave Leningrad, even in the trusted company of Avdotya, she would worry even more. Dmitri insisted that Olga should go – he had seen too many stretchered children – and he expressed his regret that the evacuation law was not compulsory. Sasha too was of the opinion that Olga should go to the country.

'She'll find friends there. And there'll be food. Farmers never go hungry. I didn't mean that,' he said quickly, for he thought of Pyotr and his family, all of whom had died for grain. 'We don't have food in the city,' he said, 'because nothing can get through. There's less chance of hunger in places where it is grown.'

But Anna was hesitant. She cried whenever she thought about it, and lately she had taken to sleeping with Olga, holding her through her own restless nights, as if she feared to lose her. The day of the scheduled departure was but a few days hence, and still Anna had come to no decision. Meanwhile Avdotya secretly prepared their packing for she knew Sasha and Dmitri would insist on their going. And when the day of the evacuation arrived, Anna was irresolute. She prayed that the railway lines to the Urals would be blocked, so that the train could not leave, thus freeing her from the need of decision.

Sasha had taken the morning off from the radio station, and he helped Avdotya with the luggage. He gave Anna her coat, her gloves and her hat, took her arm, and wordless, they all made their way to the station. It was crowded with children, and their anxious parents. But the fact that she was one of many was no comfort to Anna, and as the guard announced the boarding of the train she panicked and snatched Olga from Avdotya's hold, and cried, 'I can't do it, Sasha. Please don't make me. I can't. I'll never see her again.'

'It's best for Olga,' Sasha said. 'We must do what's best for her.'

Then Anna broke completely. And into a tirade of pent up anger. 'What do you know about these things?' she said with contempt. 'What do you know about being a parent? You weren't even here when she was born. Nor Mitya. I brought them up on my own. How could you ever understand?' She heard the echo of her spiteful words, and was appalled, for it was not she who had suffered in the camps nor missed out on the growth of her children. 'I'm sorry,' she said, drowning the echo of her tirade. 'Of course she must go. It's for her safety.' But still she didn't mean it, and she clung to Olga, willing the train to be on its way. It was Avdotya who prised Olga from her hold. She knew she was regarded as neutral, and therefore not open to blame. Anna let her go, smothering her with kisses. Olga was confused. She was excited at the prospect of a train journey and a countryside destination. To say nothing of the company of so many other children. But she was at pains to hide her excitement for fear of it being construed as disloyalty. Sasha took her in his arms. 'Olga,' he said, 'Mama and I want you to look after Avdotya. And to have a wonderful time. And to write to us often. About the friends you make, and the farm where you will stay, and about all the animals.'

Olga's face lit up with joy. Her journey had been sanctioned, and not only the journey, but her enjoyment. 'I'll miss you,' she said holding them both. 'Just you,' she said. 'And Mitya. But not the apartment.' She saw that place as a prison and the train, her way to freedom. There were farewells all round, holding each other till the last moment. Then, although many of the train doors were open the guard blew his whistle, and they rushed to the compartments. The steam puffed impatiently from the engine, and quickly all the doors were closed. But each window framed a clutch of children and waving handkerchiefs. Every travelling child waved

305

in general to every parent, and likewise the parents in their turn, and there was a certain consolation in that community of parting.

Anna was loath to go back to the apartment, to return so swiftly to a childless home. Sasha shared her reluctance, and he suggested they visit the Hermitage. It had been some time since they had been there. Such a visit required leisure and in the daily grind of their lives, there was little enough of that. But now perhaps was a moment when they could contemplate the beauties that were housed there, the paintings and the artefacts that would for ever endure, and with that promise of permanence, afford them a measure of solace.

But as they entered the gates of the museum, it was clear that the place was not as before. The usual crowd that lined up to see the treasures were now but a trickle of hopefuls who no doubt, like Sasha and Anna, were innocent of the changes that had taken place therein. The line moved quickly inside. But all hopes of a passing pleasure were dashed at the sight of the bare walls and the screaming emptiness of the salons.

'It's all gone,' Sasha said, and his whisper echoed across the halls, reverberating their loss.

'They've taken everything away,' a man said at his side.

'You knew?' Sasha said.

The man nodded. 'We come anyway,' he said. 'We come to remember. We look at the spaces on the walls and we see the Rembrandts that were there. You're standing where a Rodin was. *The Kiss.*'

Anna shivered. Let's go from here,' she said. The emptiness of the walls and the marble floors rekindled the pain of her parting with Olga.

Then the stranger put his hand on Anna's arm. 'They were taken away for safe keeping,' he said. 'When all this is over, the paintings will again hang where they belong.'

Anna smiled at him. 'Thank you,' she said.

In time, Olga would return to that place that was her rightful home.

That night the city suffered its heaviest bombardment. And its most costly. For the Badayev warehouses, that storehouse of the city's food, caught fire and the building was razed to the ground. In all the shops and larders in Leningrad, there was enough food left for twenty days. Anna thanked God that she had let Olga go.

22

It had been months since Sasha had returned to Leningrad, and still he had not seen Ivan. Nor Anna, Katya. Neither did she know how she was faring, save that Ivan had left her. The telephones were out of order, and no sooner were the lines repaired than they were once again brought down by the bombings. Anna was determined to contact her, and one day, in a lull, she braved the streets and took a tram to the district where Katya lived.

At one time, before the siege, that area had been distinguished from others in the city in that it was entirely residential, and those residences were the homes of the rich. Although since the Revolution, all men were supposed to be equal, such equality remained only a principle. For in reality there was no greater class distinction in the world than that which obtained in the Soviet Union. The rich in the land were those who worked in government departments. Hence the rich location of Ivan's residence. Katya was still there, Anna was sure. The area no longer bore its appearance of exclusivity. Bombs are indiscriminate, and the grand apartment blocks were grand no more. Many of them were but shells of their former grandeur. Anna could have been in her own district, picking her way through the rubble. She was relieved to see Katya's block was still reasonably intact. She rushed inside. The lift was out of order, and she was obliged to climb the stairs to the fifth floor. On reaching the fourth, she started to call Katya's name, expecting to greet Katya at her door. But when she reached it, it was coldly shut. She called again, but there was no reply. Perhaps Katya had taken advantage of the lull and, like all the women, had gone to forage for food. She would wait. She sat on the floor. It was lushly carpeted with a deep pile, and Anna was happy to rest there a while, in the rare silence and luxury. She thought of Olga and Avdotya, and was glad that they were safe. But she was troubled about Dmitri and Sasha. Dmitri had talked of volunteering for the Front, and Sonya said nothing to discourage him. Sasha too, might be leaving. The Broadcasting Company had suggested him as war correspondent at the front line. Soon she would be alone, and she would need Katya more than ever before. She heard steps on the stairway, and she got up and ran to the landing, but looking down, she saw a woman, dragging an almost empty bag, turn off on the floor below.

She went back to her resting place. Then began to sniff. There was a very positive smell about her, one she hadn't noticed before. Possibly, sitting there for so long, she thought, she had not noticed it, but now, after a short absence from the door, she sniffed at it with a certain foreboding. She dared to lift up the letter flap on the front door, and stick her nose inside. But quickly withdrew. She knew that smell. She knew it intimately. She sniffed it every day on her tram, and she often drove with a handkerchief on her mouth, so pungent and depressing was its odour. She opened the flap again, but this time she covered her nose, and looked inside.

There was little to see. The door of the living-room was open, and nothing looked amiss, but even without sniffing, the smell was overwhelming. There was no mistaking it. Desperate as she was to find some other reason for its acridness, she knew that that odour clung only to the dead, and that only death and nothing else could manufacture such a lethal perfume. Yet she refused to believe it. She had to get inside the apartment, before she would give it credence. She rang the bell of the apartment next door, but there was no reply. She dared to sniff at the letter flap, and the odour was musty and stale as if the flat had been untenanted for a long while. She moved down the corridor, trying each bell, and sniffing each flap. And at each one there was no reply, and the same musty smell. She concluded that the residents had left for the safe and nourished countryside, an easy option for those well connected. But she knew that Katya would never leave Leningrad. That she would do nothing for her own safety or wellbeing. That all the bonuses of

Ivan's office embarrassed her. Unless they were thrust upon her, she certainly would not seek them out.

She decided to find the caretaker. Perhaps he had keys to the apartment. She ran down the stairs, trembling with fear. She met no one on the way, and heard not a sound of habitation. She prayed that the caretaker had not deserted with the rest of them. But she found him in the basement. His door was open, and he was seated by his table, a bottle of vodka in his hand, halfway to his lips when he caught sight of her. But he did not allow her presence to interrupt that imperative movement, and he swigged amply from the bottle before putting it back on the table. Anna noticed that the room was stacked with cases of wine and vodka, and she presumed that he had the keys to all the apartments. And made no move to conceal his loot. There was a certain arrogance about the man as if he had only claimed those rights to which he was long entitled.

'Come in,' he said, and stretched the bottle towards her. Anna rarely drank, but she sensed that she would soon be in need of some sustenance. In any case the man might have been offended if she had refused. She took the bottle from his hand, and secretly wished that while he was about his looting he might have filched some glasses. She took a swig from the bottle and it oiled her throat to ease the request she was about to make, and to accept the dire consequences of his reply.

'I'm looking for Katya Volynina,' she said. 'Apartment 502.' She thought she saw him tremble at the name, but it could have been due to the alcohol. 'D'you know if she's left the city?'

'I don't think so,' he said. He had not checked on Number 502. Empty or not, he would certainly have given it a miss on his looting round. The name Volynin was not to be tampered with.

'Do you have the keys?' she asked. 'I want to see that she's well. She doesn't answer the door, but I think she's at home.' She wouldn't mention the smell.

The caretaker struggled to his feet, and crossed the room with a drunk's infinite care. He opened the drawer and took a single key, clearly the master for all the apartments. Anna hoped that he would accompany her. She would have been glad of company, for she feared what she would find. But the man didn't look as if he could make the first landing. And indeed, he didn't even intend to try. He handed her the key.

'Bring it back,' he said. 'If the door's shut, throw it through the letter-box.' He possibly intended to take his drunken self to bed. Anna was alarmed at his irresponsible manner. But she understood it. In those days of siege, it was every man for himself.

She started to climb the stairs once more, but slowly this time, for she was in no hurry to find what she feared. When she reached Katya's door, she paused, and held her breath. She put the key in the lock, but waited for some time before she dared to turn it. Then, averting her face, she opened the door wide. The stench exploded into the corridor, and she cried out, hoping perhaps that someone would hear her and come to share the burden of what she would find. But the silence was as overbearing as the smell. She knew she could delay no longer. She took her scarf, and tied it around her nose and mouth, and thus protected, though with pathetic inadequacy, she entered the apartment. And reeled. Whatever the source of the smell, it was in a state of sublime fermentation and had clearly been fizzing for some time. Her eyes began to water and she was unsure what the tears were made of. It was light in the apartment, light enough for investigation, but she felt the need for more. For company perhaps, and she switched on the central lamp of the living-room. And cruelly it spot-lit what lay centre stage on the floor. Katya, askew, and on her side, her hand vainly shielding the side of her face, a battle she had clearly lost, for the rats had eaten away half her cheek.

'Katya!' Anna screamed. For a moment she thought that she might still be alive. That she could be nursed and fed, and recover, and live a life of sorts even with half a face. She knelt down beside her. She didn't mind the smell any more, because it was the smell of a friend, and in that capacity, it was acceptable. She tried to prise Katya's hand from her face, as if to tell her that there was nothing to be ashamed of, but it was cold and stiff. She looked around the room. Perhaps there was a note, some indication of why she had laid herself down on the floor and invited the rats to a feast. But there was nothing. She looked in the larder, but there was no scrap of food. An empty milk bottle, mildewed, was the only suggestion that once somebody had lived there. They would say that Katya had died of starvation. It was a common enough cause of death in those days. But Anna knew better. Katya died because she didn't want to live any more. No more and no less than that. She had lost her faith. That faith, that had been her lifeblood, had clotted. She had died of simple despair.

She wanted to lay Katya on the bed, but she knew that with the long weight of death on her, she would be too heavy to lift, so she took a blanket from the bedroom and covered her where she lay. Then she knelt by her side and prayed. The smell no longer troubled her. Now it seemed the right and proper dressing for the life that they all led, all those victims of Ivan Volynin's Cause. And she nurtured in her heart such a hatred for Ivan, for his passionless commitment to a principle that had nothing to do with the flesh and blood to which it was supposed to apply. But above all, she hated him for his neglect of Katya and she wondered how he could find a tear to weep for her. She kissed Katya's face, then closed the door. She went down to the basement, and as she expected, the caretaker's door was closed. She decided against returning the key. She would need to come back after making arrangements for the funeral. There was no need for the caretaker to know the dire contents of the Volynin apartment.

She took a tram and went straight to the Broadcasting Company. She could not handle the event alone. She had to tell Sasha. The journey took some time because of the detours it had to make. Anna wept most of the time. She would not think of Katya's mangled face. She preferred to dwell on the beauty that was. She recalled Katya's wedding over thirty years ago, when she and Sasha had carried the ring cushions. But it was no happy memory, for most of those in attendance had died in the name of Ivan's Cause. Her bile rose at the thought of his name, and she wondered how he had been sired by those same parents of Sasha and the gentle Pyotr.

She broke the news to Sasha with no preamble and without adornment.

'Katya's dead,' she said. 'I found her on the floor of the apartment. The rats had eaten away half her face.' It was an obscene announcement, that cared not for others' feelings, but her anger and her sorrow were too weighty to care.

Sasha's reaction consisted of one word, that same word that had mangled her throat ever since the discovery.

'Ivan,' he said, and his tone was of loathing and contempt. For him, 'Ivan' was not a name. It was a symbol of all the pain and suffering that the Cause had wrought. Katya, like thousands of others, had been Ivanised.

'Where is he?' Sasha said. 'Does anyone know?' But he did not wait for a reply. 'I'll go now to the NKVD. I'll find out where he is. I'll find him.' He put his arm around Anna. 'Go home,' he said, 'and wait for me. I'll find him, I promise you. He has to go and look at her. He has to face what he has done.'

Anna gave him the key of the apartment, and she watched as he took his coat and stormed out of the station.

Going to the offices of the NKVD entailed a certain risk, but Sasha was willing to take it. The need to confront his brother was paramount. He had not seen him for many years, and he had hoped that their first meeting would be one of fraternal affection, that their differences might be put aside for a while in the joy of their reunion. But now there was little hope of that joy for even if Ivan were still capable of feelings of happiness, he was certainly not entitled to them, and a whole lifetime would not be enough to pay for that entitlement.

Sasha had no idea whether Ivan was in Leningrad, but he would ask for him just the same. He gave a false name at the desk. Alexander Volynin would not ease his passage.

'Colonel Volynin sees no one without an appointment,' the desk officer said.

'Is he in Leningrad?' Sasha asked.

'No,' the officer said. 'He returns next week. You will have to write in for an appointment.'

'Thank you,' Sasha said, and gratefully left. He had learned what he wanted to know. He decided he would return in a week and wait outside the building. There must come a time when Ivan went home, wherever that home might be.

The following week, he went back to the offices and waited outside till nightfall. There had been no bombardment all day. If the night was clear, perhaps it signalled the end of the siege. Any day now he was going to the Front, and he would feel easier if he could leave Anna in a city of relative peace.

He saw Ivan coming down the steps of the building. He was glad to see that he was alone. He looked forbidding in his Colonel's uniform, but he inspired no fear in Sasha. All he saw was the weakling under the braids, the coward under the stripes, and monstrous indifference of the being it all clothed.

'Ivan,' he called. His voice was like a summons. Ivan turned, his gun quickly drawn. 'It's Sasha,' Sasha called, realising that after such a long absence it was possible that Ivan would not recognise him.

Ivan walked towards him with measured steps, his gun still at the ready. Sasha waited where he stood for the moment of recognition. Then when it came, Ivan pocketed his gun and stretched out his arms.

'Sashenka,' he called and ran towards him. For a short moment, Sasha saw the image of his hero-worshipped brother running across the fields of Larionovka to sweep him up in his arms. But he steeled himself against such a memory. That Ivan was no more. All that was now between them was blood and even that was running thin. He allowed himself to be embraced.

'When did you last see Katya?' he said, coming straight to the point.

Ivan was startled by his manner of greeting. 'What's Katya got to do with anything?' he said. 'It's years since you and I met and you ask me about Katya.'

'Because she *is* everything,' Sasha said helplessly. 'Everything has to do with her.'

'What does that mean?'

'She's dead,' Sasha said. He watched his brother's face intently. It took on a sudden pallor that seemed to have more to do with fear than sorrow.

'How? When?' Ivan asked tonelessly.

'No one knows,' Sasha said. 'Anna went to the apartment. She

313

found her on the floor.' He felt suddenly sorry for his brother. So he would spare him the rats' supper.

'I hadn't seen her for some time,' Ivan said. 'We had grown apart.' Then suddenly he began to weep.

'It's too late to cry,' Sasha said.

'I'm crying for the past,' Ivan said. 'Our good past together.'

'That's all you've ever been able to cry for,' Sasha said. 'The past. Tears for the past are not of sorrow. They're sheer sentimentality. You would do better to weep for the present and God help us, our future. It was our present that was the cause of Katya's death.'

'Where is she now?' Ivan whispered.

'Anna arranged for her to be taken to the mortuary. It was full up, but the name Volynin seemed to open a door. A useful name,' Sasha added bitterly, 'but Katya wouldn't have thanked you for that advantage.'

'I must see her,' Ivan said. Then after a pause. 'Will you come with me?'

Sasha hesitated. He did not want to look at Katya again. 'Please come,' Ivan pleaded. 'I'm lonely, Sashenka.'

Sasha steeled himself. He did not want to pity his brother. Besides, he had deservedly earned every moment of the loneliness he now complained of. But he could not help but feel sorry for him.

'I'll go with you,' he said, 'but you must look at her alone.'

'I'll call my car.' He rushed back to the offices, and shortly a car drew up at the entrance. The driver stepped out, and opened the door for Ivan, who was coming down the front steps. Sasha went to the car, and joined Ivan in the back seat. They travelled in silence. The morgue was on the outskirts of the city. There seemed nothing to talk about, even though they had not seen each other for so many years. The matter of Katya held dominion, and it was a subject beyond words.

In time they reached the mortuary. The attendant saluted when Ivan approached, and offered his respectful condolences, though he must have wondered how the wife of such a powerful man could have died of hunger in much the same way as he and his kind were dying in the siege.

'Nobody knows that she is here, Colonel,' he offered by way of condolence.

'I'm grateful for that,' Ivan said, and Sasha felt ashamed.

'I'll wait here, Ivan,' he said. 'I've already seen her.'

The attendant opened an inner door. 'This way, Colonel,' he said. Ivan followed the man inside. The attendant wished he were elsewhere. Katya Volynina, wife of a colonel in the NKVD was not a pretty sight, and in the presence of such power, he feared he himself might be blamed for her disfigurement. He crossed the room, weaving his way between the shrouded tables. When he came to Katya's resting place he was fearful of lowering the sheet. 'This is your wife, Colonel,' he said. 'I'll leave you now. You'll want to be alone.' He forced himself to walk slowly from the room. God help that man, he thought, when he sees the face he once must have loved.

Ivan rested his hand on the sheet. He was in no hurry to uncover her. Although he had seen little of her over the past few years, he did not need to be reminded of her face. He did not think he would miss her. He had loved her once, but that love had ceased to be important. He would honour her for the work she had once done for the Cause, and for the two sons she had borne him. And there it would end. She was but an episode in his life, a simple event in his life's cycle. One did not miss such an event or mourn its passing. He would take time off to bury her, then return to his Cause. He lowered the sheet. And screamed. Outside the door, Sasha heard him, but did not move from his seat. No amount of comfort could avail his brother. Nor should it. For Ivan had to bear the burden of that cross alone. Sasha was surprised how quickly Ivan emerged from the mortuary. He looked many years older. Sasha rose to support him, for he seemed as if he would faint.

'Did I do that to her?' he whispered. The simple question implied its own answer. Sasha said nothing. He took his brother's arm and led him out of the building.

In the car, Ivan held on to Sasha's hand. 'I'm alone, Sasha,' he said.

'You have your sons.'

315

'Vassily's whereabouts are unknown. And have been for many years. And Viktor is at the Front.'

'He must come home for Katya's funeral,' Sasha said. 'You can arrange that.'

'But will he be happy to see me?' Ivan said.

Again it was no real question for Ivan knew the answer well enough.

Katya was buried the following week, giving Viktor time to take his compassionate leave. There were many officials at the funeral, officials of high rank and all in their bemedalled uniforms. Katya would not have been honoured by their presence. But it seemed that Ivan needed them. He stood in their midst, a clutch of brainwashed comrades, mourning the loss of one of their own. Sasha and Anna were sickened at the sight. They stood apart unwilling to be counted as one of their number. And by their side, stood Viktor. He too wanted no part of his father's ceremony. The coffin was lowered, and Ivan donated his shovelful of earth. Then it was Viktor's turn but he did not once look at his father. Sasha and Anna followed him with their spadesful, then moved aside. Ivan directed his officers to donate their share of earth.

Sasha and Anna turned and walked away. Viktor followed them. The sight of that mourning hypocrisy sickened them, as it would have sickened Katya. It seemed that they were desecrating her grave.

'I'll never speak to him again,' Viktor said.

'You will,' Sasha said, 'because you're his son. And because in time you will be able to forgive him.'

He looked around. The officials were leaving the graveside. Ivan remained, standing like a sentinel at the foot of Katya's grave. But Sasha would not join him. Such atonement could not be shared.

Viktor had been granted an extended leave. Ivan had manoeuvred that privilege, possibly in the hope that there would be time for reconciliation. Time to explain his Katya neglect, although in truth he could offer no explanation. But despite his frequent requests, Viktor refused to see his father, and chose to spend his remaining days of leave with Sasha and Anna. In any case, he wanted to spend time with Dmitri. Both Sasha and Anna were glad of it, for with Sasha's impending departure, they were uneasy to spend time alone together. It seemed to accentuate his leave-taking. Besides, Dmitri too would soon go away and Anna was glad to be amongst her family, which gathering sanctioned conversation that had nothing to do with farewells.

Dmitri's impending marriage to Sonya was one such topic. Anna had thought they were both too young for such a commitment, but Dmitri countered his argument with a reminder that she was younger than Sonya when she had eloped with his father. Such banter and reminiscence eased the path to Anna's lonely days ahead.

It was to be a quiet wedding. 'Only family,' Anna had said. And with infinite sadness, for that word was a trigger to tears, and a reminder of how ruthlessly that family was depleted. On Sasha's side, there was no one. His parents and Pyotr were dead, all casualties of the Cause. His remaining brother would not be invited. He no longer merited the label of family. Anna's own family was slightly less depleted, though the whereabouts of Nicolai was unknown. She had had no news of Andrei for some time. She presumed that, at the outbreak of war, he had been recalled from his posting in Berlin, but since that time she had not heard from him. His whereabouts were probably secret and she was confident that in time, when it was safe, he would be in touch with her. She missed him, especially at this time, and Nicolai too, whom over the years, she had forgiven. She hoped that wherever he was, he was safe. But most of all, she missed Olga. Both she and Avdotya wrote regularly from the country. They were safe, happy and often homesick and they prayed for the war's end, when they could all be together again. Both families, the Larionovs and the Volynins, were highly practised in reunion. Both were professional reassemblers, having practised so many farewells.

The wedding took place in the City Hall. There were no members of Sonya's family present. Her father had died when she was a child, and of natural causes, a rare legitimacy of the time. Her mother lived in Moscow, and had no means of travelling to Leningrad. So it was Anna who 'mothered' her for the ceremony, and it was Viktor who acted as best man. When it was over, they all adjourned to the war memorial. In the Soviet Union it is a time-honoured tradition that newly married couples repair to the memorial after their marriage ceremony to pay their respects to the dead of the Great War, and as they stood before the monument, both Sasha and Anna wondered whether Dmitri and Sonya's children would do likewise before a memorial to the victims of their own father's struggle. It was a depressing thought, and they were glad to leave the monument and its threat of repetition and to celebrate the wedding feast that Anna had prepared. She knew that it would be their last family reunion for a long time, and she was determined to make of it a glorious celebration. There was little to eat and drink, but with what they had they toasted a peaceful future. Speeches were in order, and each one of them made a contribution. Even Anna, whose normally shy tongue was oiled with the wines. The past had been toasted, and the present and the future. So too had all those dead. But Anna raised her glass to those absent friends. To Olga and Avdotya. To Nicolai and Andrei. And finally to Sonya's mother. It was at this last toast that Sonya rose to speak. She trembled with shyness and held Dmitri's hand the while. She had no toast to give. Just two simple words. Perhaps no one would think they were important. But in her own heart she knew that those two words would make her wholly known to her new family. That they had a right to hear them. They explained her past, her present, and with terrifying foresight, her future. She looked around at the assembled guests. 'I'm Jewish,' she said. Then she sat down. There was nothing more about her that anyone needed to know.

'What difference should that make?' Dmitri said. And the others echoed his opinion. All but Sasha, who heard in Sonya's words a terrible prophecy. And he trembled.

A few days later came the farewells. Viktor, Dmitri and Sasha left on the same train. Anna and Sonya took them to the station. There were no tears. Sorrow was private. Sonya too was dry eyed, and Anna wondered how she, who had had no rehearsal in farewells, had gathered the strength and the pride to accept them. But Anna could not hold back her tears at Viktor's farewell, for he was alone and acutely orphaned. So she kissed him for Katya, and the father whom he could not forgive.

They waited until the train pulled out of the station, then Anna and Sonya linked arms and made their way home. As she left the station, Anna turned to watch the distant steam of the train, and in so doing she saw a figure of a man leaning against the wall at the end of the empty platform. She was sure that it was Ivan, and her heart filled with pity.

But that pity was quickly disposed of. On the second day of Anna's loneliness, a letter arrived from the NKVD. It was, unsurprisingly, unsigned. Its dire information was from a source identified only as a vast bureau, peopled by men in masks, shielded in anonymity. The letter was short and to the painful point. It informed her that Andrei Larionov had been found guilty of treason and had been hanged forthwith at Lubyanka prison on 8 January 1941. He had been buried in the prison precincts, and his body could not be reclaimed.

Anna was broken. The pain of such a loss was greater than any farewell she had made with Sasha. Greater than all the sorrows of her bereaved existence. For she had loved Andrei to the limits of love that blood allows, and she knew that never in her life would she recover from that loss. In her loneliness she longed not for Sasha, not even for Olga, but for Nicolai. Some touch of him, some word, some confirmation that she did not have to bear the Larionov name alone.

But Nicolai was still flying the Larionov flag, that flag that once flew from the manor on the hill. But now it was of a different hue and of a colour mortally offensive to the Soviet eye. For Nicolai, like many White Russians of his kind, had joined the ranks of the enemy in the firm belief that a German victory would restore a rightful Tsar to their Mother Russia.

Shortly after Andrei had left Berlin, Nicolai had heeded his warning to leave the country. But not for himself. He had stayed, sensing that he was on the winning side, but he had arranged passage for Vera and his son, Nicolai, to America. That was in the autumn of 1941. Only once had he heard from them. And that quite recently, in a letter that had taken many months to reach him. They were well. They loved and they missed him. Vera had taken a job as a Russian translator, and Nicolai was in his first year of training to be an air force pilot. Nicolai dared not imagine the consequences of this last piece of information because it entailed a confrontation between father and son on opposite sides. But his decision had been made. A return to the old regime in his country would prove to be for everyone's good and would signal that his lifelong struggle had not been in vain. Meanwhile he daydreamed of a family reunion, himself, Andrei and Anna, in the great ceremonial hall of the Larionov estate.

The war was going well for the Germans and for the first three years of hostilities, the Russians bore the brunt of their attack. Nicolai had joined a regiment led by a certain General Vlasov, a Russian officer, who, like Nicolai, sniffed the scents of victory on a deserter's side. In view of his history of Tsarist loyalty, together with his age – Nicolai was in his fifty-seventh year – he was given the rank of colonel, and for the first time in many years, he felt he had been awarded the respect that was due to him. But such honour would not be his for very long. For slowly the tide of German victory began to turn. In the summer of 1944 the Allies landed on the Normandy beaches, thus opening a second front for the German armies to breach, and all over Europe panic orders were given to retreat. It was in such a context of frenzied withdrawal that Colonel Nicolai Larionov made his first visit to a prisoner-of-war camp. It lay in the mountains and housed hundreds of Russian soldiers and airmen who had lost their fight for freedom. It was to be Nicolai's first encounter with his erstwhile compatriots, and he prayed that no sudden sentimentality would weaken his resolve. He was riding in a jeep with General Vlasov. During their service together they had become close friends and constant companions. Their car followed that of General Emil Lister, whose charge was to organise a selective and discreet retreat. The prisoner-of-war camp was his present target.

As they drove into the camp precincts, Nicolai heard the sound of gunfire. It was an ominous sound to echo in such a place, a place of supposed neutrality and peace. A place in which men had laid down their arms in surrender and despair, cursing their bad luck. Men for whom it was all over, the patriotic zeal, the enemy hatred, but above all, the fear. For here in this place, unarmed, uncalled

320

upon, there was nothing of which to be afraid. Nothing but bore-
dom, and the impatience of waiting for the hostilities to be at
an end. So why the gunfire, Nicolai wondered, and finding no
explanation, preferred to turn a deaf ear to the sound.

The cars were met by a Colonel Heinrich Swale, the Camp
Commandant. General Lister accompanied him to his office but he
motioned Vlasov and Nicolai to wait outside. From time to time,
in their co-operation with the German High Command, Vlasov
and Nicolai were subject to such humiliating orders, but it was the
price they had to pay for their desertion. Neither side trusted the
other, but each recognised the advantages of their co-operation.
On this occasion Lister was particularly anxious to negotiate privately, for his brief was the dissolution of the camp to prepare for
retreat. Vlasov and Larionov need never know the details of that
preparation. He studied the papers on the Camp Commandant's
desk. Orders from Reichsführer Himmler himself. *Liquidate all
prisoners*.

Outside the hut, Nicolai fretted at the continual noise of gunfire,
and he felt it incumbent on him to investigate its source.

'I'll walk a little,' he said to Vlasov, and limped slowly away in
the direction of the sound. Its source was not difficult to locate,
and the sporadic puffs of smoke in the distance indicated the site
of the firing. His pace quickened. He was apprehensive. He feared
what he would find. Shortly he came upon a clearing in the camp.
An open field surrounded by the prisoners' huts. In the centre of
the field was a large pit. On one side of its perimeter stood a line
of prisoners, shovels in their hands. On the opposite side, and
facing them, stood another line, empty-handed, their heads bowed.
Someone shouted an order to fire, and the prisoners fell, one by
one in domino fashion, into the open pit. Nicolai could not believe
what he saw. Would not believe it. He rushed towards the pit.

The prisoners were shovelling earth onto the bodies while
another line of condemned men formed meekly on the other side.
Nicolai screamed.

'Butchers,' he shouted. The firing squad ignored him. Another
round of fire was their sole response. Nicolai watched the men fall,
and at the sight of their tattered Soviet uniforms, his heart turned

321

over. A love and longing for Larionovka, for his lands, his peasants, his stern yet loving Mother Russia, overwhelmed him entirely, and he sank to his knees and begged forgiveness for his treachery. He looked up and saw Lister and the Camp Commandant walking towards the pit. Behind them, at an offensively subservient distance, walked Vlasov. Nicolai wanted to kill them all. He limped towards them.

'Stop all this,' he shouted, his voice breaking with horror. By now he had reached them.

'Colonel Larionov,' General Lister said. 'What is it that troubles you?'

'You cannot allow this, General,' Nicolai said. 'You have no right.'

'These men are mere partisans. They have no rights,' Lister said with disdain.

'They are soldiers of the Red Army.' Nicolai looked at Vlasov. Surely he would voice some objection. Those dead in the pit were his people. But Vlasov looked at the ground as if something of desperate interest was taking place at his feet.

'I wonder sometimes what side you are on, Colonel Larionov,' Lister said.

'What about the Geneva Convention?' Nicolai shouted.

General Lister laughed. 'I'm afraid that your beloved Stalin forgot to sign it. These men have no rights in international law.' He walked to the rim of the pit. 'Carry on,' he shouted to the officer in charge. 'All prisoners must be liquidated by sundown.'

Nicolai rushed towards him, reaching for his gun. But Lister drew, and without preamble, and with infinite disdain, shot Nicolai squarely between the eyes. He watched him fall, and heard the sound that came from his dying lips. 'Larionovka.'

Nicolai had too little time to itemise all his loves, but the name of Larionovka encapsulated them all. General Lister kicked at his body and rolled it like a football into the pit. 'Let him lie with his own scum,' he said. He turned to Vlasov with a look of warning. But Vlasov had gone. He was waiting obediently in his car.

PART EIGHT

23

The Germans never recovered their advantage and by 1945 the war was over. All over the Soviet Union families were reunited, and those long-practised Volynins once again reassembled. Sasha, Dmitri and Viktor. In the offices of the NKGB Ivan Volynin, now promoted to General, celebrated with the officers of high command, amongst them Marshals Zhukov, Molotov and Khrushchev. For a moment even Stalin himself dropped in on the celebrations, and laughingly insisted that Ivan call him Koba in respect of their first meeting in the Siberian snows. Ivan looked around him, laughed and drank with each of them and tried to convince himself that these were his family. He thought of Viktor. He knew that he had been promoted to Colonel, and that he had been awarded the gold star of a Hero of the Soviet Union. He was proud of him and longed for a reconciliation. He thought too of Vassily, his long-lost elder son. Of Katya, he dared not think at all. And not only because she was dead. But because of the futility of her dying. And for the same reason, he could hardly bear to think of Pyotr. But he could think of Sasha, although he, like Viktor, was estranged. He had to face the fact that the only family he had was the Party. To hell with the kith and kin, he thought. He raised his glass.

'To victory,' he said. 'And to the Party.'

The others raised their glasses in toasts, and he wondered whether any of them had homes to go home to. He was suddenly overcome by a pall of depression. A sense of loss and loneliness overwhelmed him. And it angered him, for, as a staunch and long-serving Party member, he had no right to such petty human feelings. But he could not help but think of what he would do when the victory celebrations were all over, and he saw himself alone in his apartment, with only his dangerously human thoughts for company. It was then that he decided to go that evening to visit Sasha, and hopefully to find some warmth of family.

When the victory parade was over, he returned to his bachelor rooms. He wondered whether he should go to Sasha's in his uniform. He knew that it was forbidding, and that it inspired respect and fear. But it was exactly that that gave him confidence. Without it he felt a mere peasant from Larionovka. So he decided to preserve his shield. Moreover, he added an extra medal to his already amply beribboned lapel. Then he called his driver, and requested a government car, one with clear markings, so that no one would be in any doubt as to who rode within. Despite all his trappings, he set out with little confidence, for though amply equipped against an enemy, in the face of family, he was totally unarmed.

In Sasha's apartment, they were celebrating quietly. And in reminiscence. Anna was leafing through a photograph album, one that had been salvaged from the ruins of the manor on the hill. Beside her sat Olga, and through the photographs Anna apprised her daughter of her lineage. Sometimes the photographs were blurred, or the faces forgotten, and then Avdotya would remember and add a story to that remembrance. Thus Countess Tatiana and Count Dmitri were celebrated, and even Count Fyodor, Olga's great-grandfather, though the manner of his demise was not deemed fitting for Olga's ears. Then there were photographs of Andrei and Nicolai as children, and Anna wept on seeing them. She had not heard from Nicolai for many years, but she presumed that he too was lost to her.

'But we have little Andrushka,' Avdotya said, and she nursed the baby in her arms.

Andrushka was the latest addition to the Volynin family. The year-old son of Dmitri and Sonya had taken a Larionov name and thus cemented once and for all that perilous union. The baby was in the care of his grandparents. Dmitri and Sonya had gone for a few days to Moscow to celebrate victory. And also to attend Viktor's wedding. That Hero of the Soviet Union, that reluctant

Volynin, was to marry Natasha, a nurse whom he had met through Dmitri and Sonya. Anna was happy to look after Andrushka for a while. As her first grandson, he confirmed the continuity of the Larionov line, and in her mourning for Andrei she was comforted by her love for Andrushka. And Avdotya was delighted. She somehow felt naked without a baby on her arm.

'I wish I had a photograph of Katya,' Anna said.

Then the front doorbell rang. Anna jumped in apprehension. Even though victory was celebrated and there was a reasonable chance for peace and goodwill, a summons to the door was still heard with fear. And still fearfully ignored. Somehow the doorbell presaged yet another farewell, another parting and more years of waiting in hope or despair.

'Don't answer it,' she shouted, and was alarmed at the panic in her voice.

The bell rang again.

'I'll go,' Sasha said. 'There's no need to be afraid. It's Victory Day.'

But when he saw Ivan on the threshold, and in full menacing uniform, he wondered whether he had a right to complacency. For he was reminded of another time when he had been taken by that same visitor, and in that same uniform, though less beribboned than now, but with the same menace and foreboding. He began to regret that he had answered the door. Before greeting him, Sasha peered around him to see whether his henchmen were at hand, but the corridor was empty.

'Have you come for me on your own, this time?' Sasha said. He could not pretend to be pleased to see his brother. They had last met at Katya's funeral and that meeting had been far from cordial.

'I've come to wish you and your family . . .' Ivan hesitated. He wished he could sound less formal. But the uniform did something to his voice. It seemed to inject it with a tone of superiority. 'Sasha,' he tried again, 'I've come to wish you a happy Victory Day. I hope you won't turn me away,' he said.

No, I won't, Sasha thought. Though he couldn't count on Anna's welcome. His brother would have to take his chances.

'Come in, Ivan,' Sasha said. 'I'm glad to see you.' And was, truly, for despite their differences, Ivan was his only remaining sibling. 'We have a guest,' he said as he led Ivan into the living-room.

Anna turned her back on him and busied herself with the photographs. Avdotya who, for old times' sake, would gladly have embraced Ivan, hovered in her greeting, in deference to Anna's hostility, but she gave him a smile and hoped that that would convey to him where she stood. Ivan went towards her and embraced her, and Avdotya was embarrassed by the attention shown her, which she had in no way invited.

'This is Andrushka,' she said, grasping a neutral subject. 'Dmitri's little boy. And Sonya's.'

'He's named after Andrei,' Anna whispered from her corner. 'You recall my brother Andrei, perhaps,' she added with bitterness.

'I came to wish you a happy Victory Day,' Ivan pleaded once more. But this time Anna positively turned her back on him.

'Your Olga is beautiful,' Ivan said. He was doing his best, but in many ways he wished he'd never come. 'And Dmitri. How is he?' He thought that a show of concern for his brother's family might soften Anna's heart.

'He's in Moscow,' Olga said, and in friendly fashion, for her uncle had found her beautiful. 'They've gone to Moscow for Viktor's wedding. That's why we've got Andrushka.' She was surprised at the silence that ensued, then realised that perhaps she had spilt the secret. 'Didn't you know?' she whispered.

There was no point in pretending otherwise. 'No,' Ivan said. 'I didn't know. I wasn't told.' His face paled and he looked suddenly old. If he'd been alone he would not have bothered to control his tears. 'Who is he marrying?' he asked, coldly, as a formality, as if to confirm his indifference.

'Her name's Natasha,' Sasha said.

Any other name in the Russian lexicon would have been benign enough, but 'Natasha' rang from the gallows. Its echoes and all the sorrows that it implied had dogged him since his young manhood. 'Is she pretty?' he managed to ask.

'She looks like Katya.' This from Anna in her corner. She did

328

not turn to look at him, she knew it was an arrow she had hurled, and she would take no pleasure in his grimace of pain.

'She's very pretty,' Sasha said. 'Shall we drink to her?' he hurried on. 'Let's drink to them both, and to victory.'

'No.' Anna stood up. 'We shall not drink,' she said. 'Not with him. Never. There's too much blood on his hands,' she shouted. 'Katya's blood, my parents', my brothers'. Even his own brother's. No, we shall not drink. Not with this murderer.'

'Anna,' Sasha whispered, appalled. 'Ivan is a guest in our home. Forgive her.' He turned to where Ivan had stood, but the space was empty. He heard the opening of the apartment door, and its shutting, with infinite sorrow. He looked at Anna and for the first time in their long life together he hated her.

'*Now* we shall drink,' Anna said. Her voice was close to hysteria. 'We'll drink to all those who never lived to drink.' She took the vodka bottle and poured an untempered measure into the nearest glass to hand. Then she drank it in one despairing gulp, seeking oblivion from her terrible memories and Sasha's love, now so undeniably frayed.

Avdotya went to her side, and cradled her head in her embrace. Sasha took Olga's hand and left the room.

'Was it all my fault, Papa?' she asked.

'Of course not. He had to know somehow,' he said. 'It was best coming from you.'

'I think Mama's very cruel,' she said.

He was tempted to agree with her. But such disloyalty would have been unforgivable. 'She gets upset easily,' he said, but with little feeling. At that moment, he wondered whether he would ever love her again. 'Go to bed, my sweetheart,' he said. 'Tomorrow we'll go to the Summer Gardens.' He kissed her goodnight tenderly, then went to his own study. There, he poured himself a vodka, and then another, drowning those feelings for Anna that he had never felt before, and of which he was deeply afraid.

In his apartment Ivan was doing likewise and for the same reason. They would all earn their oblivion that night, but each of their mornings would be terrible.

*

329

Although Viktor and Dmitri had grown up together, and despite Ivan's hostility, had become firm friends, it seemed that in the weeks after the end of the war, that friendship had frayed. Perhaps on Dmitri's part it was sheer envy. Viktor's Hero's Medal, and the adulation that it inspired, irked Dmitri in the extreme. Moreover, he was himself frustrated. He had applied for so many hospital posts and had not even been called for an interview. He was bitter. He felt that his wartime service merited a greater reward than idle unemployment. As a result of his frustration he found his marriage irksome, and at this moment, on the eve of Viktor's wedding, he was deeply jealous of his friend's happiness.

They were walking along Moscow's Tver Boulevard. Viktor and Natasha were arm in arm. Dmitri and Sonya walked one on each side of them. On one corner a brass band was playing and couples were dancing in the street. Viktor stopped, took Natasha in his arms and kissed her. Sonya looked across at Dmitri but he looked at his feet.

When they continued walking, Dmitri said, 'Did you call your father, Viktor?' He couldn't bear their happiness. He wanted somehow to dampen it.

'I did order a call,' Viktor said. 'But then I cancelled it. I just don't want him to come.'

'You'll be sorry,' Dmitri said. 'I was glad to have my father at my wedding. You could phone him now. He could still be here by tomorrow.'

'I don't want him here,' Viktor said. 'It's as simple and as sad as that.'

Sonya whispered to Dmitri to drop the subject. 'I just think he'll regret it,' he hissed at her.'

'People are different,' Sonya said. 'Especially fathers.' She took Natasha's arm, and dragged her laughingly away from Viktor, hoping that the two men, once alone together, could recall their old friendship. Viktor protested at the separation.

'You've got your whole lives together,' Sonya laughed. She took Natasha's arm, and they walked ahead. Looking around she was relieved to see Viktor and Dmitri in close and serious conversation.

Later that night they all adjourned to Viktor's apartment. Dmitri no longer persuaded him to ring his father. Sonya was right. People were different. He decided that for everyone's sake he must put his frustrations to one side. At least until after the wedding. And no doubt after that, his fruitless search for a job would nurture those feelings once more.

In the morning, Natasha rose early. She had an appointment with her best friend, Vika, who was making her wedding dress. They would have a final fitting, then Vika would make the necessary adjustments. Natasha promised to be back in the apartment by early afternoon, and in ample time for the wedding ceremony.

The dress required little adjustment. Vika had excelled herself, and the two girls left her shop in good time, early enough in fact to allow for a leisurely stroll down the boulevard. Natasha carried the dress that had been tissue-wrapped in a cardboard box and she held it before her as she walked. She had saved long and hard for the material and had queued outside the shop a whole long day. Now she bore it before her like a hard-earned trophy. It would please Viktor and that was all in her life she wanted to do.

'Come along, Vika,' she said. 'You walk so slowly.'

'There's plenty of time,' Vika said. 'In any case, you're supposed to be late. Brides always are.'

There were few people about. Most were still abed, nursing victory hangovers. A car was coming towards them, and slowed down at the kerb. Two soldiers got out of the car and approached them. From their uniforms it was clear that they were of high army rank. One was blond, young and good-looking. The other was bald and slightly older. When they reached Vika and Natasha, they did not exactly block their way, but it would have been difficult, without obvious manoeuvring, to walk past them. They stopped and saluted knowing that at the sight of their uniforms, the girls would at least give them the time of day.

'Excuse me,' the younger one said, saluting, 'may I have a word with you?'

'We're in a hurry,' Natasha said.

'Just one word then,' Vika invited. She found the man attractive; she would have welcomed a partner to take to Natasha's wedding.

'My name is Colonel Smirnov of the Guards,' the man said.

'Major Antipenko,' his companion said, and gave a gallant salute.

'And I'm Veronika,' Vika said. 'And this is Natasha.'

Natasha was anxious to get on her way. Viktor would be waiting and this was no time to strike up a new friendship. 'Come along, Vika,' she said. 'We'll be late.'

'We came from Germany only yesterday,' Smirnov said. 'We want to celebrate, and we have no one to keep us company. Except other officers. We have a banquet tonight. Would you be so gracious as to accept our invitation?' He bowed in exaggerated fashion and Vika was quite captivated.

'We're busy,' she said. 'Alas. But Natasha's getting married. This evening. A pilot, a Hero of the Soviet Union. And a colonel, like you.'

'That calls for congratulations,' Smirnov said, and he rushed back to the car, and returned with a bouquet of flowers.

'It was for our banquet table,' he said, 'but now it's for the bride.' He handed them to Natasha.

'No, thank you. Really,' Natasha said. 'Vika, we have to go.' Vika's dalliance was beginning to annoy her.

'Oh take them, Natasha. It's like a fairytale. It'll bring you good luck.' Then she whispered in Natasha's ear, 'Can I invite the colonel to the wedding?'

'Of course, if you want,' Natasha said. 'But for heaven's sake, let's go. Viktor will be worried.'

'You could come to the wedding, Colonel,' Vika offered. 'Your friend too.'

'That is indeed a generous invitation. Better far than drinking with a lot of fellow officers. Where is this wedding?'

Natasha murmured the address. She did not want to appear inhospitable.

'That's on our way,' the major said. 'We'll drive back and drop off and tell the others. Two minutes. Then we can all be on our way. Come.' He took Vika's hand, and brought her to the car.

'You can follow us later,' Natasha said. She was suddenly nervous. Vika was already in the car.

'Come,' Smirnov said, taking her arm, 'you'll get there quicker by car.'

His touch was gentle, rather like a brother's, and it inspired a little trust. She let him guide her to the car and settle her inside. He himself sat in the front with Antipenko who was driving. As they drove off Natasha caught a look that passed between the two men and a thumbs-up sign, one of victory. For indeed, they had accomplished their mission. The waylaying of a couple of girls, who had to be pretty and clean. Vika and Natasha were more than qualified.

'We'll be there in five minutes,' Smirnov said. 'Ten at the most. Then we can celebrate your wedding.'

Natasha did her best to believe him. She held her carton close to her chest. Like a shield. She knew Moscow well enough to know that they were nowhere near the quarter where Viktor was waiting. Nor were they driving in that direction. They seemed to be making for the outskirts of the city.

'Where are we going?' she dared to ask.

'Not far now,' Smirnov said. 'It's only a little bit out of our way.'

What he said did not worry her. It might have been the truth. It was the way he said it. It was his tone. For his voice had lost its flirtatious edge. It had gone back into uniform, and had assumed its duty as an officer if not a gentleman.

Natasha looked at Vika and whispered in her ear. 'I'm frightened,' she said. Vika said nothing. Her silence simply confirmed her own fears.

The car turned down a lane. A high brick wall lined one side of it, and on the bend there was an iron-gated entrance. The gates opened magically as the car approached and closed as magically behind them. But this was no fairyland. The metallic thud of the gates behind them was the fearful signature of a prison. The car wove around a circular drive and stopped in front of a large house.

'Don't be long,' Vika said. 'We'll wait for you.' She still held out some hope that they had been telling the truth, that indeed they had to stop off for a while before accompanying them.

Smirnov turned around. 'Let's go in for a few minutes,' he said. 'Just one little drink. I want to show you off,' he said. His voice was flat and unsmiling. His mission had been accomplished. Trimmings were now redundant. He got out of the car, and opened the passenger door. Antipenko did likewise on the other side.

'I don't want to go in,' Natasha said. She knew that whatever battle was in store was already lost. She was trembling.

'Leave me alone,' Vika screamed as Antipenko roughly pulled her out of the car.

Natasha clung to her carton of wedding dress. Somehow it seemed to her more important to protect that than her own person. But it was suddenly snatched from her, while Smirnov, with his other arm, dragged her from the car.

'We want to see you in your wedding dress,' he laughed. 'You're going to do the only thing you're good for.'

Both girls began to scream. Smirnov pulled Natasha towards him, and slapped her hard across the face.

'Leave her alone,' Vika screamed, but got the same treatment from Antipenko for her pains.

'You should feel honoured, you little whores,' Smirnov said. 'D'you know where you are?'

They were both too frightened to reply. In any case it didn't matter where they were. Wherever it was, it was not a good place for them.

But Smirnov was going to tell them anyway. He considered he had pulled off a coup, and he was going to make sure that everybody knew about it. 'You are guests of the greatest man in the Soviet Union,' he said. 'Well, almost the greatest,' he amended, fearful of eavesdropping. 'The great Beria has asked for you.'

It was like a clap of thunder. Beria. The Chief of Security. And the most hated and feared man in the whole of the Soviet Union. And possibly the ugliest. His fame as a womaniser was widespread, and rumoured with horror and disgust.

'Please, no,' Natasha whimpered. 'I'm to be married.'

'When the great man has finished with you,' Smirnov said. 'And others too,' he added. 'There are always those who are grateful for crumbs from his table.'

By this time, they were inside the house, dragged there like pathetically resistant rag dolls. A cheer went up from the banqueting-hall as they entered.

'Mission accomplished!' Smirnov roared. He lifted Natasha's bowed head by the hair. 'Let them look at you,' he ordered. 'You too,' he turned to Vika.

The officers at the table viewed the trophies.

'Not bad,' one of them said.

'Oh, a lot better than that,' Smirnov crowed. 'This one was on her way to her wedding. Here's her dress.' He threw the carton onto the table.

One of the officers picked it up, and took it to the head of the table. Beria sat there, salivating. With his podgy, sweating fingers he loosened the string, tore at the cardboard and the tissue that covered the dress. Then he laid it in front of him on the table and roughly fingered its silk.

'What better way to deflower it than with champagne?' he roared. He called for a bottle and ordered it opened. Then he poured a little down his throat and over his uniform and then onto the dress on the table. He emptied the bottle over the silk, smoothing it out the while, so that every fold would be touched by his filthy baptism. Then when it was done, he held it up.

'Which one is the bride?' he roared.

'This one,' Smirnov said, pushing his trophy before him.

'Take her to my room,' he said. 'And let the other one wait in my ante-chamber. The bride will come first.' Then he threw the dress at Smirnov. 'Prepare her,' he said.

The girls were dragged from the room. Both were beyond screaming. Natasha looked at Vika as she was taken away and she wondered whether she would ever see her friend again. Or indeed anybody that she had ever known. She trembled with terror and part of her fear was that she was not what they supposed her to be. Since Viktor had returned from the war, she had lived with him, and she was terrified that on discovering that she was not a virgin, Beria would order her death. She prayed that he would be too drunk to notice, and even so drunk that he could not perform. But she knew it was asking for a miracle.

She found herself in a vast bedroom. She heard Vika weeping

through an adjoining door. There were scuffles and she dared not think of what was happening to her. Smirnov threw the dress on the floor.

'Take all your clothes off,' he said. 'Then put it on.'

She was grateful that he didn't make a move to help her. He seemed happy enough to watch. She was not shy of him, and she was grateful for that. The man was a beast, and she was relieved that her innate modesty had deserted her. It helped to view him as he was. A piece of perverted scum. When she was naked, she didn't even bother to turn her back on him. She picked up her dress, and struggled into it. It was soaking wet and she had to tug at it to cover herself. And as she felt its wet silk on her flesh, she started to cry for what it had become.

Smirnov smiled. A woman's tears were a turn-on. His boss would be more than satisfied. He ordered her to lie on the bed. She obeyed and sat on its black silk quilt. She lay down and noticed for the first time the mirror on the ceiling and the mirrored walls around the bed. She shut her eyes. Whatever would happen to her on that bed, she would not witness it. She would do everything she could to erase the whole event from her memory. She would be blind to it, and deaf to it, and she would stiffen her body to any sense of it. She would etherise herself entirely. Then she would go home and marry Viktor and they would live happily ever afterwards. She willed it to be so, but she knew too, and with absolute certainty, that even if she survived the ordeal, she would be utterly destroyed.

She heard Smirnov approach the bed, but she would not open her eyes. She felt his rough hands on her legs, and she tried not to tremble. With one movement he spread them wide.

'Stay like that,' he ordered. 'And don't move. That's how he wants to find you.

She heard him move away and the closing of the door. But still she would not open her eyes. 'I am someone else,' she said to herself. 'Natasha is not here.' She listened for a sound from Vika. The silence behind the door frightened her. She prayed that Vika, too, considered herself elsewhere.

Shortly she heard the door open. She pictured him behind her closed eyes, and his ugliness appalled her.

336

'I heard your husband-to-be is a pilot,' she heard him say. She heard too the sound of his undressing. But she didn't answer him.

'Is it true he is a pilot?' she heard again, and again she gave him her silence. And felt her face sting.

'Answer when you're spoken to,' he said.

'Yes,' she whimpered. 'He's a pilot.'

'That's good,' she heard. 'In that case, he is often away. And you will be brought here for my pleasure.' Then she felt the whole weight of his body on top of her, and she wept for her dress that it was so sullied. And now so ripped as he roughly turned her over and had his bestial way, grunting obscenities the while, which drowned her screaming. He rested only a little while, then turned her over so that he lay viewing himself in the mirror, and once again he grunted his way to completion.

She felt him rise from the bed. Perhaps she could go home now, she thought, and marry Viktor. It couldn't be all that late. She would tell him she had lost the dress and gone to look for it. She would hide her pain and force her eyes open when he made love to her. Then she heard Beria's voice.

'Smirnov,' he called.

The door opened. 'Just once, comrade,' she heard Beria say, 'while I have a schnapps. Then I shall be back.'

And so it began all over again, with comings and goings, and opening and closing of doors, but all the time with the eyes firmly shut and Natasha elsewhere. Then for a while, she seemed to lie alone, and she dared to open her eyes. There was no one in the room. She lifted her head and tried to rise from the bed. But every bone in her body throbbed with a dull ache. She forced herself to stand and as she rose, her wedding dress, the shreds of it, stuck to the quilt and she saw that it was covered with blood. She wondered where Natasha was. Then saw her clothes on the floor, and slowly she equated them with the person that she was. That Natasha had never been elsewhere, that it was Natasha, promised to Viktor, who had been thrown on that blood-stained bed, and on whose body and spirit havoc had been wrought.

She dressed, her fingers trembling, knowing full well who she was, and what had become of her. She thought suddenly of Vika, and then dared not think about her. She was tempted to call out her name, but she did not want to draw attention to herself. She would creep out of the room, and somehow grope her way out of the nightmare. Perhaps once outside, she would wake, and find that it was still light, and Vika would be running behind her telling her that there was plenty of time. She turned the knob on the door and looked outside. No one was about and not a sound could be heard. She crept down the corridor. She remembered the way she had been dragged. There had been no stairs, and it had taken little time from the banqueting-hall. Somewhere she heard the sound of heavy snoring and it comforted her for she knew she would not be heard. Shortly she found the dining-hall. The source of the snoring. Some officers were slouched on the table, their heavy breathing gurgling in the puddles of spilt wine. Then she ran. With terror in her heart, and fear in her heels. And a thundering relief too, that she would survive.

It was when she found herself in the street, in the silent dawn darkness, that she broke down and wept. And she wondered whether her survival would be worth surviving.

24

When Dmitri and Sonya had arrived at Viktor's apartment that evening for the wedding celebrations, they were aware of a certain unease amongst the guests. The wedding table was ceremoniously set, plates of delicacies punctuated by beribboned bottles of champagne. On a side table a pile of wedding presents. Unopened, and every thing and everybody in the room appeared to be waiting. And the room's silence underlined their patience. Dmitri caught sight of Viktor on the balcony and he went straight to him. 'What is it?' he said. 'What's happened?' For something clearly was amiss.

'Natasha's not here,' he said.

'You mean you haven't seen her since this morning? Since she went to collect her dress?'

'She didn't come back,' Viktor said.

'Well, something must have happened to her. Have you rung the police?' Dmitri was concerned.

'Nothing's happened to her,' Viktor said. 'She takes good care of herself. She probably changed her mind, that's all.'

It was clear he felt he'd been jilted and so did all those others waiting inside, cloaked in their silent pity and embarrassment.

Sonya joined them on the balcony. She had overheard their conversation. 'That's impossible,' she said. 'She loves you. Something must have happened to her. We must do something.' She now shared Dmitri's concern. She took him aside and whispered to him that he should make enquiries. Meanwhile she stayed by Viktor's side.

'Perhaps the dress didn't fit,' she said feebly. 'Perhaps they're still trying to get it right.'

'I phoned Vika's,' he said. 'Two hours ago. There was no reply.'

'She would never change her mind, Viktor. I know Natasha. She loves you. She talks of no one else.'

'We've all been deceived,' Viktor said.

In another room in the apartment Dmitri was on the telephone. It had taken some time to get through to the police department, and when eventually he did, he could talk to no one who would take him seriously. Moreover, they all appeared to be drunk, an opinion confirmed by the background noises of laughter and cork-popping. 'It's victory time,' they kept saying. 'Hundreds of people go missing. She'll come back when she sobers up.'

Then Dmitri had tried the hospitals. Every casualty department in Moscow. But there was no news of either Vika or Natasha. Dmitri had a niggling feeling that perhaps his friend had been jilted after all. He wondered whether he should play host and open the champagne. At least drinking would give the guests something to do and something to take their minds off their pity. But it seemed illegal to open champagne when there was nothing to celebrate. He was afraid to join the guests. As the would-be groom's best friend, he might be pumped by them for information. So he went quickly through the room and onto the balcony once more. It was getting dark and a firework party had already begun on the balcony of a neighbouring apartment. Viktor turned his face away. He was sick of victory and all its celebrations. He wanted to go away somewhere and hide. He wished they would all go home.

'Tell them to go, Dmitri,' he said.

'Let's give her a little longer,' Sonya pleaded. 'There must be some good reason why she's late.'

'She could have telephoned,' Viktor said, and to that there was no answer.

They waited on the balcony, saying nothing. It grew quite dark and they heard movement behind them, and the scraping of chairs. Guests who were leaving, hoping their leave-taking would go unnoticed. And in deference to that, Viktor, Dmitri and Sonya remained on the balcony and did not look around. It was like a game of hide-and-seek, in which there would be no seeking. But the three were infinitely relieved that the guests were taking their leave. They gave them time, and when they thought that the coast was clear they left the balcony for the warmth of the empty room. The wedding table was untouched, but Dmitri noticed that the pile of beribboned presents was gone.

'I think we all need a drink,' Dmitri said, and though there was precious little to celebrate, he uncorked the champagne. He gave no toast. Nothing on earth seemed appropriate. So they drank silently. Glass after glass and bottle after bottle, and with each drink all three of them grew more and more sober. Nearby a church bell struck the hour, and they counted the four chimes. Natasha would not come, they knew. Nothing had happened to her. She had simply changed her mind. Poor Viktor.

Sonya shivered, and she went to close the balcony door. The fireworks still sprouted from the opposite apartment, silent and full of colour. Their sporadic light illuminated the street below, and before shutting the balcony doors, Sonya went outside to catch the burgeoning dawn. She leaned over the balcony and saw a figure huddled on a bench below. She could not decipher whether it was a man or woman but whatever it was, it was a figure crouched in despair. She waited for another firework whose light would give a further clue. When it came, she started. The figure was without doubt a woman. It was possible that it was Natasha. She didn't want to raise any hopes by calling her name. It might well have been somebody else, and even if it was Natasha, she was clearly in no mood for response. She said nothing, but went back into the living-room. Then she excused herself, noisily opened the bathroom door, then rushed downstairs into the street. The figure was still huddled on the bench, and as she approached it she recognised Natasha. Partly with relief, but principally with fear, for though it was a comfort to know that she was alive, her state was clearly one that gave rise to anxiety. She called her name. The figure did not stir. It remained huddled in sublime indifference. Sonya went to the bench, and sat at Natasha's side. She knew that words were futile, so she took her in her arms. Natasha heaved with sobbing,

341

and Sonya let her cry it out, whatever the terrible 'it' was that troubled her.

Then after a while she said, 'Come, Viktor is waiting for you.'

'It's all over, Sonya,' Natasha said. She allowed herself to be helped to her feet, and Sonya guided her to the building. Outside she stopped suddenly.

'Are there people there?' she whispered.

'Only Dmitri and Viktor,' Sonya said. She took Natasha's arm and led her to the lift.

'No. Let's walk,' Natasha whispered. She was shivering, but Sonya knew that it was not from cold and she wondered what hell had been Natasha's in her absence. Natasha took the stairs very slowly. She seemed to be in pain. At the top of the flight she rested on the banister. 'I want to die,' she said. Sonya held her for a while then guided her into Viktor's apartment.

He was standing by the window when he heard Dmitri's gasp. Then he turned. 'Natashenka,' he whispered. He went to her and made to fold her in his arms, but she shrank from him, curling herself into her body. Untouchable. Sonya sat her down on a chair. She motioned to Dmitri that they should leave the room, but as she turned away Natasha said, 'No. Please. Stay.' So she sat by her side.

'What happened?' she asked. Perhaps Natasha would find it easier to tell a woman.

'Beria,' Natasha said.

Then Viktor knew, and so did the others, that Natasha had gone mad. Dmitri even went so far as to giggle. When she heard that sound Natasha rose, gathering a strength that astonished her. She picked up the nearest plate on the table. It was laden with caviare and lemon slices. She took her time with aim, time enough for Dmitri to remove himself from the line of fire. But he was so astonished, he stood rooted on the spot, and the plate winged him on the cheek lacing his face with blood-stained caviare.

'You're mad,' he managed to shout at her. He had lost all sympathy. But Viktor and Sonya wondered whether she was so mad after all.

'What about Beria?' Viktor said.

342

Natasha had vented her spleen, and the relief had loosened her tongue. Now the terrible words tumbled out of her mouth with no respect for chronology or structure. 'Beria,' she said again. 'He raped me. In his house. Kidnapped. Vika and me. Where is his house?' she interrupted herself. 'First Beria, then the colonel, then the major, then Beria again. And again. Where's Vika?' Viktor went towards her and tried to touch her. But she shrank from him. 'Don't touch,' she screamed. 'He touched. Beria touched.'

Viktor sat on the floor by her side. He was as broken as she. 'I'll kill him,' he whispered.

Sonya signalled again to Dmitri who was nursing his cheek with bitter resentment. Together they went from the room. In the hall Sonya whispered, 'She's not mad, you know. She's telling the truth.'

'I'm going to phone Papa,' Dmitri said. 'God knows what Viktor's going to do. Ivan has to know about it.' He picked up the telephone. Sonya went to close the living-room door. From inside she heard Natasha's pleading voice. 'Don't touch me. Never. Never.'

When the phone rang in Sasha's apartment, he was startled out of his sleep. Anna awoke immediately with that hangover fear from her dreams that Sasha would once again be taken. But at least this sound wasn't the doorbell. Arrest was impossible by telephone. Yet at that time of the night, the news could not possibly be good. In her mind, she quickly checked on her family. Parents dead. Beyond any more pain. Likewise, Andrei. Olga was in the next room. Asleep. Likewise little Andrushka. That left Nicolai and Dmitri. She had not heard from Nicolai for many years, and often she thought that he must be dead. That left Dmitri, whom she knew to be in Moscow. But anything could have happened to him. She got out of bed and followed Sasha into the living-room.

'Mitya?' she heard him say when he picked up the phone. So it wasn't Dmitri who was in trouble.

'What is it, Sasha?' she whispered. She watched his face grow pale. Occasionally he said, 'No. No. That's terrible.'

'What's terrible?' she almost screamed at him.

'Just a minute, Mitya. I must tell Mama. Natasha's been raped,' he said to her. 'She's all right. Yes, Mitya, I'm listening.'

Anna noticed how his hand trembled on the receiver. 'Of course I'll come,' she heard him say. 'And I'll bring Ivan.'

'No!' Anna shouted, as he put down the phone. It was worrying enough for him to go away at all. To go in Ivan's company spelt disaster.

'I have to go, Anna,' Sasha said. 'They're in terrible trouble. They need family.'

'But I need you. Olga needs you. It's terrible what's happened to Natasha. But Viktor will look after her.'

'It's more than rape, Anna,' he said. 'It's who raped her. Beria no less. My brother's boss. Viktor says he's going out to kill him. I *have* to go, Anna. And I have to take Ivan.' Then she saw how serious it was.

'Beria,' she spat the name. 'How did he find her?'

'She'd collected the wedding dress. She was on her way back to the apartment with her friend. They were kidnapped. It happened in Beria's house. That's all I know.'

'That's more than enough,' Anna said softly. 'I'll pack you a bag.'

He dressed hurriedly. 'I won't phone Ivan,' he said. 'I'll go straight to his apartment.'

'Be careful of him,' Anna said. 'Here,' she took a gold locket from around her neck. 'Give this to Natasha,' she said.

'But it was your mother's.'

'It has helped me through troubled times. Tell her to wear it. It will help her.'

Sasha kissed her. 'I'm coming back,' he said. 'I'll do what I can, and I'll come straight home. This is no parting.'

Anna smiled. 'I'll try and believe you.'

He took a cab to Ivan's apartment and instructed the driver to wait at the door. He rang Ivan's bell, and knocked on the knocker, and felt a certain pleasure in waking his brother at the crack of dawn, as his brother himself had so often done to others. On so many doors and with so much terror. Now Ivan's heart could miss a beat. Now Ivan could wonder about all those labour camps he'd

344

never seen. Now Ivan could tremble at all the dawns that he had witnessed for others.

'Who is it?' Ivan trembled.

'Sasha. Open the door.'

He heard the unbolting of many locks and chains and it pleased him to know that even his brother lived in fear.

Then he saw him, his hair dishevelled, and a bewildered look in his eye.

'What d'you want?' Ivan said. He was far from welcoming.

'Get dressed,' Sasha said. 'We're going to Moscow.'

'Nonsense,' Ivan said. 'I wasn't invited to my son's wedding. In any case I have work.'

'There's no wedding,' Sasha said. 'And you have work in Moscow. The most important work you ever did.'

'What's happened?' Ivan asked. 'I'm not moving until you tell me what's happened.'

'Your job has happened, that's what. And the job may be lost for you.'

It was enough to get Ivan going.

'I'll tell you in the train,' Sasha shouted after him.

Happily there was an early-morning train to Moscow. Sasha insisted on breakfast before telling Ivan the purpose of their journey, and they were both settled in the dining car before Sasha began.

Ivan heard the tale at first with mocking disbelief. 'She's lying,' he said. 'It's impossible.'

Sasha was patient. 'What would be the point of making up such a fantastic story on the day of her wedding? I'm afraid it's true, Ivan. Beria is well known to be a monster, with women as well as other things. I'm not even going to bother to convince you,' he said with disgust, adding, 'but you should know Viktor has it in mind to kill Beria. Dmitri says that nothing will stop him. That's why you're going to Moscow.' He let Ivan think about that for a while.

'What can I do?' Ivan said. He was in panic.

'You must try and talk to him. Forget your job. Forget your boss. Talk to your *son*. He's bereaved. He's broken.'

'Why didn't you go to the wedding? You were invited, weren't you?' Ivan said. He was still deeply hurt that he had been ignored.

'I wanted to go,' Sasha said, 'but I couldn't if you weren't invited. I told Viktor so. I tried to persuade him to ask you. But he won't forgive you for his mother.'

'And you expect me to humiliate myself and ask him to forgive me?' Ivan's voice was raised.

'No,' Sasha said wearily. 'Not your son. But your Comrade Stalin, he can throw shit in your face, your beloved Beria, he can piss on you, but you'll lick both their arses. And for what? For promotion. For rank. You deserted Katya and let her die in filth because she criticised the Party. Because you wanted promotion. And to have her around was an impediment. Well, you've got your promotion. And that's *all* you've got.'

Now it was out, and there was some relief in it. He looked at Ivan's face, and saw the tears course down his cheeks. 'Have I lost you too?' Ivan said.

Sasha touched his brother's arm. 'God help me, Ivan. What have we got if not each other?'

After that few words passed between them until they reached Moscow. At the station, they took a cab straight to Viktor's apartment.

But Viktor had already left. He had sat up all night listening to Natasha's weeping. Dmitri and Sonya sat with him. From time to time he had gone into the bedroom, and perhaps had tried to touch her, but outside the bedroom door they heard her screaming. Then he had gone into the bathroom, showered and shaved, and returned to the living-room, resolute.

'I'm going to kill him,' he said. 'I'm going to bomb his house. There's no other way.'

'That's madness,' Dmitri said. 'You'll be shot.'

Viktor ignored the remark. 'I want you to take Natasha to Leningrad. You have to keep her hidden.'

'Viktor, you cannot do it. I won't let you,' Dmitri said. He stood up and tried to block Viktor's path to the door. But Viktor brushed him aside.

'I couldn't live if I didn't do it,' he said.

'You won't live in any case,' Dmitri shouted after him. For he was gone, and they heard his furious feet on their way to his revenge. Sonya began to weep. She knew that she would never see Viktor again. Then suddenly Natasha appeared in the living-room. 'Where's Viktor?' she said.

'He'll be back soon,' Dmitri whispered. But he knew that Viktor would never come back. That Natasha was already a widow.

'We must eat something,' Sonya said. And she went to prepare breakfast.

It was then that Sasha arrived with Ivan. 'Where's my son?' Ivan said. No preamble. No greeting.

Natasha looked at him. So this was Viktor's father. He whom he called Ivan the Terrible, and she understood why he'd not been invited to the wedding.

'I'll go and help Sonya,' she said, and she limped into the kitchen, unable to bear his presence.

'Is that her?' Ivan said when she had gone. He could not bring himself to pronounce her name.

'That's Natasha,' Sasha said coldly.

'Where's Viktor?' Ivan asked again.

'I can't tell you,' Dmitri said.

'We have to know, Mitya.' Sasha put his arm around his shoulder. 'He'll do himself harm. We have to find him.'

'He's gone to get his revenge.'

'But where?' Ivan shouted. 'And how?'

'He's gone to the airfield. He's going to bomb Beria's house. I couldn't stop him.'

Ivan shivered. But not for the fate of his son. He saw his career crumble about him. He saw the bleak dawn that others had seen, others whom he had witnessed. He stormed into the kitchen. Sasha and Dmitri followed him.

'Last night,' he shouted in Natasha's direction, 'when you were there, did you use my name?'

'For God's sake, Ivan,' Sasha spluttered.

But Ivan persisted. 'Well, did you, or didn't you?'

'I don't remember,' Natasha whispered.

'My God, you're a monster.' This from Sonya. Hitherto she had held her tongue on all matters concerning Dmitri's uncle. She had kept her terrible opinion to herself. But now she had to shield Natasha. 'Can you think of nobody else except yourself?' she screamed at him.

Ivan noted her comment in silence. But he vowed that it was a remark Sonya Volynina of Jewish birth would dearly pay for. He wanted to hit her, but for the moment he controlled himself.

'I shall find him,' he said. 'Sasha, you stay here, in case he phones.'

'His name's Viktor,' Natasha sobbed.

But Ivan ignored her. 'Persuade him to come back. And don't mention that I am here.' He had the sense to add that, for he knew that Viktor would come nowhere near him.

'Shall I come with you?' Dmitri offered.

'You stay here and make sure she doesn't leave the apartment.' He didn't want company. Especially family. He wanted no witnesses to what he had in mind to do. They would never understand it.

He rushed from the apartment and called a cab, directing the driver to the military airfield.

'I have no permit,' the driver said.

Ivan flashed his insignia, and the man trembled and cursed his bad luck. He did as he was told and prayed for a return journey to his wife and children. When they reached the airport checkpoint, Ivan once again identified himself, and the driver furtively crossed himself and drove inside. He pulled up at the entrance and quickly left his seat to open the passenger door, a gesture he would never have made in the course of his driving day. He hated himself for his obsequiousness, but he, like most of his compatriots, lived in terror of what his fare represented. It was better to appear to be on their side. He even managed a little bow and scrape as Ivan alighted from the cab, though he could happily have spat on him. But that he saved until he was out of the airport and for the grass verge that surrounded it.

Ivan held his insignia before him, and paths were cleared for his progress.

'I'm looking for the office of Colonel Viktor Volynin,' he addressed one of the guards.

The man bowed slightly and said he would lead the way. In time they reached Viktor's door. Ivan noted how his son's name was inscribed on a brass plate, and beside it, as a recent addition, a star, the emblem of a Hero of the Soviet Union. For a moment he felt proud, but not for long, for his son was about to stain that honour, and his momentary pride soured into shame. He strode through the door. There was no sign of Viktor in the office. Its sole occupant was a young lieutenant who sat at Viktor's desk. On seeing the insignia, he quickly stood to attention and gave a salute. Ivan brushed the greeting aside.

'Where is Volynin?' he asked.

'I don't know, sir. I haven't seen him.' He blushed as he spoke, and the colour was not lost on Ivan.

'You're lying,' he said.

The lieutenant trembled. He was Viktor's closest friend. They had flown together many times. He suspected that this man was Viktor's father. Viktor had spoken about him often enough. He knew he was a man to inspire terror, and at this moment the lieutenant did not feel himself to be an exception to that rule. Yet he would not betray his friend. He knew where Viktor was, and he guessed what he was about. For only an hour or so earlier he had stormed into the office in a state of near hysteria. He had been a wedding guest the night before. He was one of those who waited, and slunk away, unwilling to face the jilted groom. He had no idea of what had happened to Natasha and he was afraid to ask. But he knew that his friend's frenzy was connected with the almost-wedding feast. Viktor had asked him to get his plane ready. He had told him that he would be taking off at eight o'clock that evening. He said he was flying alone, and he swore his friend to secrecy. He had taken with him a detailed aerial map of the Moscow suburbs. And as he left, he had said farewell as if he would never return.

'I'm not lying,' the lieutenant said, though every syllable trembled. 'I haven't seen him.'

'Why are you trembling?' Ivan said.

'The NKGB inspires fear in everybody,' the lieutenant said. They were the first words of truth he had spoken.

349

·Ivan gave a flicker of a smile. 'And that's as it should be. Don't you think so, Lieutenant?'

He nodded. He was prepared to agree with anything, but he would not divulge the whereabouts of his friend.

But Ivan did not need his co-operation. In broad outline he knew what Viktor was about. He could do without the details even if this man knew them. And perhaps he didn't know them. He might even be telling the truth.

'Thank you, Lieutenant,' he said, and he left the room. He went straight to the offices of the Air Defence Command. Once again his insignia more than eased his passage. More salutes, more obeisance, and a strong odour of fear. He addressed himself to the colonel in charge.

'Are any planes scheduled to leave here today?' he asked.

'None at all, sir,' the colonel said.

Ivan smiled. 'I think you may be wrong,' he said. 'I have information that one plane will leave the airfield. I do not know its take-off time. I order you to put your anti-aircraft batteries on alert. As from now. The plane is piloted by an enemy of the Soviet Union. It must be shot down.'

'Your orders will be obeyed, sir,' the colonel said. He could not understand them. He knew the flight schedules, and he knew with absolute certainty that today the field was idle. But orders were orders. He hoped for his own sake that the secret police were mistaken.

From the Air Defence Command, Ivan made his way to the control tower. Space was cleared for him in front of a radar screen. He did not explain his presence. The technicians need not know. In any case, he had lost the words to explain. He would wait. And wait in silence. He looked at his watch. It was five o'clock in the afternoon. He would wait. He prayed that he would not have to wait long, but in what was left of his heart, he prayed that he would have to wait for ever.

In Viktor's apartment they were waiting too. At least Sasha was waiting. Dmitri, Sonya and Natasha, exhausted by their night's terror, were sleeping, while Sasha kept vigil. The phone did not ring, and there was an ominous silence. Which was suddenly

350

broken by a thud outside the apartment door, and the sound of scurrying footsteps in the hall. Sasha waited, trembling. He allowed the silence a while, then crept to the front door and cautiously opened it. And stifled a cry. A body lay there. A woman's body. Her clothes were torn, and no effort had been made to cover her nakedness. He dared to look at her face and thought that she might once have been pretty. But the eyes were now bulging and the tongue lolled in her open mouth. About her neck was a tightly wound stocking, her killer's signature. He knew that she must be Vika, Natasha's friend, and he knew too that Natasha must never know. He ran to wake Dmitri, and whispered to him what he had found. Together they lifted her body, and laid her gently on the balcony. Then they covered her.

'It's poor Vika,' Dmitri confirmed. 'And they'll be back. You must take Natasha straightaway, Papa,' he said. 'You must take her to Leningrad. I'll see to the body. But you must go quickly.'

Sonya was woken but they told her nothing, except that she should wake Natasha. They were leaving, Sasha told her, and Dmitri would explain when they were gone. Sonya did not question him but gently woke Natasha from her fitful sleep, and within a very short while they were on their way to the station.

The train for Leningrad did not leave till eight o'clock. And it was only seven. But the train was waiting at the station, so they were able to board. Sasha settled Natasha comfortably in a corner seat, and held her hand. Then he remembered the locket that Anna had given him. He took it out of his pocket.

'I have a gift for you, Natasha,' he said. 'From Anna, my Anna. It belonged to her mother and she sent it to you.'

'But why?' Natasha said. 'She doesn't even know me.'

'Viktor loves you. And that's enough for us to know.'

'But will I ever see him again?' she said.

It was not a subject for speculation, and both fell silent.

'We will soon be home,' Sasha said after a while. 'You will be safe there.'

And so will I, he thought, and Anna won't worry any more. But he itched for the train to take off, for as long as he was in Moscow, the site of Natasha's terror, he could feel the shadows behind him.

351

He tried to be patient. He recalled that much of his life had been spent waiting. And always for freedom. As he was waiting now. And somehow, with all his long practice, waiting never became easier.

In the control tower Ivan was waiting too. And for a freedom of a kind. His own. His own exoneration. He looked at his watch. It was almost eight o'clock. He sensed that whatever he was waiting for, was about to happen. He felt it in his stomach, with a certain sense of sad inevitability. He noticed that those around him were suddenly on guard. Then a searchlight beam that seemed to sprout astonished from the earth swept across the airfield and came to rest on a single aircraft rolling slowly down the runway. Ivan stared at the radar screen forcing himself to witness that Isaac-sacrifice on which God would turn His back.

The control tower command spoke into the microphone that linked the tower with Air Defence Command.

'Flight number 104 has just taken off from Moscow field,' he said. 'Unauthorised,' he added sternly. Ivan forced himself to stare at the screen. Again he was a witness. But this was not like a dawn witnessing. There one watched the flesh and blood of treachery that would soon be no more. But here he was looking at mere pictures. He watched the flashes of light from the barrage about the plane, and when they missed he was exalted. In his heart he urged the plane to dodge the fire. 'Where is it now?' he dared to ask the officer.

'Over the suburbs,' he said.

Still Ivan prayed for the plane's escape. This was a game he didn't want to win. He wanted desperately to order them to hold their fire. The plane had ceased dodging and was flying level. It was preparing for its lethal discharge. And then the fire hit it. Square in its offensive face, and it spun like a Catherine wheel, a splintered flower in the night. It was over. Ivan put his head in his hands. He wondered what name his son had called as he spiralled to his death. Possibly, like Pavlenkov, he had called 'Natasha'. The wheel had come full circle.

PART NINE

25

Sasha glanced at his watch. It was just after eight o'clock, and he wondered why the train still idled at the station. He glanced out of his window and to his horror saw the cause of the delay. A colonel and three soldiers were marching down the platform and making their undeniable way to Sasha's carriage. It was too late to escape and a fleeting image of Siberian snows flashed across Sasha's eye.

They crashed into the compartment. Natasha cowered. The nightmare face of Smirnov startled her eye. He took her roughly and handed her over like a parcel to one of the soldiers. 'Put her in the car,' he said.

She made no protest. She had convinced herself that she would never see Viktor again, so she had little appetite for further life. She went with the soldiers almost willingly.

Not so Sasha. As the soldiers grabbed him, he put up a tremendous fight. But the years he had paid in hard labour in the camps, had wasted his body's strength. Yet he struggled, thinking of Anna and how yet again he would leave her, while they pinned him to the ground, and pistol-whipped him until he fell into a merciful faint. He woke to find himself handcuffed and shackled, propped up in the corner of a travelling van. Out of his bruised eyes he saw his guards, and he noticed that his coat was stained with blood. He wondered painfully what had happened to Natasha, as Natasha was wondering about him. She too was travelling, and in Smirnov's car, which at that moment turned into the drive of Beria's house where once again she would be called upon to do her duty.

Sonya and Dmitri returned to Leningrad the following day. And they came laden with all the dire news. Ivan had had the temerity to call at the apartment, ostensibly to collect Viktor's belongings. He had itemised the events of his day. Viktor's manner of death, which he regretted, Sasha's arrest, and Natasha's suitable return to the Beria mansion. He had ignored Sonya during his visit, but he had been particularly friendly towards Dmitri.

'I have lost a son,' he had said, 'and you, a father. And God knows for how long. I would like to be a father to you. If you need any help, I shall be there.'

Sonya would happily have killed him. But what angered her even more was Dmitri's acquiescence. He even thanked him for his offer. How unlike his real father he was.

And all this news they brought back to Leningrad. To Anna, who had heard it all before. She took to her bed, devastated. She did not think she could endure another Siberian widowhood. She clung to Olga and Avdotya, and thanked God for their company.

The years passed. Life was hard. There was little money, and Anna was too frail to go back on the trams. The year turned on her half-century and she thought about Sasha, her milk-sibling, whose year was turning in the Siberian snows. Sonya visited her often bringing Andrushka, who lightened their lives. But Dmitri came seldom. Sonya excused him. He was looking for work. For some reason he could not find a hospital post suitable to his experience. Money was scarce for them too. Anna could see that she was not happy. Dmitri blamed her in his frustrations. He remembered his Uncle Ivan's offer when Viktor had died. He had been wary of visiting him, but as each workless day passed, and with every post rejection, he was tempted to take up his offer. After all, his mother needed money, to say nothing of his own needs, and with his father in a labour camp he was the sole provider. Thus he talked himself into using his uncle, but he would say nothing to Sonya or his mother. So one Sunday, when Sonya had gone to Anna's, he took himself to Ivan's apartment.

He had made an appointment and on the telephone, Ivan had been full of welcome. He lived in a Leningrad suburb, in an apartment building strictly reserved for high-ranking government officers. Dmitri was impressed by its opulence. In spite of employ-

356

ing servants, Ivan himself answered the door. Dmitri had not seen him for several years. Their last meeting had been a fraught one in Viktor's apartment in Moscow. He felt it would be in his interest to make no reference to that meeting, nor indeed to the name of Viktor which, by all paternal laws of nature, must still stick in Ivan's throat.

His uncle looked well. Though older than his own father, he looked considerably younger, and Dmitri was sadly reminded of his father's camp absences. His uncle had never undergone such privation. His fitness and health had never been interfered with. Dmitri felt resentful, and was relieved to have no scruple in asking his uncle for favours. His uncle owed. Of that there was no doubt in his mind. He had every right to use him.

Ivan directed him to his study, and asked him to wait. He had a phone call to make, but would be with him shortly. Dmitri was glad to have a little time on his own, time to examine his uncle's study, and perhaps find clues there of the man whom everyone feared and whom no one believed was human. A large portrait of Stalin dominated the room. The eyes were cruel and penetrating. Anyone who passed through Ivan's study would feel immediately under surveillance. The portrait seemed to stamp the room with an impersonal cold aloofness, and Dmitri sought an object or any effect that would mark this room as belonging not just to any Party Official but to his uncle, Ivan Volynin, who had once been his father's hero-worshipped brother. He found those effects on a side table. Framed portraits of Ivan's family. There were many of Viktor. Viktor as a young pioneer, Viktor as cadet, and as a captain, standing in front of his plane. And central to the Viktor display was his Hero's medal, set in a bed of red velvet, and framed in ebony black. A portrait of Katya was set on one side as if she had nothing to do with Viktor but was there for form's sake. Ivan's family sat neatly in silver frames, and possibly in the only form that he could accommodate them.

'It's good to see you,' Ivan said as he came into the room. 'I hoped one day you would call.'

'Is there news of my father?' Dmitri asked.

'I only know that he is in a camp in Siberia,' Ivan said. 'I

357

presume he is alive. Otherwise I would have heard. Will he ever learn his lesson, that dear brother of mine?' Ivan laughed, and Dmitri felt slightly resentful.

'Perhaps there are lessons he doesn't wish to learn,' he said. 'He accepts that he must pay the price.'

'I'm sorry about that,' Ivan said. 'I miss him. Now he is the last of my family.'

Dmitri wondered whether those were just words. Spoken for form's sake, but without heart. He tried to imagine his uncle alone, without his uniform and medals, vulnerable in his pyjamas perhaps, alone in his bed at night, unable to sleep. What did he think about? Where did he allow his thoughts to wander? Dare he think of Pyotr. Of Katya? Of his lost son, Vassily, perhaps? And most dangerous of all, of Viktor. Perhaps he dwelt in that only area where death did not lay at his door. The memory of his father, Vassily. Safe, manageable, secure. That he could recall. For that memory he could shed a tear. But for others he could manage only a silver frame.

'But your father will return,' Ivan said. 'He always does. Now let's talk of you, Dmitri. First, I shall pour you a drink.' He went to his cabinet and poured two vodkas. 'What shall we drink to?' he said. He seemed in jovial mood, a temper so rare in his uncle, that Dmitri was puzzled. Perhaps age had mellowed him a little, or the thought perhaps that having lost Viktor, nothing could touch him further. For he had indeed 'supp'd full of horrors'.

'I'd like to drink to my future,' Dmitri said, 'which at the moment looks pretty bleak.'

'We'll drink to that,' Ivan said, raising his glass. 'Is that why you have come to see me?'

Dmitri downed his drink. 'I hope you can help me, Uncle,' he said. He sat himself down. He needed to confide in Ivan, and for that he needed comfort. He was glad when Ivan drew up a chair beside him.

'I'm thirty-two years old,' Dmitri said. 'I've been a qualified doctor for over ten years. I'm a decorated lieutenant colonel. I was in complete charge of a military hospital. My record is good. No one could deny that. But when the war was over, it wasn't easy to get a decent post. At the moment I'm deputy head of a health commission. It's a paltry job. It has little to do with medicine. But it's all that I am offered.'

He noticed a smile flicker on his uncle's lips, as if he understood his dilemma. And only too well.

'Have you applied for other jobs?' Ivan asked.

'Yes. Just last week. It's head of a department in the Ministry of Health in Moscow. It's just my kind of work. I went for an interview. They told me they were very impressed with my qualifications. They asked me lots of questions. How long I intended to stay in Leningrad? Did I have children? That sort of thing. Then they asked me about my father. I had to tell them. I had a letter from them yesterday. They had found someone else they said. But I know from friends who work there that the job's still open. It's my father, Uncle,' Dmitri said. 'As long as I have to divulge his record, I'll never get a job.'

Now Ivan smiled openly, and poured them both another vodka. 'You don't understand anything, do you?' he said.

'What do you mean?'

'Your father's got nothing to do with it, Dmitri. Nothing at all. I can vouch for that.'

'Then what's the reason? I can think of no other cause.'

'It's very simple, Dmitri,' Ivan said. He was still smiling. 'You are not offered a job, a proper job, that is, because your wife is Jewish. Divorce your wife and you'll get a job the following day. That I can promise you.'

'Then I'll get a divorce,' Dmitri said. He did not hesitate, and Ivan warmed to him. Here was a man after his own heart. A man whose priorities were abundantly clear. 'I don't intend to suffer all my life because of my relatives,' Dmitri said.

'Let's drink to that.' Ivan poured more vodka.

'I'll do it tomorrow,' Dmitri said. 'May I ring you then, Uncle, and let you know I'm clean?'

His choice of word was astonishing, but it had seemed to Dmitri to be the right and proper word.

'As soon as you are "clean", as you put it,' Ivan laughed, 'I

359

shall set the wheels in motion. Now drink up, and go about your business.'

Dmitri thanked him profusely. It had been a happy meeting and he resolved that he would come more often. He felt his uncle must often long for company.

'Do come again,' Ivan said. 'I've enjoyed our little chat. And my regards to your mother,' he added, though those, too, were only words.

When he reached home Sonya was putting Andrushka to bed. He was particularly loving to her, stroking her face and tousling her hair. She was surprised because of late he had been cold towards her, and irritable, and she ascribed it to his frustrations in his career. Perhaps now he had at last found a job worthy of his qualifications. But she would not enquire. He would tell her in his own time.

'When you've put Andrushka to bed, I want to talk to you,' he said. He kissed their son, and went into the living-room, and waited for her. While she was bathing their son, he took the opportunity to phone a lawyer friend. At the time, divorce was easily obtained under Soviet law. Between consenting partners all that was necessary was the signing and countersigning of a couple of forms. For this they had to attend the District Court House, and swear before the presiding magistrate. All this information Dmitri gathered from his phone call. His friend did stress, however, the word 'consent'. Both partners had to agree to the divorce. It was this crucial aspect that would form the basis of his talk with Sonya. He expected some initial resistance, but he was confident that finally she would agree.

When she came into the living-room, he rose and sat her comfortably on the settee. This unaccustomed solicitousness of his worried her, and she half expected that he wanted a favour of her. She was sad that she had grown to mistrust him so. She did not respond to his friendliness, but that did not faze him.

'We need to talk,' he said.

'I'm listening.'

He told her about his visit to Ivan, and she did not attempt to hide her displeasure. She hated Ivan. From Anna she had heard how he had treated Katya, and she had seen for herself what he had done to Viktor. How different Ivan was from Sasha.

'Why did you go to him?' she said angrily. 'Did you go to kowtow for favours?'

So he gave it to her straight. He couldn't be bothered with a preamble. He was rather glad that she had given him cause for irritation. 'I want a divorce,' he said. And then, 'I *have* to have a divorce.'

Sonya was aghast. She thought she had not understood him. But then he repeated it, and she had to believe what he said. She knew that lately their marriage had been uncertain, but she thought he still loved her. And she had no doubt about her own loving feelings for him. Her limbs trembled and she felt the onset of a fever. 'Is there someone else?' she said. It seemed to her to be the only explanation.

Dmitri laughed. 'Of course not.' Then regretted he had been so abrupt. 'It won't change anything,' he said. 'It's just a stupid formality.'

'But why do it at all? Was it *his* idea?' She could not bring herself to pronounce his name.

'It has nothing to do with him. It's my idea. I can't stay married to you, Sonya. It's because you're Jewish. That's the only reason. And as long as I have a Jewish wife, I'll never get a decent job. I love you, Sonya, and no paper is going to change that. You must understand. It's the best for all of us.'

She took his outstretched hand. What he had said made sense of a sort. She had often suspected that her religion was his career impediment.

'But what will happen to us?' she asked. 'Can't you live with me any more?'

'There's a job in Moscow. I think I could get it.'

'With his help, I suppose,' she said with contempt.

'Yes, with his help,' he shouted. 'And I'm not above using it. He *owes*. He owes for my father, for my mother, for Katya, for Viktor. He *owes*. Why should I scruple to use him?'

'Then he will owe for us too. He will separate us.'

'But it won't be for ever,' Dmitri said. 'Things will change.

361

There'll come a time when it won't matter whether you're Jewish or not.'

'There will never come such a time,' Sonya said. 'There has never ever been such a time. Nowhere in the world, and certainly not in the Soviet Union.'

He could not disagree with her, but he had to hold out a measure of hope. 'We have to assume that it will happen. In time. In Andrushka's time may be.'

'But until that time?' she asked.

'I shall live in Moscow. I'll come and see Andrushka when I can.'

She noticed that he'd made no mention of herself, and she knew that despite his provisions and his promises, her marriage was truly over. She knew too that there was little point in withholding her consent to a divorce, because she knew that in Dmitri's heart, he had already left her. She believed him that there was no other woman. It was just that she was a Jewish nuisance who hampered his career. How like his uncle he was, she thought. And shivered.

The following day, they went together to the District Court. There the magistrate witnessed their signatures. As he scanned Sonya's distinctly Jewish maiden name he nodded. He had understood. No questions were asked. He declared them divorced and wished them each well on their ways. The next couple who entered his chambers were to be married. With different forms and with only a small modification in his vocabulary, the ceremony was exactly the same.

That same day, Dmitri left for Moscow, leaving Sonya to break the news to his mother. Like all bullies, Dmitri was a devout coward.

Anna was deeply upset at the news. Both for Sonya and for her wayward son. She blamed Ivan. He had influenced him. Of that she was sure. She blamed Sasha too for his frequent absences, and Dmitri's lack of fathering.

'A woman cannot do everything,' she moaned. She insisted that Sonya come and live with her. She could find work, and her child would be cared for. 'Work will take your mind off things.' She spoke from her own experience. In earlier days the trams had been her lifeline.

Sonya took little persuasion. She regarded Anna and Sasha, when he had been there, as her family. Dmitri had often complained that she spent too much time with them. Now she hoped he understood why. It was where the loving was, and loving was home.

So the women lived together, Sonya, Anna, Olga and the ageing and loving Avdotya. And together they prayed for Sasha's return.

In the Siberian snows, Sasha longed for it too. But as much as he yearned to be with Anna once again, he dreaded it with equal intensity. For something had happened to Sasha in the camp. He had fallen in love. He had not looked for it. And it had not sought him out. It happened. Simply that. As naturally as the night that follows day.

The prison camp was situated in a forest, and its work programme was tree felling. It was situated near a lumber mill, about two miles downstream. It was backbreaking work, and the older prisoners found it particularly arduous. But it was not a cruel camp. In Sasha's experience, and he was something of a veteran, the treatment of prisoners was less harsh than he had known in his time. If a prisoner was injured in his work, he was treated in the camp hospital, and was allowed to rest there until his injuries were healed. It was on one such occasion that Sasha fell in love.

He had been in the camp for about three years, and one day, while stripping the branches from the trees, preparing the trunks for their journey downstream, the axe had slipped from his hand. It had landed on his leg and cut deep into the flesh. His comrades had carried him to the hospital where he lay for many weeks in recovery. Although in pain, he was grateful for the rest, and for the comparative warmth of the ward. He'd been allowed books to read, and he had a stock of forbidden pencil stubs, and under cover of reading Lenin's *Collected Works*, he scribbled his journal in its margins. His writings kept him alive. As long as he bore witness, he felt he would survive.

It was mid-morning. Always a quiet time. Outside he could hear

363

the rhythmic chopping of the wood, and it surprised him that such backbreaking work should produce such a melodious sound. He looked up for a moment and was startled to see a gold locket swinging gently before his eyes. At first he thought he had a fever and was hallucinating. For a moment he even wondered whether he might have entered heaven. He watched it for a while, mesmerised. Then the locket was lowered, and he saw that a hand was attached to it. A woman's hand and by its almost-white and frayed cuff, the hand of a nurse. He thought suddenly of Anna, and recognised the locket as hers. One that had belonged to her mother. But he remembered too that years ago she had made it over as a gift. He grasped the hand in wonder and without seeing her face he whispered, 'Natasha.'

'You remember,' she said, and came to sit by his side. For a while they simply looked at each other. Both found the other aged, their faces lined with furrows of hope. But furrows of resistance too, those creases of stubborn survival. Smile creases which they gave each other now, and with an embrace they blessed the miracle that they had found each other in this terrible place.

'Tell me. Tell me all, Natasha,' Sasha whispered. 'How long have you been here?'

'Only a day,' she said. 'I was in a camp near Sverdlovsk. My son, Viktor, was born there,' she said. Then, 'Viktor's son,' she added quickly. 'He looks like Viktor. You'll see.'

'Is he with you?' Sasha was astonished.

'I have a little room here,' she said. 'A nurse's room. We live together. Come, I'll show you.'

She helped him on to his crutches. Sasha was trembling with excitement. Just the simple act of finding a face from his past life in this place, was miracle enough. And that it should be Natasha, family almost, seemed to him to be a gift beyond compare. He hobbled after her, still thinking it was all a dream.

Her room was tiny and without windows. There was a narrow iron cot on one side, and on the other, a child's trestle bed. By the table, perched on a stool was a little boy playing with pieces of cardboard. He was thin and clearly undernourished. In every day

364

of his short life he had gone hungry, and he had that pallor on his skin that accepts hunger as the norm.

'He looks like Viktor, doesn't he?' Natasha pleaded.

'The image,' Sasha said. The child had to look like Viktor, else he could have had Beria's features, or those of any one of the savages who had used her. He took the child on his knee. 'I'm your grandfather, Viktor,' he said. 'Grandfather Sasha.'

'Grandpa's a writer, Vitya,' Natasha said, 'and if you're good he'll tell you stories.'

Over the next few months, Sasha went often to Natasha's room and poured his stories into Viktor's eager ear. They were like a little family together, and each of them wondered at their happiness. At night when Viktor was in bed, he and Natasha exchanged stories of their lives since being prised apart in the train at Moscow station.

Natasha's story was a tale full of horrors. She still found much of it unbelievable. So over their months together, she told it in instalments. How she had been returned to Beria's house and become the whore of the Party. How she had been tossed from one officer to another. Everyone's contemptible toy. How, when they discovered she was pregnant, they'd sent her promptly to a labour camp. And how she had blessed them for that move, for anywhere on earth was preferable to the hell in which she dwelt. Sasha wondered how she could have endured it. Her womanhood had been totally ravaged, yet throughout she had maintained and still wore that dignified pride. With all their humiliating torment and cruelty, they had not managed to destroy her. She was made of woman, through and through.

'There's something else,' she told him one day. 'It's worse than anything that I've already told you.'

'Tell it to me only if you need to,' Sasha said.

'I hesitate,' Natasha said, 'only because it will hurt you as much as it hurt me.'

'Then we must share it.'

So she told him about Viktor and how his father had betrayed him. How he had ordered his plane shot down, and watched its disintegration on the radar screen. 'Beria told me,' she said. 'A true man of the Party. That's what he called your brother.'

Sasha was stunned. He felt sick. He wondered how Ivan could go on living with such a monstrous crime on his head. He didn't want to hear any more. He put his head in his hands. His brother was dead for him.

In her own mourning, Natasha comforted him, and out of their grief, they drew a greater strength and will to survive. For survival was their only form of revenge.

And it drew them closer in loving. A loving that came not out of hunger or of long deprivation. Nor even out of a simple human need. Both knew that it could have happened at any time and in any place, and that, wherever they were, it would last for ever.

26

It was 5 March 1953, and a great blessing fell on the Russian people. Joseph Stalin, in whose name millions had died, the begetter of the great terror and the unimaginable fear, finally gave up his sullied ghost. And though the people mourned and publicly wept, a finely tuned ear would have heard a great sigh of relief throughout the land. And behind closed doors the muffled sigh of laughter and celebration. For a monster had been laid to rest. People crept into churches and pretended to pray for his rotten soul, but in truth they wished him to the fires of hell and they thanked God for their deliverance. And none more so than Anna, who saw in the tyrant's death the possibility of Sasha's return.

And indeed, one of the consequences of Stalin's end, was the release of thousands of prisoners who were victims of his repression. When the news was announced in Sasha's labour camp, the prisoners did what they thought they were obliged to do. They wept. And with exaggerated cries. But there was jubilation in their hearts. It was the best piece of news they'd had in years, and through their crocodile tears it was hard to suppress their joy. In time the orders came for their release. Sasha and Natasha were together when they heard the news and their joy was mixed with sadness. For though both welcomed the freedom they had yearned for, they knew that that freedom spelt the end of their romance. Not of their loving – both were assured of that – but of their togetherness, which in Leningrad, would be impossible.

'Where will you live?' Sasha felt bound to ask her. 'You must stay in Leningrad.'

'I'll find somewhere,' she said. 'I have friends there as well as in Moscow. If they're still alive,' she added. 'Viktor will miss you. You've been a father to him over the years.'

'And still shall be,' Sasha said. 'That must not change. And need not,' he added. 'A seven-year-old boy needs a father.'

But they were words, and Natasha knew it as well as he. They were words that could not relate to the reality of home. To the reality of Anna. Sasha's words belonged to the exile. Elsewhere they were futile. As was their loving. And though both rejoiced in the prospect of their freedom, they dreaded their future separation.

A date was arranged for the general release of the prisoners. A special train was to take them to Moscow. The authorities advised their next of kin. Whether or not they were well enough to travel, the authorities wanted to be rid of them. The stigma of Stalinism had become an embarrassment.

When Anna received the news, she gave thanks to God. It was almost eight years since she had last seen Sasha, and those years had been hard for her. Dmitri's behaviour had saddened her. She regarded his divorce as an act of immoral cruelty. And now he had remarried. And one whose father moved in Ivan's circles. He was not generous with Sonya, and rarely came to Leningrad to see his son. But Olga was a blessing to her. She had grown beautiful, full of care and loving. She had done well at school, and now she was completing her training as an interpreter. Sonya too was a wonderful companion, and the presence in the house of little Andrei did much to comfort her loneliness.

But recently there had been another sorrow. Avdotya, who had been ailing for some time, had died. She had lived to see the death of Stalin, and with the last of her strength, she had rejoiced. Then a day later she was no more. She was Anna's last link with Larionovka, and Anna missed her terribly. So when news came through of Sasha's release, Anna was confused. So many events had crowded in on her, it was difficult to accommodate yet another radical change. Moreover, she was nervous. Her vanity made her so. She had aged, she knew, and it showed. She wondered if Sasha could still love her. Olga teased her that she was still beautiful and so did Sonya, and they insisted that they would dress her up to go to Moscow to meet him. But she balked at it. She would feel easier seeing Sasha in the familiar surroundings of her home, rather than risk a sudden encounter on a bleak railway station. She would inform Dmitri of his father's arrival, and thus ensure that at least one of the family would be there to greet him.

Dmitri was not happy with the assignment. But he could hardly refuse. His father, with his subversive history, would be an embarrassment to him. He had remarried Svetlana, the daughter of a KGB official whom he had met socially through Ivan. Over the years any reference to his father had not been encouraged. He himself still harboured a bitter resentment against him. It had begun in his childhood as a very natural resentment against an absent father. But lately that resentment had found a political rationale that was far more comfortable to accommodate than his childhood bitterness. The sudden reappearance of his father in Moscow was a nuisance to say the least, and he would do his utmost to return him to Leningrad as soon as possible. Moreover, he would keep Svetlana well away. So he went alone to the railway station. Ivan had told him what to expect. His father would be accompanying Natasha and her son, Viktor, named after his father. Ivan had broken that item of news with a certain gentleness. As if he himself would look forward to meeting her. Over the years, Ivan had grown mellow, and Dmitri was of the opinion that his uncle was ready to atone. That in his isolated power, he was in truth a very lonely man, and that he might be glad to house his grandson and Natasha, whose name of late he had been able to articulate without pain. But he would not come to Moscow to meet them. He would wait for them to return to Leningrad.

The station platform was crowded. Families clung together with a certain apprehension awaiting the arrival of those whom they had not seen for several years. Many of the women were constantly checking their hand mirrors, primping their hair, pinching their cheeks, ruing the lines that years of loneliness had etched on their faces, fearful of never being loved again. When the first hint of steam was seen along the platform they turned away and began to weep. Over and over again, in their lonely years, they had rehearsed this very moment, but no amount of practice had prepared them

369

for its shuddering reality. So they wiped the tears from their faces, smudging their so carefully prepared disguises, and in doing so, achieved an indifference to a beauty they knew only as skin deep, and allowed themselves, unadorned, to surrender to reunion.

Dmitri walked amongst the crowd, but he did not feel one of them. He noticed a number of KGB officers amongst them. For some returning prisoners, freedom could never be guaranteed. Dmitri stood aside, at the end of the platform, and watched the sorry crowd of ragged prisoners alight from the train. With their pallid look of hunger and longing, their rags for clothes, and their battered, roped luggage, it seemed to Dmitri that they all looked the same, and he was surprised that some of the waiting women were so quickly able to claim their own, and for some reason their loving embraces sickened him. Amongst them all, he did not hope to recognise his father, or Natasha for that matter, so he looked for a child who might resemble Viktor. He walked down the platform and actually passed his father by as Sasha alighted from the train.

Sasha was wearing the same clothes in which he'd been arrested nearly eight years ago on this very platform. But now they hung on him, as if borrowed for the occasion. He took Natasha's suitcase and set it down. It was to have been her honeymoon case, bought for her by Viktor so many years ago. And it had indeed seen a honeymoon of sorts. Sasha himself had no luggage. Simply a satchel which he clung to as if his future depended on it. Which indeed it did. For it housed that manuscript he had written in the camp, bearing yet further witness to the hell that had been theirs. In all his wanderings and incarcerations, Sasha's luggage had been a simple manuscript, of a moral weight hard to bear. The luggage of a witness, with its nuisance bulk, unwieldy, insistent, its contraband screaming to be declared.

He helped Natasha down from the train and he took Viktor's hand. He fully expected somebody to meet them. He scanned the platform for a face that he could recognise as Anna. Or Olga. Dmitri or Sonya.

'Let's go,' Viktor was saying, tugging at Sasha's arm. 'I want to see the Kremlin. And everything.'

On the journey, Sasha had told him about Moscow, and had promised him a sightseeing tour.

'Be patient, Vitya,' Natasha said. 'There's plenty of time.' She did not look around the platform. She expected no one to await her return. But she feared that Anna might be amongst those waiting women. Anna, whom she had never seen, whose locket she wore, and whose love for Sasha she had shared.

'Let's wait a while,' Sasha said. 'Someone may be here to meet us.' He guided them both to a bench, and they sat together, huddled in their rags, both dreading and longing for greeting.

Dmitri passed them by, and gave them a cursory glance. The man's coat or what was left of it, caught his eye. It was indeed familiar. He walked a little distance, then turned and gave its wearer another furtive glance. The man was old, thin, bearded and looked like any of the other travellers. Yet Dmitri felt a pull of blood on looking at him. The woman by his side might well have been Natasha, as she might have been anybody else. And that child with them. Ivan had told him there would be three of them travelling together. They were sitting there, waiting, and it looked as if no one was claiming them. He had a feeling that they would do as well as any other. He retraced his steps. He stopped a little distance from them. He was too old to call 'Papa', and in any case, those days were over. So tentatively, he called, 'Father.'

A number of old men along the benches looked up, hope gleaming in their eyes. But at the sight of the source of the sound, they turned away sadly. This smartly dressed man in his neat blue pinstripe suit, could in no way be equated with the family they had left behind. But Sasha looked at him, and knew him at once, not by recognition, but by the pull in his heart. He got up and went to embrace him. 'Mitya,' he called.

He clung to his son for a while, but felt a strange reticence in his embrace. Sasha was uncomfortably aware that his rags were soiling his son's immaculate attire. But he clung to him nevertheless. He was entitled to his son's embrace. Then he called Natasha and Viktor. 'You remember each other,' he said.

Natasha drew Viktor to her side. 'Vitya,' she said. 'This is your Daddy's best friend.' She said it as much for her own reassurance

371

as to remind Dmitri of what Viktor had once meant to him.

Dmitri smiled at her, but it was a smile of infinite pity.

'Where is Sonya?' Sasha asked.

It was a question that Dmitri had dreaded. 'We're divorced,' he said. 'We weren't getting on.' He dared not give his father the Jewish explanation. 'She lives in Leningrad with Anna,' he hurried on. 'And Andrushka. I'm married again.' Thus he gave them the whole story, and he hoped that his father would accept it without question. Which Sasha did, hearing the panic in his son's voice. Anna would tell him the true story later.

'And Anna?' he asked.

'She is well,' Dmitri said, omitting that he had not seen her for some time. 'So is Olga. Mother was nervous of coming to Moscow,' he added. 'She wanted to meet you at home.'

'Well, I've promised Vitya Lenin's tomb, and Red Square. And his father's grave,' he added. 'But can you first take us to your home, where we can wash, perhaps?'

He thought it a reasonable request to make of his son, so he was unnerved by Dmitri's confused response.

'It's – it's difficult for me to take you home,' he said. 'We live with Svetlana's parents, and – well – he's a – in the KGB. I don't want to cause anyone embarrassment. But I've booked a table at my favourite restaurant,' he hurried on, 'and two rooms in a hotel.' As he spoke he heard the meanness of his offer.

'We don't need a hotel. Or a restaurant,' Sasha said. He tried to control his anger. 'We will make our own way,' he said. He took Vitya's hand, and motioned Natasha to follow.

'Let me give you some money,' Dmitri pleaded.

'I have money,' Sasha said. 'Don't trouble yourself further. It was good of you to meet us. Now you can go back to your father-in-law.'

And they left Dmitri standing. Bewildered, hurt, and furious. But Sasha was equally hurt. He had reared a son who had grown up to be ashamed of his father, and the wound was deep, and far more painful than anything he had suffered in the camp.

'Goodbye, Dmitri,' he said. He could not utter the loving 'Mitya'.

'Perhaps we shall meet in Leningrad. You will be more than welcome in my home.'

'Can we go to Red Square now?' Vitya asked.

Sasha was grateful for the boy's presence. In front of him there could be no violence, for Sasha was astonished at his sudden feelings of aggression. He had to get away. And quickly. He hurried Natasha out of the station, and to the baggage check where they left her small luggage. But Sasha clung to his satchel, his witnessing. Now, after his sour meeting with his son, it seemed to have an extra dimension. For not only was it a testimony, it was now a vindication.

His mood was low, and Natasha tried to comfort him. But Vitya would not let him be depressed. He owed the boy the tour he had promised.

They took a tram to Red Square and joined the line outside Lenin's mausoleum. Vitya jumped up and down with impatience and excitement, but when at last they entered the tomb, he was infected by the silence and the awe of the place. And the shivering presence of ghosts. The bodies of Stalin and Lenin lay side by side, and Sasha could not resist a bitter smile. Lenin would not have been happy with his bedfellow. Afterwards they spent a little while in Red Square, and Vitya watched with wonder as all Sasha's prison tales came alive. And all the time he was running. Never in his young life had such space been his. Without confines. No boundaries, no limits, no barbed wire or watch tower. For the first time he understood the meaning of the word 'freedom'. Only as he grew older would he learn that freedom too had its fences.

Their next port of call would be a painful one, but Natasha insisted on it. They took a tram to the suburbs of Moscow to visit the Military Cemetery. She felt sure that Viktor must be buried there. She felt that if she could see his grave, it would afford her the final proof that he was no more. For until that day his death had been pure hearsay. They found the caretaker in his lodge and enquired as to the whereabouts of Viktor's grave. The man took down a ledger and ran his finger down the V entries. Then, 'Volynin,' he read slowly. 'Viktor Ivanovich?'

'That's right,' Sasha said.

'I'll show you.' He led them through the maze of paths between the graves. He walked with a measured and confident tread. Of all the hundreds of graves in that cemetery, he knew the location of every one. He stopped in front of a mound of earth. 'This one,' he said. Then he left them, partly for their own privacy, but mainly because he was ashamed of the state of the tomb. Clearly no one had been there since the burial, and even then perhaps, it had been swift and without ceremony. It looked like a grave of shame. Whoever had buried him there, had managed nothing more than the compulsory marker. Natasha, Sasha and Vitya stood by the grave and read its legend. *Colonel Volynin, Viktor Ivanovich 17 November 1919–9 May 1945.* There was no mention of his Hero's Medal. The grave was overgrown with tall grass and weeds.

Natasha knelt beside it. 'This is where your father lies, Vitya,' she said. 'Now we shall make his bed beautiful.'

She went once more to the caretaker's lodge and shortly returned with gardening tools. The three of them set to work. And silently. They cut the grass and weeded. Then they trimmed the edges of the plot. Natasha cleared the plaque nesting her fingers in the groove of each letter, imprinting his name upon her hand.

'I'm glad we came,' she said, when their work was done. 'He will know that I was here. With his son.' She did not weep. She had mourned him long enough. She had mourned his absence. Now the confirmation of his death was something of a relief and she looked at Sasha and smiled. 'Now we can go on living,' she said.

They went straight back to Moscow station. There was an hour before the train left for Leningrad, and though it was waiting at the station, both Sasha and Natasha were wary of boarding. They had waited on that same train before. They realised then how hungry they were, that they had not eaten since leaving the prison camp. They were glad to have something to do to occupy their time. In the station buffet they tasted foods whose flavours they had long forgotten, and their meal was like a safari into a distant land. Few words passed between them. Both were aware of the parting that was to come. Natasha excused herself for a minute, and Sasha watched her go to the telephone. Vitya was almost asleep on his bench. Sasha took him on his lap. He knew that he would miss this boy most of all.

When Natasha returned, she was smiling. 'I will be met in Leningrad,' she said. 'Irina, my friend. She has room for us.' She was relieved, as much for Sasha's sake as for her own. 'We can board the train now,' she said. 'It leaves in five minutes.'

Vitya had fallen fast asleep, and Sasha carried him to the train. They managed to secure a carriage on their own. Sasha was impatient, willing the train to leave. Natasha put her hand on his arm. 'No one will come,' she said. 'We are not a threat to them any more.'

'Freedom has its own threats,' he said. He pictured the station platform in Leningrad, and his waiting family. Somewhere in that crowd was Anna. He would expect her to have aged, as he himself had done. He knew she would be nervous, fearing that their love would not have stood the test of his last absence. And he feared it too. And not only because of Natasha. His love for her was of a different kind, frailer perhaps, because it had not been fed by history. And no rival, neither his nor Anna's, could trump that history. No, his fears lay in another direction. Dmitri had been a sore disappointment. Would Anna blame him for that? Would she blame him for his divorce and for his questionable remarriage? He would not tell her about Dmitri's greeting on Moscow station, though it would probably come as no surprise. Could she now find it in her heart to forgive him, and could he guarantee that he would never be absent again? He clutched the satchel to his chest. Stalin was dead, and there was hope of a greater freedom. But his comrades who had died in the camps must not be forgotten. His work must be published, or else they would have died in vain. He wondered whether the new freedom could afford to embrace his testimony. He would fight for it. All his life he had fought for that freedom, and if he again were to pay for it with captivity, he would let himself be taken. Saying, as he always said, 'I shall come back. Do I not always come back?'

Natasha had fallen asleep. She did not want to think of her parting with Sasha. And sleep was a refuge from such thoughts. Though they were now nearing Leningrad, he would let her sleep

375

until the last moment. He watched her. She had that vulnerable look that sleep bestows, but he knew that even awake she bore it, for the scars of a victim last for ever.

The train slowed. Sasha looked out of the window, and in the failing light he saw the outline of the platform and the shadowy silhouettes of those waiting. He woke Natasha gently. She opened her eyes with an immediate awareness of where she was, for even in sleep, she had not left Sasha's side. He took her in his arms and kissed her, and she knew that he was telling her that they would not kiss again. She woke Vitya and steadied him to his feet. Then they shuffled into the corridor and waited for the train to stop. Sasha was the first to alight. He knew that his apprehension could only be fed by delay. So quickly he helped Natasha and Vitya down, and scanned the platform for those who would meet him.

'Sasha!' His name rang down the platform and gave him a strange sense of assurance. That stating of his name confirmed that he had not been forgotten. And more. That his return was joyous and welcome. It was Sonya whom he recognised first, and the girl by her side must be Olga, he thought. She looked so much like Anna as a girl, that for a moment, Sasha felt he was back in Larionovka in his love-sick boyhood. She was running towards him. 'Papa,' she called, and fell into his arms. Then he knew his age, and he embraced her with all that fatherly love of which she had been deprived. Over her shoulder, he saw Sonya again, and on her arm, reluctant and shy, that love of his, that half-century love. At a distance, she stopped and looked at him, and he made no move to approach her. Both needed a moment in which to believe in the reality of his return, in the promise made so many years ago, that promise that he had not broken. Both needed to recall their years together, their sorrows and their joys. In that moment they acknowledged the history that they had shared, that they had both survived. Then they drew towards each other, as if magnetised, and gently took each other in their arms in silent embrace. Natasha stood aside and watched them. And with some relief. For she knew that what had happened in the prison camps had in no way touched that long and stubborn partnership. Then Sonya came towards them with Andrushka. He was not much older than Vitya. Sasha

376

hastened to introduce them, for he saw, through their possible friendship, a continuation of the link between himself and Natasha.

'And this is Natasha,' he said to Anna. 'Viktor's Natasha.' He took her hand and guided her towards his family. Anna looked at them both and knew in an instant that they had been lovers. And she wondered who indeed was Vitya's father.

Then someone called Natasha's name. A woman rushed towards her. Her friend, Irina. They greeted each other with tearful affection. 'This is my friend, Irina,' Natasha said.

'Come,' Irina said. 'I have a car waiting.'

Natasha was about to say her farewells to Sasha and his family, when Sonya said, 'Look over there. By the bookstall. I don't believe it.'

They all turned to stare in that direction. Ivan stood there, unsmiling, a bunch of flowers in his hand. He had had the sense not to wear his uniform, and his lack of medals and cloth of authority underlined his isolation and loneliness. Sasha looked at him, and for a moment pitied him, but he resolved himself against greeting. He moved away and the others followed him. All but Natasha. She stood alone, and stared at him. She had no intention of greeting. It was just that his very presence stunned her. Her amazement rooted her to the spot. Had he come to gloat? Or to make amends perhaps? The flowers in his hand were an offering of a kind. She watched him as he came towards her, mesmerised by each step, her heart swelling with such a hatred, that she thought she might explode. Her body was smouldering and she was certain that one word from this man, this murderer, would ignite it. Yet she did not move. Could not. And a certain perverse curiosity fixed her where she stood. He held the flowers in front of him, both as a shield and an offering. When he reached her, he attempted a smile. 'I hope you will make your home with me,' he said. 'You and my grandson.'

'We'd rather sleep in the streets,' Natasha said, marvelling that out of her sublime fury, she was able to speak at all. 'As for your flowers,' she spat at him, 'put them on Viktor's grave. It's *his* forgiveness you need. Not mine.' She turned, grabbed Viktor's hand, and rushed to join Irina.

Sasha and his family had watched the encounter from the far

377

end of the station. They saw the refusal of the flowers and Natasha's cool and contemptuous dismissal of that great man of power. They watched him standing there alone, and amongst them, only Sasha was moved to pity. But though it was the first time in almost eight years that he had seen his brother, he did not go towards him. Viktor's ghost had shadowed him from the Military Cemetery, and that ghost was a monumental hurdle to a fraternal encounter. He turned away. It was not only Ivan that he pitied, but the whole of Mother Russia that he embodied. He was anxious to get home and to the safety and warmth of his family, and he realised with stubborn regret, that despite his power and his wealth, Ivan had no home to return to.

Later that night as they were preparing for bed, Anna said, 'We must not lose touch with Natasha. Vitya and Andrushka could be friends.'

'Of course we shall be in touch. She will need our support.'

Anna began to undress, but shyly, hiding herself from him.

'We have both aged,' Sasha said. 'It makes no difference to our loving.' He went towards her and fumbling, undid the buttons on her dress. 'I have ten thumbs,' he laughed.

'Is that child yours?' Anna said suddenly.

He distanced himself from her. The question surprised him. It had never occurred to him that she might consider that possibility. But she had every right to, of course. He and Natasha had been together for so long.

'Vitya was two years old when Natasha came to the camp,' he said. 'He was born in Sverdlovsk, the first camp she was sent to.' He grasped Anna's shoulders. 'He's Viktor's child, Anna. Whether he looks like him or not. He *has* to be. The alternative is unthinkable. Why, even that brother of mine is prepared to view him as a grandson. And he has no more proof than Natasha.'

'Poor Natasha,' Anna said. 'We must care for her.'

In bed, she asked him what he intended to do, now that he was free.

'I have a little money saved,' she said. 'There is no urgency. But I noticed your satchel,' she smiled.

'My luggage,' he laughed. 'My testimony. Tomorrow I shall look for a publisher,' he said.

Anna trembled. Stalin was dead, but the habit of hammering on twilight doors dies hard.

27

When Stalin died, there was no obvious successor, and for a while a collective leadership held the reins of power. But out of that leadership, one man emerged. Nikita Khrushchev. Khrushchev was not one to be invested with absolute power, and in comparison with the Stalinist era, his reign was benign. The dreaded secret police were slowly stripped of their power, and the head of security, the infamous Beria, was shot. At the twentieth Party Congress in 1956, Khrushchev delivered his famous anti-Stalin speech, in which the former leader was revealed as the monster and tyrant that he was. De-Stalinisation was now official. The town of Stalingrad was rebaptised Volgograd. Stalin's body was summarily removed from the mausoleum, and Lenin slept easy. With hindsight, the biggest blot on the Khrushchev regime occurred shortly after his assumption of power. Hungary, Russia's neighbour, sniffed the smell of tolerance from over the border, and took it as a licence for their own freedom, and they revolted against their Communist regime. In answer, Khrushchev sent in Soviet tanks, and the sad revolt was quickly crushed.

So although on the surface, a greater tolerance existed in the Soviet Union, there were still pockets of fierce repression. Freedom of speech and freedom to publish were still unknown. A man did not speak his mind nor publish his thoughts. Else he would hear the knocking on his twilight door. In the light of these restrictions, Sasha found it difficult to secure a publisher for his latest novel. He took it to many publishing houses where it was read and secretly admired and celebrated. But not one of them dared to publish it.

At best it would mean the closure of their business; at worst a spell in a labour camp.

'What shall I do?' Sasha asked one of them.

'It will never be published in this country,' he said. Then he smiled slyly. 'Make what you will of that.'

The inference was clear. If the manuscript could be smuggled out of the country, it could possibly be published abroad.

'Forget that I said that,' the publisher said, for it was a deeply seditious statement.

'I didn't hear it,' Sasha said obligingly, and he left the office. He was deeply depressed. He had no contacts amongst foreigners, and in any case it would be folly to put a stranger at risk. And criminal too. It would be a mode of behaviour that his manuscript had been at such pains to condemn. He saw no way out. He found it difficult to start on a new novel so long as this one would not see the light of day. And he had so much to write about. And all of it was about the Russian darkness that no one dared to enter. Anna tried to comfort him. She even enlisted Natasha's help, knowing how much he valued her friendship. But Natasha could do little to lift his depression. He tried not to infect his family with his melancholy, but Olga especially was affected by it, and the sheer unfairness of it all.

Olga no longer lived at home. As an interpreter for foreign guests, she was housed in a hostel especially set aside for those in her profession. She was entitled to her own room and kitchenette. Other facilities were shared. The hostel was administered by a warden who was clearly in the pay of the KGB, that most recent title for Internal Security. Surveillance of that kind was part of normal life in the Soviet Union. Olga accepted it. Her job entailed contact with foreigners, so the government was entitled to keep a watchful eye on those in her profession. Every Sunday, when there were no tourists to serve, she would go home. Sunday was a family day, and since Sasha's release, it was more than just a family gathering. It was an opportunity for Olga to read her father's latest novel. He would not let the manuscript out of his house. He knew full well that it was regarded as seditious, and anyone found in possession

381

of it would be culpable. That manuscript was his sole responsibility, and it was only within his walls that it could be read.

It was on one such Sunday, when the family was assembled at lunch, that someone knocked on the apartment door; and caused that time-honoured reflex fear at the table. Olga ran to hide the manuscript, which she had left open on the side table, though she knew that no hiding place could escape a KGB search. Anna visualised yet another parting. 'I can't go through it again,' she whispered.

'I'll go,' Sasha said, and already he rehearsed his farewell. 'I shall come back,' he said to himself. 'Do I not always come back?' He went to the door and inside they listened for the summons.

'My name is Billy Crichton,' they heard. 'I'm from the American Consulate, and I'd like to talk with Anna Volynina.'

The voice sounded friendly enough. There was no summons in its tone. Moreover, it asked for Anna, she who didn't write books, who had never openly dissented, who had prayed behind closed doors, and cursed behind her hand.

'May I come in?' they heard.

Then Sasha was leading him into the living-room. The man was casually dressed. Moreover, he wore a smile that hid nothing more than pleasure.

'This is my wife,' Sasha said, taking Anna's hand, 'Anna Volynina. And my daughter and daughter-in-law, Olga and Sonya.'

Crichton shook hands around the table, and Sasha invited him to sit and share their meal. But he had already eaten, he said. He seemed anxious to get away, for he sat on the edge of his chair, a temporary stance, prepared for takeoff. Around the table they looked at him, trying not to stare, waiting for him to begin.

'I have a message for you, Anna Volynina,' he said. 'It's from a friend of mine in Washington. His name is Nick Larion. He says you are his aunt.'

Anna paled, and tears started in her eyes. 'Nicolai,' she whispered.

'His son,' Crichton said. 'I have a picture.' He put his hand in an inside pocket, brought out an envelope and handed it to Anna. She opened it and laid the photograph on the table. She recognised

Nicolai at once, and gave a shriek of delight. Then noticed that in the photograph he looked much younger than she expected. And the boy at his side was but a child.

'That's Nick,' Crichton said, pointing to the youngster. 'He's thirty-five now. That's his mother. She's still alive.'

'And his father?' It was Sasha who asked for Anna's sake.

'He died,' Crichton said. 'In the war. He fought on the German side. I think that's why Nick changed his name.'

'Nicolai dead,' Anna whispered. 'But there is a son. The Larionovs still exist. I thought I was the last of them.'

Sasha put his arm around Anna's shoulder. 'Tell us about Nick,' he said to Crichton. 'And why you've come to see us.'

'He's coming here next week. With the Peace and Friendship tour. He's a journalist. He works on the *Washington Post*. And he wants to see you.'

'Oh yes, yes, we must meet,' Anna said. 'But how? Sasha is under surveillance. We know it.'

'I have a friend. He lives near the Consulate. A Russian, a frame maker. He's absolutely trustworthy. I'll send Nick there on Friday. Three o'clock. Here's his address,' he said, handing over a slip of paper. 'It's all arranged.'

'Are you sure it will be safe?' Sasha asked. 'No one must be put at risk.'

'In my job, I daren't risk suspicion,' Crichton said.

'I'm an interpreter on that tour,' Olga suddenly admitted. 'For the three days they are in Leningrad.'

Crichton was silent for a while. 'I think it will be better if nobody knows he's your cousin. I'll write and tell him that. He must keep quiet as well. It's best for all of you. He speaks good Russian, by the way, but he does not want that known.'

'But I'll see him at least.' Olga was excited. 'I never knew any of the Larionovs.'

'Your Uncle Andrei,' Anna reminded her.

'I was a child. I don't remember him,' Olga said.

When Bill Crichton had gone, Anna stared at the photograph. She was sad and joyful at the same time. The continuation of the

Larionov line was a source of great pleasure to her for somehow it blunted the pain of her brothers' deaths.

Olga rose from the table and retrieved the manuscript from its hiding place. 'Papa,' she said. 'Nick Larion, or whatever he calls himself, is a way of getting this to America.'

'Never,' Sasha said. He was angry that Olga had even thought of it. 'Nobody has the right to put anybody else at risk.' He was so angry, that Olga thought that he had clearly been tempted to such a manoeuvre, and it was an anger against himself that he expressed so vehemently. He crumpled into his chair and lapsed into his usual melancholy. He had seen an avenue of freedom, and he cursed those moral scruples that made him turn his back. Olga could have wept for him.

The following day, she attended the usual Monday briefing for interpreters. The session referred entirely to arrangements for the Peace and Friendship tour. Georgi Kirichenko, the supervisor, who made no bones about being a KGB agent, was addressing the small gathering.

'This visit to Leningrad', he said, 'has a strict programme, and you must stick to it. And always be on the lookout. We cannot rule out the possibility that some of the visitors are agents for the CIA. If anybody behaves suspiciously, it is your duty to inform the authorities. You have the telephone number. Keep it with you at all times. Otherwise, behave in a friendly manner. We want to make a good impression.'

Olga was surprised that she had not been relieved of the assignment. The KGB were careful. Every visitor to the Soviet Union was vetted, and if they had been thorough enough, they would have discerned the Volynin/Larion connection. She concluded that it was reasonably safe to assume that they were ignorant of any relationship. For she had a plan. She intended to take full responsibility for smuggling her father's manuscript out of the Soviet Union. Her cousin's visit was an opportunity not to be missed. She had to take advantage of it, for without publication, she could see no end to her father's melancholy. She returned to her room in the hostel, and she spent the whole evening composing a letter to that cousin whose kin she must not acknowledge. She told him who she was, and that she had a great favour to ask of him. She explained her father's dilemma, and asked quite bluntly if he would be prepared to take the manuscript to the States and arrange for its publication. She added that on no account should her father know. A simple nod or shake of the head would be an adequate reply, and if a nod, she would make further arrangements. If Nick were willing, she knew she would have to spirit the manuscript out of her father's desk. She trusted to luck that he would not miss it until it was too late to subvert it, which was more than probable for it depressed him even to look at it.

The interpreters, English, French, German and Spanish, assembled at the tourist hotel early on Thursday morning. The tour was divided according to language needs, and out of the dozen or so travellers in her care, Olga recognised Nick immediately. And he, her, though both were at pains to hide it. In Nick's face, Olga saw traces of her mother's gentle features. And in Olga, Nick discerned his father's strength and stubbornness. She smiled at him, but it was part of the permitted and general smile of welcome.

That morning they were to go to the Hermitage. It was a visit that allowed opportunities for close contact. Especially after the picture viewing when the tourists gathered in the museum shop to buy souvenirs. Nick was looking through a file of postcards, and Olga approached him, and slipped the letter into his side pocket. Then under cover of translation, she whispered to him that it was there and that he should read it in privacy. Then she went to see to the needs of the other visitors in her charge. She was very, very careful for it was not wise to trust anybody. She knew that colleagues kept watch on each other. Everybody was on the lookout for promotion, for that meant the possibility of interpreting trips abroad. And abroad meant defection and freedom. But every day on the job, Olga promoted the society that she loathed, and envied all those foreigners who had the sense to disbelieve her.

The following morning the group were taken on a tour of the city. They gathered together in the foyer of the hotel, and, at once, on seeing her, he nodded vigorously. She smiled, then regretted it, for out of the corner of her eye she caught sight of Kirichenko, who might well have noticed their exchange. But the morning went

385

smoothly and she felt herself in the clear. That afternoon, Nick was due to meet her parents, and in their absence from the apartment, she would collect the manuscript.

Sasha and Anna arrived at the frame maker's apartment a little before three o'clock. And found Nick already waiting for them. The frame maker showed them into a little room, and then withdrew, knowing their need for privacy. For a while, they said nothing, then slowly Nick moved towards Anna and embraced her.

'I know a great deal about you, Aunt Anna,' he said.

'Did your father talk about me?'

'All the time.'

She started to cry. 'But he never knew that I forgave him,' she said.

'Yes he did.' Nick comforted her. 'Uncle Andrei told him in Berlin. My mother told me the whole story. After father died. And now I've met the man who was the cause of it all.' Then he folded Sasha into his embrace, and they were silent once more.

Nick had brought photographs with him, those that his father had taken from the Larionov house on the hill. And Anna had brought her collection, and much of the afternoon was spent sharing the past and the present between them. Sasha felt very much an outsider. In his mind the Larionovs appeared sudden foreigners, and he realised, perhaps for the first time, the enormous courage that Anna had drawn upon to leave her tribe.

'I have never regretted it,' she said to Nick, and she took Sasha's hand.

'I shall have such a story to tell my mother,' he said. 'Perhaps one day, you can come and visit us. Both of you,' he said. 'Is that day so far away, d'you think?'

'We work for it. All the time,' Sasha said. 'It has to come. Perhaps not for us. But for Olga and her generation. Your Peace and Friendship tour is just the beginning.'

They left the frame maker's flat separately. Although the parting was sad, both Sasha and Anna had a sense of elation. Their meeting with Nick had been proof of continuity. As long as the Larionovs survived Anna was relieved of the burden of carrying the name alone. She took Sasha's arm.

'For the first time I am allowed to feel like Anna Volynina,' she said.

They walked home through the park like a young courting couple, and when they reached home there was no sign in the apartment that Olga had been and gone.

She went straight to Nick's hotel. This was the only risky part of the operation. She covered the manuscript in brochures and tourist information, so that if she were questioned in the lobby of the hotel, she would have an alibi of sorts. She waited. She had made no arrangement with Nick but she knew that he would return to the hotel after his meeting with her parents. She was relieved when she saw him coming in through the doors. She did not go towards him, but she placed herself in the way that he would cross the hall. When he neared her, she held out the brochures. He took them from her smiling. Then whispered, 'It will go through the Consulate.' Then she shook his hand, and loudly wished him a safe journey home. He would be leaving the following day and though she'd had little opportunity to know him, she knew that she would miss him terribly.

She returned to her room in the hostel and considered that her mission had been accomplished. The manuscript would be on an American publisher's desk before her father, with luck, would have noticed it was missing.

In the morning, she accompanied her group to the airport as part of her duties. Kirichenko was on the bus, and she made a point of ignoring Nick and sitting as far away from him as possible. On arrival at the airport, her last duty was to help the travellers through Customs. Again she left Nick to see to himself. Most of them passed through Customs with ease, but Nick was stopped and ordered to open his luggage. She shivered, praying that the manuscript was safely in the Consulate. She felt a figure move to her side and without looking she knew that it was Kirichenko. She dared to look at him and even give him a smile, but she expected immediate arrest. She looked back at Nick, and was relieved to see that he appeared totally unperturbed although they were ransacking his bags like ferrets. Everything they contained was laid out on the table. Containers and clothing were shaken. Even toothpaste

387

was minutely examined. And Nick seemed to be smiling all the while. She wished he would look more serious. Eventually the frustrated customs officers abandoned their search and instructed Nick to pack his bags. He took his time, smiling all the while, which did little to improve the officers' tempers. Kirichenko moved from her side and made his way to the Customs table. Olga feared Nick's arrest. So she was surprised to see her supervisor actually help Nick with his packing. But it did not please her. Assistance from such a quarter was sinister. When the packing was done, he actually shook Nick's hand, and watched him to the gate of departure. On reaching it, Nick turned, and Olga froze as he lifted his hand to her, a huge smile creasing his face. She did not return his smile. She was terrified because with his smile he had clearly incriminated her. She shuddered at his sheer lack of intelligence. She stood there long after he was gone, fully expecting her arrest. But Kirichenko walked past her without a word. It was some while before she dared to move, then, afraid of calling attention to herself for loitering without purpose, she walked out of the Customs hall, and took a bus into the city. The fear did not leave her and at night she lay in bed waiting for the twilight knocking. But nothing happened. She reported each day for work and everything appeared normal, and she ceased to be afraid. She was nervous of going home on the following Sunday in case the manuscript had been missed. But no mention was made of it. Sasha's melancholy seemed to have lifted, and Anna seemed more at peace, and she ascribed their changes of mood to Nick's visit. Indeed, they never stopped talking about it, and it irritated her as she recalled his parting gesture. But Kirichenko had said nothing since his departure, though Olga thought he kept a sterner eye on her than usual.

Shortly afterwards, Russia sent its first man into space. Yuri Gagarin was the earth's first cosmonaut, and when he returned from his bizarre voyaging, he was fêted all over Russia. He was due to visit Leningrad, and the streets of the parade were festooned with garlands, streamers and balloons. The whole of Leningrad turned out to greet their new-found hero. Amongst them, Sasha and his family, and Olga with some of her colleagues. And close to her, mingling with the crowd, though with his eye fixed firmly upon her, stood Kirichenko. He did not look in a celebratory mood. The news he had received that morning from one of their agents in New York had given him nothing to smile about. Apparently a manuscript, written by one Alexander Volynin, had found its recent way to a publisher's desk and was at that very moment in the process of excited translation. Kirichenko would do what had to be done. Punishment was easily meted out. Not so easy was the explanation to his superiors of his oversight. It might mean demotion or worse and he was going to make sure that that Volynin woman would pay for it.

There was a fanfare of trumpets, which heralded the approach of the Russian hero. Dressed in a white air-force dress uniform, he stood erect in a white soft-top car flashing that smile that he had brought home from another world. Olga reached on tiptoe to have sight of him, and she felt herself being lifted from behind. She turned and saw two young men smiling at her.

'Now you can have a king-size view,' one of them said. And she did. But only for a split second, for she felt herself turned swiftly. The grips on her waist tightened, as she was carried away from the parade.

'Papa!' she screamed.

Sasha turned, and saw her panic-riddled face, and he knew that hers was no carnival lift, but a crass KGB abduction. He alerted Anna, but there was nothing they could do, except fight their way through the crowd to follow her, in time to see her hauled into a police van and driven away.

Like father, like daughter, Anna thought bitterly. But she said nothing. She just couldn't understand it. 'But why?' she whispered. 'What could she have done?' But Sasha knew. His instincts told him, and he was proud of Olga for what he suspected she had done, but he would have given his own freedom to assure hers. They hurried home. On reaching his apartment he went straight to his desk drawer and found it, unsurprisingly, empty.

Inside the police van, Olga tried to keep calm. She knew that her arrest must have something to do with her father's manuscript. There could be no other reason. She would deny all knowledge of it, but she had little hope that they would believe her. The two plain-clothes officers who had offered her that generous lift sat one each side of her. She was offended that she found them both so good-looking, and it pained her that they should earn their living in such a way.

'Where are you taking me?' she asked.

'Back to your room,' one of them said. 'We have a search warrant.'

The news gave her some relief. There was nothing in her room that could incriminate her. Perhaps they thought they would find the manuscript there. For despite her father's history of surveillance and arrest, she was still strangely naïve regarding the methods of her captors. When they reached the hostel, they gripped her on each side and dragged her inside. One of them kicked open the door of her room, sat her on a chair, and began his search. It was silent in the hostel. All its inhabitants were celebrating in the streets, and Olga seethed with a sense of deprivation. Yet she was glad that no one was around to witness her humiliation. She sat there helpless, and enraged as the officers tore her room apart. They opened the drawers and threw all their contents onto the floor. They wiped her dressing-table clear, shattering the glass containers. Yet they did not seem to be looking for anything. They were not searching with any purpose, unlike the Customs officer who had rifled Nick's luggage. These men's search seemed to be a mere destructive formality. She watched as one of the men lifted the mattress from the bed, and with one hand took a small package from his pocket. This he threw onto the box springs. He made no effort to hide his planting. Indeed, after placing the package, he looked at Olga and smiled as if after a deed well accomplished.

'What have we here?' he said.

'You ought to know. You just put it there.' The words burst out of her with her last vestige of courage. Now she fully understood that the manuscript export had been discovered, and that any charge would do to convict her.

The officer opened the cellophane wrapping, and dipped his finger inside. Then he put the white powder on the tip of his tongue, and smacked his lips. 'First-class heroin,' he said, 'and enough here to be dealing. Come, let's go.'

390

He took her roughly by the arm, and pulled her into the corridor. The other officer followed and together they bundled her into the van. Olga trembled. She had heard rumours of trumped-up charges, and had found them hard to believe. Now she was the victim of one such charge and she dreaded what was to become of her. She thought of her parents, those two so long practised in partings, and she was saddened by the further sorrow she had brought upon their house.

But neither of them would give in to despair. 'I shall go to the police station,' Sasha said. 'I'll make enquiries. We have to know what's happened to her.'

'No.' Anna was firm. 'That's what they're waiting for. If you go you'll never come back. You stay here. She might be allowed to phone. I shall go the station. They won't take me. I'm no use to them.'

Sasha tried to stop her, but he knew she was being sensible. It would have been folly for him to present himself to the authorities. He kissed her. 'Take care,' he said. 'And come back soon.'

She smiled at him. 'I shall come back,' she said, mocking his usual farewells. 'Do I not always come back?'

She made her way to the police station, gathering anger as she walked. She must not be timid, she knew. They would take advantage of that. No, she would demand her rights, then realised sadly that in her country people had no rights at all.

At the station, she announced herself to the desk officer, and demanded to see her daughter.

'One moment, madam,' the officer said.

Then he left his desk and disappeared into the inner office. Shortly afterwards he returned, and led her through a corridor and into a room where a KGB officer sat at his desk. He rose when she entered and courteously offered her a seat. Anna was wary of his politeness, and had she the strength, she would have preferred to stand, but after her long walk she was tired and she feared that her fatigue would lead to timidity. She leaned on the arm of the chair.

'I want to see my daughter,' she said.

'That's impossible, I'm afraid,' the officer said. 'The prisoner has no visitors until after the trial.'

'Trial?' Anna's knees weakened and she was forced to sit down. 'What is she charged with?'

'Drugs.' The officer was curt. 'Heroin. Possession and possibly dealing.'

'It's a lie!' Anna screamed, and tried to hold back her tears. 'My daughter has never taken drugs.'

He leaned forward with manufactured sympathy. 'I have children too, Madam Volynina,' he said, 'and I sometimes think I don't know them at all. In these cases, my sympathies are always with the parents.'

'Thank you,' she said, rising. 'I don't want your sympathy. I say again, my daughter has never touched drugs. This is a trumped-up charge.' She thought she had better say no more, in case it would backfire on Olga. She went to the door, but her heart was breaking, and with it, what was left of her pride. She turned to him. 'I beg you,' she said, 'as one parent to another, let me see my child.'

But that sympathy that he had formally claimed was gone. 'After the trial,' he said. And then for good measure he added, 'After the sentence.'

So she was guilty, and the trial was a mere showcase, that was clear. The officer had spelt it out.

'I'll see myself out,' Anna said, her pride returning. So had his courtesy it seemed, for he rose and opened the door for her. For a moment he felt genuinely sorry for her. She was not likely to see her daughter again for at least two years. And after that the Volynin girl would be marked for the rest of her life.

Anna took a cab back to the apartment. She didn't have the strength to walk. She felt defeated. Sasha was waiting for her at the door, and he crumbled at her report. He knew there was only one thing he could do. But he could not mention it to Anna. It would throw her into even deeper despondency.

'I'm going for a walk,' he said. 'I have to think.'

'Come back,' she said. 'Make sure you come back.' Anna knew, and Sasha knew that she knew, that he was about to call on Ivan.

It had been many years since Sasha had seen his brother. He recalled the last time at Leningrad station when Natasha had rebuffed Ivan's invitation to make his home with her. Eight years ago, yet a day rarely passed without a thought for him. Of late he had heard nothing of him. Perhaps he had retired. He was old enough, though the KGB were not fussy about calendar. There was no reason for Sasha to visit Ivan, except for a favour, and he would make that abundantly clear. Ivan was the only person who could help his daughter.

He took a cab into the suburbs. He had remembered the address but he had forgotten the number of the apartment, and he was obliged to ring the caretaker's bell.

'Could you give me the number of Ivan Volynin's apartment?' he said. 'I'm his brother.' He felt he ought to give his credentials in order to gain admission.

The caretaker looked at him with infinite pity. 'If you're his brother,' he said with disdain, 'then you should know that he was deprived of his apartment some four years ago, when he was shamefully dismissed from office.'

There was no question which side the caretaker was on. Sasha was shocked. He could not imagine Ivan out of his beribboned uniform. 'Could you tell me where he lives now?' he asked.

'I heard he'd moved to an old people's home. I don't know where.'

Sasha felt tears sting his eyes. He couldn't imagine Ivan as a registered old man. The information stunned him into acknowledgement of his own ageing and of the years that had passed and lined the faces of them all. The Larionovs, the Volynins, those who were left of both houses, those who had spanned over half a century of sorrows. The caretaker closed the door, but Sasha stayed there for a long while, wondering what he had come for, conscious only of the years that had passed and the separating sorrows of their lives. He would not enquire as to Ivan's whereabouts. He had come for fraternal favour, but it was clear that Ivan was no longer in a position to grant it. He did not want to witness his brother's ageing. His present way of life was probably what he had earned, and no more than he had fully deserved. So he went back to Anna and blessed her for the years of her support.

But Ivan did have a visitor that day. And the first in many

years. Four years ago, he had been one of the many casualties of de-Stalinisation. Overnight he had lost status, office and privilege. His apartment was given over to his successor, and when he returned home from his last day in office, he found his bag and baggage on the street. The caretaker, who hitherto had wiped his feet and minded his manners at Ivan's every appearance, now thrust a piece of paper in his hand that informed him of his new address. The caretaker had noted it. It lay in a run-down part of the city reserved for those whom society had discarded. In handing it over, he made no attempt to hide the glint of triumph in his eye.

Ivan had few possessions. Despite his former wealth, he had never been acquisitive. His prize possession was his portrait of Stalin, signed 'To Ivan' by the great tyrant himself. This he had hung on the wall of his new and miserable quarters, and to view it gave him a measure of solace that blunted the edge of his bitterness. But it had not hung there for long. A few days at most, then Matron, fearful of her position, had ordered him to take it down, but out of pity had allowed him to keep it hidden in his room. So he was still able to look at it from time to time, one ear cocked for the footfall outside his door.

Over the years, he had had no visitors. His erstwhile friends in the Party had been dismissed as ignominiously as himself and most kept themselves to their embittered selves. Some had shot themselves in their despair, and for them Ivan had nothing but contempt. For he lived in hope. In time, Stalin would be seen once more as the redeemer. No less than that. And his portrait would once again hang on Ivan's privileged wall.

Apart from those other inmates of the home, Ivan saw no other people. Sometimes he thought of visiting Sasha, but his pride forbade it. He went for long and solitary walks, and exercised daily and with frenzy, for he had somehow to take his mind off his mind. For to recall his past life and past deeds, was very painful. Over the years he came to be addicted to solitude, and he resented any threatened intrusion.

So he was none too pleased that day when Matron knocked on his door and told him that he had a visitor, and without waiting for his expected rebuff, she showed the caller into his room.

394

He was a man of middle age, robust, but with a certain shyness, for he hung at the door when Matron had left, waiting perhaps for some sign of recognition. He smiled, hoping to declare that he was not a hostile visitor. Ivan stared at him. He did not know this man, but by his faltering heartbeat, he knew that he was kin, that he was of his own flesh and blood, and that once there had been love between them. A love that had persisted till now. For a hallucinated moment, he thought the man was Pyotr, so closely did he resemble him, and his eyes filled with unaccustomed tears as the ghosts of his past paraded with stubborn insistence.

'Vassily,' he said, and he stretched out his hands to greet him.

Vassily fell into his father's embrace, and held him close, as if to contain his body wracked with sobs. It seemed that in that moment, all those tears that Ivan had systematically sent back to where they came from over the years, all those tears so proudly unshed, now flooded out of his unmanageable past in a deluge of unmodulated confession. Vassily knew it for repentance and it astonished him.

'How did you find me?' Ivan said after a while.

'I have never lost touch with you,' Vassily said. And indeed, over the years, he had followed his father's career with horror, disgust and undisguised contempt, but always with a stubborn love that deeply offended him. He could not help himself. For his father, that man who had deprived him of any true parenting, was still the target of his life's loving. He knew about his mother's death; he knew too about Viktor. The knowledge of both should have cured him of his loving. But they had only served to augment his compassion. Over the years he had been tempted to contact his father, but he had feared his wrath. Now, having learned that he had been stripped of his power, he dared to risk encounter. And more than that. He had resolved to ask his father to make his home with him. The child who owes least, pays most. He released his hold on his father. The sobbing had ceased.

'Tell me, tell me,' Ivan said. 'What have you done? Where have you been all this long separation?'

'I'm a farmer,' Vassily said. 'And have been for many years.'

'Like Pyotr,' Ivan whispered and the tears came again.

'I have a farm. About a hundred kilometres from here. Wheat,

395

mainly. A few cattle. It's a good life. I have a wife, Maria, and three sons. We all work together on the farm.' He paused. Then, 'There's room for you,' he said. 'You would be very welcome. I invite you, and so do Maria and the boys.'

'I would be a burden to you,' Ivan said.

'No.' Vassily was adamant. 'You're healthy. You're strong. You could help on the farm. You needn't be lonely any more.'

'I have deserved my loneliness,' Ivan said.

'I won't let you pay that price. Please think about it, Papa.'

It was at the sound of that word, unheard for so many years, that Ivan broke down completely. 'My son,' he sobbed. A word equally strange, and he said it again, as if he had to practise it, for it had been part of a lexicon anathema to the Party. He was glad he was able to say it. And to feel it too. With all his heart. But he knew that only *he* could hear it. It was too late, and too undeserving for its echoes to resound in his son's ear. Nevertheless, he said it again. And again. And it was like music in his ears.

'Will you come?' Vassily asked. 'You could stay at first for a visit. And then you could make up your mind.'

Ivan heard a certain pleading in his son's voice. 'Have I not damaged you enough?' he said.

Again Vassily embraced him. 'Please think about it, Papa,' he said. 'I shall come again in two days. That will give you time. Maria will prepare your room. Then I shall hope to find you packed.'

Enough had been said. Words had passed between them that had both healed and opened wounds at the same time. Now was the time for silence. Vassily smiled. 'In two days,' he said, 'we shall begin a new life together.' He went to the door. 'I'm glad I came, Papa,' he said.

Ivan smiled, but he could say nothing. His mouth was full of long-forbidden rusted words – 'son', 'father', and above all, 'love' – words that in their long embargo had swollen in dissent, and to release them now would have shaken the earth.

When Vassily had gone, Ivan took the portrait of Stalin out of its hiding place. He held it in front of him and through a blur of tears, he viewed its distortion. He trembled at the feelings that overcame him, and the sudden threat of the truth that would not

396

be denied. He would face it. He had to. He had to acknowledge those years that he had lost, that past that he had wasted and abused, that faith so drastically misplaced but above all, those words that he had strangled in his throat. From his desk he took a Swiss knife, a relic from his Party days, and with swift and angry movements of its blade he slashed to pieces his god that had failed. And he took by the scruff of its unwieldy neck that unmanageable past of his, and he forced himself to face it, direct in its squalid eye. First his brothers Pyotr and Sasha. Both victims of his silence. His mother too, and the village of Larionovka. Then Andrei, supposedly his friend, whose sentence had once again silenced him. Andrei, for whom he had made no plea. Then Katya, whom he had never fully valued, and whom he had criminally neglected, she too had to be faced, and her forgiveness beseeched. As for Viktor, he knew he could never lay his ghost, but he could at least take a while of what was left of his time, to confront what he had done. That too he met with flickering eyes, and Ivan knew that it was a crime beyond God's gift of forgiveness. And finally Vassily, whose amnesty still throbbed in the room, and Ivan knew it was the hardest encounter of all. He could live with his obscene silences, his cowardly collusion, his neglect. Yes, even with his filicide he could live. The ghosts of Pyotr, Andrei, Katya and even Viktor could stalk his life for ever. Yet he would survive. But Vassily. There was the rub. The love of his first-born. He whose 'Papa' had not stuck in his throat. Vassily and his heartbreaking *decency*. Unsurvivable.

Downstairs, in her quarters, Matron was making herself some lemon tea when she heard the shot. She rushed upstairs and from room to room. Any one of her charges could have fired a gun, for most of them had had enough. Outside Ivan's room, she found a clutch of geriatrics, throbbing with triumphant survival. She turned them away from the door. Then entered. She steeled herself against the gruesome spectacle on the floor.

Ivan had shot himself through the mouth and pieces of him were strewn about his body. At his side lay the slashed portrait of Stalin. Matron smiled. She was glad that at last Ivan Volynin had come to his senses.

Who knows who Ivan's Natasha was, what name he had called out before his finger moved? It could have been 'Katya', 'Pyotr', or a choked 'Viktor'. But more probably it was Vassily, his first-born, that object of his greatest love and his greatest regret.

PART TEN

28

Olga's trial, if it took place at all, was closed to the public. But her sentence was rumoured outside the court. Eight years' hard labour. Location untold. Sasha and Anna had waited all day outside the courthouse, hoping for a glimpse of her. By nightfall, they had to accept that Olga had been spirited away, and by now was on her journey to the snows. But she would return. Both Anna and Sasha knew about returns and they were practised with patience. Time passed. Olga's absence was a sorrow, but despite their long acquaintance with melancholy, her parents were not immune.

'Will we live to see her again?' Anna said one day.

Sasha kissed her cheek. 'We're sixty-eight years old,' he said, 'and we're still too young to give up hope.'

They were as old as the century, and the year of that anniversary was a blemished one for the Soviet Union. Its new leader was Leonid Brezhnev. Khrushchev had been removed from office four years before, but unlike most of his predecessors, he was allowed to die naturally in his bed some seven years later. But Brezhnev was bad news for human rights, and the old fears, never wholly lost, now returned with a vengeance. Brezhnev left his first menacing visiting card in Prague in August of that year. Czechoslovakia, a satellite of the Soviet Union, was tempted to a taste of democracy, and received the same response as Hungary some years before: Soviet tanks in their streets. The rebellion was quashed very quickly, and many Czech lives were lost.

Amongst those who manned the tanks that entered Prague that August was Vitya Volynin, son of Natasha, and hopefully of Viktor.

Natasha had watched her son's growth with close and fearful attention. She needed to think that he was Viktor's son, and she rejoiced whenever she recognised a Volynin trait. But occasionally he behaved as if he came from a Beria stable. On those occasions, Natasha turned her back. Physically Vitya resembled Natasha, so his appearance gave no clue as to his sire. His choice of profession was no clue either, although like Viktor Volynin, he had chosen to serve his country in an identifiable uniform, rather than in dubious plain clothes.

He had just returned from Prague, and his mood was sullen. He was twenty-two years old, and too young to have seen the sights that Prague offered that summer. And that he saw them through the narrow observation slit of the tank made them no less gruesome to view. Rather that narrow lens seemed to heighten the terror that reigned on the bloodied streets of Prague in those times. Through it he had seen a hand's breadth of a crowd, hurling rocks, stones and insults at the tanks. Then a streak of fire as a flaming torch was thrown. But his eyes were fixed on a young boy, sitting peacefully in the line of his tank, and he saw how he poured a wafer-thin stream of petrol over his body, and calmly set it alight, and through his isthmus lens, Vitya saw freedom on fire. It burned his inner eye and left a scar that he knew would never heal. He dared to wonder what he was doing there, shooting down men who were guilty only of claiming their human rights. He recalled the stories that Sasha had told him when he was a young boy in the camp. Sasha had fought like these men, and for the same freedoms, yet here Viktor was playing the part of their persecutors. It was as if he were killing his own family. He was deeply disturbed. He didn't know what he ought to be feeling. If he gave way to his true nature, it could be construed as disloyalty. So when he returned from Prague he kept his mouth shut, afraid of his ambivalent feelings.

But something strange was happening in the Soviet Union, a phenomenon never seen before. There had always been dissidence, but it was felt in the heart and stifled there. A few, like Sasha, had expressed their feelings, and had paid a heavy price. But dissidence cannot be suppressed for ever, and often it takes but one event to prompt it out of hiding, to give it a licence for public display. That event was the Soviet invasion of Czechoslovakia. The result was public protest and demonstration on the streets. In all the large cities of the Soviet Union, people had not seen its like before.

Vitya came home on leave, and on his way from the station, he caught sight and sound of the demonstrating crowd. His first reaction was one of fury, because he knew that had he been out of uniform, he might well have been part of it. But on the other hand, he had just arrived fresh from combat, and it angered him that this demonstration seemed to negate the risks he had taken.

Natasha was overjoyed to see him. She shared her apartment with Sonya. Their sons were close in age and in friendship.

'Andrushka will be so glad that you're home,' Sonya said.

'Where is he?' Vitya asked.

Sonya was hesitant. Seeing his uniform it might have been tasteless to tell him that Andrushka had gone to the demonstration. But Natasha told him. She felt he was entitled to know.

'What does Andrushka know?' he said with contempt. 'He's out there encouraging our enemies to take advantage of us. That's all we need. He doesn't understand what's going on.'

Natasha shivered. That was Beria talk. She turned a deaf ear. 'Let's not speak about it,' she said. 'I'll make supper.'

It was not a good homecoming, and the women dreaded Andrushka's return. But when he did come home, the two friends were so happy to see each other that there was no room for argument. After supper, they went out to a bar, and out of their mothers' presence they had to be honest with each other.

'Why did you go to the demonstration?' Vitya asked.

'You're in the army, Vitya,' Andrushka said, 'so you don't have any choice. But I don't think we have any right to move against Czechoslovakia.'

'Their Government asked for our help,' Vitya said. 'To put down an uprising.'

'So we send in tanks and blow the city apart. People were killed.'

'They are armed,' Vitya insisted. 'We have to defend ourselves.'

'You don't sound terribly convincing. Or convinced,' Andrushka said.

Vitya wasn't. But he was at pains not to show it. His problem

403

was the image on his retina. That offensively stubborn image of the Czech boy on fire. What hell must have been his, and the rest of his compatriots, if death were preferable? 'They are armed,' he said again.

'What's happened to you, Vitya?' Andrushka said. 'You used not to be like this. Does a uniform change a person so radically? We had no right to go in there in the first place.'

Vitya shut his eyes in the hope of erasing the burning image. 'I'm putting my life at risk out there,' he said. 'I come back on leave and my best friend is out demonstrating. You make loyalty ludicrous. And patriotism – outdated. I . . . oh, for God's sake, Andrushka, we'll never agree. Let's get drunk.' Which is what they did as an alternative to a fraying friendship.

When they returned to the apartment, they found Sasha and Anna there. They had heard of Vitya's home leave and had come to welcome him.

'I don't want to talk about it,' Vitya said at once, pre-empting any argument that might ensue. 'I suppose you were at the demonstration as well,' he said.

'No,' Sasha said. 'I'm not one to go into the streets. I *write* my dissent. Here it is.' He handed them a book. 'I had a visitor today,' he said. 'Bill Crichton, you remember, Nick's friend, from the Consulate. He brought it to me.'

It was a copy of his novel, translated into English, that book for which Olga was paying an eight-year price. They crowded around it. Even Vitya shared their enthusiasm.

'He said it's a bestseller in America,' Anna said. She knew that Sasha was too modest to offer that information.

'That's good news,' Sasha said, 'and it makes me happy. But it's also bad news. Crichton told me that I may have to pay a price for its success.'

'They won't take you away again.' They all said it, almost in chorus. But none believed that he was safe. That once again they would hear, 'I shall come back. Do I not always come back?' and they wondered whether Anna could bear another parting.

'Come,' Sasha said, sensing their fears, 'we have reason to celebrate. Let's enjoy each day that God gives.'

They were happy to be absolved from further speculation, and so they sang and drank and talked of the past, that sad yet safe area that had at least been survived. But in the morning they all woke with the sobering thought that 'Volynin' was once again an unsafe name to bear.

But it was not Sasha who paid the patronymic price. It was Andrushka. The KGB eye was on him and had been for some time. His presence had been noted at demonstrations. But so had hundreds of others. But Andrushka Volynin bore that dubious name. Moreover, his mother was Jewish. Besides, he did more than demonstrate. He painted. And his paintings did not conform to Brezhnev's taste in art. He had the effrontery to display them, too, and had gathered around him a small number of painters who would be judged equally subversive. They had formed an open-air exhibition of avant-garde work. Their paintings were displayed in a square in a suburb of Leningrad. As yet they did not dare the city. This exhibition was a trial run, a rehearsal for a more defiant and more public show. Passers-by were curious, and they stopped and viewed the presentation. But not for long. For they could smell its subversion and did not want to be seen to be part of it. So they hurried away. Some, more brave, lingered awhile, astonished at the artists' audacity and courage. For in the paintings they saw the threatening hope of change. They idled there, marvelling, then heard the menacing thunder of bulldozers approaching the square. And they fled, unwilling to be found in such dissident company.

The artists panicked. Some were rooted to the ground in fear. Others ignored the bulldozers and rushed into their paths in an effort to save their work. But the vehicles were upon them and they had to flee to the pavements. And from that vantage point watch how their work was pulverised and ground into the dirt. None of them spoke. They just stood there, astonished. Then looked to Andrushka for some kind of guidance. But there was clearly no help to come from that quarter, for they saw him surrounded by men in that plain-clothes uniform of the KGB and they watched as they bundled him into a large black car. His arrest was so swift, they could barely believe it. It seemed a nightmare, but they saw the shattered remnants of their work on the square, the squashed

405

frames and pulped pictures, proof that what had happened had not been a dream. They were a group no more. And they knew that without a leader they could not be a viable voice of dissent.

When Andrushka did not return home that evening, Sonya was frantic with worry. She knew about the exhibition and had warned her son against it. Now she feared the worst. She was alone with Natasha. Vitya had returned to Prague, and Natasha had her worries enough. But she was supportive.

'I think you should ring Dmitri,' she said. 'Andrushka's his son, and he must be told.'

Sonya was wary of phoning Dmitri. For many years, a monthly cheque, signed by an anonymous lawyer, was her only contact. 'It's the middle of the night,' she said. 'I wouldn't want to disturb him.'

Natasha laughed. She had to, else lose her temper. She marvelled at Sonya's appetite for punishment. 'He's treated you like a dog all these years. And you don't want to disturb his sleep. Poor Dmitri. We should all worry about Dmitri. For heaven's sake, Sonya,' she said. 'Think about yourself for a change.'

'What time is it?' Sonya asked. She was afraid to phone Dmitri, but she was even more afraid of Natasha's scorn.

'It's almost three o'clock,' Natasha said. 'He has to be told.'

Sonya went to the desk to look for the number. Dmitri had given it to her some years ago with strict instructions that it should be used only in a case of emergency. Well this was urgent enough, she considered, and with trembling fingers she dialled. It rang for a little while and she became more nervous with each ring. Then she heard Dmitri's voice. Or was it Dmitri's voice? She could not be sure. So she asked to speak to Dr Dmitri Volynin.

There was a pause on the other end of the line. Then, 'There is no Dr Volynin here,' Dmitri's voice announced.

'But this is his number,' Sonya whispered.

'This is the number of Doctor Suvorov.'

Whatever name he was offering, Sonya was now certain it was Dmitri's voice that gave it out. A sudden rage overtook her. 'Doctor Suvorov,' she said, 'or whatever you call yourself, this is Sonya. Your son, Andrushka, has been arrested. I thought you ought to know.'

'I have no son,' Dmitri said, and put the phone down.

Sonya crumpled into a chair.

'What is it?' Natasha asked.

So she told her that Dmitri had changed his name. With his father's dubious reputation, and his Uncle Ivan's dismissal and death, Volynin was no longer the flavour of the month. But worse than that, he had denied Andrushka. '"I have no son," he said.'

Natasha cursed him under her breath. 'We must tell Sasha,' she said.

'No,' Sonya was firm. 'It will hurt him terribly, and he's worried enough about Olga. I don't know what to do.'

'You don't have any choices,' Natasha said. 'We just have to deal with it ourselves. First we must find out where he is. And for that, we'll have to wait until tomorrow.'

Sonya did not sleep the rest of that night. She was listening for Andrushka's key in the door. Dmitri's renunciation of his father's name deeply saddened her. But his refusal to acknowledge his son was more painful. Andrushka had never been close to his father – over the years, Dmitri had neglected a relationship of any kind – but now he would rage at his cutting off. Or perhaps it would be a relief to him, that in hating his father, he was only obliging him.

The two women went to the police station early in the morning. At first the officer in charge denied any knowledge of a Volynin, and Natasha told him that they would wait until he refreshed his memory. That took him the whole morning. When they approached him again, he told them that Volynin was at another station, and would be held there until his trial. He was not allowed visitors.

'What station?' Natasha demanded.

'I am not at liberty to tell you.'

'What trial? What is he charged with?' Sonya was frantic.

'His trial is on Thursday,' the officer said. 'You will hear the charges in the court.'

There was nothing more that they could do. Except to wait two long days until the sentence, and afterwards to learn to live with its injustice.

Dmitri's treachery angered Natasha even more than it enraged Sonya. Natasha would have given her life to be sure of that name

Volynin, and with absolute assurance to attach it to her son, Vitya. And attach it without a shadow of doubt. For his provenance nagged at her. His recent leave from Prague had often hinted at a Beria siring, with his defence of killing in the name of the Party. And it had pained her. But she had heard his crying in his bed at night, bewailing the sights he had seen, with a Volynin compassion. So she hated Dmitri that he could so lightly discard such lineage. He was a rogue Volynin, like his Uncle Ivan. Her Vitya was like Sasha and poor Pyotr.

By the day of the trial both women were exhausted through anxiety and lack of sleep. They feared too that they might not gain entry to the court. They remembered Olga's so-called trial; they prayed that they would see Andrushka, even if he were to be imprisoned.

They reached the court house and were relieved to be admitted without ado. The public benches were not crowded. Little knots of people were scattered along them, families, Sonya presumed, sitting in fear and trembling of the outcome. It was clear that many prisoners were to be tried that morning, and there was a small relief in that, for whatever crime they were charged with, if crime it was, was diminished in importance because of its many participants. Moreover, they were not to be tried separately, for they were led into the court as a group, and aligned before the judge. On entering, Andrushka surveyed the benches hopefully, and smiled when he caught sight of his mother and Natasha. He even gave them a little wave of greeting, and Sonya's heart turned over. Their backs were towards the spectators as they lined up in front of the judge, who sat there, irritated, anxious to get it all over and done with, as if the trial were a nuisance interruption in his daily routine. He took the paper that the clerk handed to him, and he read out the names of the prisoners. His voice was loud and sonorous, and he enunciated the roll call very slowly, giving each name a certain dignity, which seemed to augur well for his decision. But it was simply a performance. When he came to the end of the list, he looked at the men, shifting his eyes from one face to another with an expression of gathering contempt. Then he scooped his scorn into one fiery breath. 'You are charged with being enemies of the Soviet State,' he said. 'You will each receive treatment, and sentence will follow accordingly.'

A terrible gasp oozed out of the well of the court, as the crowd envisaged the so-called 'treatment' of son, brother or lover. Then some women started to scream, and the judge ordered the clearance of the court. Sonya and Natasha did not move. They could not believe what they had heard.

'Andrushka,' Sonya called. She went towards him. She wanted to touch him, to imprint on her hand a rubric that would endure, a seal of some duration that would keep him always at her side. She ran towards him, but an officer barred her way.

Andrushka turned towards her, and despite the tears in his eyes, he smiled. 'I love you,' he mouthed as he was led away, and Sonya mouthed it back to him, their first and last letter of his incarceration.

She couldn't believe that it was all over. She didn't even understand what the 'it' was. Yet she understood that the apartment would be empty of him for God knew how long, that Leningrad itself would be hollow without him. That he would not be there for Olga's return to freedom, or Vitya's army leave. That he would suffer, and perhaps watch his youth evaporate. But he would smile. That was the message he had given her. He was a Volynin. Like his grandfather, he would survive.

But his 'treatment' took some surviving. The prisoners were handcuffed and loaded on to a van that took them to a treatment centre outside the city. Here diagnosis was to be made, and according to that diagnosis, sentence was passed. There were two possible verdicts. One, that you were insane and therefore qualified as a patient in a psychiatric hospital; and the alternative, that would label the offender as a troublemaker, and he would be sent direct to a labour camp. There was little to choose between them, for both were designed to destroy the mind and the body.

The prisoners were hustled into a room. Since their trial there had been no talk between them. And not even before, for each was unknown to the other. Andrushka had looked carefully at each one of them. He recognised no painter amongst them. None looked like a thug or hooligan, and each gaze was bewildered and innocent.

But he was determined to converse with none of them. In his Grandfather Sasha's stories of the camps, he remembered those government spies planted amongst the prisoners, posing as them. He looked at those in his company, and despite their innocent features, he suspected each and every one of them. It saddened him that he should doubt them, for in that suspicion, he was already losing his own innocence.

Their names were called one by one. All of them were nervous, but it was a relief when their turn came. Waiting was frightening and induced imaginings of fearful prospect. Andrushka was one of the last to be called. He was no longer smiling. He had waited too long, and he was frightened. They directed him to a room bare of furniture but for a table and three chairs. Three nondescript men sat at the table, and there was not a single clue on their faces as to what their business was about.

'You are charged with being an enemy of the Soviet State,' one of them said.

There was no answer to that except a look of bewilderment, which Andrushka gave them as an automatic response. And which didn't please them.

'Do you disagree with the verdict?' another one asked.

'I don't know what it means,' Andrushka said.

'It means exactly what it says. In displaying your decadent art, you are imitating the degeneracy of the West, and in so doing, you proclaim yourself an enemy of the State.'

'Art cannot develop in a closed society,' Andrushka said. He was doing himself no good but he persisted. 'It is the duty of the artist to challenge accepted forms.'

The three men looked at each other and between them floated a smile of pity.

'You are a dissident,' one of them said. 'On your own admission. We, in the Soviet Union, regard dissent as a disease. And you, comrade, are deeply infected. Your condition is one of creeping schizophrenia. But do not despair. With your co-operation we can cure you. It may take months or even years. It depends entirely on you.'

Andrushka didn't know what they were talking about, but theirs

410

were frightening words, and he dared not wonder what would become of him. One of them pressed a button on the desk, and a guard entered and gripped Andrushka's arm.

'Minsk,' one of the men said.

The guard dragged Andrushka out of the room. In the corridor another guard was waiting.

'Minsk,' the first guard said.

Andrushka was shunted to his second escort, who pulled him outside and shoved him into a waiting-room. There were four men already inside, waiting there on the floor. Minsk bound, all of them, and they knew that Minsk was no longer just the name of the town.

Minsk was a verdict. A verdict of insanity. The town housed a notorious hospital for mental diseases, and was the site of appalling psychiatric abuse. As he waited in the van with his silent companions, Andrushka tried to recall whether Grandfather Sasha had mentioned Minsk in his stories. But the word rang no bells. In those places where Sasha had lingered the priority had been the breaking of the body, in the hope that the spirit would crumble too. But the verdict of Minsk referred only to the spirit, and as a side effect, the body would take its natural toll.

Two more prisoners joined them in the van, and shortly they took off in the darkness. Not a word passed between them during the whole journey. Nobody trusted his neighbour.

They travelled most of the night. The men slept fitfully but even in their wakefulness they did not utter a word to each other. Then on arrival at the hospital, their silence broke. Their common fear of the place rendered that silence unnatural and the need to communicate was paramount.

'I'm Sergei,' the man beside Andrushka said.

'Andrushka. Andrushka Volynin.'

'Any relation to the writer?'

Andrushka warmed to him. 'My grandfather,' he said.

'Is that the reason you're here?'

'It helps, I suppose,' Andrushka said. 'But actually, I'm a painter. And you?'

'I don't paint and I don't write. I'm what's called a parasite. That's my crime. Parasitism. They call it a disease.'

'I don't understand,' Andrushka said.

But there was no time to explain. An orderly ushered them into a room, and told them to strip and shower. Then they were given pyjamas and led into an empty ward. Andrushka was disappointed that there were no other patients there. Old-timers perhaps, who knew the ropes, for the place and its purpose were beyond anyone's understanding. Once in their pyjamas they were told to get into bed, to sit up and to await orders. Sergei managed to secure the bed next to Andrushka, but they were too far apart for whispered conversation. There was a great temptation to lie down and sleep. The overnight journey from Leningrad had been arduous and fearful, but by now fatigue had overcome their fears and it was difficult to stay awake in a situation designed for sleeping. But one of the men in a bed opposite Andrushka's ignored the order, and curled himself up into the rough sheet and settled himself with the intention of making up for his lost night. But not for long. Out of nowhere, an orderly sprang to his bedside, and struck his body with a truncheon that was hanging at his waist. The astonished inmate sat up with a loud groan of pain and understood once and for all that Minsk was no rest-cure. The orderly looked round the ward. He said nothing, but in his look was the nuance 'Let that be a lesson to you all'. The injured prisoner cried out in pain hugging his hip with his arms. He had been hurt without doubt, but what pained him more was the affront, the unjustifiable attack, and there was murder in his heart. He looked at the orderly, and with what was left of his strength, he spat on the floor. The rest of the inmates watched the insult and trembled for him. And admired him too. For his courage and his pride. The orderly crossed once more to his bed, his hand on his truncheon, and once again he landed it on the man's body. And again the silent look around the ward. The other men sat up even straighter in their beds, proclaiming that they had received the message. And all felt ashamed of themselves for their lack of support for one of their own kind. The victim's groans had ceased. They hoped he had mercifully fainted from the pain. He lay against the pillows, his eyes closed. The orderly looked at him with contempt, then returned to his sentry point at the door.

412

Sergei turned his head to look at Andrushka, but his face was blank. He did not dare to pass him any expression.

Shortly afterwards another orderly entered the ward pushing a trolley. The men hoped for some refreshment and were disappointed to find the trolley loaded with bottles of various sizes. It was drug time, and this, the early morning round. The trolley moved from one bed to another, and a pill was given to each prisoner. The same kind of pill, Andrushka noticed, to each man, since they all came out of one bottle. The orderly stayed by the bed and himself placed the pill in the prisoner's mouth. Then he gave him water, the prisoner swallowed and the orderly examined the man's mouth to ascertain that it was empty. This was the procedure along the row of beds. When the trolley reached Sergei's bed, Sergei had the courage to ask what he was being given.

'Something that will make you better,' the orderly said.

'But I'm perfectly well,' Sergei said. 'There's nothing the matter with me.'

'That's what you think,' the man said. 'But you are deluded. Open your mouth.' He thrust the cup of water into Sergei's hand. Sergei knew there was no point in argument. He opened his mouth and obediently swallowed. He had made his protest. There was nothing more he could do. The trolley went on its round, and all waited for it to reach the injured man's bed. When it did, it passed by swiftly, as if its occupant was already beyond drugs of any kind. When the round was finished, the orderly told the men to get out of their beds, and as they obeyed, he himself dragged his first victim out of bed. The poor man could barely stand. He was dazed and still in pain, and he clearly did not know where he was. He clung to the orderly's arm, grateful for its support. He even managed a small smile of gratitude. It was obvious that he did not recognise the man who had abused him. He took the pill that the orderly offered him, and smiled again as if it was going to make him all better. Andrushka looked at him with horror. This place took in sane people and systematically drove them mad. He cursed his bad luck that he had not been sent to a labour camp. He waited for whatever pill he had been given to take its effect.

They were told to make their beds and to collect brushes and buckets of water from the orderly room. Each man was to scrub the area around his bed and then share the main floor of the ward between them. The task was accomplished in silence, and when it was over and the buckets put away, they returned to the ward and found themselves with nothing to do. All the men were desperately tired and itched to go back to bed, but without being told, they knew it was forbidden. There were no orderlies in the ward. It seemed that they were left to themselves, and they gathered as one around the first victim of their sentence. There were no chairs in the ward, and the man was sitting on the floor. They crouched beside him.

'I'm all right, I'm all right,' he protested. 'It will take more than that to break me. I know someone who was here before. I made a mistake. You must do what they say. Always. They'll put words into your mouth and you've got to repeat them. Even though they are against your nature. It's the only way you can get out of here.' He clutched at his painful side. It was so clearly an effort for the man to speak, that it would have been cruel to encourage him to further explanation. They would have to exercise patience and wait to reach him, for the man, with his hearsay, was a manual on survival.

There was nothing to do, and the men assumed that the enforced idleness, day after day, was part of the punitive procedure. But no one had issued a rule against conversation. It was an opportune time to get to know each other. It was Sergei who suggested they sit in a circle, and introduce themselves. Andrushka recalled his grandfather's tales, and his warnings about spies in the camps. He looked around the circle, and found no clues. For men in pyjamas automatically assume a look of innocence. But he would take no chances. He would give the simple facts about himself, facts already known, but he would be careful to offer no opinions. He was tempted to give this advice to the others, but refrained, for he might well be offering it to the mole in their midst.

Sergei offered himself first. His crime, he said was parasitism. He was a Jew, and wished to emigrate to Israel. His application for a visa automatically rendered him unemployable, and he was fired from his job as a technician in a laboratory. He had tried for various jobs, but failed even with the most menial. He had been out of work for six months. Thus he qualified as a parasite. 'That's my story,' he said, and said no more.

Andrushka was relieved. Perhaps Sergei had heard Sasha stories too. His own turn was next. He gave his name proudly. He hoped that 'Volynin' would echo its own message. 'I am a painter,' he said. 'I was arrested for exhibiting my works in a public square. I am accused of being avant-garde and therefore an enemy of the State. That's all about me.'

Then it was his neighbour's turn, one Evegny, who was a writer expelled from the Writers' Union. He said no more, and didn't have to, for it was quite clear that expulsion from the Writers' Union marked him as an enemy of the State.

And so the round of introductions continued. A few of the men were like Sergei, naïve visa seekers. The injured man gave his name as Vanya. 'I was caught teaching Hebrew,' he said. 'Anti-Soviet agitation, they charged me with. I'm like all of you. An enemy of the State.' He managed to smile, despite his pain.

The conversation then turned to more domestic matters. Where did they live, were they married and did they have children? There was much laughter amongst them, and growing friendship.

'I feel quite elated,' one of them said.

'It's the pill they gave us,' Vanya told them. 'I know about pills too. The feeling doesn't last long.'

Shortly they were ordered to carry in the dining-table and chairs. Chairs were only allowed for eating, and had to be removed together with the table after the meal. The men were hungry, but the fare was far from satisfying. As Vanya had foretold, the sense of elation quickly evaporated, and in its place, a lethargy overcame them, laced with a pall of depression. They heard how their own and each other's speech became slurred and they resorted to silence in terror of listening to their own deterioration. When the meal was consumed, they were ordered to clear the table and the chairs, and wash their single dish and spoon. Without furniture the ward looked like a prison cell once more. They were told to stand by their beds for the roll call, though there was no way anyone could have escaped the ward. They answered to their names like zombies.

415

When they were ordered to bed, there was no relief amongst the men, for depression had overtaken their fatigue, and they longed for the pill of oblivion. Some of the men had begun to cry.

'Weep away,' Vanya said, as they climbed into bed. 'It's part of the disease.'

The men tossed and turned and groaned from time to time. Andrushka covered his head with the sheet, and sniffed at the despair within, the rancid aroma of hopelessness, bequeathed from one prisoner to another. He dared to wonder what had happened to the bed's last occupant, and that thought brought tears to his eyes. So he cried with the rest of the men until mercifully sleep overcame him.

But not for long. Another trolley round awakened them, and the same pill-taking procedure. But there was no elation after the second dose. Just an aggravated lethargy. And so it continued throughout the day. Two more trolley rounds, a miserable supper, and a blurred bedtime.

Every day, though the men had lost count of calendar, proceeded in the same way. It was clear that mornings were the best time when they could talk to each other and still consider themselves human. Andrushka organised an exercise class that started after the taking of the morning pill. All the men joined in with enthusiasm for each knew the necessity of keeping the body fit. But all were weakened by hunger and their limbs were geriatric in their movements. Andrushka noticed that Evegny went about his press-ups with a frantic vengeance, as he tackled all the exercises. It was as if he was in competition. His zeal was unnerving in such a place, and Andrushka had to tell him to take it easy. But he would not let up. With every press-up, he annihilated the system that had incarcerated him. It was his method of survival, and after a few days Andrushka left him to his own vigorous devices.

But on the seventh day of their imprisonment, Evegny obliged the authorities and went round the bend. It happened in the afternoon at the onset of zombie time. He started to scream. Blood-curdling cries, so that the others marvelled at the strength that he found to produce them. Then he went to the far wall of the ward, and started to bang his head against it, screaming all the while. It was a brick wall, and he was likely to do himself great injury. But no one went forward to stop him. It seemed that in Evegny's madness, he had become untouchable. So they were relieved, when three orderlies, alerted by the screams, darted into the ward, and folded the raging Evegny into their rough embrace. They plaited him into a straitjacket, but the fight had already gone out of him. Another orderly appeared with a stretcher and a syringe. Evegny yielded to their treatment. They carried him on to the stretcher and one of them plunged the needle into his leg. Then they wheeled him out of the ward. Inside it was zombied and silent once more, and the men would never have believed that anything untoward had happened. They had been hallucinating perhaps. But the echoes of the screaming still reverberated from the walls, proof of an event that had terrorised them all.

Evegny never returned to the ward, and the men were afraid to enquire as to his welfare. But his breakdown had taught them a lesson: that with the greatest ease one could go mad in this place. There was nothing to do, no book to read, no paper or pen with which to write. No communication with the outside world. But worst of all there was no clue as to how many days or weeks were passing by. But through the windows of the wards the seasons proclaimed themselves. During his time in that prison, Andrushka counted two snowfalls, and twice he saw how the snow turned to slush. Twice he saw flowers bloom and die, and he guessed that two of his birthdays had passed in his ignorance. In all that time, none of the men had been seen by a doctor, nor was called for examination of any kind. For two years of mornings they had exhausted each other's minds and each other's opinions. Indeed they had begun to hate each other, not for what they were, but that they were part of each man's nightmare. Perhaps that was part of the treatment too, Andrushka thought. He talked to himself often, trying to probe a change of heart. But in truth he had to confess that his incarceration had changed nothing. It had aged him, no doubt, he could see that from his skeletal body, and it had, no doubt, impaired his body's health. But his opinions had in no way changed, and he thanked God for that. If he were released now, his paintings would still be a statement of anti-Soviet agitation.

417

This thought gave him courage, and that night, for the first time since his imprisonment, he slept without dreaming.

The following day, he woke refreshed. He took his pill, ate his meagre breakfast, and scrubbed his share of ward. Then he started on his exercises. The notion of a class had long evaporated. Andrushka was no longer anyone's teacher. Most of the men had dropped out in their lethargy. Others exercised on their own, and in separate places. Then an orderly interrupted their exertions, and announced that today the men would be examined. His announcement was greeted with a sigh of euphoria, for whatever the examination entailed, it was an event. And it meant a movement of a kind. From one room to another. A chance perhaps to view furniture that wasn't beds. Faces that hitherto had not been seen. A picture on a wall perhaps, and even the ecstatic sight of a calendar. The men primped their hair, and straightened their pyjama jackets. They wanted to look their best. And their sanest. With Vanya's coaching over the years, they all had their answers ready. They would agree with whatever was suggested to them, and in their hearts they would beseech God to forgive their treachery.

Sergei was the first to be called. The men wished him luck. They pitied him rather, that he was the first, for those who remained would hope to learn something from his report, and each of them, because of this transfer of information, hoped that he would be the last one to be called. They waited for Sergei's return. But after a while a second name was called, that of Vanya, who could not profit from Sergei's account. And then, after lunch, a third name, and still neither Sergei nor Vanya had returned. Hope lurked in the men's hearts that they had been released, and it was almost too much to bear. When Andrushka's name was called, he imagined his homecoming. But on his way out of the ward, he saw Vanya on his return. And he looked as if he had been broken. There were no outward scars, but from his bent gait and shuffling steps, it was clear that his spirit had been sorely bruised. But Sergei hasn't returned, Andrushka thought. There was still hope.

He was led down many corridors. His feet had long been accustomed to the length of the ward, and then a turn towards a second length, and turn after turn until his promenade was done. But now there was a kind of freedom in not having to retrace his steps, to be able to walk without hindrance, to turn occasionally to the right or the left and to view the long distance of freedom. At last they came to a door and he was ushered inside. The examination room, with its table and two examiners' chairs. Andrushka stood in front of them. He stood erect, in the obedient position, his mouth chock-a-block full of his prepared deception.

'Volynin,' one of the men said, his voice not unfriendly, 'how are you feeling?'

'I'm well, thank you,' Andrushka said.

'Are they treating you nicely here?'

Andrushka was disheartened by the man's tense. It implied that they could still go on treating him, nicely or otherwise.

'Thank you,' he said. 'I have no complaints.'

'It seems that you have given no trouble here,' one of the examiners said. 'But what's going on in your mind? That's what interests us.'

'In which respect, sir?' Andrushka asked.

'With respect to your paintings, for example. Have you had any thoughts about the purpose of an artist in the Soviet Union?'

Andrushka was fully prepared for the question and had rehearsed its answer many times. Yet he stumbled on it. He didn't want to give the impression of rehearsal. He punctuated his piece with many pauses for thought and reflection.

'I have thought of little else,' he said. 'I was wrong. I was arrogant. I was . . . I was imitating the West. I . . .'

'Go on,' the examiner encouraged.

'I . . . I shirked my duty as an artist,' Andrushka said, as the words curdled in his lying mouth. 'I have come to the conclusion, that Comrade Brezhnev's taste in art –' he hoped to God that Brezhnev was still in power – 'I think his taste in art is a moral one. And a right one. If ever I had the opportunity to paint again, I would try to be worthy of his . . . his criteria.' He felt sick, and he would not have been surprised if blood had spurted from his mouth in protest.

He saw the examiners smile with satisfaction, and he marvelled at their abject stupidity.

419

'We're going to give you a chance,' one of them said. 'You will be released, but you can be sure that we will keep a stern eye on you. The orderly will take you to get your clothes.'

But Andrushka couldn't move. His knees were jelly. And a sudden sadness assailed him as he thought of Vanya who had clearly not practised what he had preached. 'You can go now,' the man said again. 'The orderly will give you money for the train to Leningrad.'

Andrushka forced his feet off the floor. 'Thank you,' he said. He had to remember his manners, and he practically walked backwards to the door. As he reached it, one of the men called after him. 'Your father sends you his regards. Don't let him down again.'

Once outside the room, Andrushka gave way to his trembling. This last piece of information had unnerved him considerably. He knew nothing of his father's change of name, but even as a Volynin, he rarely thought of him. And when he did, his feelings were devoid of affection. He suspected that his father had used his influence for his release, but had let him languish there for God knows how long to teach him a lesson. He was in no way grateful. He had no appetite to see his father ever again. But he thought of his mother and could not bear to wait to see her. And Sasha and Anna, Natasha, and to find warmth in all their loving. He ran to the orderly room to collect his clothes. He noticed a calendar on the wall. The present date was ringed in a red plastic frame. It informed him silently that he had been in Minsk for close on three years, and he was glad he had had no idea of how much of his life had been frittered away.

They gave him the suit he had arrived in. It hung on him with astonished reacquaintance. For the body which it now clothed was a stranger to its girth. The orderly made no comment on his bizarre appearance and he gave him money for his ticket and a little extra for food. Then he directed him the way to the station.

The sudden smell of fresh air intoxicated him and he wondered if, after three years indoors, he could ever acclimatise. He reeled like a drunk along the streets, and had to pause from time to time to steady himself. His release had been so swift and so unexpected that he felt endangered on his own, and for a moment he wished himself back in the safety of the ward, with the frayed companionship of familiar faces. He wondered where Sergei was, and what had happened to Vanya. He looked down at his clothing and considered that he must look very strange. He passed by shop windows, but avoided his reflection in the glass. He was glad to reach the station, and to settle himself in the waiting train. He huddled into a corner. When people joined him in the compartment, he pretended to be asleep. He did not want to talk to anybody. He tried to think of the joys of his homecoming, but the echo of those sullied words that had obtained his release still haunted him. He thought of Vanya, and with a certain envy. Envy for that principle of his, that, for all his tutoring and practice, he could not bring himself to betrayal. And he felt unclean, unworthy of his freedom. The train started to move, and he covered his face to hide his sobbing.

29

When he arrived at Leningrad station, Andrushka phoned his mother to apprise her of his freedom. He would have wanted to surprise her, but he knew that she would be shocked by his appearance. Sonya broke down when she heard his voice and it was a little while before she could speak to him. Then, 'Get a taxi,' was all she could say. 'I'm waiting for you.'

The phone call had not surprised her. She was expecting it. Over the years of Andrushka's absence, Sasha had tried to make contact with Dmitri. But he could not be traced. So Sonya had been forced to tell him about his son's change of name. Sasha was mortified, but nevertheless, he went to Moscow to plead for his grandson. At the hospital he asked for Dr Suvorov. The name stuck in his throat with the bile of betrayal. Dmitri had kept him waiting, and his belated greeting was cool.

'I'm only concerned about Andrushka,' Sasha said, making the purpose of his visit immediately clear. He had not seen his son since their abortive meeting at Moscow station some years ago. He mourned his son's distance, and its reasons more than depressed him, but he respected Dmitri's need to lead his own life, and over the years he had done nothing to dissuade him. 'Only about Andrushka,' he said. And then added, for good measure, 'Your son.' He thought of Ivan and his son Viktor, and looking now at Dmitri, the parallels were frightening.

'I can do nothing,' Dmitri said. 'To acknowledge him as my son would be very embarrassing.'

'Meanwhile he rots in a psychiatric ward. Your *son*!' Sasha practically screamed at him. 'Embarrassing,' he said with contempt.

'Exactly,' Dmitri said. 'I'm not prepared to jeopardise my career on behalf of my wayward son.'

Sasha stared at him. He had even begun to look like Ivan. 'Is that your final word?' he said. 'Won't you even think about it?'

'I've thought about it often enough,' Dmitri said. 'I'm sorry about it, naturally.'

'Naturally?' Sasha wondered as to the true nature of that 'naturally'.

'Yes. Naturally,' Dmitri repeated. 'There's nothing I can do.'

'Then I have no alternative,' Sasha said. He rose and made to leave. There was threat in his step and it was not lost on Dmitri.

'What does that mean?' he asked.

'It's very simple,' Sasha said. 'I shall go immediately to the head of this hospital, and I shall declare myself. I shall offer him my history of subversion, camp by terrible camp. I might even leave him a copy of my latest novel, smuggled out of this country, and published in America. And after that, I shall tell him that Doctor Dmitri Suvorov, or whatever you call yourself, is my son.' He looked at Dmitri. 'D'you think you might find that *embarrassing*?' he asked. '*Naturally* embarrassing?'

'I'll do what I can,' Dmitri said helplessly. He watched his father go to the door. 'How's mother?' he asked.

'She sends her love. She made me promise I would give it to you.'

'And mine to her,' Dmitri whispered.

But Sasha was not moved. 'Get on with it,' he said, and he left the room without farewell.

It was shortly after that meeting, that Andrushka was called for examination. So that his phone call from Leningrad station came as no surprise to Sonya. But her joy was boundless. Sasha and Anna were quickly informed. Olga, too, who had completed her sentence. And Natasha, and Vitya, who was, at the time, on leave from army duties. And all converged on Sonya's apartment, and waited to greet their loved one's return.

They were horrified at the change in him, and there seemed no sense in hiding their concern. In fact, they all wept at the first sight of him. He was so thin, so pale, so dispirited. Sasha's heart turned over. He had seen that look so often before. It was not Andrushka's spare frame that worried him. That, with good nourishment, could be repaired. But in his sunken eyes, he saw the look of abdication that no nourishment could erase. That offended look that forbade all future happiness, that resignation in the eyes that longed for death to close them. Andrushka would not recover. Minsk had broken him. Sasha took him in his arms. His first and only grand-child. He had hopes still for Olga, but she too was still recovering from eight long years of isolation. This country of ours has not served us well, he thought. He held Andrushka close, and Andrushka knew that he understood everything.

Andrushka was glad to be home, glad to be amongst those who loved him. But he was not joyful. The image of Vanya was seared on his retina, and he knew that so long as it was there, he would never paint again. And if he couldn't paint, what else was there left for him to do?

In his absence, Vitya had been promoted to captain. For his part, he was overjoyed to see his cousin. Natasha delighted in their friendship, for it underlined the 'Volynin' in her son. 'Tell us about it,' he said.

'Later,' Andrushka mumbled.

Olga heard him, and she knew that 'later' was 'never', and would always be 'never', so long as one remembered those who were left behind. For she too had a 'Vanya' in the iris of her eye.

'Perhaps now, we can all be together for ever,' Anna said. 'The Volynins won't go away again.'

They drank to that, but in their hearts they had little confid-ence of togetherness. Dissidents were never safe, and of those, the Volynins had their fair share.

The following year, it was announced, President Nixon was due to visit the Soviet Union. It would be the first visit of an American President in office, and Brezhnev didn't want any trouble. Lately, dissenters had been getting quite big for their boots. They were actually risking the streets with their protests and their banners. Brezhnev wanted the cities of the Soviet Union thoroughly clean for the President's visit. So he sent out an order to round up the dissidents known to be troublemakers. And though Sasha had never carried a banner in his life, nor taken to the streets in protest, his name was included on Brezhnev's list. Possibly his translated novel was the cause.

So they came for him, two days before the Nixon visit was due. Sasha understood the reason for his arrest, and it did not overdisturb him, for he assumed that he would be held in custody only for the duration of the visit, and that when the President had left, the banners of protest could once again litter the streets. So he packed his usual luggage of current manuscript and toothbrush and let himself be taken. So confident was he of a swift return that he made no formal farewell to Anna, and Anna did not insist on it, for she too was of the same optimistic mind. Olga simply pecked him on the cheek.

'See you in a few days,' she whispered.

But it was a lot more than a few days, before they saw Sasha again. Much more, and three months passed before there was communication from him. When Anna saw the Siberian postmark she felt for certain that she would not live to see Sasha again, and his lack of farewell, and hers too, now ground a hole in her heart. He wrote that he was in Petroska.

By my usual standards he wrote, *this is a de luxe camp. I work indoors in the machine shop and the work does not tax my strength. I love you and miss you. I shall come back. Do I not always come back?*

He had said his farewell at last. Anna smiled. He would come back. And come back with a new manuscript. A satchel full of trouble. It would never end. But that was his life. And hers too.

So she and Olga moved back to Sonya and Natasha's apartment. A united front of women alone. Together with Andrushka, now so broken, so resigned, so withdrawn, that his gender was an irrelevancy. The months passed. From time to time Vitya came home on leave, his Beria/Volynin ambivalence more and more acute on each visit. It was not the happiest of times. Months turned to years and there was talk of war. Another Hungary. Another Czechoslovakia.

425

But this time at further distance. And of longer duration and greater casualty. Afghanistan.

It was Russia's Vietnam. And like Vietnam, it ended in withdrawal and defeat. The Soviets supported a puppet government in Afghanistan, which had for many years been under the threat of a Muslim faction, who were fighting for an independent Muslim state. The fundamentalists were well armed and well supported. An uprising was imminent. The Soviet Union's tanks and soldiers entered on cue, with the intention of swiftly quashing the rebellion. But this was no Czechoslovakia. This was guerrilla warfare and on cunning terrain. The war lasted almost a decade and its toll was terrible.

Vitya's regiment was one of the first to leave for the front. In his heart, Vitya was reluctant to take part in this war. It was a civil one, the worst of all. Brother fighting brother, and he, a stranger, giving the order to fire. And even as he left for the battleground, he resolved that after the war, he would return to civilian life. He thought he might like to be a farmer, and he envisaged a future with a wife, a couple of children, an old farmhouse, which would have room and welcome enough for his mother and Sonya. And Andrushka of course. The thought of his so-loved friend pained him. On each of his leaves, Andrushka's withdrawal seemed more acute. He seemed remote from life, dwelling in another place, a place that gave him no peace. He would come to the farm, Vitya decided. He could wander through the fields, and perhaps he might want to paint again. Vitya often daydreamed in this fashion, and such thoughts blunted the edge of his fear and loathing of battle.

Each Soviet unit was under the command of an Afghan officer. It was not a situation conducive to comradeship, or even co-operation. Vitya was at odds with his Afghan from the outset, whose only advantage, as far as Vitya was concerned, was language. His knowledge of military tactics was minimal. Their supply column was crossing the arid wasteland. The lead vehicle was approaching a narrow pass. It was guerrilla terrain and Vitya knew that a narrow pass was favourable to ambush, a known guerrilla tactic. He suggested that the column make a detour, but his Afghan commander ignored his advice. He ordered the column forward. And the inevitable happened. The wheels of the lead vehicle set off a pair of mines, and they stood helpless and watched as the Jeep exploded in a ball of fire. What looked like an arm was seen to fly in the air and land some distance from the vehicle. All that was left of some mother's son. Vitya choked back an 'I told you so', and the commander gave the order to charge. Vitya was horrified. It was an invitation to a massacre. The guerrillas were pouring through the pass. Hand-to-hand fighting was their forte, and though their weapons were outdated, they were far more efficient than modern armoury when engaged at close range. The result was slaughter. And on both sides. Eventually the guerrillas withdrew leaving their dead behind. The assault was over, and the commander gave orders to load their own dead on to the wagons and to return to base.

'We cannot leave these bodies behind,' Vitya said. 'Every man is entitled to burial.'

'Let them bury their own,' the commander said.

It was an order that Vitya had to refuse. 'I'll see to it,' he said. 'I'll follow on with my platoon.'

The commander looked at him in disbelief. 'You're disobeying orders,' he said.

Vitya ordered his platoon to unload the shovels from the wagon. 'I'm aware of that,' he said. He walked over to a foxhole. Inside lay the body of a guerrilla, a musket covering his chest. From his weapon, he could have been a fighter in the American Civil War. Vitya bent down and closed the dead man's staring eyes. As he did so, an Afghan soldier jumped across the hole, then spat into the grave. And in broken Russian he said, 'What side are you on, Captain?'

The commander left with his troops to return to base. Vitya stayed with his men until the burials were complete. His second-in-command, Vladimir, worked by Vitya's side. Over the years of their army service, they had become close friends. Vladimir had often been witness to Vitya's unmilitary compassion, and he admired it, but he sensed that this time, in positively disobeying an order, his friend might have gone too far.

'There'll be trouble, Vitya,' he said.

'I'm expecting it. Let's get the job finished and go.'

On their way back to the base, they had to pass through a small village, and Vitya was surprised to see his Afghan commander and soldiers assembled in the square. Ranged in front of them were the villagers, clustered in family groups, the terrified children hugging their mothers' skirts. The situation looked ugly. Clearly the commander suspected that the village housed guerrillas, possibly the very guerrillas who so lately had decimated his platoon. He was questioning an old man, and butting him in the stomach with his rifle. The man fell to the ground to avoid the blows. Vitya, from his viewpoint, was appalled and he rushed into the square, snatched the rifle from the commander's hand, and had to curb his temptation to strike him. 'Leave him alone,' was all he managed to say. Vladimir looked on, and dreaded Vitya's return to base.

And with cause. On his return, the Afghan commander had gone immediately to the Russian commander's office to detonate. His fury was sublime. He had been humiliated in front of his troops. He demanded an immediate apology.

The commander tried to placate him, but his fury did not abate. He gave the impression that an apology was only a beginning. He would demand a great deal more.

As soon as he was gone, Vitya was sent for. 'Good luck,' Vladimir said.

'Will you do something for me?' Vitya asked.

'Anything. What do you want?'

'I want you to be my witness.' He remembered Sasha's stories, and the duty of every witness to tell his tale. Vitya sensed that soon he would have a story to be told, and that he himself would not be around to tell it. 'If anything should happen to me, Vladimir,' he said, 'I want it to be known.'

'Nothing will happen. You'll get a good dressing-down. May be you'll have to apologise. And that will be the end of it.'

Vitya put his hand on Vladimir's arm. 'But I won't apologise,' he said. 'I'm not sorry, and I want that to be witnessed too.'

Then Vladimir was very concerned. 'You have to apologise, Vitya,' he said. 'Sorry is only a word. It doesn't have to come from your heart.'

'If you'd grown up with Sasha Volynin,' Vitya laughed, 'you'd know that words are precious. And they must not be misused. I am not sorry,' he said again, 'and I won't apologise. Wait for me. With so little to say, I don't suppose I shall be long.'

Vitya stood to attention before the commander's desk. He saw that his face was purple with rage, clearly a hangover from the Afghan's visit.

'What in God's name d'you think you're doing, Volynin?'

'Sir?'

'You know exactly what I'm referring to. I gather you humiliated a senior officer in front of his troops.'

'He was beating a civilian, sir. That's against all military rules.' Vitya had decided to stand his ground.

'You are not here to judge the actions of our allies,' the commander said. 'And certainly not when you are in the field.'

'But, sir –'

'There are no "buts". It's not a question of whether you approve or disapprove.'

'Soldiers fight soldiers,' Vitya insisted. 'They don't fight civilians.'

'In a civil war, there are no civilians,' the commander said. 'Least of all in a barbaric country like this one. You will go to the Afghan commander at once, Volynin, and you will apologise. Profusely. And I hope, for your sake that it will satisfy him.'

Vitya did not move. 'No, sir,' he said.

The commander hardly believed what he'd heard. 'What was that?' he said.

'I said no, sir. I shall not apologise. I am not sorry. Those people were peasants. Proud people. Close to the earth. When I looked at them, I wondered what we were doing here. Why can't we let them make their own lives?'

'I don't believe what I'm hearing. This is treachery, Volynin,' he shouted.

Vitya stared at him. And suddenly a great sense of freedom flooded his heart. And all those words that over his ambivalent years he had never dared to utter now broke in a deluge on his lips, craving release. And he uttered a phrase that crystallised them all. 'I can't kill any more,' he said. 'I can't kill. And I won't.'

The commander rose. 'Come,' he said. He left the room, and Vitya followed him. Outside on the compound Vitya noticed that Vladimir was waiting, and he was glad that he was in the witness stand. The commander got into his Jeep and ordered Vitya to drive. Swiftly and unseen, Vladimir took the nearest Jeep and followed them. But at a distance. He had a feeling that what was about to happen was not for public view, and that he must not be caught as spectator. They drove a few miles as Vladimir kept his distance. They were in the countryside. There were no villages in sight. It was bare terrain, and silent, a terrain that could keep secrets to itself. Vitya was driving into a valley, and its depth was ominous. From Vladimir's viewpoint it looked like a descent into hell, and he had a frightening sense that at the bottom of the valley they would come to a stop. He was sure of it. So sure, in fact, that he took a small side route, and parked his Jeep at a point that gave out over a panoramic view of the valley itself. He trembled when he saw Vitya's Jeep come to a halt. He knew with fear and sorrow what he was about to witness. His friend's respect for words was going to cost him his life.

He saw Vitya alight and go to stand with his back against a tree. He was clearly fulfilling an order. Vladimir couldn't see his face from his distance, but he suspected that his friend was smiling. The commander didn't even bother to get out of the Jeep. He simply levelled his pistol at Vitya's heart, and pulled the trigger. The shot echoed offensively down the whole length of the valley, and reverberated across the adjoining hills in requiem. Vladimir saw how the commander moved into the driving seat, turned the Jeep, and steered it into the ascent. Vladimir crouched down in the sandy grass, and as the Jeep passed his hiding place, he thought he heard the commander singing.

He waited a while, giving the Jeep time to return to the base, then he drove down to the bottom of the valley. He rushed over to his friend's body. Perhaps he was not quite dead. Perhaps there was still time to save him. But Vitya was still. And he was smiling. Vladimir cradled him in his arms and wept unashamedly. He sat

430

thus for a while, then he took the chain from Vitya's neck, and emptied his pockets of all his personal belongings. Amongst them were photographs, one of a family group, and one, a single, of a beautiful woman whom Vladimir took to be Vitya's mother. If he survived this war, he decided, he would return them to Vitya's family, and play the role of witness as Vitya had wished.

He scratched at the earth with his hands. He looked in the Jeep for a suitable tool to dig a grave. The jack would more than do. He worked with a fury, cursing the commander and the Russian army in general. He had been a witness. And he would tell. Yes, he would tell. He would go to the top and he would tell. He would scream the injustice from the roof tops. He would be a witness of whom Vitya would have been proud. He dug the grave deep. He would not skimp on his labours. Then when it was ready, he laid Vitya inside, kissed him gently, and covered him. He fashioned a small cross from twigs that lay beneath the tree, and he knelt by the grave and prayed. Then sickened, he returned to camp.

It was a month or so later that Natasha received a notice from the War Office announcing that her son, Viktor Volynin, had been killed in action, and her screams echoed around the city. *He died in the service of his country*, the note had said, as if that patriotic sacrifice were to make his death more palatable. The house was filled with great mourning. For the first time in many years, Andrushka gave voice to feelings of a kind, and they heard him sobbing in his room. When, in due course, the letter arrived from the War Office informing Natasha that her son's body was coming home, it changed the tenor of the mourning. It gave it a sense of finality. It made it terminal. If she could see Vitya's body, Natasha thought, she would believe it. Then she could begin to live with her sorrow.

She was given a time to call at the Military Recruiting Office. Natasha and Sonya went together with Andrushka, who had expressed his need to see his friend. There were many gatherings of families in the courtyard. Each of them had come to see what they had dared not believe. A row of zinc coffins stood on trestles under an awning. A recruitment officer who wore a black armband, and a suitably mournful expression, was directing families to the coffin that held their loved one. He looked down his list, and called out, 'Volynin.'

Andrushka was the first to move forward. Then he waited for the women, and gently put his arms on their backs, guiding them to the appropriate bier. 'This is your son's coffin,' the recruitment officer said. 'And I'm very sorry,' as he had said a dozen times that morning. They stared at the zinc casing, and they wondered if that was all they had come to see. Natasha looked around and saw that the other families were mumbling amongst themselves. A nameless zinc box with a number was clearly not going to satisfy anybody.

Natasha touched the officer on the arm. 'Open the coffin, please. I want to see my son.'

The officer was taken aback. Nervous too, because he knew that the other families had overheard this woman's request. 'It's not customary, I'm afraid,' he said. 'We've never had such a request before.'

'Well, here it is for the first time.' It seemed that Andrushka had finally discovered a will to live. His voice was strong and authoritative. He was to be counted. 'Open the coffin, as Madam Volynina requests.'

There was a sudden silence around them. The other families were waiting for the outcome. They were on Natasha's side, and they would happily let her speak on their behalf.

'I'm sorry,' the officer said, 'but it's out of the question. It's against the rules.' He felt the others crowding in on him, and he heartily wished himself elsewhere.

'Then I'll get something and I'll open it myself,' Natasha said. Then screaming, 'I want to see my son.'

'It's impossible,' the officer stammered.

'Open that coffin or, I swear, I'll kill you,' she said.

'Wait one moment, madam,' he said, and he scuttled like a rabbit into the building.

Shortly afterwards, he returned in the company of four soldiers. There was safety in numbers. But one of them carried a large spanner and wedge. They went straight to the Volynin coffin, and with trembling hands, they prised it open. The other families withdrew. Now that the woman had had her way, her grief could be private.

But they heard Natasha shriek. 'That's not my son,' she said, viewing a body that was twice Vitya's age, and though somebody's husband, was no grief of hers. She sank to her knees, sobbing, 'I never saw my husband's body, and now I shall never see my son's.'

'Open the coffins,' a voice called from the crowd. 'Open all of them.'

Then it was Andrushka who spoke. 'No, in God's name,' he begged them. 'They're all the same. Any dead body has gone into any coffin. Don't torture yourselves further. They're only bodies, and your sons, your lovers, your fathers, their souls have gone to heaven long ago. Let's just pray for them.' Then he knelt on the stones, and the others joined him in prayer. Sonya watched her son in wonder. Vitya had died but Andrushka had been resurrected.

Andrushka's return to life certainly lightened the gloom in Natasha's apartment, though she knew it as a grief from which she would never recover. She longed for Sasha. His presence would have been a comfort. In the camps, he had been a father to Vitya, and Vitya had loved him in return. Sasha would have understood her grief, and shared it. But there had been no word of his possible release, and Anna feared she would die without him. Only Sonya was buoyant, and being strong, she shared the others' sorrows.

Then one night, quite late, when the women were about to go to bed, the bell rang in Natasha's apartment. The women looked at each other and shared the same thought: 'Which one of us is guilty?' Each of them had Soviet sins to atone for, and for which they had not yet paid. Natasha herself, for her outburst at the coffin; Sonya, simply because she was Jewish; and Anna for her loyalty to the dissenter. To say nothing of Olga and Andrushka, known offenders, and already with records. The bell rang again as they wondered which of them was best placed to answer the door. And it was Anna who rose, out of long-rehearsed habit perhaps. Or perhaps she half-hoped that they had come for her.

There was no glass in the front door, so no shadow could give her a clue as to the caller. She hesitated before opening, and the bell rang again. Behind her, Andrushka and the women trembled.

Slowly Anna turned the handle and in the chink of the opening, she saw that well-known satchel, chock-a-block full of trouble. She giggled like a young girl and threw the door open wide.

'It's Sasha,' she called out with joy.

He took her in his arms. 'I'm back,' he said.

And then they said it together: 'Do I not always come back?'

They did not go to bed early that night. There was too much to tell. And sorrow to share. Viktor's death moved Sasha profoundly, and he wept as if he'd lost his own son. His grief was a strange comfort to Natasha. Her own burden seemed somehow lightened by his presence.

That night in their room, Anna asked Sasha about his new novel.

'It's happier than the others, Anna,' Sasha said. 'It has more hope. Things are going to change. I feel it.' He took her hand. 'This time I missed you more than any other absence. In my time, I have hurt you, my love, but I have never, never ceased to love you. You must believe that.'

'I do,' Anna said, 'and sometimes it's been quite a burden. Shall we go to bed?' she said shyly. 'I've never got used to sleeping alone.'

With Sasha's return, life resumed a semblance of normality. And one day Andrushka started to paint. The gesture was one of those old Volynin orders to survive.

Then, some months after Sasha's return, the doorbell rang again. But this time, it was in the middle of the day, and the sun was shining and there was nothing ominous in the ring. Natasha answered the door. A young man stood there, a bunch of flowers in his hand. He wore an army uniform, and one sleeve of the jacket was doubled and pinned. He smiled at her, and Natasha knew that in some way he was linked to Vitya.

'I'd like to speak to Madam Volynina,' he said.

'Which one?' Natasha asked. 'There are three of us here.'

'I think it's you,' he said, recalling her photograph. 'I'm looking for Vitya's mother.'

'Come in,' she said. 'You must meet Vitya's family.' Natasha was so overcome that she had to share this man, whoever he was, with others. But he could not bring bad news, she thought. That

434

had been brought, and grieved over. 'What's your name?' she asked.

By now she had urged him into the living-room, where the rest of Vitya's family waited.

'My name is Vladimir Rozhkov,' he said. 'I was Vitya's second-in-command. I came home a few weeks ago and I was in hospital. I lost an arm as you can see. But everything's all right now. I came to see you as soon as I could.' He handed over his flowers to Natasha. She sensed that he had something of importance to say, and in a way she wanted to delay it. She offered him tea, cakes, but he declined. He sat on a chair that Andrushka offered him, and he said, 'I saw Vitya die.'

They looked at him. Had he come to tell them that? That which they knew already?

'He was not killed in action,' Vladimir said flatly. 'I have to tell you this.' They noticed how tears started in his eyes. 'I have to tell you how he died. I promised him.'

'Thank you so much for coming,' Anna said. 'You bring a little of him home to us.'

'We were in a village,' Vladimir began, and slowly he unfolded his tale. 'When he went to see the commander, I think he knew what was going to happen to him. It was then that he asked me to be a witness. He told me about you, sir,' he nodded in Sasha's direction, 'and said that you had taught him the importance of witnesses. I promised him. I waited outside the commander's office, and when they came out, they both got into a Jeep. Vitya was driving. I followed them. They drove into a valley, and I parked my Jeep, unseen, but at a vantage-point. From there I saw the Jeep stop, and Vitya alight and walk towards a tree. It was silent, and the commander thought it would remain a secret. But I saw him. He shot Vitya from the car, then he drove back quickly to the base. After a while, I drove down the valley and I buried him. It's a pretty little place,' he said, 'sheltered in hills.' Then, with his one hand, he extracted Vitya's belongings from his pocket and laid them on the table. 'This is all he had,' he said.

They were silent around the table. Then Sasha rose, and from the vodka bottle, he poured a glass for each of them. 'Let's drink to

435

Vitya,' he said, and looking at Natasha, he added, 'a true Volynin.'

Yes. It was proof. There was no longer any doubt in Natasha's mind as to Vitya's paternity. Whatever ambivalence her son had felt in his short life, he had died a Volynin.

At supper that night, they gathered around the table in almost festive mood. Vladimir was urged to join them, and he told story after story of Vitya's army adventures. 'He told me that when the war was over, he would buy a farm. And he said that all of you would live with him.' He looked around the table. 'All of you. He loved you very much.'

Towards the end of the meal, Anna called for silence.

'I am eighty-one years old,' she said. 'And I want to go home.'

30

It had all begun in Larionovka, and as far as Sasha and Anna were concerned, it was there that it would end. In their eighty-second year, they were both going home.

They knew that the village would be radically changed, but never beyond recognition. For nothing could erase their common memory. Or indeed their common history. And Larionovka was where their forefathers lay, and those small plots of earth gave them an inalienable territorial right. Larionovka, however disguised, was their home. Both of them knew that there was little time left to them. They had come home together to die.

The little station was as they remembered it. Modernisation had passed it by. But the taxis outside were new, and were Sasha's and Anna's first taste of the radical change that had overtaken their village. For though it was still small, it didn't look like a village any more. The streets were no longer cobbled but they were narrow as of old. The single-room huts had given way to small houses, and they were all crammed together in terrace fashion, but of no fashion at all.

The first stop was the church, or what they hoped was still the church. But on arrival, they found it closed. Closed for worship. But not simply closed – it was padlocked, as if worship were forbidden. But the graves were still there. Overgrown, neglected, but undeniably the resting place of their lineage. They picked their slow way through the broken tombs. And slowly their past unfolded, and it enveloped them in gentle embrace. The Count Larionov lay under a raised weedful mound, and on either side of him, Marfa and the governess, Miss Cameron. Despite their status in life, in death they had merited equal measurements of earth. Sasha recalled how, so many years ago, he and his beloved Pyotr had buried them, without priest and without ceremony. Anna thought of Nicolai and Andrei, both lying in unknown and dishonoured graves. And her mother, buried in Moscow. 'In the olden days,' she said, 'all the Larionovs lived their lives together, and they all lay dead together. But we will lie together, you and I,' she said.

They tidied the graves as best they could, then crossed the churchyard to the small Volynin holding. Their graves were side by side, Vassily and Maria, but like the Larionovs, away from their children. Ivan was buried in Leningrad, and only God knew where Pyotr lay. Sasha stroked the gravestones and tended them as well as he could. As he did so, he was aware of someone watching him. He looked up and saw a man, possibly his own age, who was staring at him with some curiosity. When Sasha caught his eye, he looked away embarrassed, and pretended to be concerned with a grave alongside him. Sasha spared him the embarrassment and did not look again. But as he and Anna were leaving the graveyard, the old man looked at them and made a few tentative steps towards them. 'Is it possible?' he said.

Sasha tried to put him at his ease. 'In this place, anything is possible,' he said.

'Volynin?' The man asked. 'And . . . and . . . the little Countess?' Sasha stared at him. 'Oleg?' he tried. 'Oleg Lukashov?'

The old man cackled with laughter. 'You remember me,' he said. 'Countess,' he explained, 'we were in school together, Sasha and I.'

The men walked towards each other and embraced, and wept for all the history they shared.

'Come, come,' the man said, 'come to my house. Please, please. My wife is there. Klara. In the same class,' he laughed. 'You will remember her. Oh God, you are good,' he sang to himself as he led the way out of the cemetery. He turned to them. 'We're the only ones left, Klara and I,' he said.

'I thought everyone had gone,' Sasha said. 'Except Avdotya.'

'Avdotya,' Oleg crooned. 'The lovely Avdotya. We lived close to her. Outside the village. We were spared. Advotya went to Leningrad.'

'To live with me,' Anna said. 'She died some years ago.'

'God bless her,' Oleg said.

When they reached his street, he started calling, 'Klara.' A number of women came to their doors, not in answer to the name, but in some hopeful response to an event, for life was clearly monotonous in Larionovka.

'Klara, Klara,' he kept calling.

At last, Klara appeared on the doorstep.

'I have the Countess,' Oleg shouted, beyond himself with excitement.

'And the Tsar, I suppose,' Klara shouted back, 'and you're bringing them home to tea.'

'That's right,' he said, reaching his door. 'Not the Tsar, God be thanked, but the Countess, and look, a Volynin.'

Klara stared at them. 'Sasha,' she said, and broke down into uncontrollable tears. 'Sasha Volynin,' she sobbed. 'Pyotr, Ivan.' The image of the whole family crowded in on her and she wept at having found one survivor of her childhood.

'Come, come, Klara,' Sasha said. 'This is no time for tears.'

'No. Come in,' she said. 'We'll drink to your return. And Countess,' she said, and she could not disguise a creaking curtsey.

'Not Countess,' Anna said. 'Just Anna.'

At first, they were shy with each other, but the vodka thawed them, and clarified their recall. The time passed swiftly as they talked of old times. The distant past, in their ageing eyes, was sharply focused, and names and events long forgotten, now assumed their rightful and proper place.

'Have you come back here to live?' Klara asked.

'We must find somewhere. Somewhere to rent. Will that be difficult?' Sasha said.

'No, there is room,' Oleg said. 'Tonight you will sleep here, and tomorrow we'll go to the Hall to find accommodation.'

'The Hall?' Sasha asked. 'What's that?'

'It runs all the affairs of the village.'

'Where is it?' Anna said.

439

Klara and Oleg were silent. They clearly did not want to answer that question. And so obvious was their reluctance, that Anna instinctively knew where the Hall had placed itself.

'In our house?' she whispered.

'Yes,' Oleg said. 'They rebuilt it. Now it's just offices. I'm sorry.'

'I'll get used to it,' Anna said. 'We'll go tomorrow, Sasha.'

It was a strange night that the two old lovers spent together. For in that place, they became as children again.

'We are blessed,' Anna whispered.

'Indeed we are. And we must thank God for that,' Sasha said. 'But remember,' he laughed, 'however old we are, we are still too young to count our blessings. That way lies resignation. And I have a new book to finish, and you have to read it. We are just beginning, you and I,' he said.

And both stretched their old limbs in a great clutch after life, and Anna even looked forward to returning to her old home.

But next day, as they made their way there, it seemed that she was old once more, into her real years, and her pace was accordingly slow. Sasha took it for reluctance, for nervousness, and he did not hurry her.

The manor house was not difficult to recognise. The façade had been reconstructed in its original style, though the seams of the new work were highly visible. But the grounds, as Anna remembered them, had almost disappeared. There was a patch of lawn in front of the house that looked pathetically at odds with the classic columns of the façade. The rest of the garden and its woods were built upon, in row after row of terraced houses. It was violation of the worst kind. For it had made ugly what was once so beautiful.

'I will not cry,' Anna said, catching Sasha staring at her. 'It's functional. The land has provided somewhere for people to live.'

'You talk like a Party member,' Sasha laughed. 'It's hideous. There's no reason why, with the same money, they couldn't have made it beautiful.' He paused. 'Shall we go inside?' he asked.

'Slowly,' Anna said. 'We are crossing almost a century.'

He put his arm around her, and guided her up the steps, and both expected to arrive in the grand foyer. But what greeted them was a warren of little doorless, windowless cubicles, and they were affronted.

'Was this my house?' Anna said. She looked around desperately for some clue as to its past grandeur, and looking up, she saw it. The rose in the ceiling, from which the vast chandelier had hung. For a moment she thought she saw its dazzling shimmer, and even heard a snatch of crystal music.

She smiled at Sasha, and he, knowing her so well and so lovingly said, 'But there's no room to dance.'

They wandered around the maze of rooms and enquired the whereabouts of the office for accommodation. They were directed upstairs. The narrow steps were about a third the width of the original grand staircase and the curving balustrade was now a fantasy. That which had once been Anna's nursery was decimated into bureaucratic boxes, and Anna no longer tried to translate the architecture of her childhood.

The officer in charge informed them that there was one unit available that answered to their entitlement. He unfolded a map of the estate, and pointed out its situation. 'It's just opposite the Hall,' he said. 'That cluster of units with the grass surround.'

Sasha squeezed Anna's hand and smiled. Both knew that they were going back to the conservatory. 'I haven't been so happy in a long time,' Anna said.

With the help of Oleg and Klara, they moved into their new home. It had one room, a tiny kitchen and bathroom, and was smaller, Sasha reckoned, than the hut in which he'd lived as a child. It was already furnished with the wherewithal to sleep, sit, and cook, and Anna and Sasha rejoiced in their freedom from possessions. With the exception of Sasha's books. Andrushka brought them himself from Leningrad, and built shelves and a makeshift desk for Sasha to work on. He was halfway through his novel, and he was working at it very slowly, for he knew that so long as it was unfinished, he was immortal.

So the time passed, and at the turning of every year, they celebrated their birthdays, and thanked God for their blessings, but did not count them. Sasha's book progressed, and every evening he would read to Anna his day's work. He noticed how her health was failing, though she was at great pains to hide it. He dared not think of how he could live without her. He pressed on with his work, but made the decision to hold back his last page until the day when she would leave him, and then he would write his final words and acknowledge his own mortality.

This last book, begun in the machine shop of Siberia, was more hopeful than any other. It was written with a writer's prophetic eye and ear, and that optimism was seen to be justified soon after his eighty-fifth birthday. For it was the year that Mikhail Gorbachev assumed the reins of power in the Soviet Union. The reforms that he promised hinted at a true revolution in Russian thought and way of life. 'The second revolution in our lifetime,' Sasha said.

Anna took his hand. 'We can go now,' she said.

He held her close. He could write his penultimate page.

Anna was right. The new order, after all their struggles, had given them a licence to leave. They had done their part, both of them. Now it was others' struggle. They could go.

She grew weaker in the following days, and each night he held her hand and read to her. Then one morning she could not rise from her bed. He sat with her all day, and read his penultimate page. When evening came, she smiled and gripped his hand.

'Sasha,' she said. 'This is not the end of our loving.'

It was her way of saying goodbye. It was her way of saying she would not return. That all she could leave him was her love, and Sasha knew that it would be too great and too wonderful a solace to bear alone.

'I can smell the flowers of our conservatory,' she said. Her hand loosened in his, and the smile that played on her lips, now surprised the whole of her face, like a swiftly rising sun, and her eyes shimmered in death's blinding light.

Sasha closed her eyes. He felt a sudden nagging hollow at his side. And he was shipped right back into their weaned infancy, and to that very first of many partings. But this time the hollow was more painful. Ulcerous. Unfillable. Hitherto, he had been able to say, 'Do I not always come back?' But now their togetherness was no longer of this life. He kissed her gently, and weeping, he went to his desk, and wrote his last words.

442

All that matters is the loving. Without it there is no beginning. And without a beginning there is little reason to reach for the end.

There are many ways of celebrating the completion of a novel, Sasha thought. A simple dying is one of them.